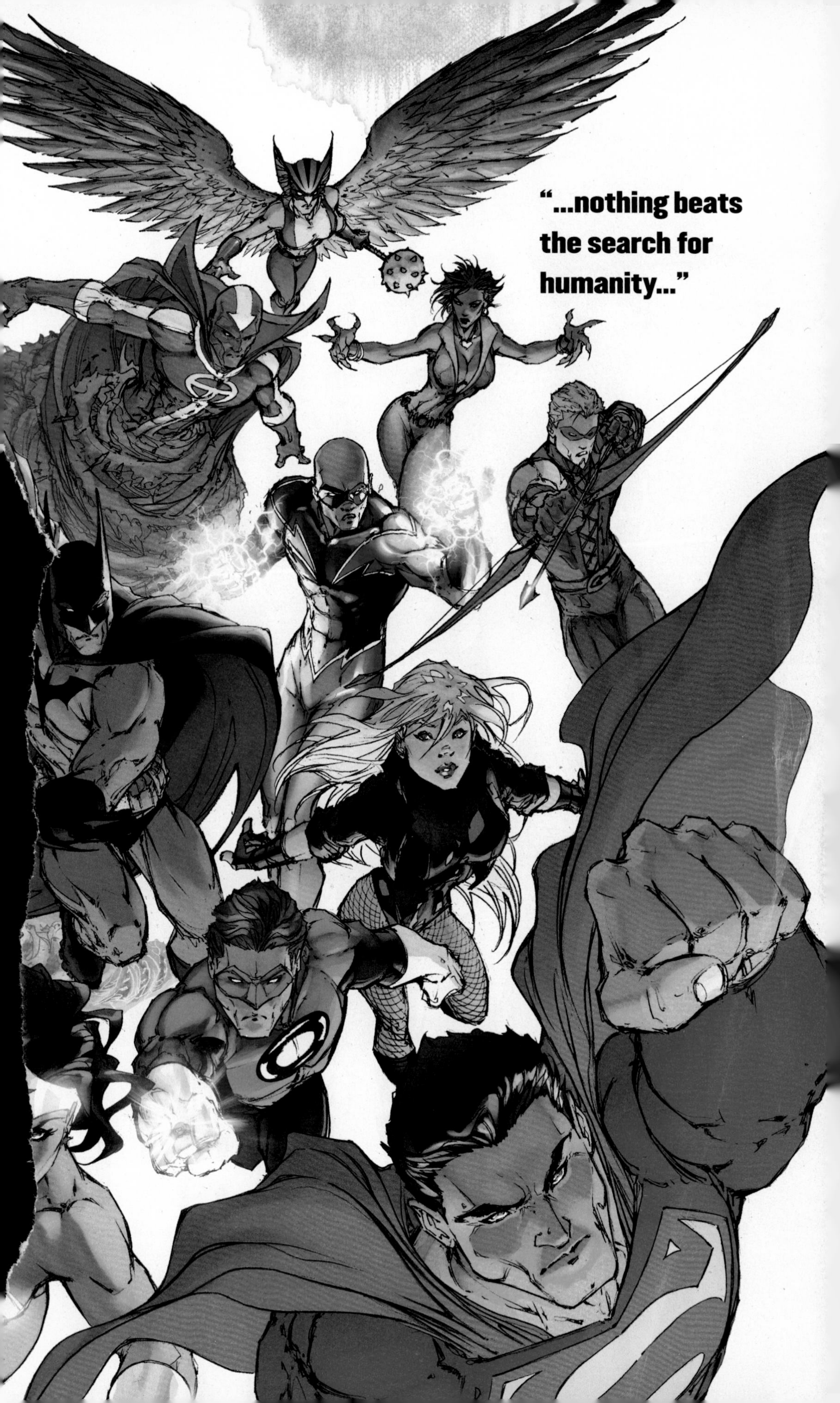
"...nothing beats the search for humanity..."

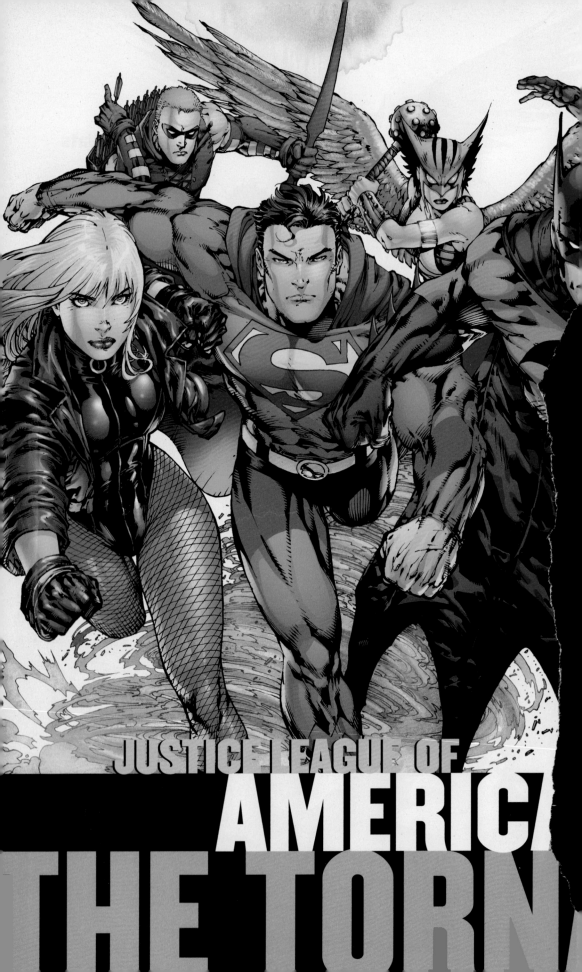

JUSTICE LEAGUE OF
AMERIC
THE TORN

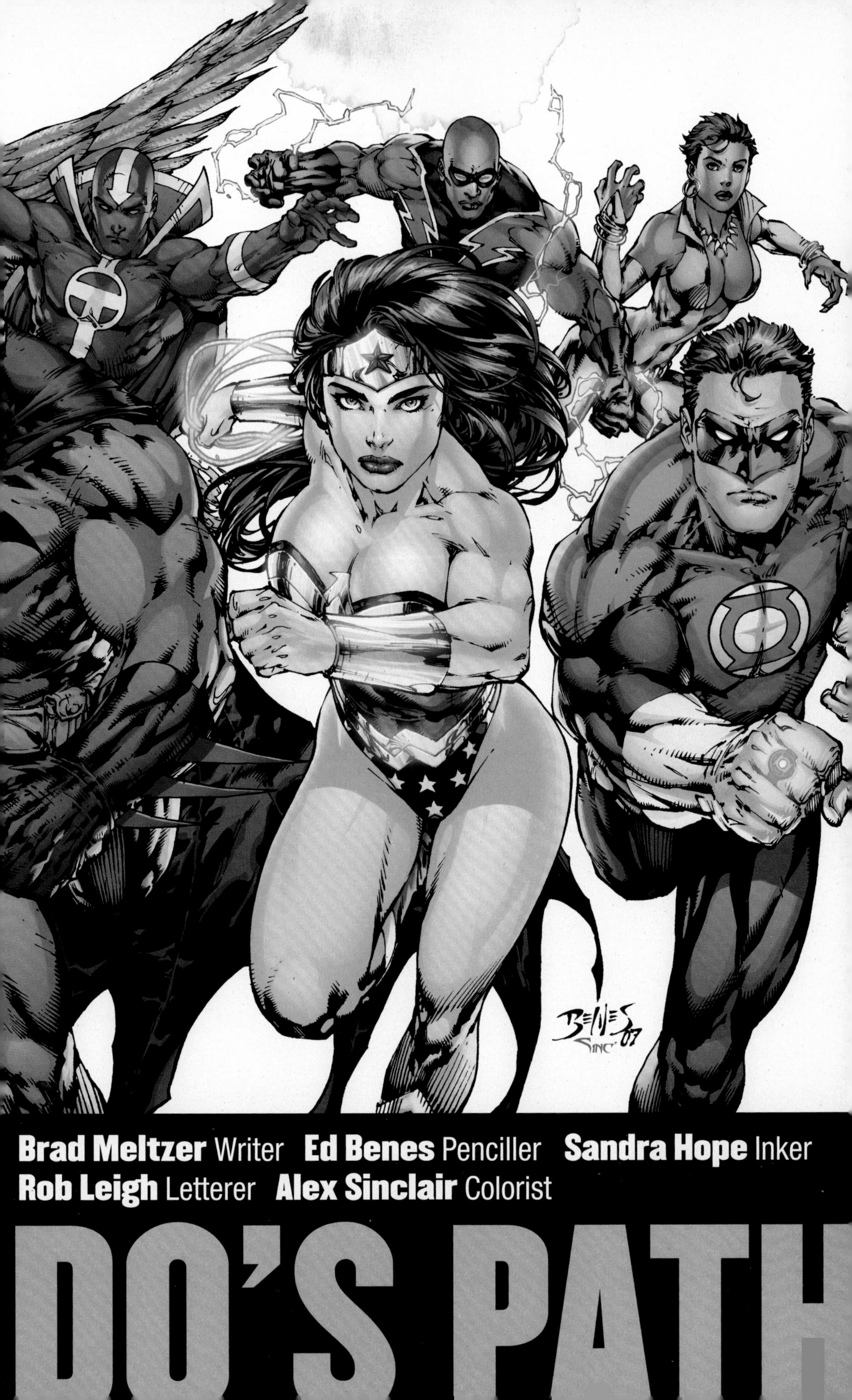

Brad Meltzer Writer **Ed Benes** Penciller **Sandra Hope** Inker
Rob Leigh Letterer **Alex Sinclair** Colorist

DO'S PATH

Dan DiDio Senior VP-Executive Editor
Eddie Berganza Editor-original series
Jeanine Schaefer Adam Schlagman
Assistant editors-original series
Bob Harras Editor-collected edition
Robbin Brosterman Senior Art Director
Paul Levitz President & Publisher
Georg Brewer VP-Design & DC Direct Creative
Richard Bruning Senior VP-Creative Director
Patrick Caldon Executive VP-Finance & Operations
Chris Caramalis VP-Finance
John Cunningham VP-Marketing
Terri Cunningham VP-Managing Editor
Alison Gill VP-Manufacturing
Hank Kanalz VP-General Manager, WildStorm
Jim Lee Editorial Director-WildStorm
Paula Lowitt Senior VP-Business & Legal Affairs
MaryEllen McLaughlin VP-Advertising & Custom Publishing
John Nee VP-Business Development
Gregory Noveck Senior VP-Creative Affairs
Sue Pohja VP-Book Trade Sales
Cheryl Rubin Senior VP-Brand Management
Jeff Trojan VP-Business Development, DC Direct
Bob Wayne VP-Sales

Cover art by **Michael Turner** and **Peter Steigerwald**
Logo designed by **Kenny Lopez**

JUSTICE LEAGUE OF AMERICA: THE TORNADO'S PATH

Published by DC Comics. Cover, introduction and compilation copyright
© 2007 DC Comics. All Rights Reserved.

Originally published in single magazine form in JUSTICE LEAGUE OF
AMERICA 1-7. Copyright © 2006, 2007 DC Comics.
All Rights Reserved. All characters, their distinctive likenesses and
related elements featured in this publication are trademarks of
DC Comics. The stories, characters and incidents featured in this
publication are entirely fictional. DC Comics does not read or accept
unsolicited submissions of ideas, stories or artwork.

DC Comics, 1700 Broadway, New York, NY 10019.
A Warner Bros. Entertainment Company
Printed in Canada. First Printing.

HC ISBN: 1-4012-1349-9 ISBN: 978-1-4012-1349-7
SC ISBN: 1-4012-1580-7 ISBN: 978-1-4012-1580-4

For my Mom,

the true creative one

in the family

—Brad Meltzer

I dedicate this book to

John Buscema, who

was my "teacher,"

and gave me the

foundation for my work.

And to my great friend,

Raimundo Nonato (Huk)

who showed my work to

editors in São Paulo, Brazil—

which is how my

career began.

—Ed Benes

INTRODUCTION BY **DAMON LINDELOF**

Okay...

You guys ever seen "Pinocchio?"

Y'know... really cute Disney movie based on the really cute classic story?

Guy makes wooden puppet... wooden puppet wants to become a real live boy more than anything else in the world? There's a whale? A bad bearded dude named Stromboli? Ringing any bells?

You DO remember it?

Cool.

Now.

Close your eyes and, if you will, imagine this — Stromboli rips off Pinocchio's arm and eats it right in front of him.

And that, dear readers, is pretty much all you need to know about the book you currently hold in your hands.

It's Pinocchio...

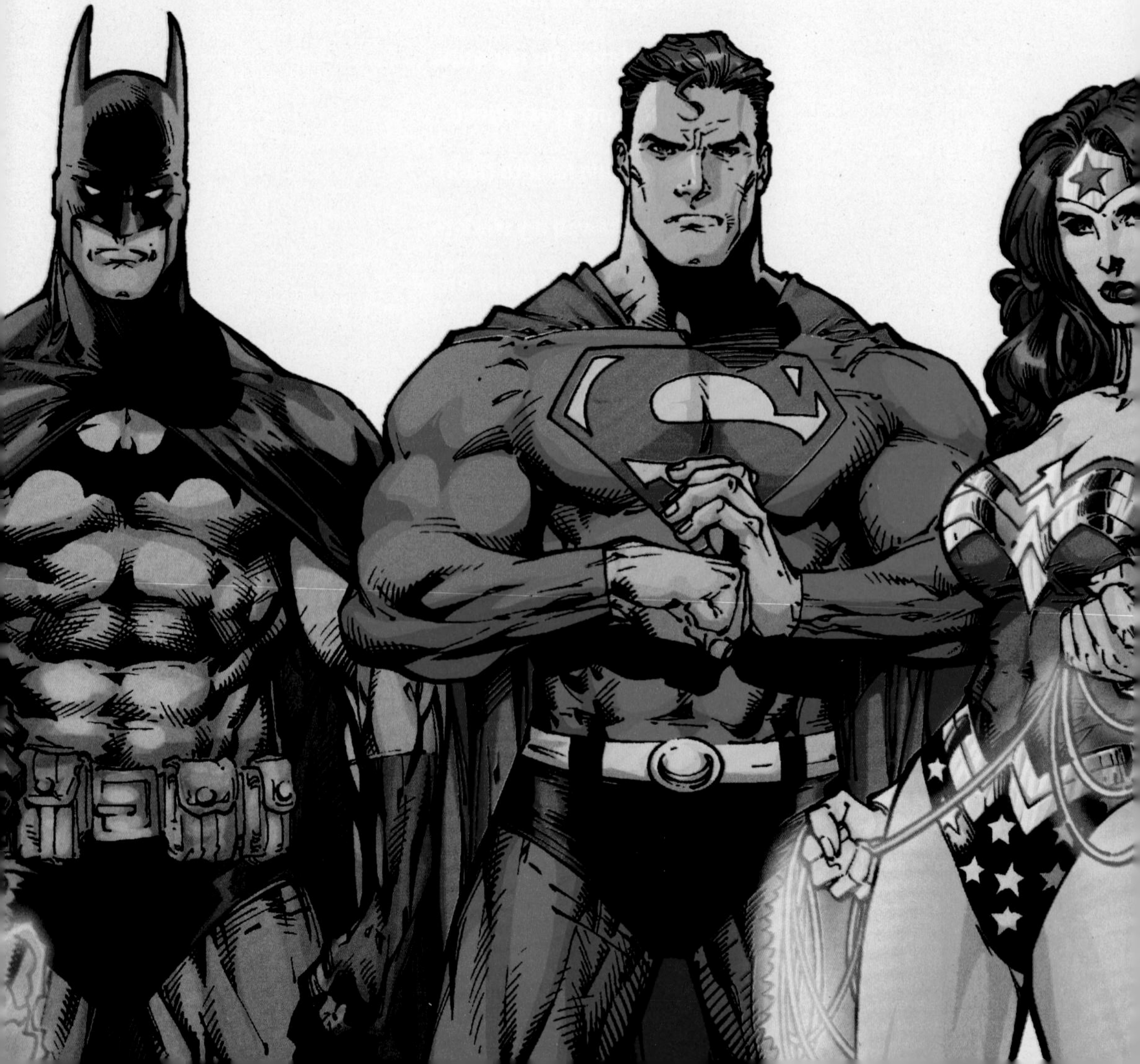

Except really, really, really violent.

Awesome, right?

Okay, okay... Perhaps I'm oversimplifying Mr. Meltzer's (he makes everyone call him that) ingenious relaunch of the JLA, but a story's a story. And in my humble opinion, the boldest approach to this book was to center it on one of the least obvious characters. And yeah, let's face it — in a universe populated by the scene-stealing Supers and Bats and Wonders and Lanterns, well...

What's the matter with giving a little love to a guy whose name sounds like it should be a highly caffeinated energy drink?

Red Tornado rocks.

And I never thought I'd write that. Or mean it.

And why does he rock? Well, unlike most superheroes, he actually wants something.

Sure, "wanting to fight evil" is glamorous (and the most common answer to the JLA's job application under "Why do you wear the tights?"), but nothing beats the search for humanity itself as a pretty sweet character motivation.

John Smith wants to be a real live boy. Simple. Beautiful. Relatable.

The fact that he can also shoot F5 Tornadoes out of his hands and fly is just the icing on the cake. No folks, it's when John discovers his sense of humor that makes this baby sing.

And yeah, yeah... there's a LOT of cool stuff on top of that. Our first look at the members of a new and improved League (you had me at Vixen, Mr. Meltzer), a kickass villain core to give them a run for their money and of course, the requisite Battle Royale with no less than a zillion Tornado robots.

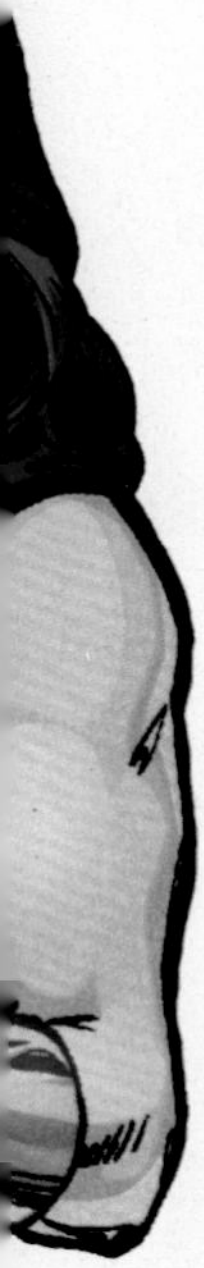

And then of course, there are Ed Benes' pencils. Do yourself a favor... turn to page 52 and take yourself a gander at THAT.

And if cutting out Ed's panel of Hawkgirl smashing Amazo in the head with her mace and firmly affixing it to my bathroom mirror so I can look at it whilst I brush my teeth every morning is wrong?

I don't wanna be right.

So let's get to it, shall we? Now that I've forced you to take a sneak peek at Reddy's detached and severely mutilated head, you're probably worried that he ain't gonna make it to the League's new roster.

Oh...

And I also kinda hinted at the fact that his arm might get pulled off and eaten at some point, too.

Well...

I was just kidding.

But if I weren't kidding, look at the bright side — you can't get your arm eaten if you're not a real live boy, now can you?

-Damon Lindelof
March 2007

Damon Lindelof is the co-creator and executive producer of the hit ABC series, Lost.

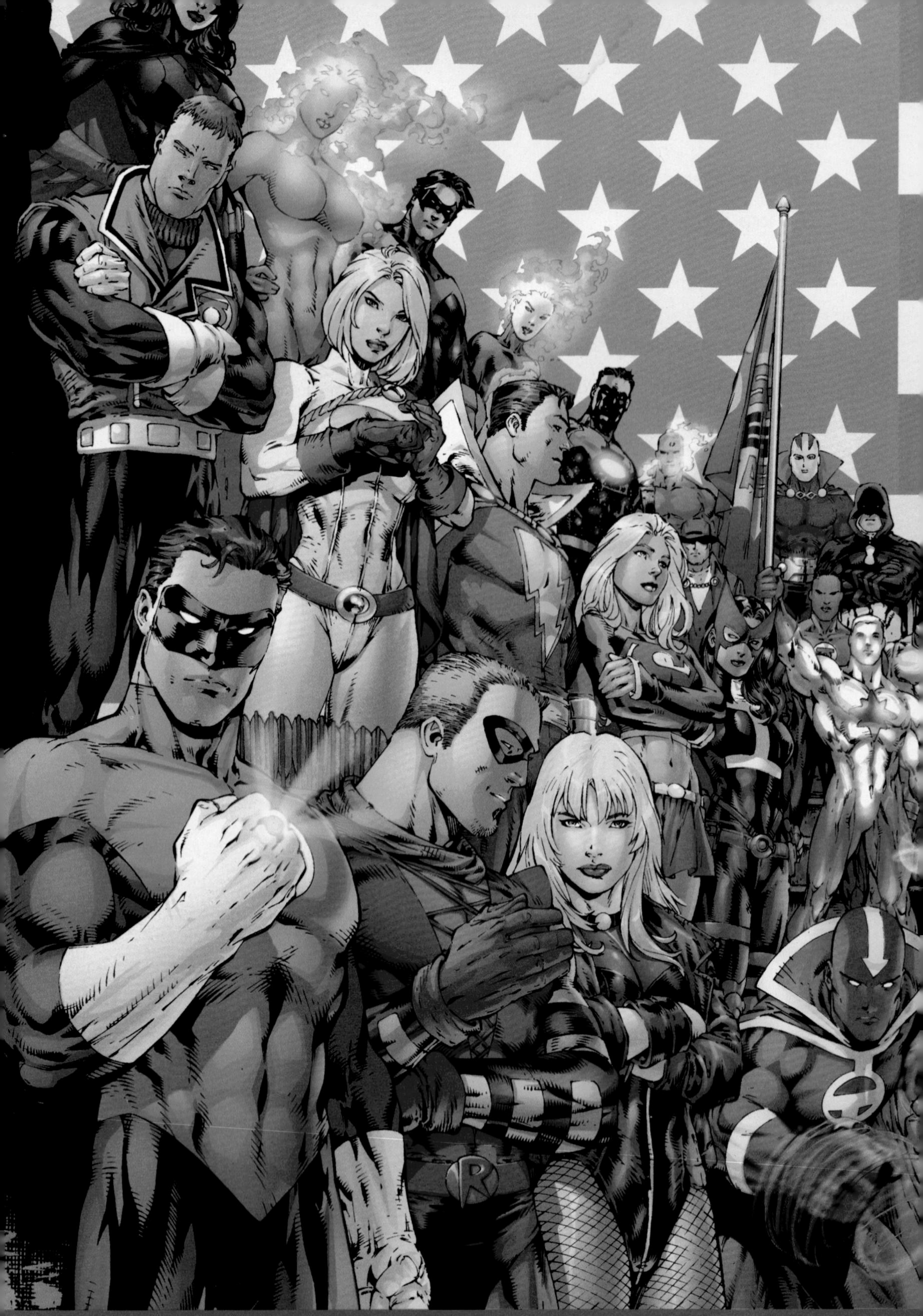

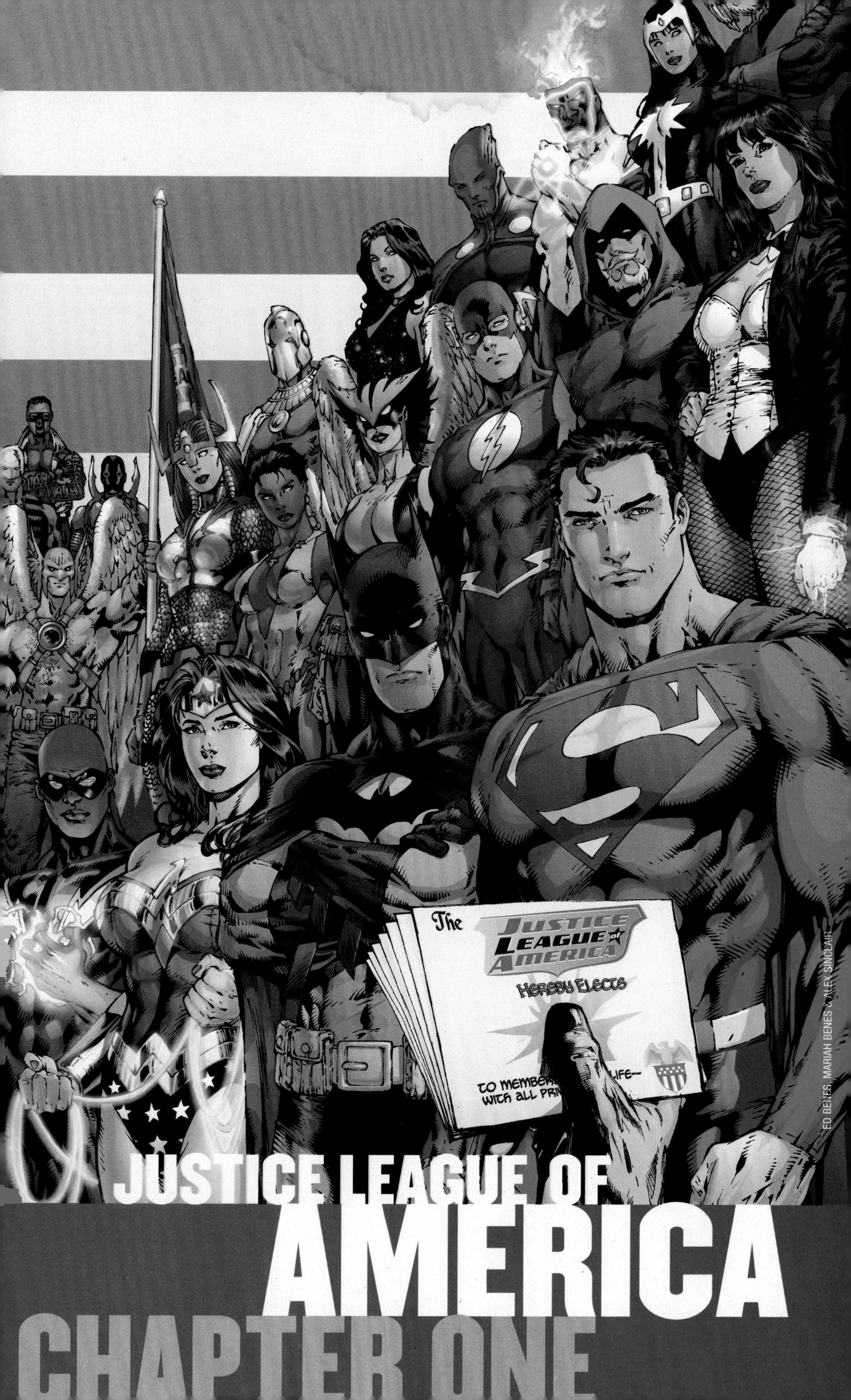
The
JUSTICE LEAGUE of AMERICA
HEREBY ELECTS
ED BENES, MARIAH BENES & ALEX SINCLAIR

JUSTICE LEAGUE OF AMERICA
CHAPTER ONE

"You're putting the band back together, aren't you?"

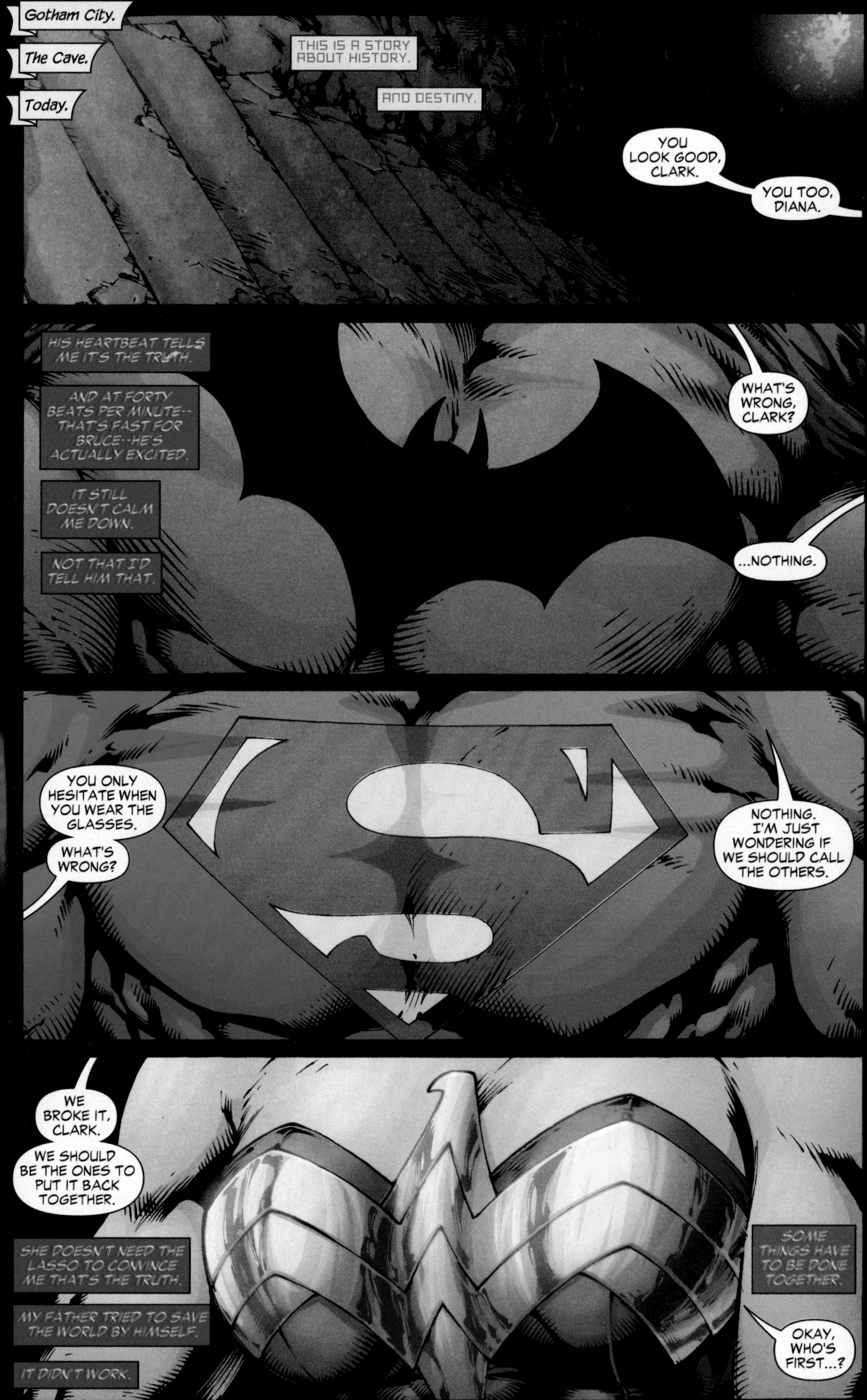
Gotham City.
The Cave.
Today.
THIS IS A STORY ABOUT HISTORY.
AND DESTINY.
YOU LOOK GOOD, CLARK.
YOU TOO, DIANA.
HIS HEARTBEAT TELLS ME IT'S THE TRUTH.
AND AT FORTY BEATS PER MINUTE--THAT'S FAST FOR BRUCE--HE'S ACTUALLY EXCITED.
IT STILL DOESN'T CALM ME DOWN.
NOT THAT I'D TELL HIM THAT.
WHAT'S WRONG, CLARK?
...NOTHING.
YOU ONLY HESITATE WHEN YOU WEAR THE GLASSES.
WHAT'S WRONG?
NOTHING. I'M JUST WONDERING IF WE SHOULD CALL THE OTHERS.
WE BROKE IT, CLARK.
WE SHOULD BE THE ONES TO PUT IT BACK TOGETHER.
SHE DOESN'T NEED THE LASSO TO CONVINCE ME THAT'S THE TRUTH.
MY FATHER TRIED TO SAVE THE WORLD BY HIMSELF.
IT DIDN'T WORK.
SOME THINGS HAVE TO BE DONE TOGETHER.
OKAY, WHO'S FIRST...?

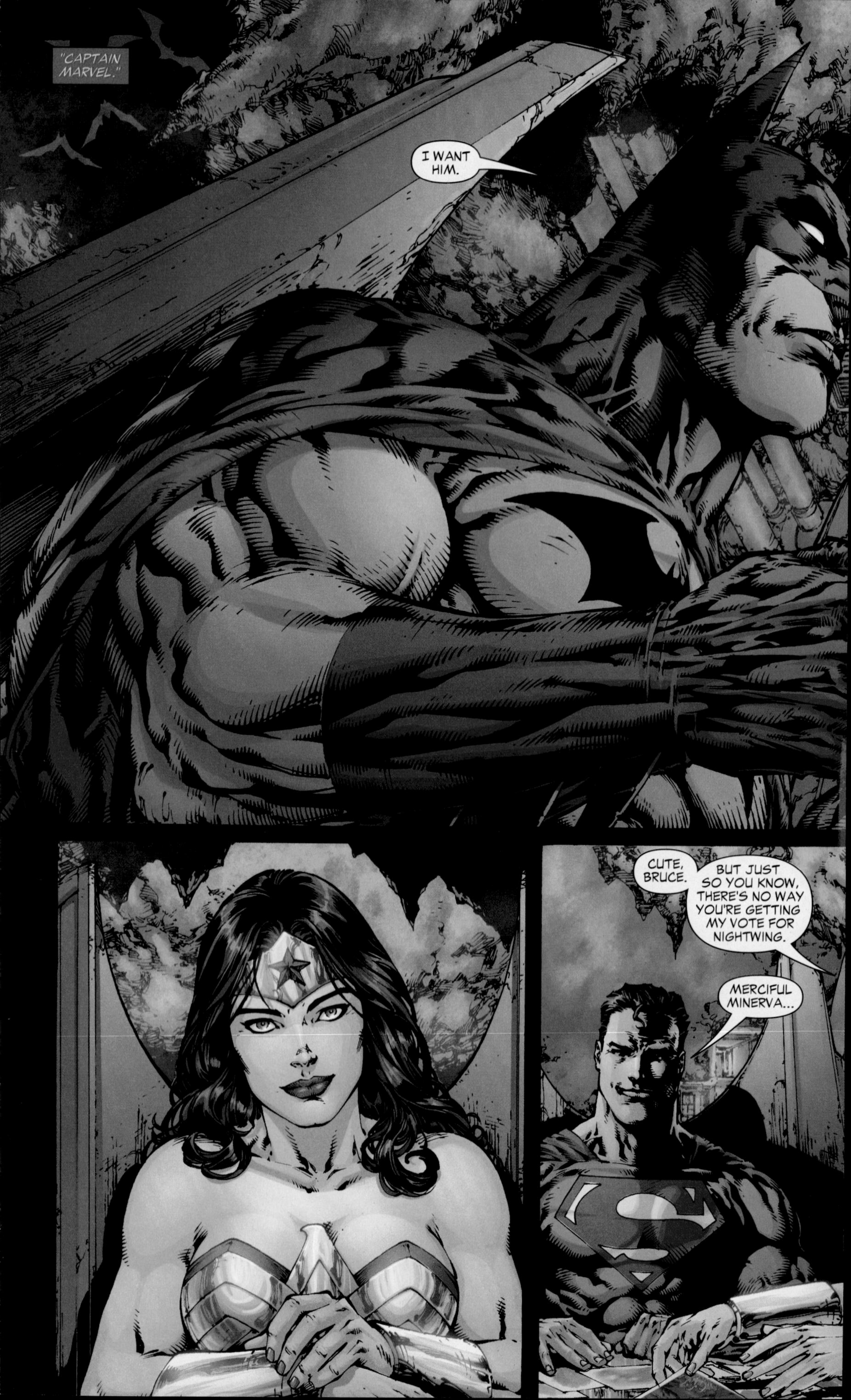
"CAPTAIN MARVEL."
I WANT HIM.
CUTE, BRUCE.
BUT JUST SO YOU KNOW, THERE'S NO WAY YOU'RE GETTING MY VOTE FOR NIGHTWING.
MERCIFUL MINERVA...

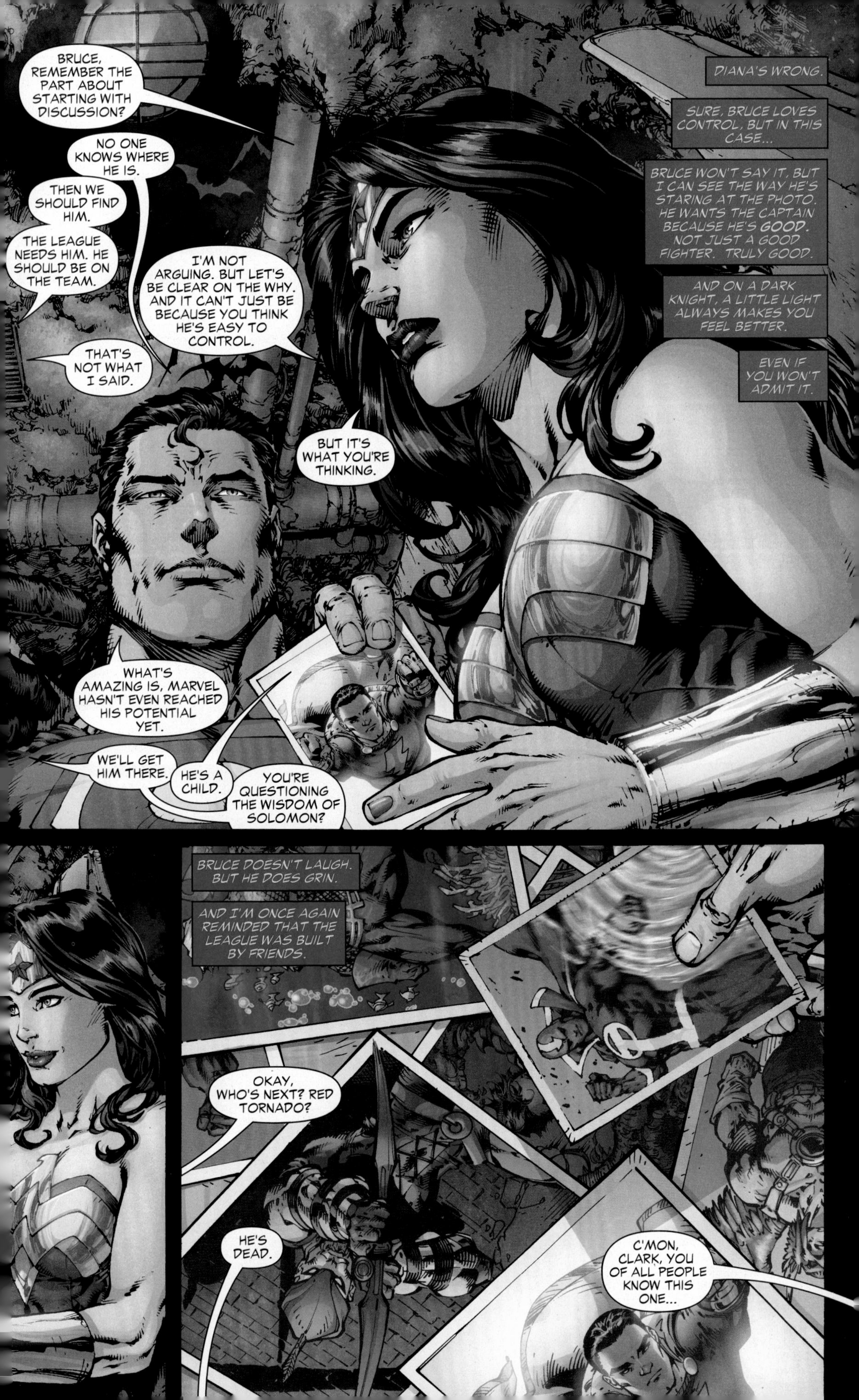
BRUCE, REMEMBER THE PART ABOUT STARTING WITH DISCUSSION?
NO ONE KNOWS WHERE HE IS.
THEN WE SHOULD FIND HIM.
THE LEAGUE NEEDS HIM. HE SHOULD BE ON THE TEAM.
I'M NOT ARGUING. BUT LET'S BE CLEAR ON THE WHY. AND IT CAN'T JUST BE BECAUSE YOU THINK HE'S EASY TO CONTROL.
THAT'S NOT WHAT I SAID.
DIANA'S WRONG.
SURE, BRUCE LOVES CONTROL, BUT IN THIS CASE...
BRUCE WON'T SAY IT, BUT I CAN SEE THE WAY HE'S STARING AT THE PHOTO. HE WANTS THE CAPTAIN BECAUSE HE'S GOOD. NOT JUST A GOOD FIGHTER. TRULY GOOD.
AND ON A DARK KNIGHT, A LITTLE LIGHT ALWAYS MAKES YOU FEEL BETTER.
EVEN IF YOU WON'T ADMIT IT.
BUT IT'S WHAT YOU'RE THINKING.
WHAT'S AMAZING IS, MARVEL HASN'T EVEN REACHED HIS POTENTIAL YET.
WE'LL GET HIM THERE.
HE'S A CHILD.
YOU'RE QUESTIONING THE WISDOM OF SOLOMON?
BRUCE DOESN'T LAUGH. BUT HE DOES GRIN.
AND I'M ONCE AGAIN REMINDED THAT THE LEAGUE WAS BUILT BY FRIENDS.
OKAY, WHO'S NEXT? RED TORNADO?
HE'S DEAD.
C'MON, CLARK, YOU OF ALL PEOPLE KNOW THIS ONE...

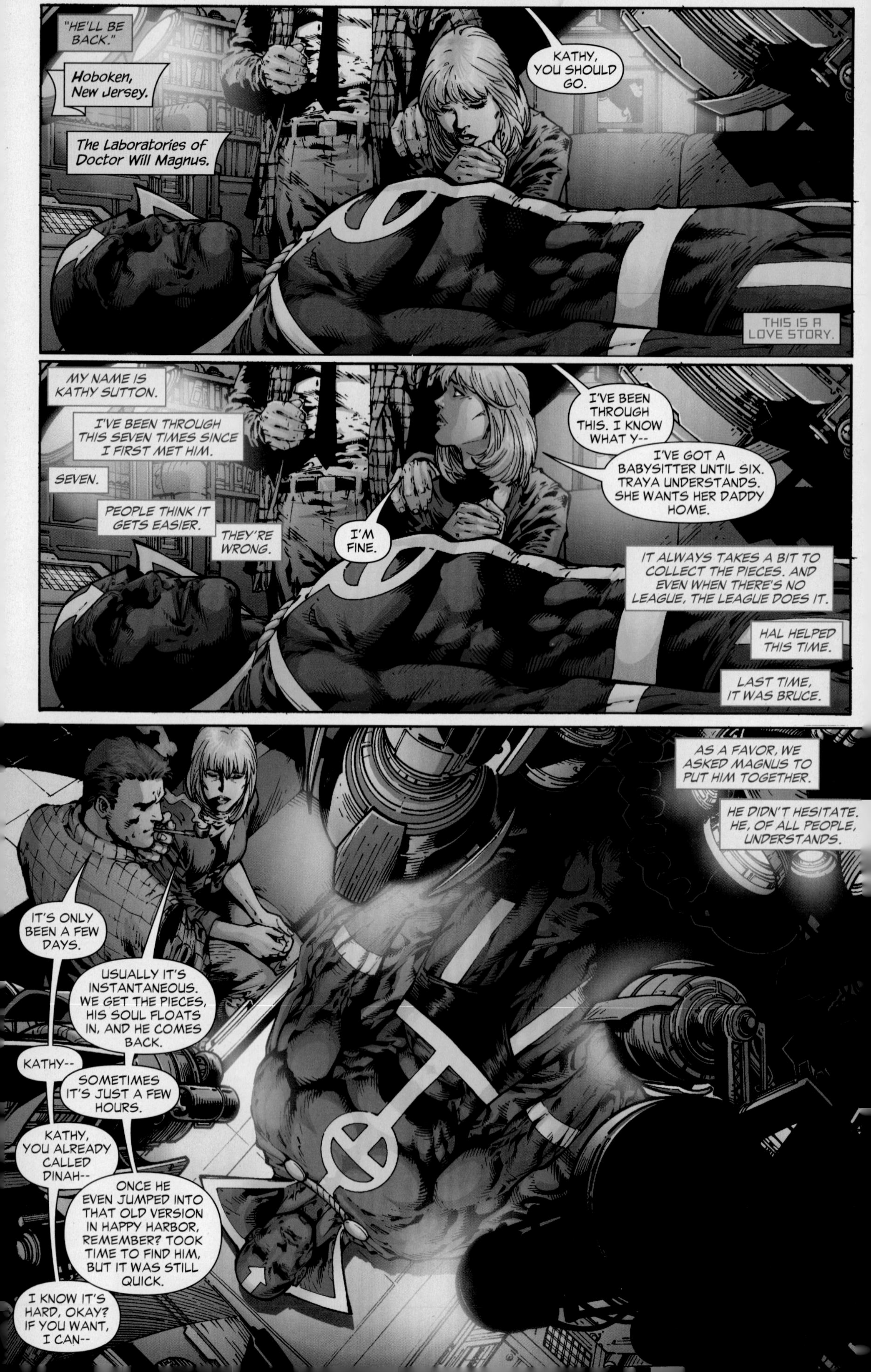
"HE'LL BE BACK."
Hoboken, New Jersey.
The Laboratories of Doctor Will Magnus.
KATHY, YOU SHOULD GO.
THIS IS A LOVE STORY.
MY NAME IS KATHY SUTTON.
I'VE BEEN THROUGH THIS SEVEN TIMES SINCE I FIRST MET HIM.
SEVEN.
PEOPLE THINK IT GETS EASIER.
THEY'RE WRONG.
I'M FINE.
I'VE BEEN THROUGH THIS. I KNOW WHAT Y--
I'VE GOT A BABYSITTER UNTIL SIX. TRAYA UNDERSTANDS. SHE WANTS HER DADDY HOME.
IT ALWAYS TAKES A BIT TO COLLECT THE PIECES. AND EVEN WHEN THERE'S NO LEAGUE, THE LEAGUE DOES IT.
HAL HELPED THIS TIME.
LAST TIME, IT WAS BRUCE.
AS A FAVOR, WE ASKED MAGNUS TO PUT HIM TOGETHER.
HE DIDN'T HESITATE. HE, OF ALL PEOPLE, UNDERSTANDS.
IT'S ONLY BEEN A FEW DAYS.
USUALLY IT'S INSTANTANEOUS. WE GET THE PIECES, HIS SOUL FLOATS IN, AND HE COMES BACK.
KATHY--
SOMETIMES IT'S JUST A FEW HOURS.
KATHY, YOU ALREADY CALLED DINAH--
ONCE HE EVEN JUMPED INTO THAT OLD VERSION IN HAPPY HARBOR, REMEMBER? TOOK TIME TO FIND HIM, BUT IT WAS STILL QUICK.
I KNOW IT'S HARD, OKAY? IF YOU WANT, I CAN--

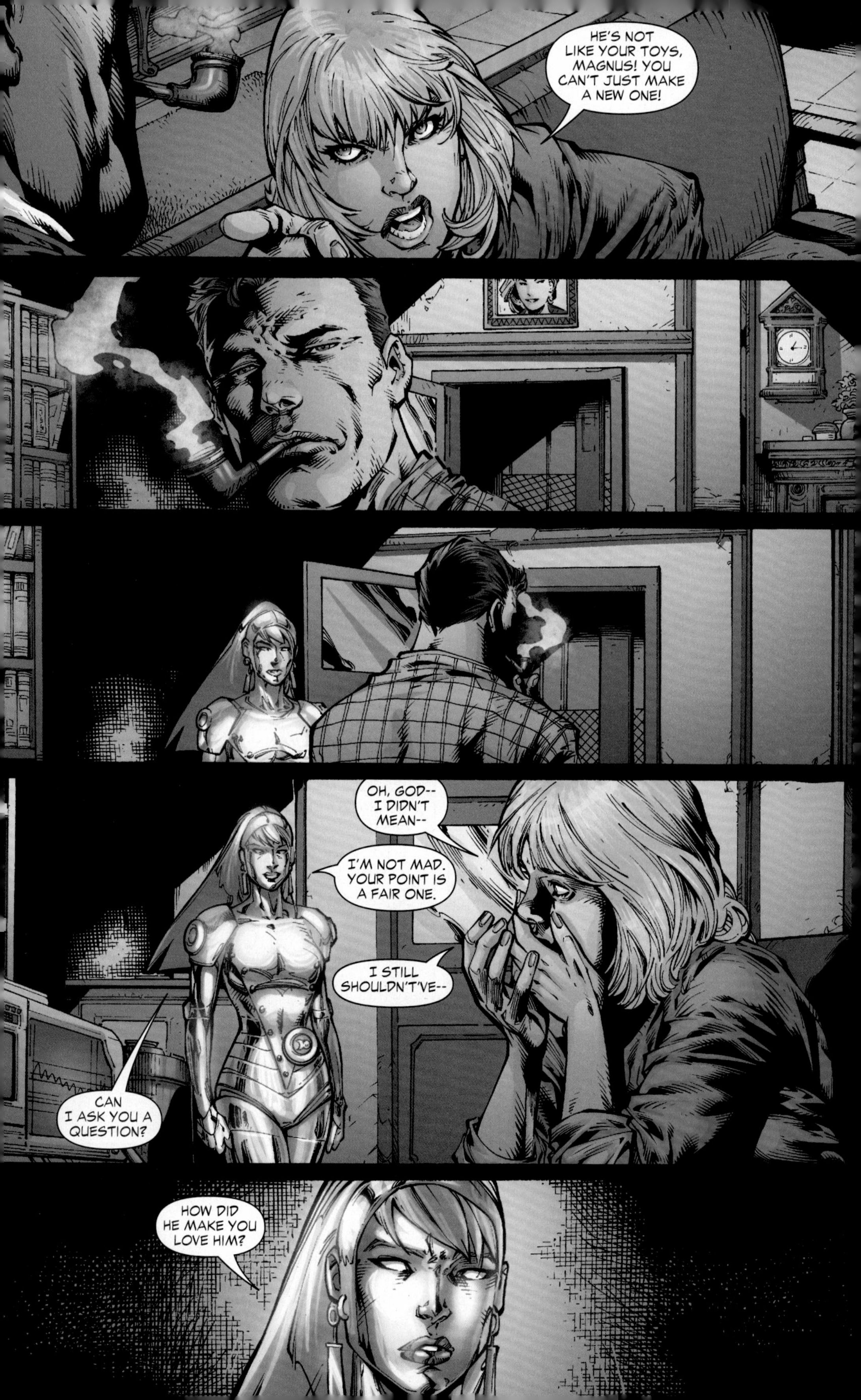
HE'S NOT LIKE YOUR TOYS, MAGNUS! YOU CAN'T JUST MAKE A NEW ONE!
OH, GOD-- I DIDN'T MEAN--
I'M NOT MAD. YOUR POINT IS A FAIR ONE.
I STILL SHOULDN'T'VE--
CAN I ASK YOU A QUESTION?
HOW DID HE MAKE YOU LOVE HIM?

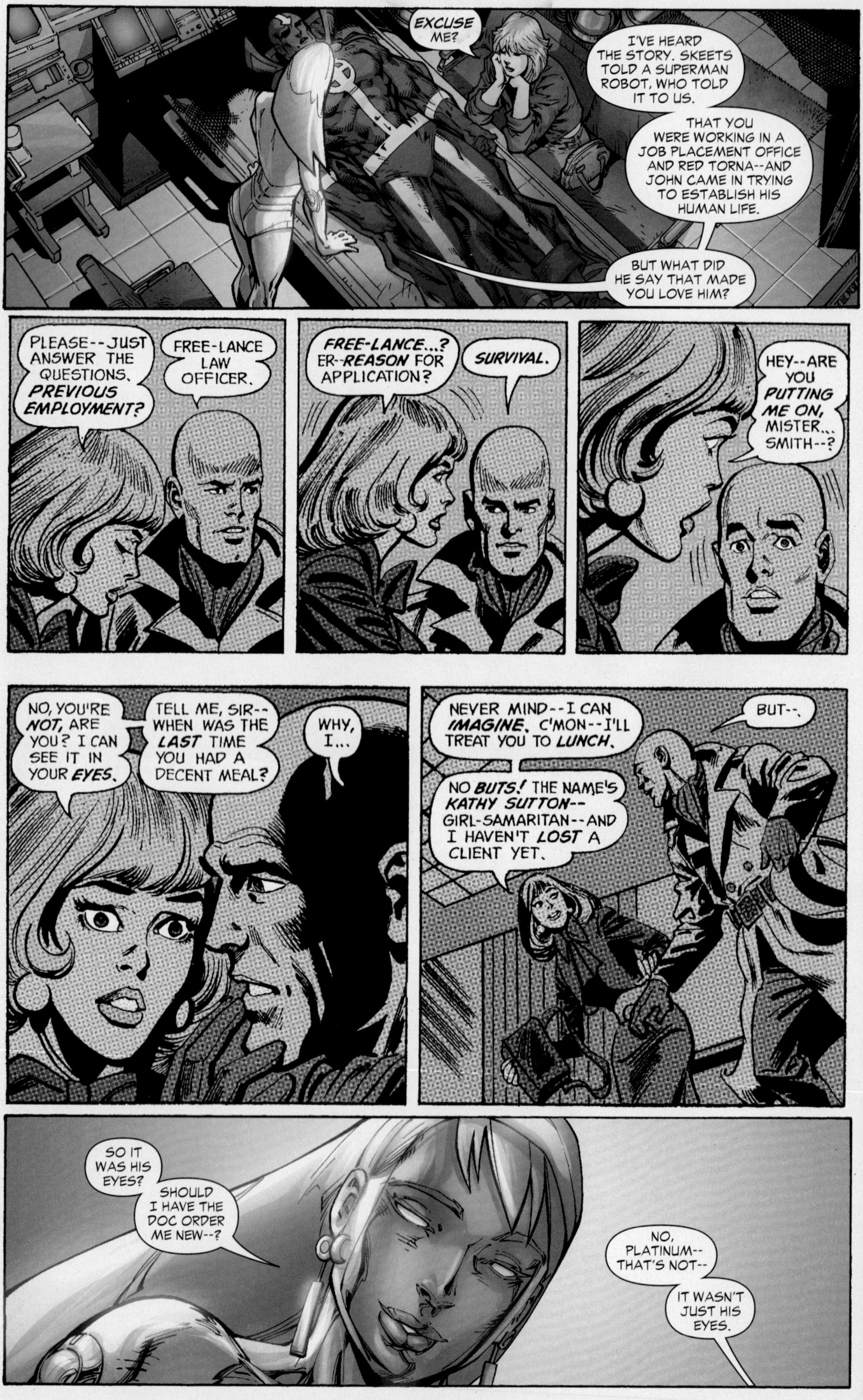
EXCUSE ME?
I'VE HEARD THE STORY. SKEETS TOLD A SUPERMAN ROBOT, WHO TOLD IT TO US.
THAT YOU WERE WORKING IN A JOB PLACEMENT OFFICE AND RED TORNA--AND JOHN CAME IN TRYING TO ESTABLISH HIS HUMAN LIFE.
BUT WHAT DID HE SAY THAT MADE YOU LOVE HIM?
PLEASE--JUST ANSWER THE QUESTIONS. PREVIOUS EMPLOYMENT?
FREE-LANCE LAW OFFICER.
FREE-LANCE...? ER--REASON FOR APPLICATION?
SURVIVAL.
HEY--ARE YOU PUTTING ME ON, MISTER... SMITH--?
NO, YOU'RE NOT, ARE YOU? I CAN SEE IT IN YOUR EYES.
TELL ME, SIR--WHEN WAS THE LAST TIME YOU HAD A DECENT MEAL?
WHY, I...
NEVER MIND--I CAN IMAGINE. C'MON--I'LL TREAT YOU TO LUNCH.
BUT--.
NO BUTS! THE NAME'S KATHY SUTTON--GIRL-SAMARITAN--AND I HAVEN'T LOST A CLIENT YET.
SO IT WAS HIS EYES?
SHOULD I HAVE THE DOC ORDER ME NEW--?
NO, PLATINUM--THAT'S NOT--
IT WASN'T JUST HIS EYES.

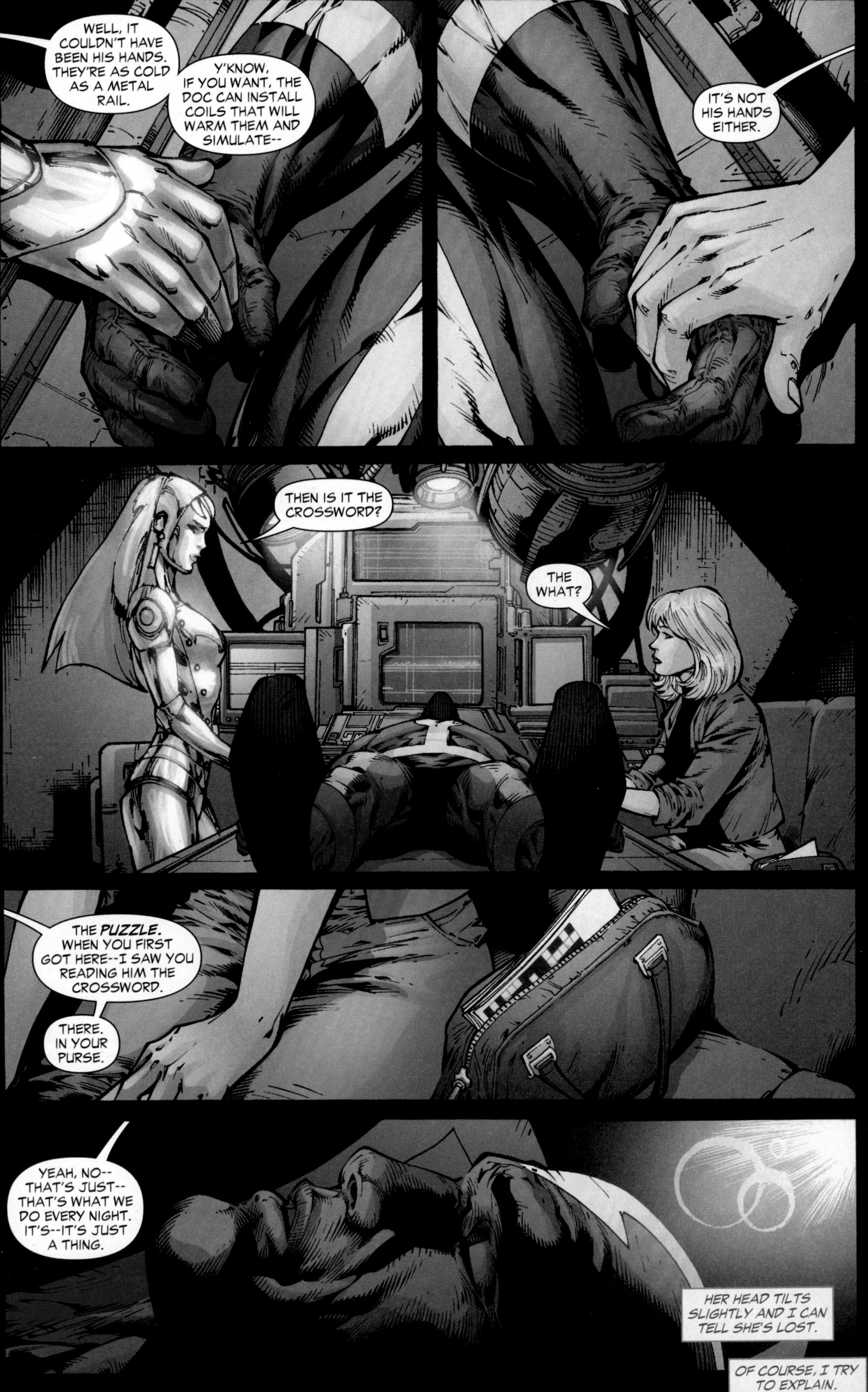
WELL, IT COULDN'T HAVE BEEN HIS HANDS. THEY'RE AS COLD AS A METAL RAIL.
Y'KNOW, IF YOU WANT, THE DOC CAN INSTALL COILS THAT WILL WARM THEM AND SIMULATE--
IT'S NOT HIS HANDS EITHER.
THEN IS IT THE CROSSWORD?
THE WHAT?
THE *PUZZLE.* WHEN YOU FIRST GOT HERE--I SAW YOU READING HIM THE CROSSWORD.
THERE. IN YOUR PURSE.
YEAH, NO--THAT'S JUST--THAT'S WHAT WE DO EVERY NIGHT. IT'S--IT'S JUST A THING.
HER HEAD TILTS SLIGHTLY AND I CAN TELL SHE'S LOST.
OF COURSE, I TRY TO EXPLAIN.

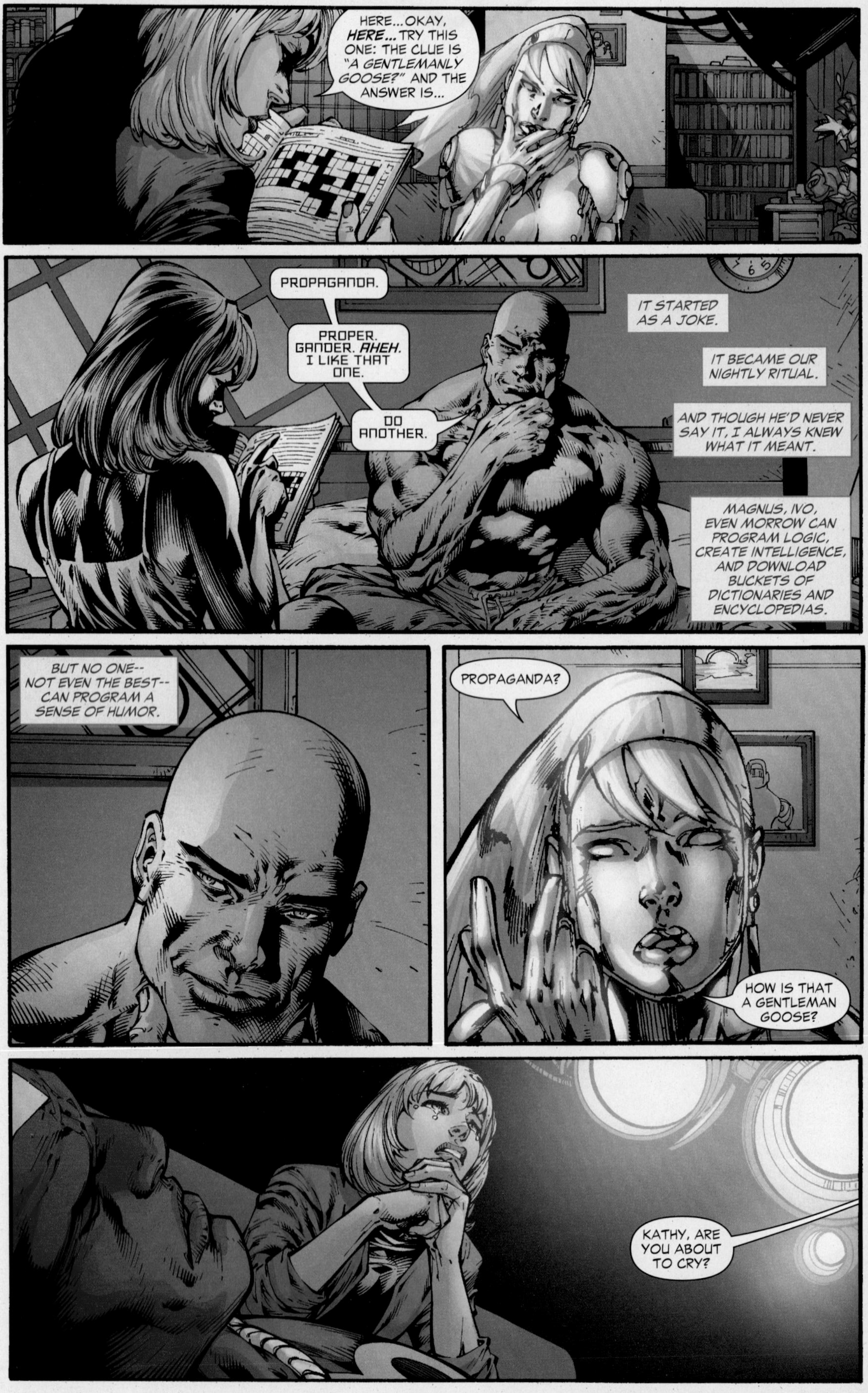

HERE...OKAY, HERE... TRY THIS ONE: THE CLUE IS "A GENTLEMANLY GOOSE?" AND THE ANSWER IS...
PROPAGANDA.
PROPER. GANDER. AHEH. I LIKE THAT ONE.
DO ANOTHER.
IT STARTED AS A JOKE.
IT BECAME OUR NIGHTLY RITUAL.
AND THOUGH HE'D NEVER SAY IT, I ALWAYS KNEW WHAT IT MEANT.
MAGNUS, IVO, EVEN MORROW CAN PROGRAM LOGIC, CREATE INTELLIGENCE, AND DOWNLOAD BUCKETS OF DICTIONARIES AND ENCYCLOPEDIAS.
BUT NO ONE-- NOT EVEN THE BEST-- CAN PROGRAM A SENSE OF HUMOR.
PROPAGANDA?
HOW IS THAT A GENTLEMAN GOOSE?
KATHY, ARE YOU ABOUT TO CRY?

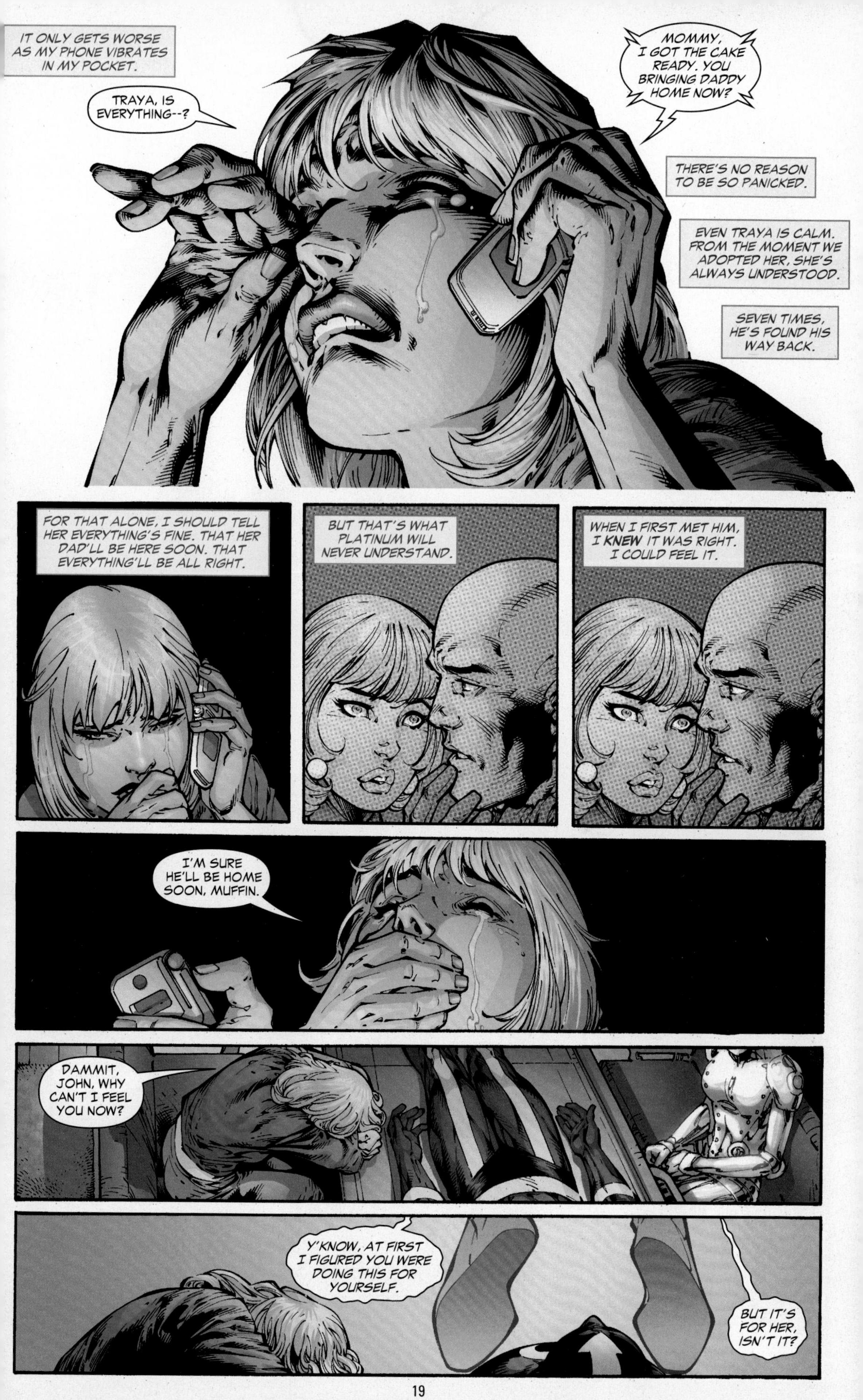
IT ONLY GETS WORSE AS MY PHONE VIBRATES IN MY POCKET.
TRAYA, IS EVERYTHING--?
MOMMY, I GOT THE CAKE READY. YOU BRINGING DADDY HOME NOW?
THERE'S NO REASON TO BE SO PANICKED.
EVEN TRAYA IS CALM. FROM THE MOMENT WE ADOPTED HER, SHE'S ALWAYS UNDERSTOOD.
SEVEN TIMES, HE'S FOUND HIS WAY BACK.
FOR THAT ALONE, I SHOULD TELL HER EVERYTHING'S FINE. THAT HER DAD'LL BE HERE SOON. THAT EVERYTHING'LL BE ALL RIGHT.
BUT THAT'S WHAT PLATINUM WILL NEVER UNDERSTAND.
WHEN I FIRST MET HIM, I **KNEW** IT WAS RIGHT. I COULD FEEL IT.
I'M SURE HE'LL BE HOME SOON, MUFFIN.
DAMMIT, JOHN, WHY CAN'T I FEEL YOU NOW?
Y'KNOW, AT FIRST I FIGURED YOU WERE DOING THIS FOR YOURSELF.
BUT IT'S FOR HER, ISN'T IT?

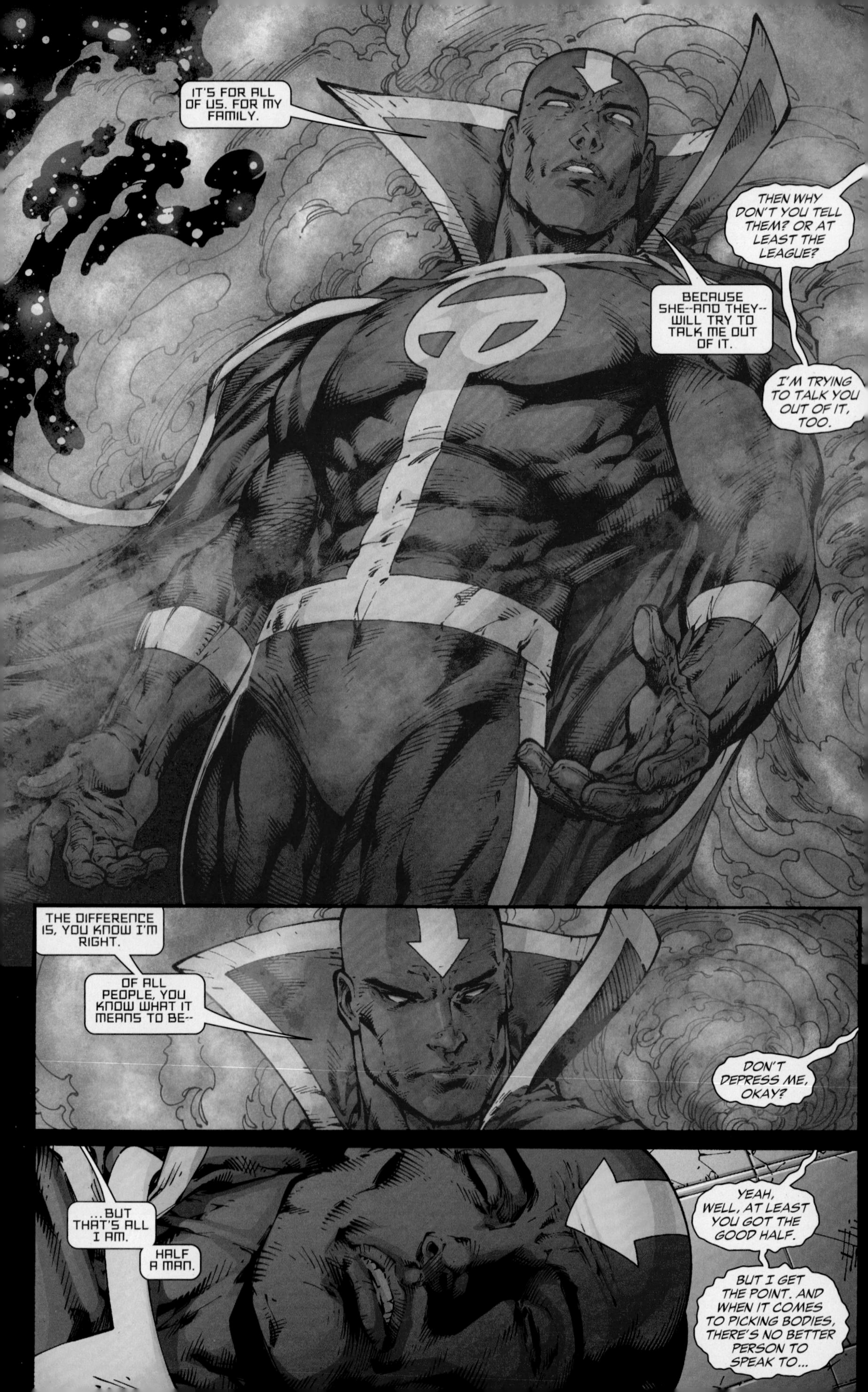
IT'S FOR ALL OF US. FOR MY FAMILY.
THEN WHY DON'T YOU TELL THEM? OR AT LEAST THE LEAGUE?
BECAUSE SHE--AND THEY--WILL TRY TO TALK ME OUT OF IT.
I'M TRYING TO TALK YOU OUT OF IT, TOO.
THE DIFFERENCE IS, YOU KNOW I'M RIGHT.
OF ALL PEOPLE, YOU KNOW WHAT IT MEANS TO BE--
DON'T DEPRESS ME, OKAY?
...BUT THAT'S ALL I AM.
HALF A MAN.
YEAH, WELL, AT LEAST YOU GOT THE GOOD HALF.
BUT I GET THE POINT. AND WHEN IT COMES TO PICKING BODIES, THERE'S NO BETTER PERSON TO SPEAK TO...

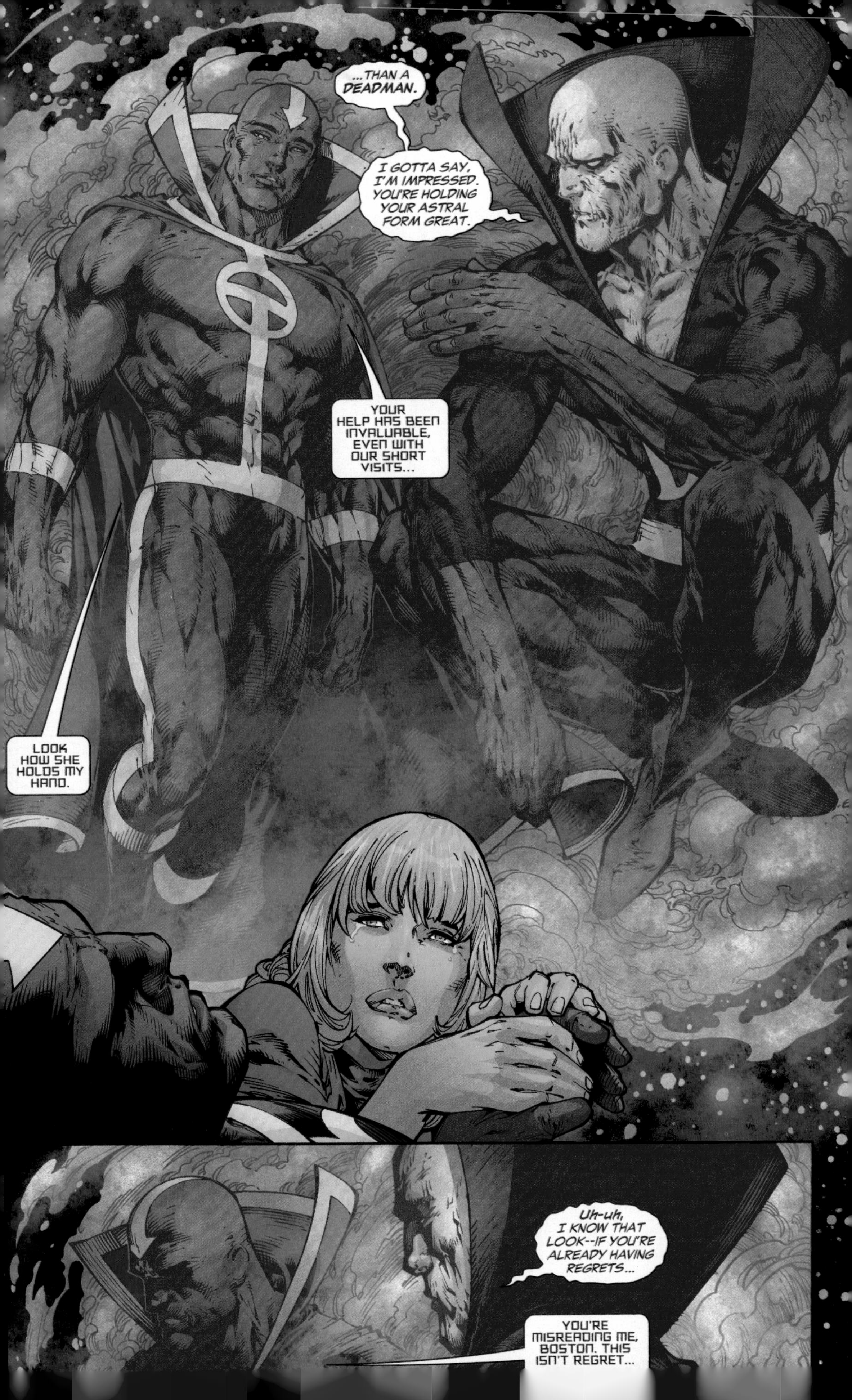
...THAN A DEADMAN.
I GOTTA SAY, I'M IMPRESSED. YOU'RE HOLDING YOUR ASTRAL FORM GREAT.
YOUR HELP HAS BEEN INVALUABLE, EVEN WITH OUR SHORT VISITS...
LOOK HOW SHE HOLDS MY HAND.
Uh-uh, I KNOW THAT LOOK--IF YOU'RE ALREADY HAVING REGRETS...
YOU'RE MISREADING ME, BOSTON. THIS ISN'T REGRET...

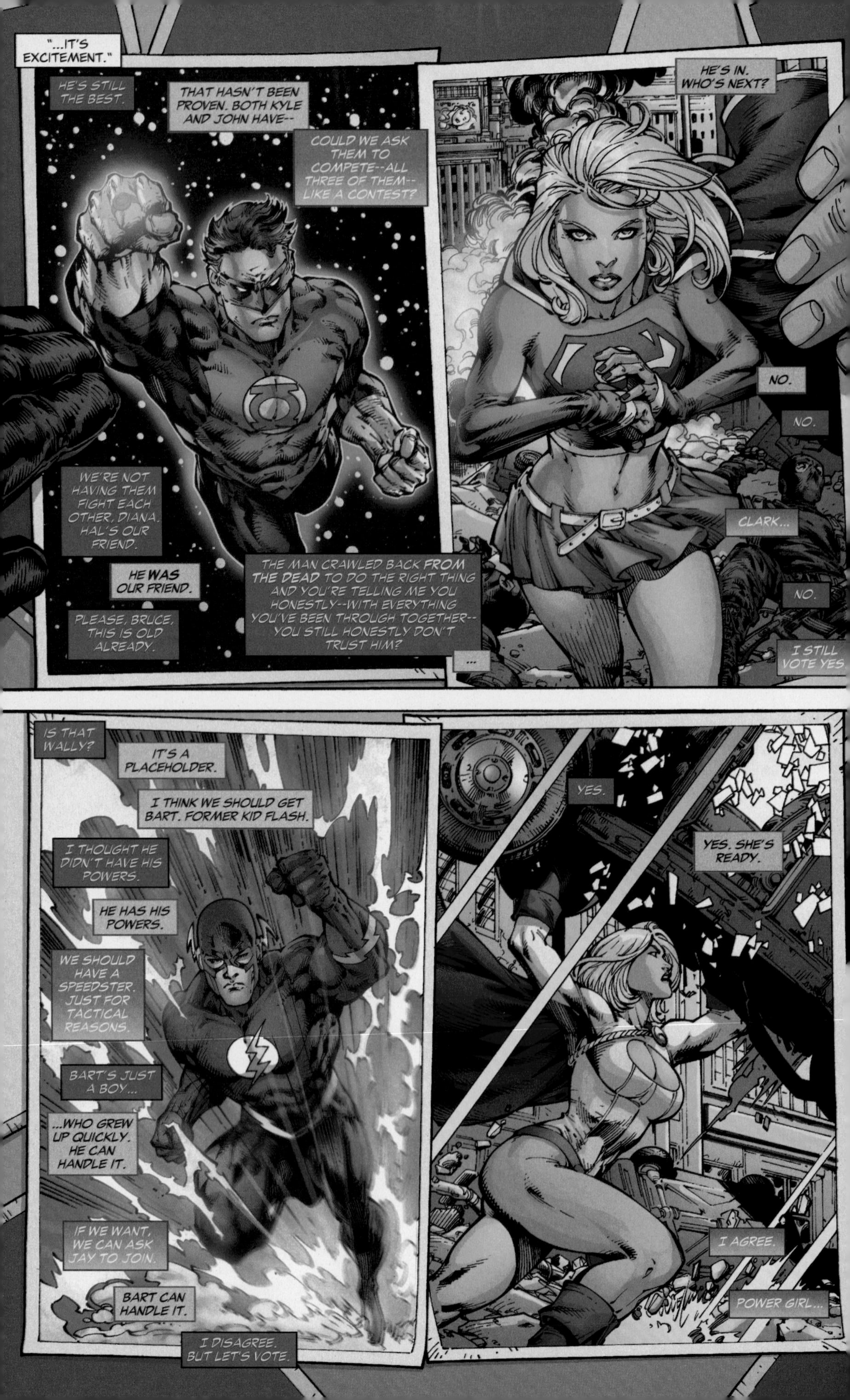
"...IT'S EXCITEMENT."
HE'S STILL THE BEST.
THAT HASN'T BEEN PROVEN. BOTH KYLE AND JOHN HAVE--
COULD WE ASK THEM TO COMPETE--ALL THREE OF THEM--LIKE A CONTEST?
WE'RE NOT HAVING THEM FIGHT EACH OTHER, DIANA. HAL'S OUR FRIEND.
HE WAS OUR FRIEND.
PLEASE, BRUCE, THIS IS OLD ALREADY.
THE MAN CRAWLED BACK FROM THE DEAD TO DO THE RIGHT THING AND YOU'RE TELLING ME YOU HONESTLY--WITH EVERYTHING YOU'VE BEEN THROUGH TOGETHER--YOU STILL HONESTLY DON'T TRUST HIM?
...
HE'S IN. WHO'S NEXT?
NO.
NO.
CLARK...
NO.
I STILL VOTE YES
IS THAT WALLY?
IT'S A PLACEHOLDER.
I THINK WE SHOULD GET BART. FORMER KID FLASH.
I THOUGHT HE DIDN'T HAVE HIS POWERS.
HE HAS HIS POWERS.
WE SHOULD HAVE A SPEEDSTER. JUST FOR TACTICAL REASONS.
BART'S JUST A BOY...
...WHO GREW UP QUICKLY. HE CAN HANDLE IT.
IF WE WANT, WE CAN ASK JAY TO JOIN.
BART CAN HANDLE IT.
I DISAGREE. BUT LET'S VOTE.
YES.
YES. SHE'S READY.
I AGREE.
POWER GIRL...

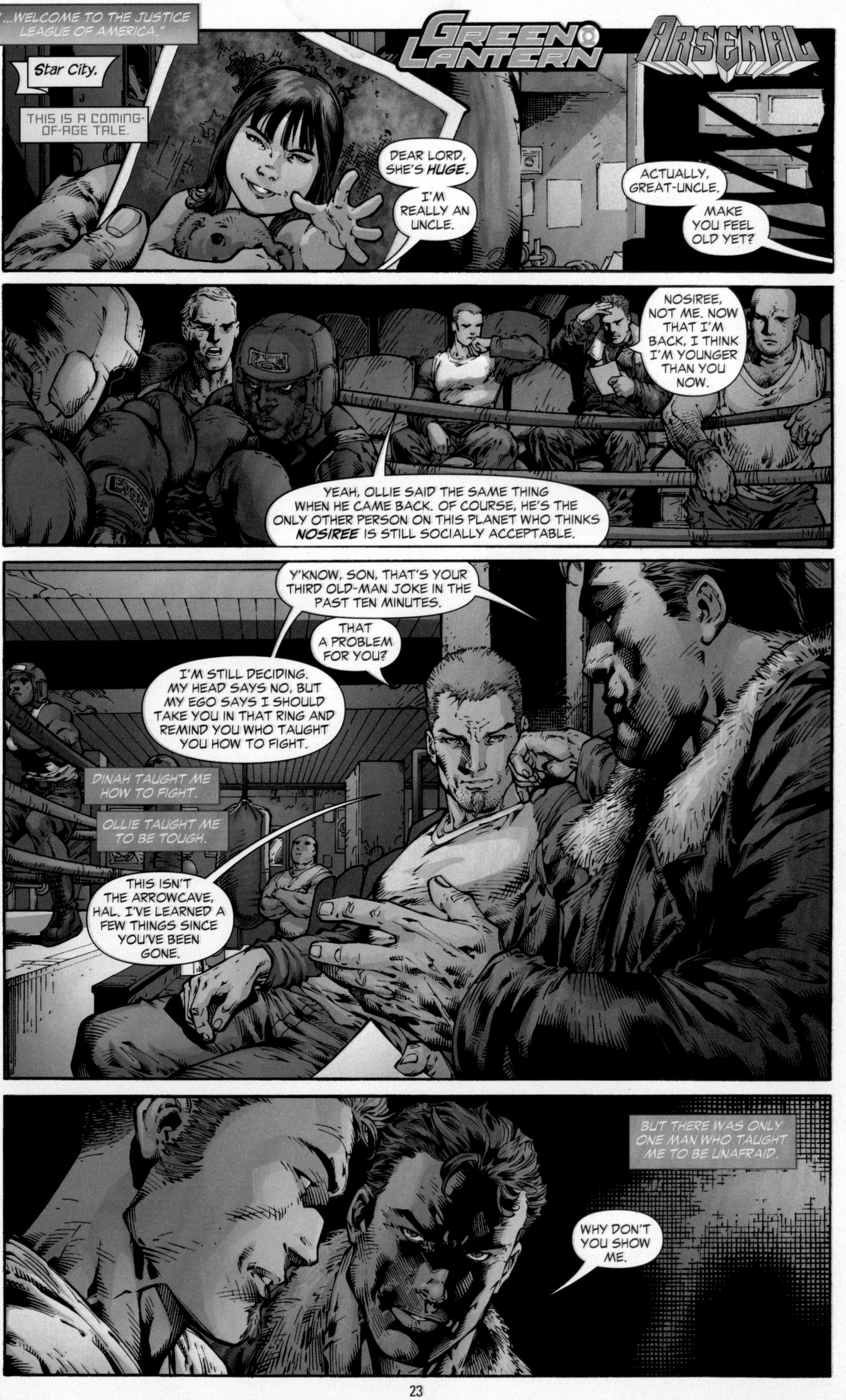
"...WELCOME TO THE JUSTICE LEAGUE OF AMERICA."
GREEN LANTERN
ARSENAL
Star City.
THIS IS A COMING-OF-AGE TALE.
DEAR LORD, SHE'S HUGE.
I'M REALLY AN UNCLE.
ACTUALLY, GREAT-UNCLE.
MAKE YOU FEEL OLD YET?
NOSIREE, NOT ME. NOW THAT I'M BACK, I THINK I'M YOUNGER THAN YOU NOW.
YEAH, OLLIE SAID THE SAME THING WHEN HE CAME BACK. OF COURSE, HE'S THE ONLY OTHER PERSON ON THIS PLANET WHO THINKS NOSIREE IS STILL SOCIALLY ACCEPTABLE.
Y'KNOW, SON, THAT'S YOUR THIRD OLD-MAN JOKE IN THE PAST TEN MINUTES.
THAT A PROBLEM FOR YOU?
I'M STILL DECIDING. MY HEAD SAYS NO, BUT MY EGO SAYS I SHOULD TAKE YOU IN THAT RING AND REMIND YOU WHO TAUGHT YOU HOW TO FIGHT.
DINAH TAUGHT ME HOW TO FIGHT.
OLLIE TAUGHT ME TO BE TOUGH.
THIS ISN'T THE ARROWCAVE, HAL. I'VE LEARNED A FEW THINGS SINCE YOU'VE BEEN GONE.
BUT THERE WAS ONLY ONE MAN WHO TAUGHT ME TO BE UNAFRAID.
WHY DON'T YOU SHOW ME.

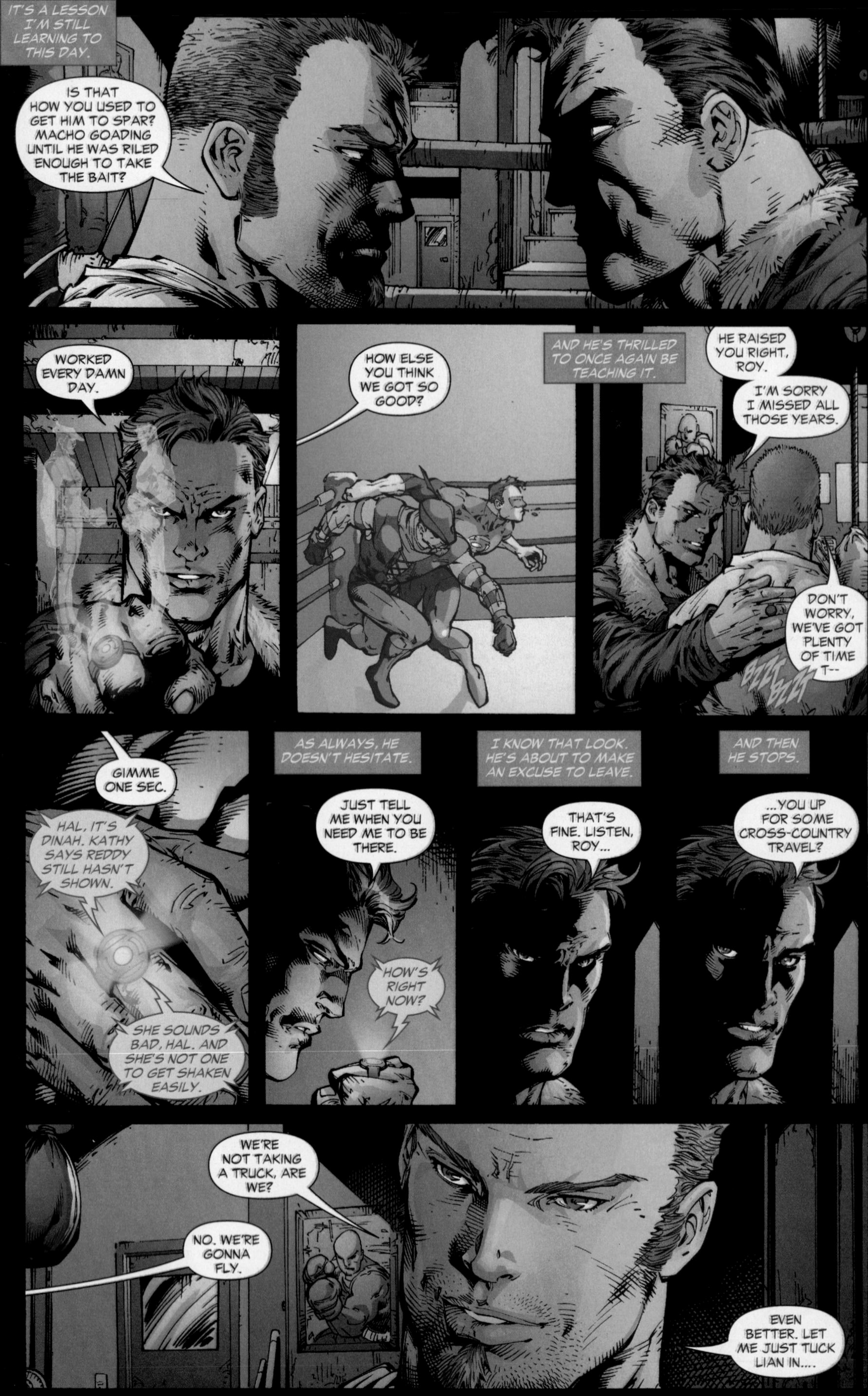
IT'S A LESSON I'M STILL LEARNING TO THIS DAY.
IS THAT HOW YOU USED TO GET HIM TO SPAR? MACHO GOADING UNTIL HE WAS RILED ENOUGH TO TAKE THE BAIT?
WORKED EVERY DAMN DAY.
HOW ELSE YOU THINK WE GOT SO GOOD?
AND HE'S THRILLED TO ONCE AGAIN BE TEACHING IT.
HE RAISED YOU RIGHT, ROY.
I'M SORRY I MISSED ALL THOSE YEARS.
DON'T WORRY, WE'VE GOT PLENTY OF TIME T--
BZZT BZZT
GIMME ONE SEC.
HAL, IT'S DINAH. KATHY SAYS REDDY STILL HASN'T SHOWN.
SHE SOUNDS BAD, HAL. AND SHE'S NOT ONE TO GET SHAKEN EASILY.
AS ALWAYS, HE DOESN'T HESITATE.
JUST TELL ME WHEN YOU NEED ME TO BE THERE.
HOW'S RIGHT NOW?
I KNOW THAT LOOK. HE'S ABOUT TO MAKE AN EXCUSE TO LEAVE.
THAT'S FINE. LISTEN, ROY...
AND THEN HE STOPS.
...YOU UP FOR SOME CROSS-COUNTRY TRAVEL?
WE'RE NOT TAKING A TRUCK, ARE WE?
NO. WE'RE GONNA FLY.
EVEN BETTER. LET ME JUST TUCK LIAN IN....

"...AND MAKE SURE EVERYTHING'S SAFE AT HOME."

Metropolis.

BLACK LIGHTNING

THIS IS A STORY ABOUT FRIENDSHIP.

MY NAME'S JEFFERSON PIERCE.

FOR TWO YEARS, I WORKED IN LEX LUTHOR'S CORRUPT ADMINISTRATION.

THE GOAL WAS TO INFILTRATE AND GAIN LUTHOR'S TRUST.

WE GOT SOMETHING FAR MORE VALUABLE THAN THAT.

WHO ELSE?

FIRST IT WAS PLASTIQUE AND ELECTROCUTIONER, WHO NOW CALL THEMSELVES THE BOMB SQUAD.

THAT'S A STUPID NAME.

THEY THOUGHT IT'D MAKE THEM SOUND SCARIER.

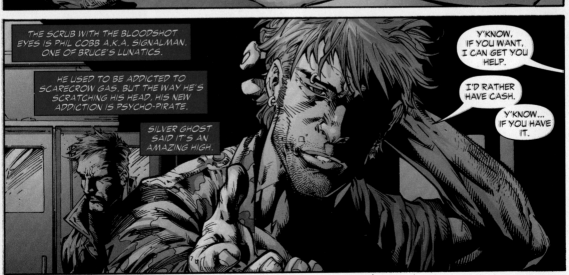

THE SCRUB WITH THE BLOODSHOT EYES IS PHIL COBB A.K.A. SIGNALMAN. ONE OF BRUCE'S LUNATICS.

HE USED TO BE ADDICTED TO SCARECROW GAS. BUT THE WAY HE'S SCRATCHING HIS HEAD, HIS NEW ADDICTION IS PSYCHO-PIRATE.

SILVER GHOST SAID IT'S AN AMAZING HIGH.

Y'KNOW, IF YOU WANT, I CAN GET YOU HELP.

I'D RATHER HAVE CASH.

Y'KNOW... IF YOU HAVE IT.

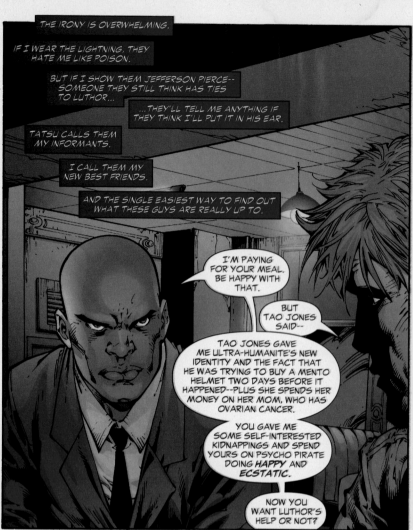

THE IRONY IS OVERWHELMING.

IF I WEAR THE LIGHTNING, THEY HATE ME LIKE POISON.

BUT IF I SHOW THEM JEFFERSON PIERCE-- SOMEONE THEY STILL THINK HAS TIES TO LUTHOR...

...THEY'LL TELL ME ANYTHING IF THEY THINK I'LL PUT IT IN HIS EAR.

TATSU CALLS THEM MY INFORMANTS.

I CALL THEM MY NEW BEST FRIENDS.

AND THE SINGLE EASIEST WAY TO FIND OUT WHAT THESE GUYS ARE REALLY UP TO.

I'M PAYING FOR YOUR MEAL. BE HAPPY WITH THAT.

BUT TAO JONES SAID--

TAO JONES GAVE ME ULTRA-HUMANITE'S NEW IDENTITY AND THE FACT THAT HE WAS TRYING TO BUY A MENTO HELMET TWO DAYS BEFORE IT HAPPENED--PLUS SHE SPENDS HER MONEY ON HER MOM, WHO HAS OVARIAN CANCER.

YOU GAVE ME SOME SELF-INTERESTED KIDNAPPINGS AND SPEND YOURS ON PSYCHO PIRATE DOING HAPPY AND ECSTATIC.

NOW YOU WANT LUTHOR'S HELP OR NOT?

LIKE THE PITCHFORK. Y'KNOW, AQUAMAN'S THING.

THEN TO MAKE IT WORSE, LAST NIGHT, DR. IMPOSSIBLE GOT ATTACKED WITH A-- READY FOR THIS?-- SOME PITCHFORK THING BEFORE HE'S GONE TOO.

DR. IMPOSSIBLE?

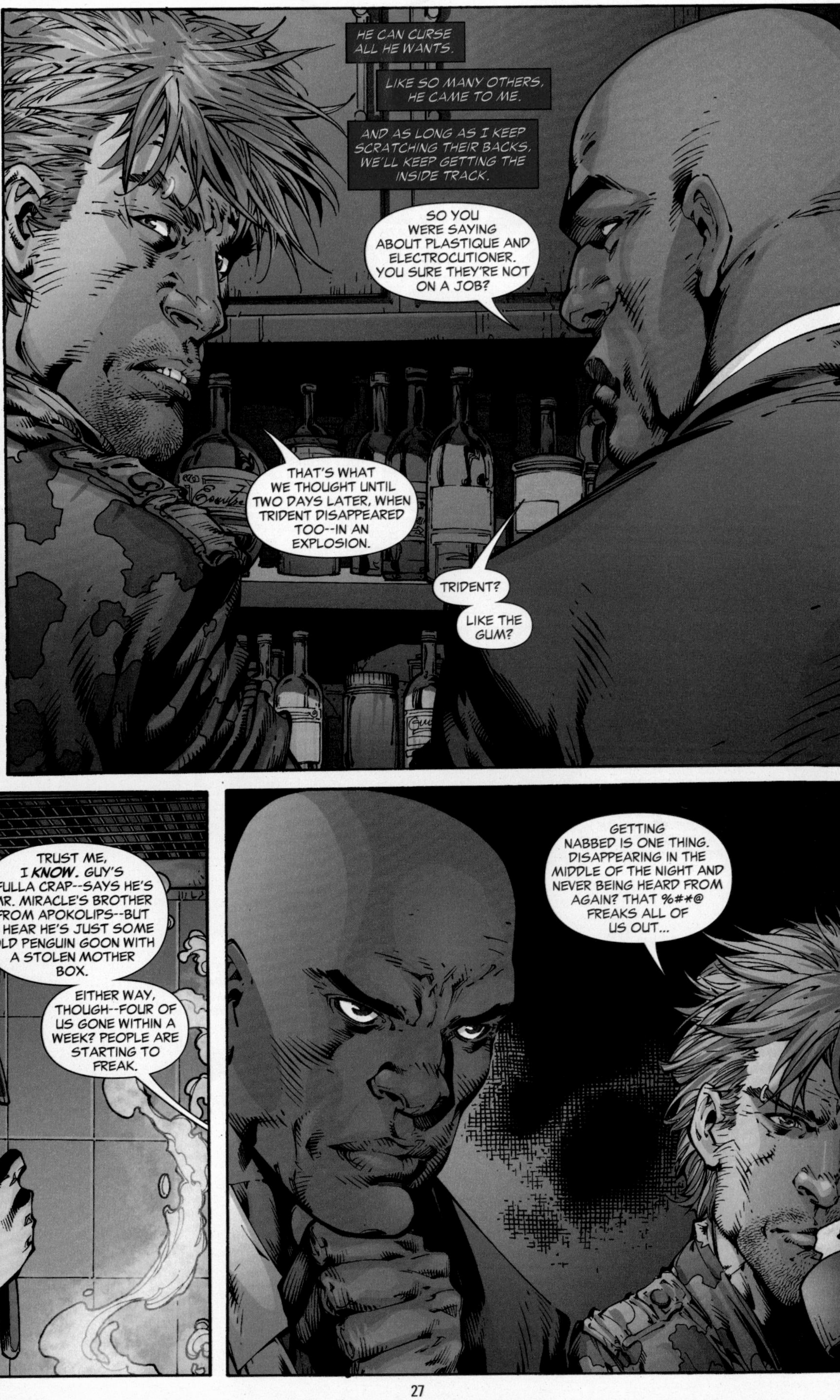
HE CAN CURSE ALL HE WANTS.
LIKE SO MANY OTHERS, HE CAME TO ME.
AND AS LONG AS I KEEP SCRATCHING THEIR BACKS, WE'LL KEEP GETTING THE INSIDE TRACK.
SO YOU WERE SAYING ABOUT PLASTIQUE AND ELECTROCUTIONER. YOU SURE THEY'RE NOT ON A JOB?
THAT'S WHAT WE THOUGHT UNTIL TWO DAYS LATER, WHEN TRIDENT DISAPPEARED TOO--IN AN EXPLOSION.
TRIDENT?
LIKE THE GUM?
TRUST ME, I **KNOW**. GUY'S FULLA CRAP--SAYS HE'S MR. MIRACLE'S BROTHER FROM APOKOLIPS--BUT I HEAR HE'S JUST SOME OLD PENGUIN GOON WITH A STOLEN MOTHER BOX.
EITHER WAY, THOUGH--FOUR OF US GONE WITHIN A WEEK? PEOPLE ARE STARTING TO FREAK.
GETTING NABBED IS ONE THING. DISAPPEARING IN THE MIDDLE OF THE NIGHT AND NEVER BEING HEARD FROM AGAIN? THAT %#*@ FREAKS ALL OF US OUT...

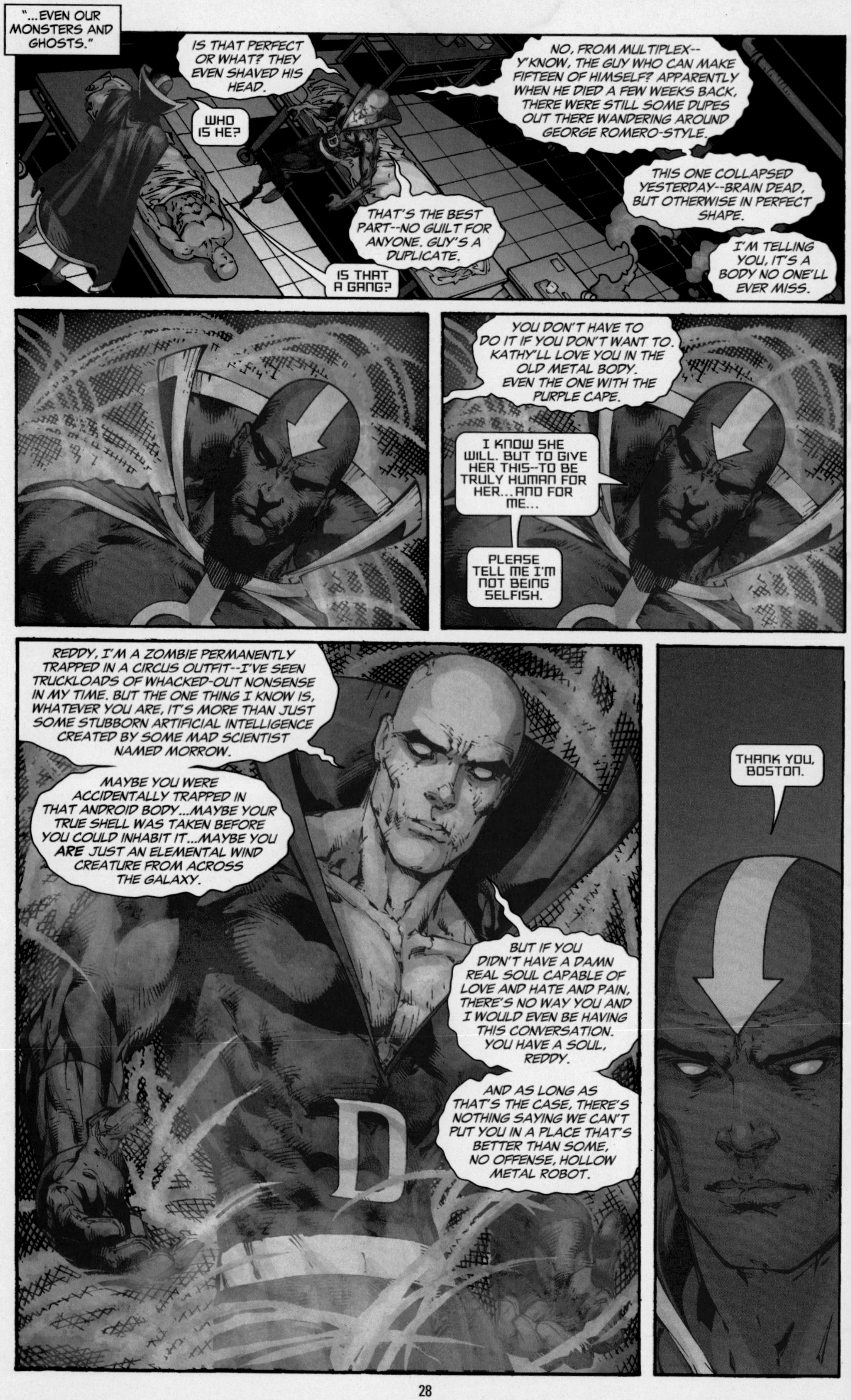
"...EVEN OUR MONSTERS AND GHOSTS."
IS THAT PERFECT OR WHAT? THEY EVEN SHAVED HIS HEAD.
WHO IS HE?
THAT'S THE BEST PART--NO GUILT FOR ANYONE. GUY'S A DUPLICATE.
IS THAT A GANG?
NO, FROM MULTIPLEX-- Y'KNOW, THE GUY WHO CAN MAKE FIFTEEN OF HIMSELF? APPARENTLY WHEN HE DIED A FEW WEEKS BACK, THERE WERE STILL SOME DUPES OUT THERE WANDERING AROUND GEORGE ROMERO-STYLE.
THIS ONE COLLAPSED YESTERDAY--BRAIN DEAD, BUT OTHERWISE IN PERFECT SHAPE.
I'M TELLING YOU, IT'S A BODY NO ONE'LL EVER MISS.
YOU DON'T HAVE TO DO IT IF YOU DON'T WANT TO. KATHY'LL LOVE YOU IN THE OLD METAL BODY. EVEN THE ONE WITH THE PURPLE CAPE.
I KNOW SHE WILL. BUT TO GIVE HER THIS--TO BE TRULY HUMAN FOR HER...AND FOR ME...
PLEASE TELL ME I'M NOT BEING SELFISH.
REDDY, I'M A ZOMBIE PERMANENTLY TRAPPED IN A CIRCUS OUTFIT--I'VE SEEN TRUCKLOADS OF WHACKED-OUT NONSENSE IN MY TIME. BUT THE ONE THING I KNOW IS, WHATEVER YOU ARE, IT'S MORE THAN JUST SOME STUBBORN ARTIFICIAL INTELLIGENCE CREATED BY SOME MAD SCIENTIST NAMED MORROW.
MAYBE YOU WERE ACCIDENTALLY TRAPPED IN THAT ANDROID BODY...MAYBE YOUR TRUE SHELL WAS TAKEN BEFORE YOU COULD INHABIT IT...MAYBE YOU ARE JUST AN ELEMENTAL WIND CREATURE FROM ACROSS THE GALAXY.
BUT IF YOU DIDN'T HAVE A DAMN REAL SOUL CAPABLE OF LOVE AND HATE AND PAIN, THERE'S NO WAY YOU AND I WOULD EVEN BE HAVING THIS CONVERSATION. YOU HAVE A SOUL, REDDY.
AND AS LONG AS THAT'S THE CASE, THERE'S NOTHING SAYING WE CAN'T PUT YOU IN A PLACE THAT'S BETTER THAN SOME, NO OFFENSE, HOLLOW METAL ROBOT.
THANK YOU, BOSTON.

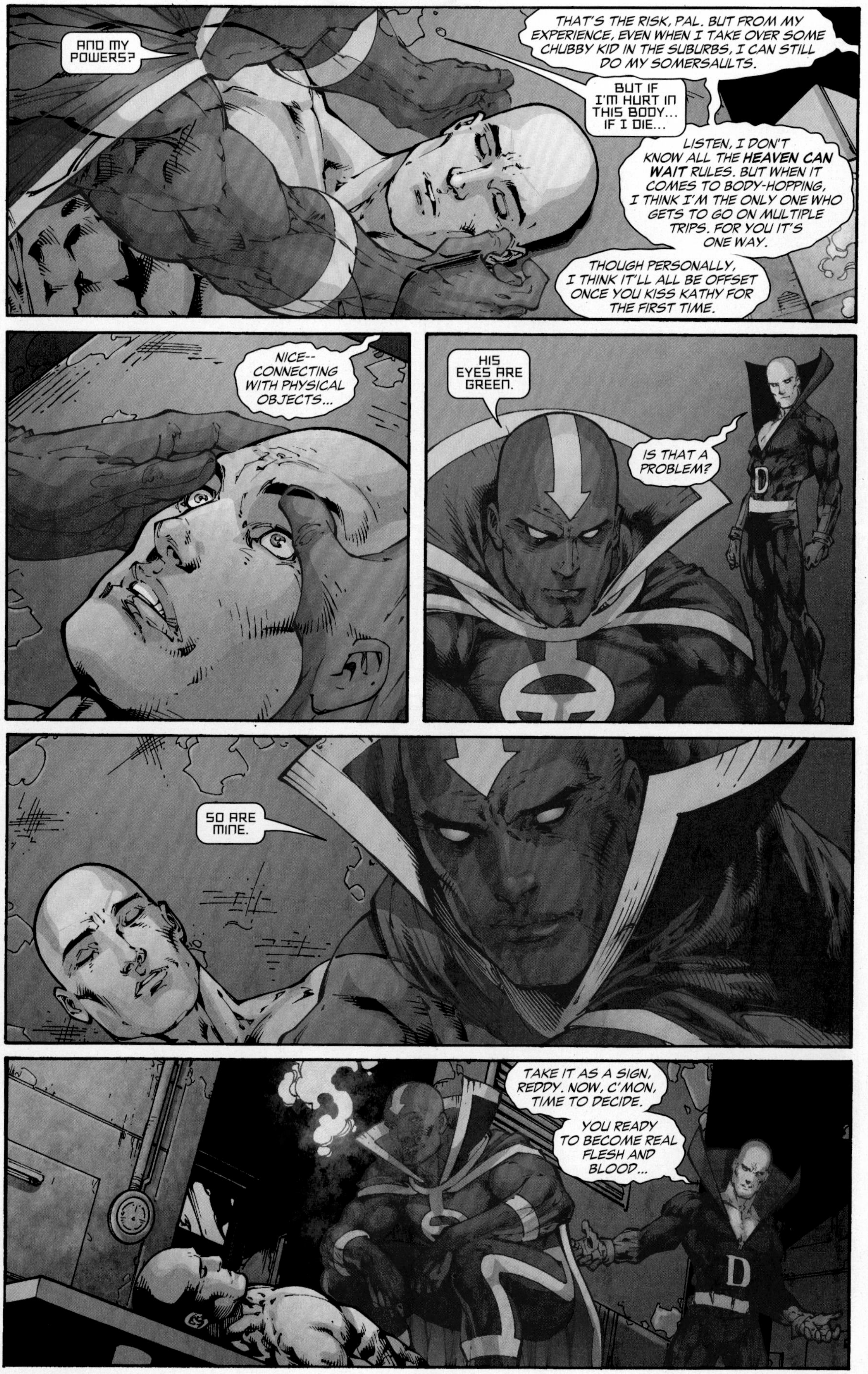
AND MY POWERS?
THAT'S THE RISK, PAL. BUT FROM MY EXPERIENCE, EVEN WHEN I TAKE OVER SOME CHUBBY KID IN THE SUBURBS, I CAN STILL DO MY SOMERSAULTS.
BUT IF I'M HURT IN THIS BODY... IF I DIE...
LISTEN, I DON'T KNOW ALL THE **HEAVEN CAN WAIT** RULES. BUT WHEN IT COMES TO BODY-HOPPING, I THINK I'M THE ONLY ONE WHO GETS TO GO ON MULTIPLE TRIPS. FOR YOU IT'S ONE WAY.
THOUGH PERSONALLY, I THINK IT'LL ALL BE OFFSET ONCE YOU KISS KATHY FOR THE FIRST TIME.
NICE-- CONNECTING WITH PHYSICAL OBJECTS...
HIS EYES ARE GREEN.
IS THAT A PROBLEM?
SO ARE MINE.
TAKE IT AS A SIGN, REDDY. NOW, C'MON, TIME TO DECIDE.
YOU READY TO BECOME REAL FLESH AND BLOOD...

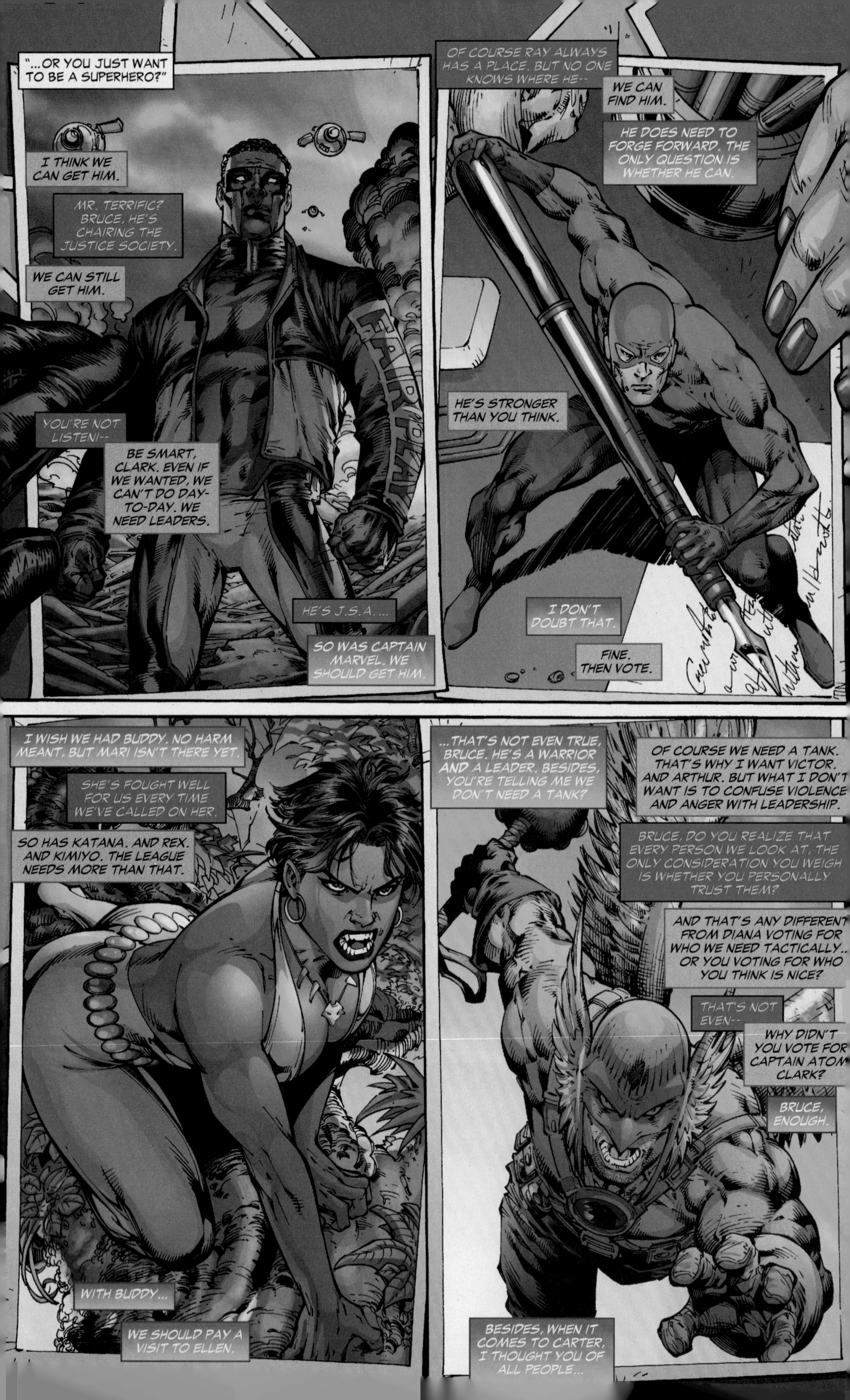
"...OR YOU JUST WANT TO BE A SUPERHERO?"
I THINK WE CAN GET HIM.
MR. TERRIFIC? BRUCE, HE'S CHAIRING THE JUSTICE SOCIETY.
WE CAN STILL GET HIM.
YOU'RE NOT LISTENI--
BE SMART, CLARK. EVEN IF WE WANTED, WE CAN'T DO DAY-TO-DAY. WE NEED LEADERS.
HE'S J.S.A. ...
SO WAS CAPTAIN MARVEL. WE SHOULD GET HIM.
OF COURSE RAY ALWAYS HAS A PLACE. BUT NO ONE KNOWS WHERE HE--
WE CAN FIND HIM.
HE DOES NEED TO FORGE FORWARD. THE ONLY QUESTION IS WHETHER HE CAN.
HE'S STRONGER THAN YOU THINK.
I DON'T DOUBT THAT.
FINE. THEN VOTE.
I WISH WE HAD BUDDY. NO HARM MEANT, BUT MARI ISN'T THERE YET.
SHE'S FOUGHT WELL FOR US EVERY TIME WE'VE CALLED ON HER.
SO HAS KATANA. AND REX. AND KIMIYO. THE LEAGUE NEEDS MORE THAN THAT.
WITH BUDDY...
WE SHOULD PAY A VISIT TO ELLEN.
...THAT'S NOT EVEN TRUE, BRUCE. HE'S A WARRIOR AND A LEADER. BESIDES, YOU'RE TELLING ME WE DON'T NEED A TANK?
OF COURSE WE NEED A TANK. THAT'S WHY I WANT VICTOR. AND ARTHUR. BUT WHAT I DON'T WANT IS TO CONFUSE VIOLENCE AND ANGER WITH LEADERSHIP.
BRUCE, DO YOU REALIZE THAT EVERY PERSON WE LOOK AT, THE ONLY CONSIDERATION YOU WEIGH IS WHETHER YOU PERSONALLY TRUST THEM?
AND THAT'S ANY DIFFERENT FROM DIANA VOTING FOR WHO WE NEED TACTICALLY... OR YOU VOTING FOR WHO YOU THINK IS NICE?
THAT'S NOT EVEN--
WHY DIDN'T YOU VOTE FOR CAPTAIN ATOM, CLARK?
BRUCE, ENOUGH.
BESIDES, WHEN IT COMES TO CARTER, I THOUGHT YOU OF ALL PEOPLE...

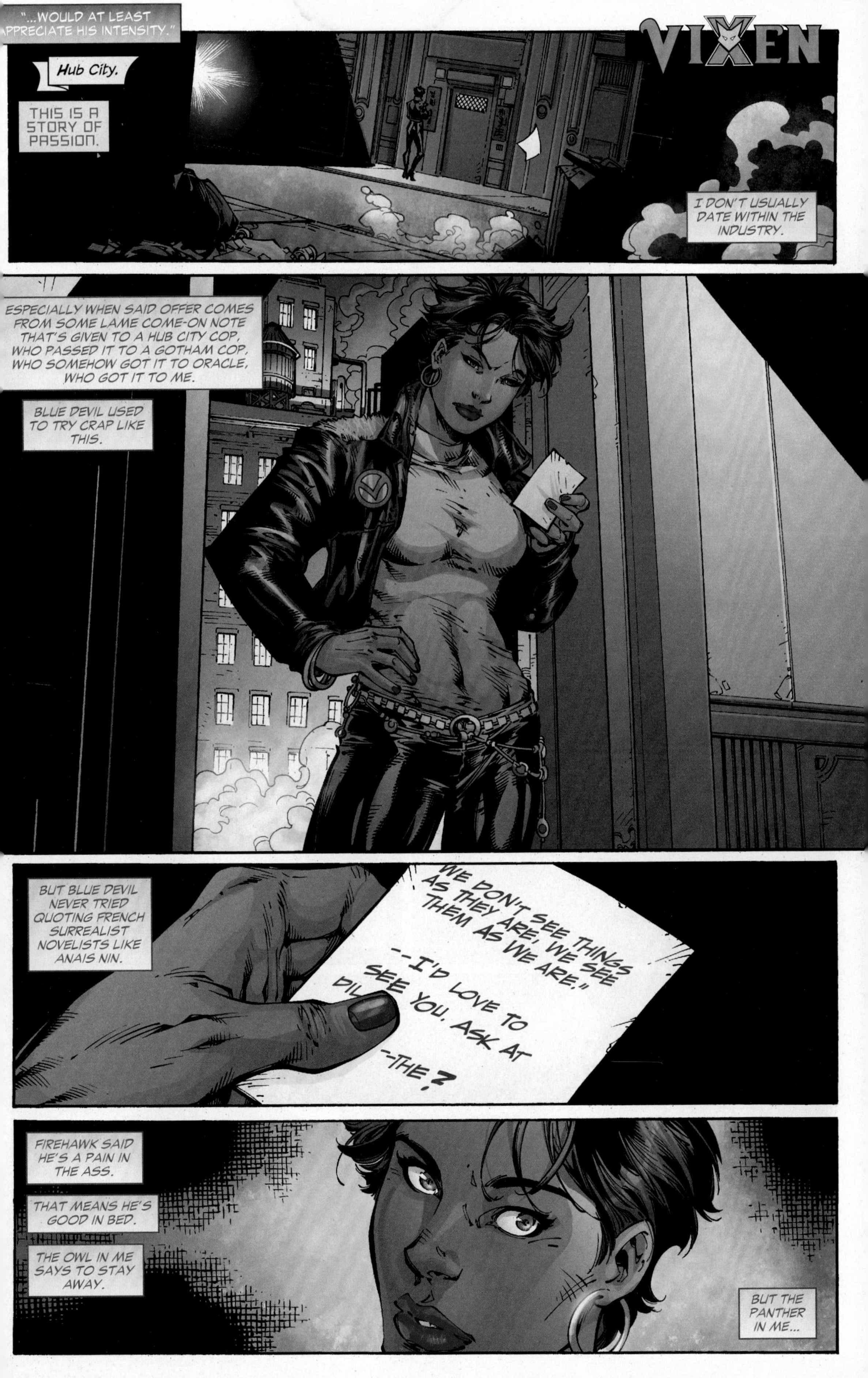

"...WOULD AT LEAST APPRECIATE HIS INTENSITY."
VIXEN
Hub City.
THIS IS A STORY OF PASSION.
I DON'T USUALLY DATE WITHIN THE INDUSTRY.
ESPECIALLY WHEN SAID OFFER COMES FROM SOME LAME COME-ON NOTE THAT'S GIVEN TO A HUB CITY COP, WHO PASSED IT TO A GOTHAM COP, WHO SOMEHOW GOT IT TO ORACLE, WHO GOT IT TO ME.
BLUE DEVIL USED TO TRY CRAP LIKE THIS.
BUT BLUE DEVIL NEVER TRIED QUOTING FRENCH SURREALIST NOVELISTS LIKE ANAIS NIN.
WE DON'T SEE THINGS AS THEY ARE, WE SEE THEM AS WE ARE."
--I'D LOVE TO SEE YOU. ASK AT
--THE ?
FIREHAWK SAID HE'S A PAIN IN THE ASS.
THAT MEANS HE'S GOOD IN BED.
THE OWL IN ME SAYS TO STAY AWAY.
BUT THE PANTHER IN ME...

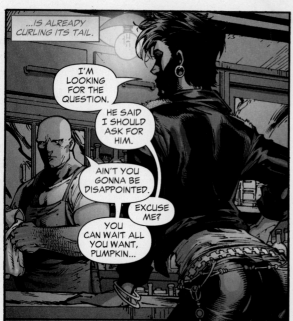

...IS ALREADY CURLING ITS TAIL.

I'M LOOKING FOR THE QUESTION. HE SAID I SHOULD ASK FOR HIM.

AIN'T YOU GONNA BE DISAPPOINTED.

EXCUSE ME?

YOU CAN WAIT ALL YOU WANT, PUMPKIN...

I FEEL THE BIRDS FIRST. SEAGULLS AND TERNS.

...BUT THE QUESTION AIN'T OPERATED OUT OF HUB CITY FOR OVER A YEAR.

DANGER'S COMING.

THEN I FEEL THE TIGER.

ANGER OVERWHELMS ME.

THE PLACE LOOKS EMPTY.

LOOKS AREN'T EVERYTHING.

DOBERMAN.

THEY'RE ALREADY HERE.

SNFF SNFF

LION.

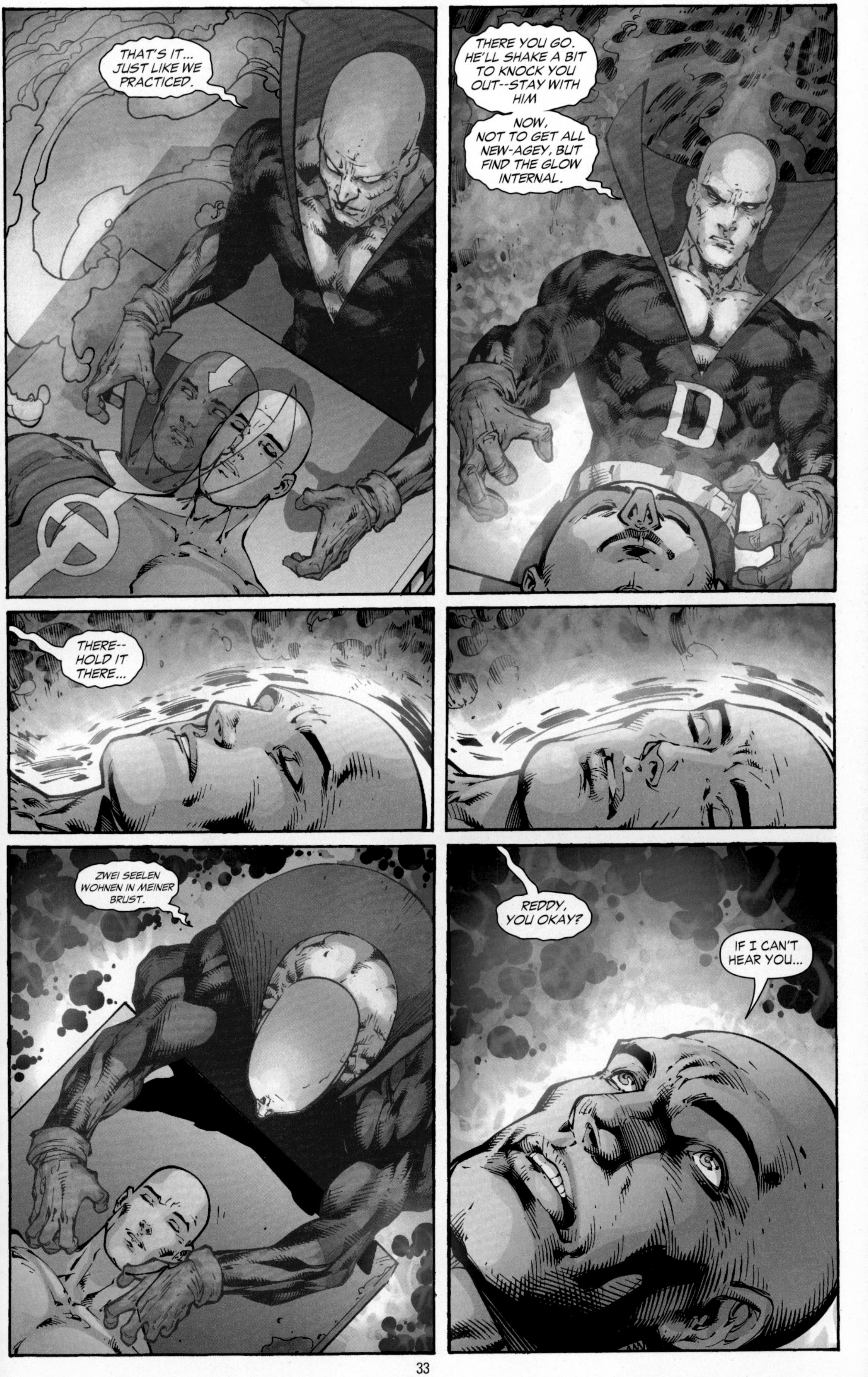
THAT'S IT... JUST LIKE WE PRACTICED.
THERE YOU GO. HE'LL SHAKE A BIT TO KNOCK YOU OUT--STAY WITH HIM
NOW, NOT TO GET ALL NEW-AGEY, BUT FIND THE GLOW INTERNAL.
THERE-- HOLD IT THERE...
ZWEI SEELEN WOHNEN IN MEINER BRUST.
REDDY, YOU OKAY?
IF I CAN'T HEAR YOU...

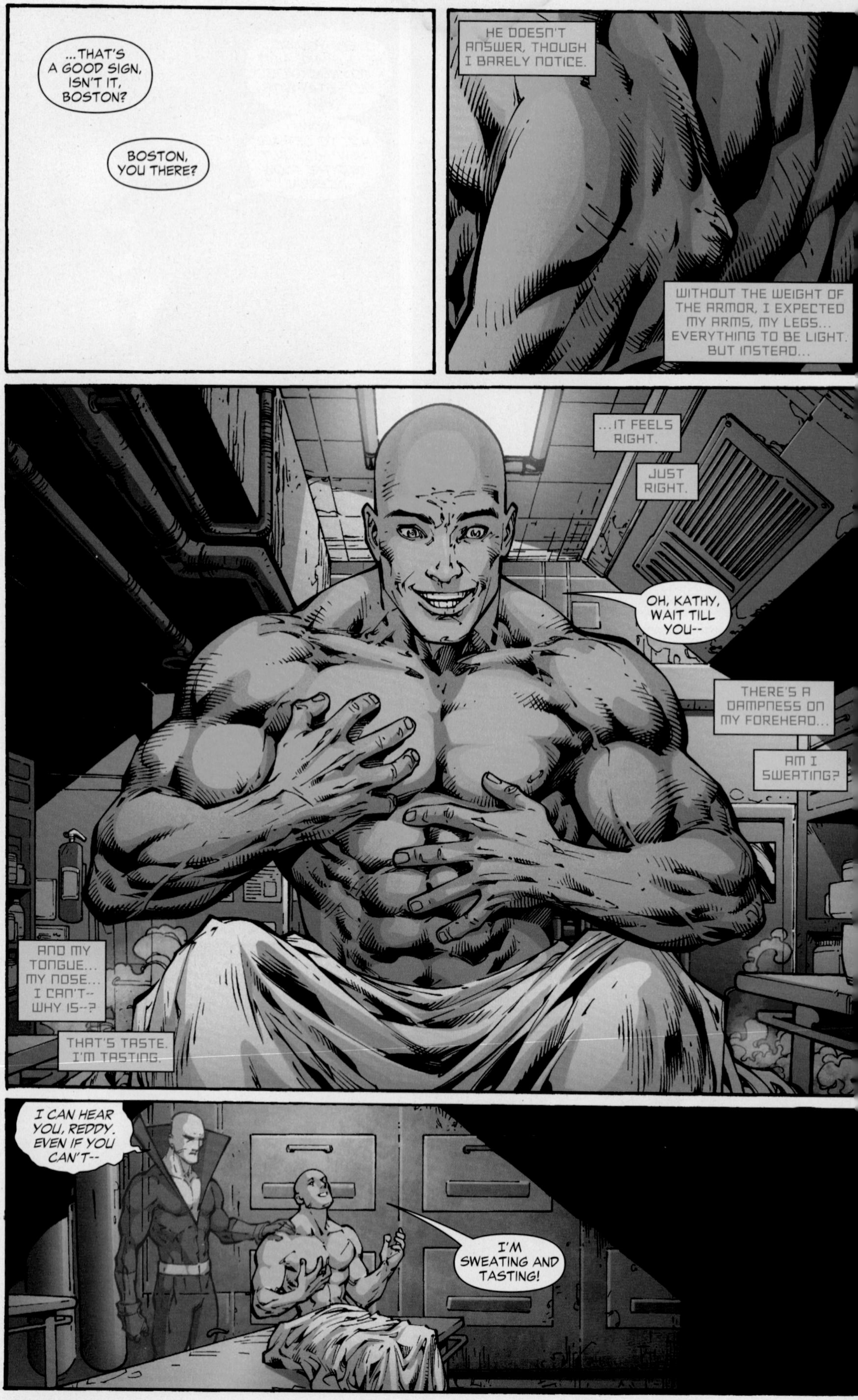
...THAT'S A GOOD SIGN, ISN'T IT, BOSTON?
BOSTON, YOU THERE?
HE DOESN'T ANSWER, THOUGH I BARELY NOTICE.
WITHOUT THE WEIGHT OF THE ARMOR, I EXPECTED MY ARMS, MY LEGS... EVERYTHING TO BE LIGHT. BUT INSTEAD...
...IT FEELS RIGHT.
JUST RIGHT.
OH, KATHY, WAIT TILL YOU--
THERE'S A DAMPNESS ON MY FOREHEAD...
AM I SWEATING?
AND MY TONGUE... MY NOSE... I CAN'T-- WHY IS--?
THAT'S TASTE. I'M TASTING.
I CAN HEAR YOU, REDDY. EVEN IF YOU CAN'T--
I'M SWEATING AND TASTING!

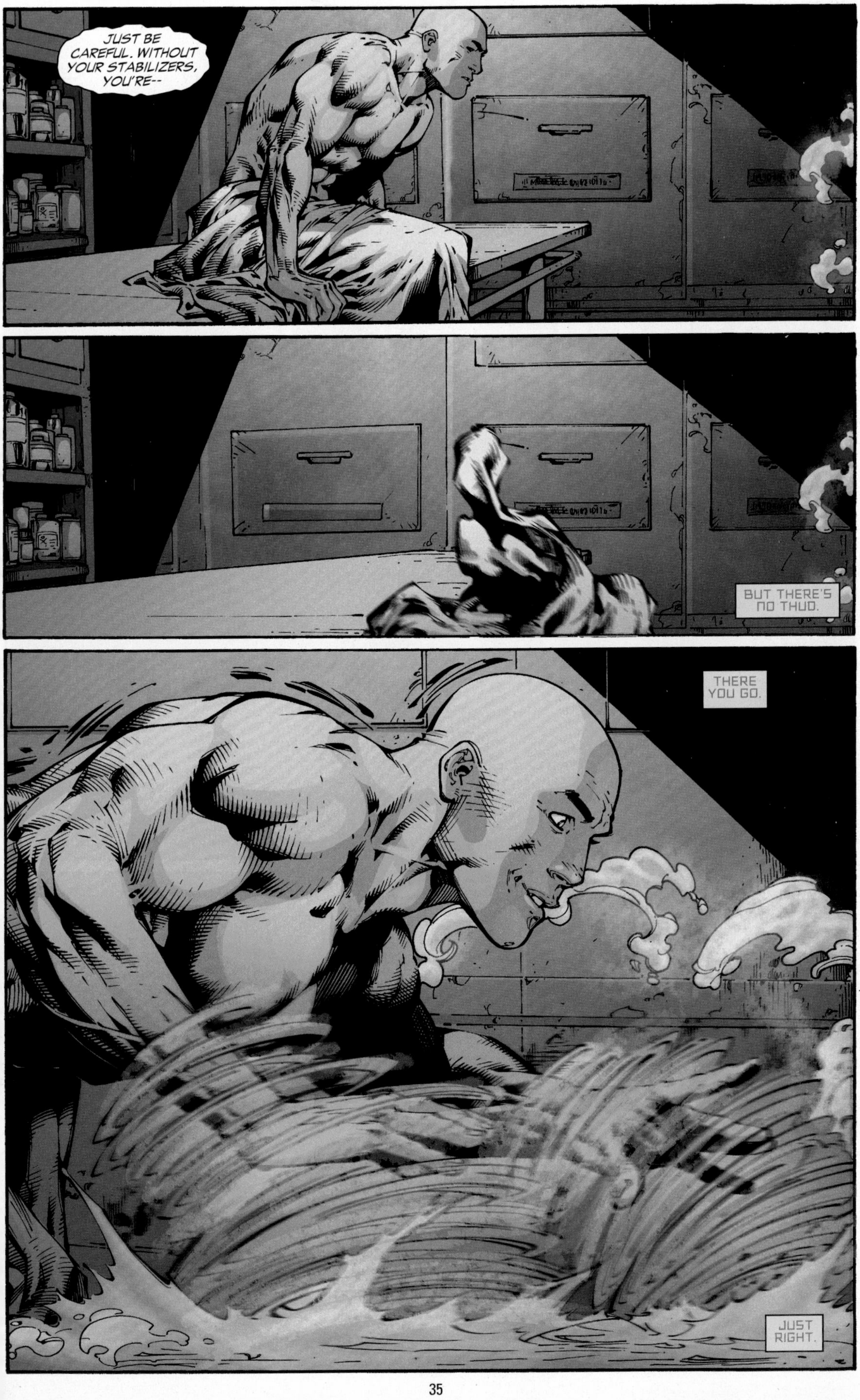
JUST BE CAREFUL. WITHOUT YOUR STABILIZERS, YOU'RE--
BUT THERE'S NO THUD.
THERE YOU GO.
JUST RIGHT.

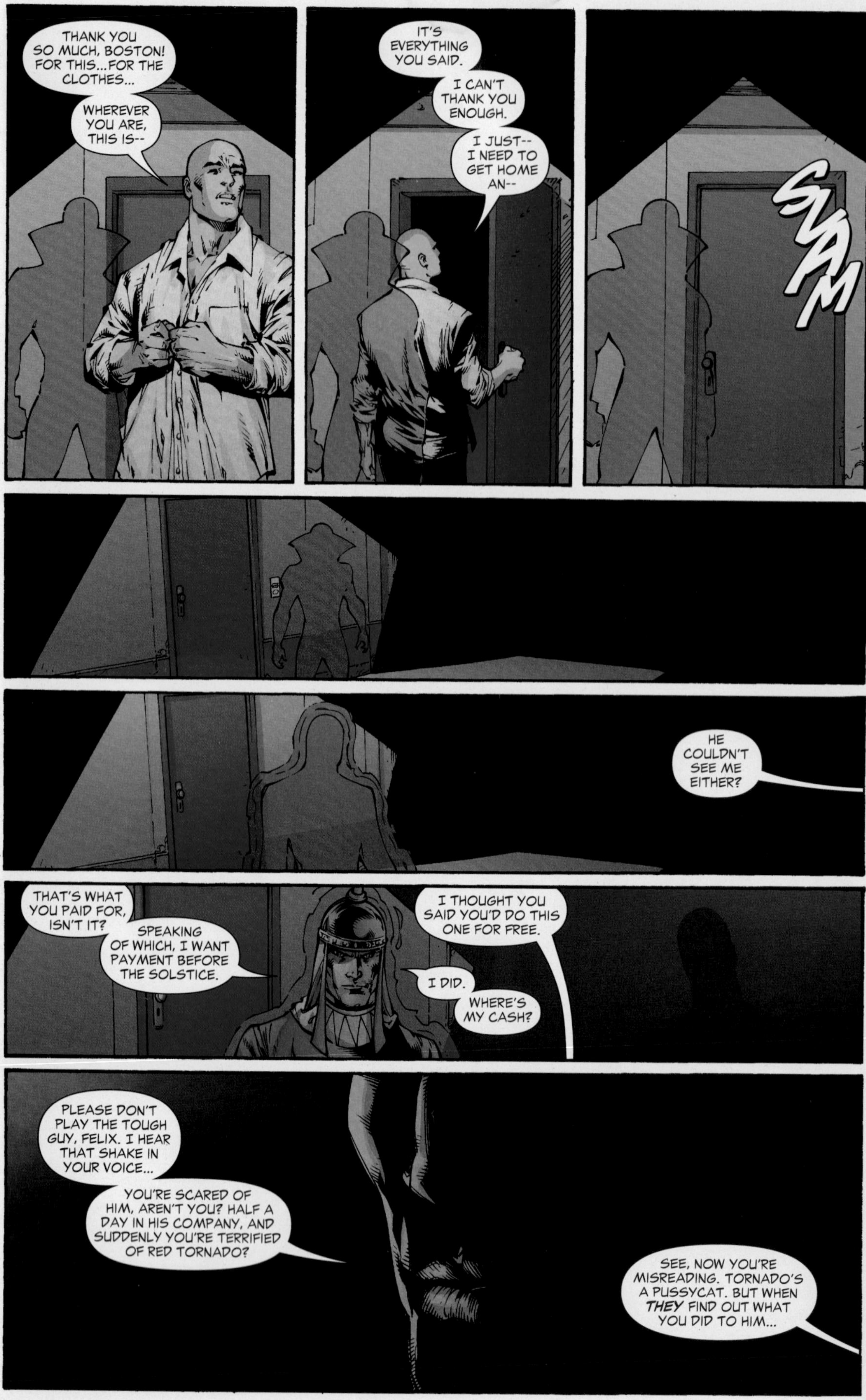
THANK YOU SO MUCH, BOSTON! FOR THIS...FOR THE CLOTHES...
WHEREVER YOU ARE, THIS IS--
IT'S EVERYTHING YOU SAID.
I CAN'T THANK YOU ENOUGH.
I JUST-- I NEED TO GET HOME AN--
SLAM
HE COULDN'T SEE ME EITHER?
THAT'S WHAT YOU PAID FOR, ISN'T IT?
SPEAKING OF WHICH, I WANT PAYMENT BEFORE THE SOLSTICE.
I THOUGHT YOU SAID YOU'D DO THIS ONE FOR FREE.
I DID.
WHERE'S MY CASH?
PLEASE DON'T PLAY THE TOUGH GUY, FELIX. I HEAR THAT SHAKE IN YOUR VOICE...
YOU'RE SCARED OF HIM, AREN'T YOU? HALF A DAY IN HIS COMPANY, AND SUDDENLY YOU'RE TERRIFIED OF RED TORNADO?
SEE, NOW YOU'RE MISREADING. TORNADO'S A PUSSYCAT. BUT WHEN *THEY* FIND OUT WHAT YOU DID TO HIM...

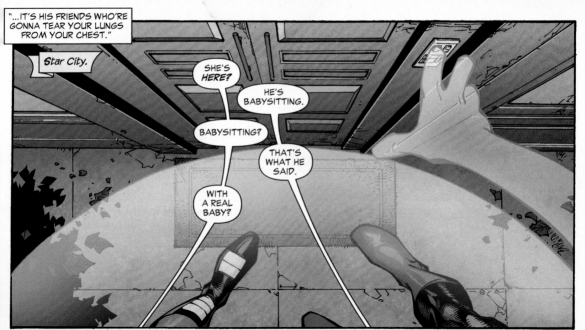

"...IT'S HIS FRIENDS WHO'RE GONNA TEAR YOUR LUNGS FROM YOUR CHEST."

Star City.

SHE'S *HERE?*

HE'S BABYSITTING.

BABYSITTING?

THAT'S WHAT HE SAID.

WITH A REAL BABY?

NO JOKE, DINAH. BABYSITTING. RIGHT NOW.

YOU'RE SERIOUS? AW, JEEZ--THIS IS GONNA BE...

AWKWARD.

WHAT'RE YOU--?

WAIT, CAN ANYONE SEE--?

THAT'S WHAT THE GREEN BUBBLE'S FOR. WE'RE INVISIBLE.

I KNOW THOSE LOOKS.

YOU'RE PUTTING THE BAND BACK TOGETHER, AREN'T YOU?

HOLD ON, I'LL GET MY BOW.

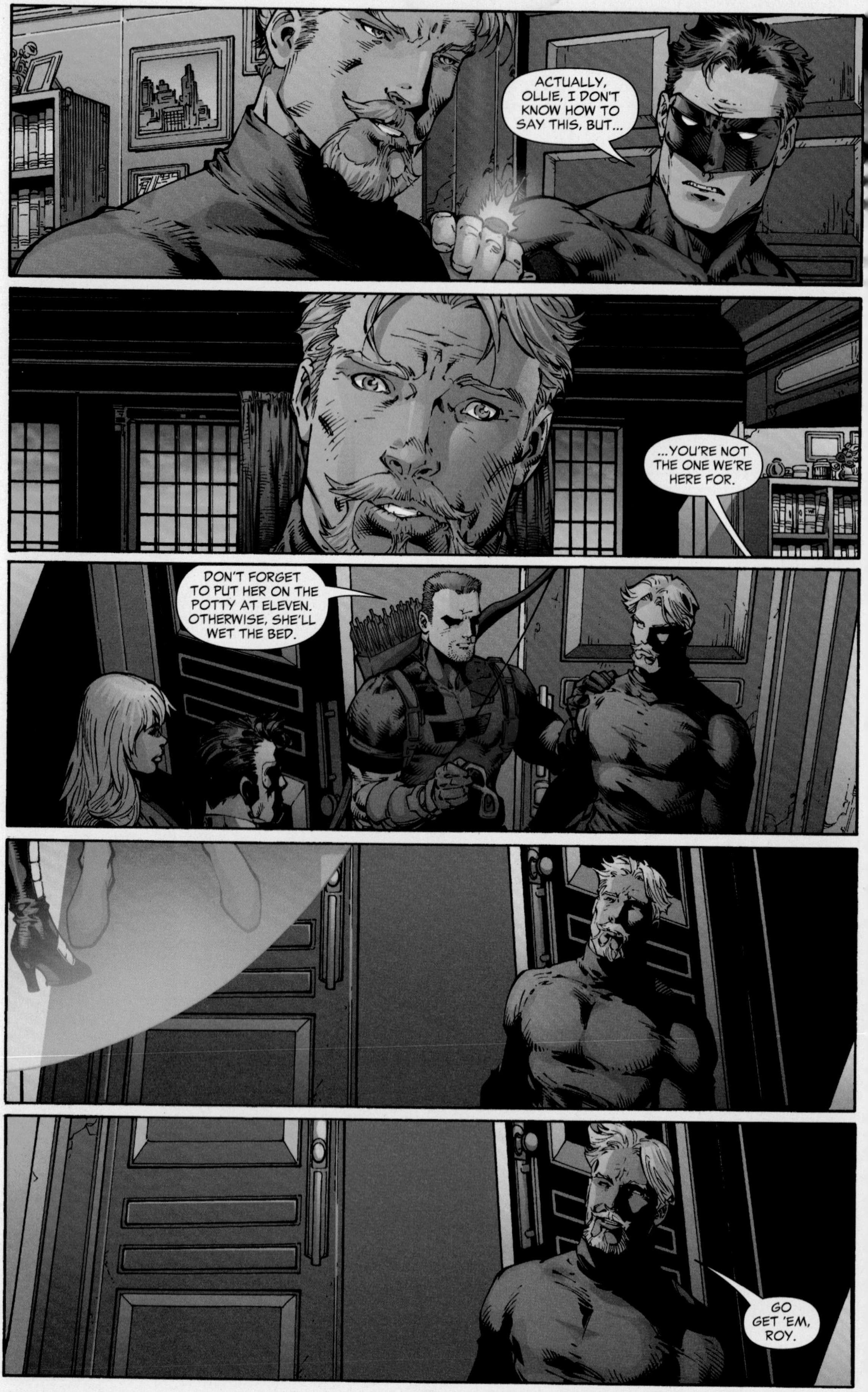
ACTUALLY, OLLIE, I DON'T KNOW HOW TO SAY THIS, BUT...
...YOU'RE NOT THE ONE WE'RE HERE FOR.
DON'T FORGET TO PUT HER ON THE POTTY AT ELEVEN. OTHERWISE, SHE'LL WET THE BED.
GO GET 'EM, ROY.

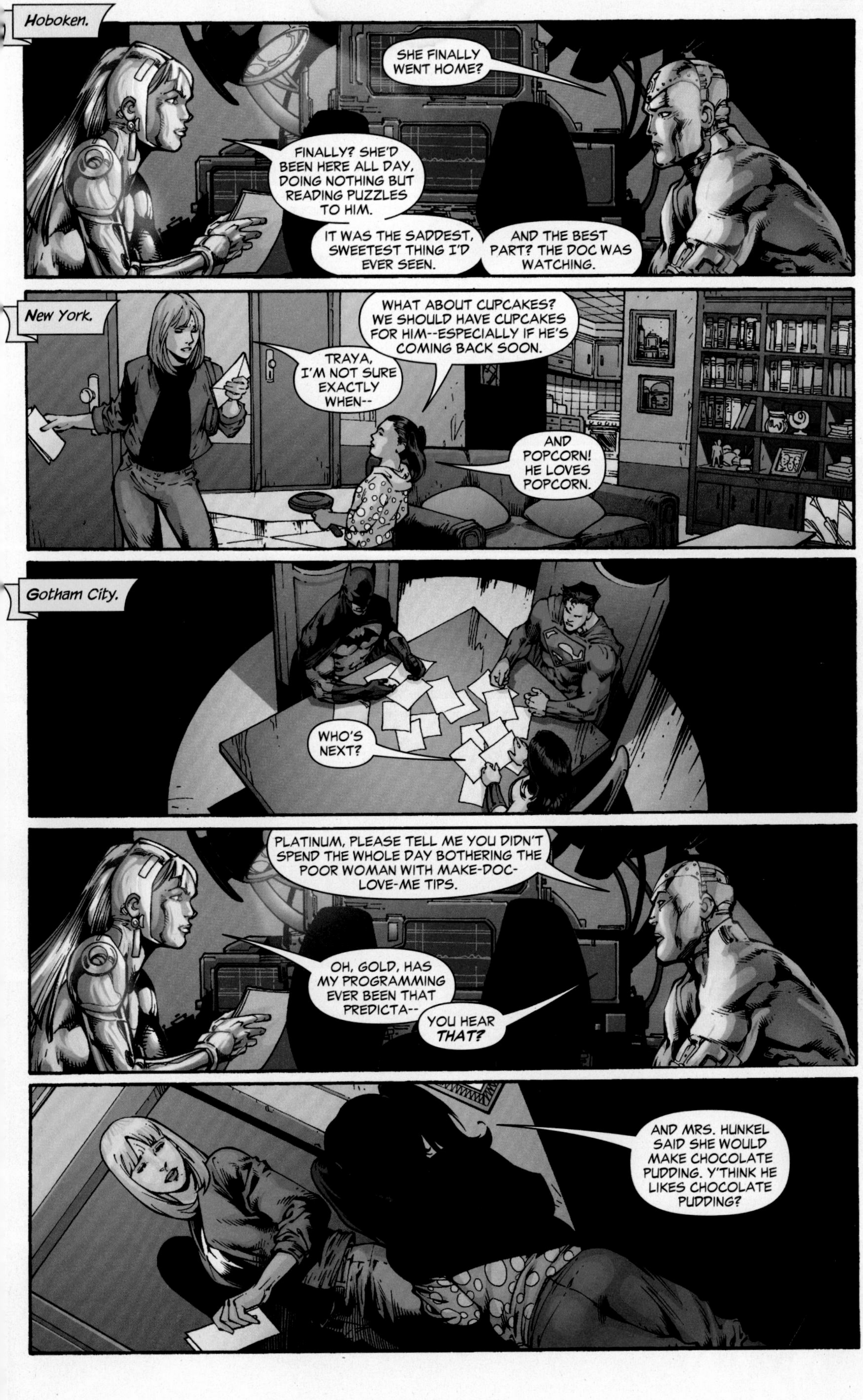
Hoboken.
SHE FINALLY WENT HOME?
FINALLY? SHE'D BEEN HERE ALL DAY, DOING NOTHING BUT READING PUZZLES TO HIM.
IT WAS THE SADDEST, SWEETEST THING I'D EVER SEEN.
AND THE BEST PART? THE DOC WAS WATCHING.
New York.
WHAT ABOUT CUPCAKES? WE SHOULD HAVE CUPCAKES FOR HIM--ESPECIALLY IF HE'S COMING BACK SOON.
TRAYA, I'M NOT SURE EXACTLY WHEN--
AND POPCORN! HE LOVES POPCORN.
Gotham City.
WHO'S NEXT?
PLATINUM, PLEASE TELL ME YOU DIDN'T SPEND THE WHOLE DAY BOTHERING THE POOR WOMAN WITH MAKE-DOC-LOVE-ME TIPS.
OH, GOLD, HAS MY PROGRAMMING EVER BEEN THAT PREDICTA--
YOU HEAR *THAT?*
AND MRS. HUNKEL SAID SHE WOULD MAKE CHOCOLATE PUDDING. Y'THINK HE LIKES CHOCOLATE PUDDING?

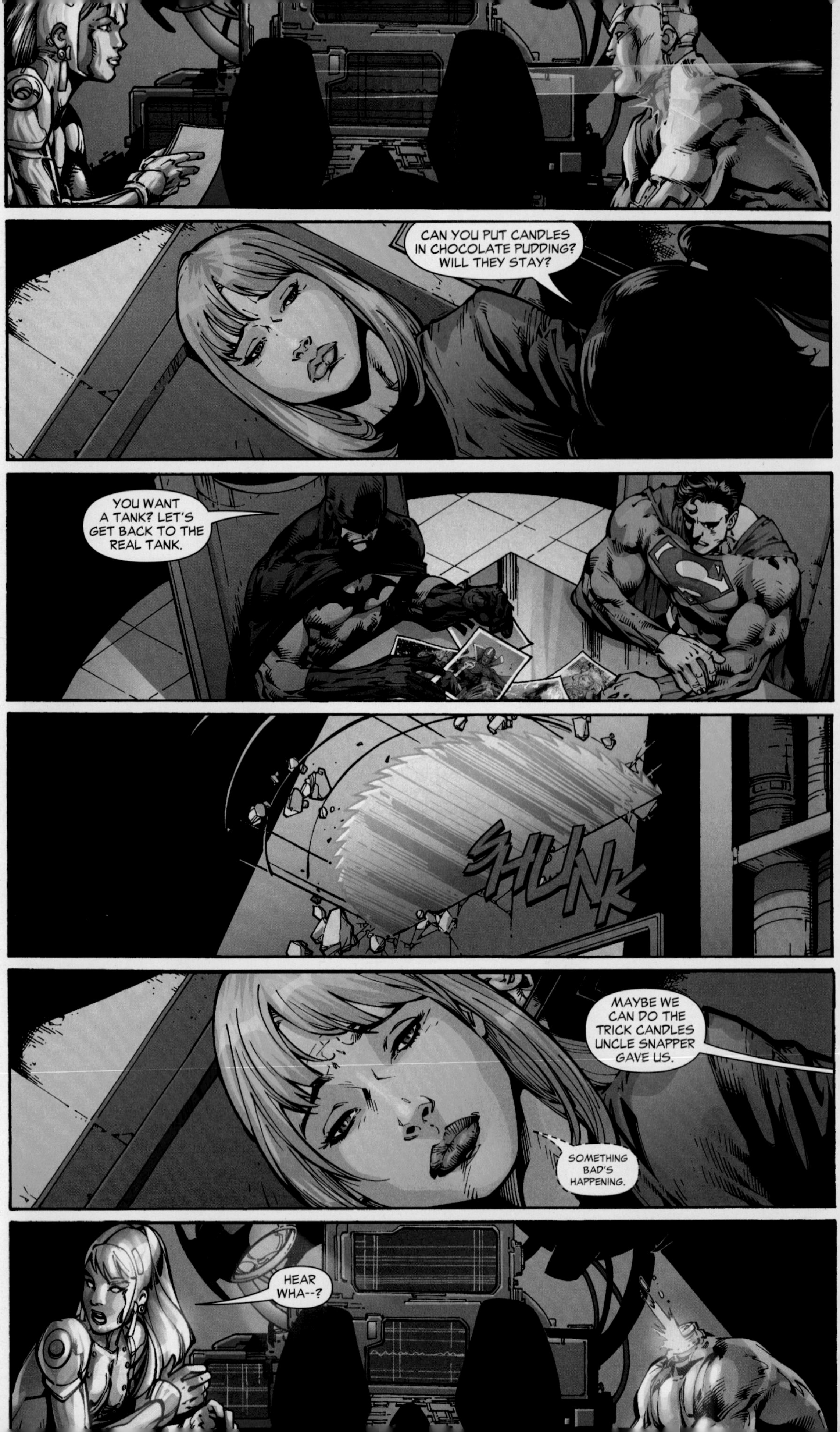
CAN YOU PUT CANDLES IN CHOCOLATE PUDDING? WILL THEY STAY?
YOU WANT A TANK? LET'S GET BACK TO THE REAL TANK.
SHUNK
MAYBE WE CAN DO THE TRICK CANDLES UNCLE SNAPPER GAVE US.
SOMETHING BAD'S HAPPENING.
HEAR WHA--?

5D
SUTTON/SMITH
NOK NOK
MOMMY, SOMEONE'S AT THE DOOR!
GOLD?
SWEET CREATOR! GOLD!
WAIT, WHO ARE--!? HOW DID YOU GET IN HERE?
BRUCE, JUST BECAUSE CARTER--
FORGET CARTER.
YOU EVER TAKEN THE TIME TO SEE WHAT TORNADO'S MADE OF? HE'S NOT JUST A ROBOT, DIANA.
AT THE DOOR! Y'HEAR THAT?
DADDY'S BACK!
MODEL GOLD: OFFLINE
MODEL PLATINUM: OFFLINE
ALARM ENGAGED.

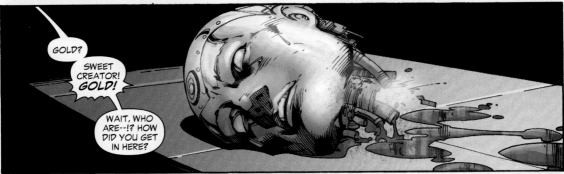

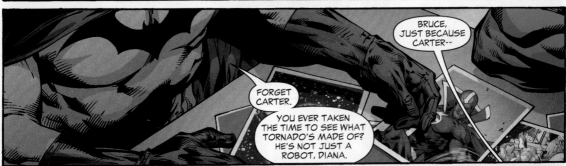

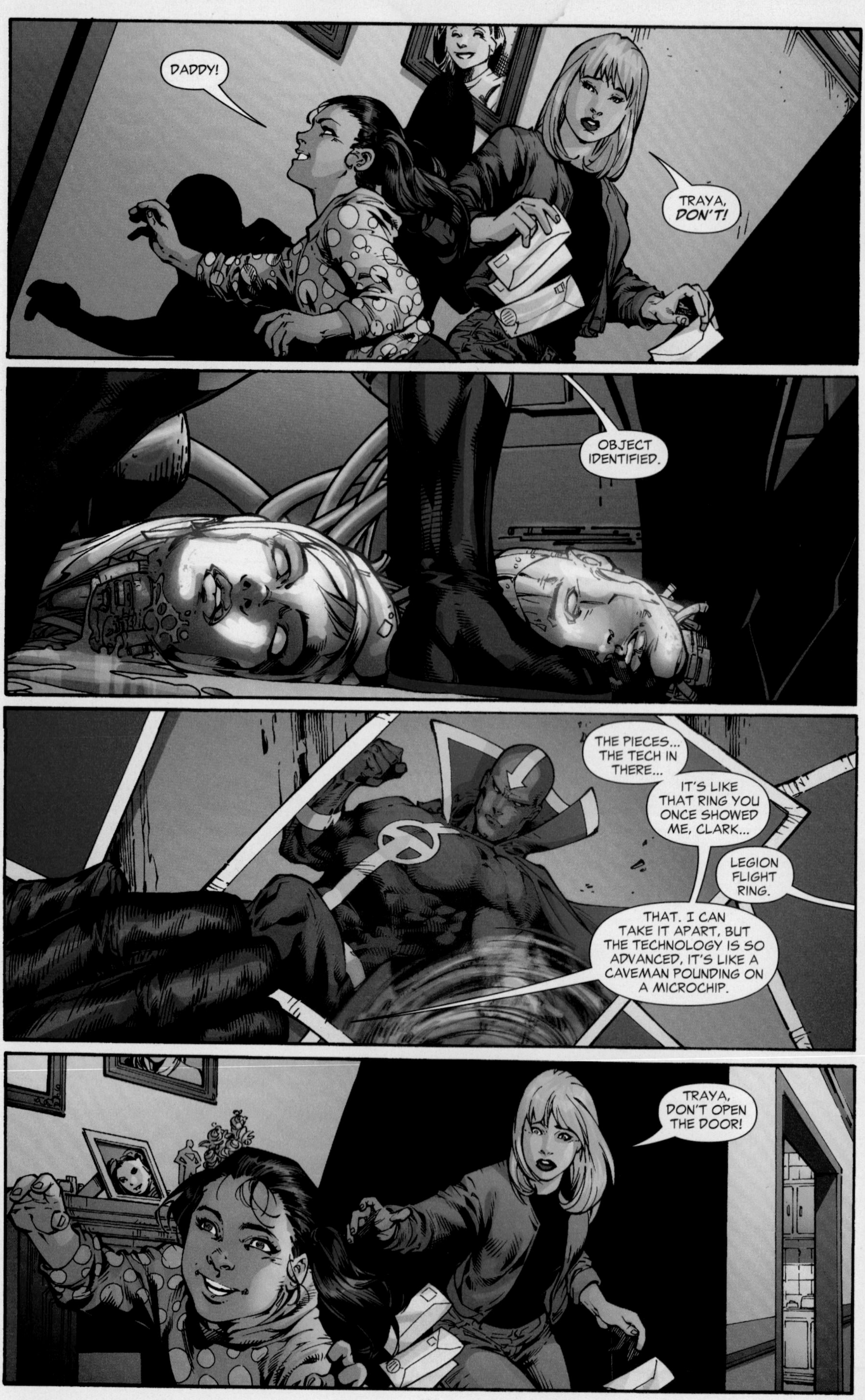

DADDY!
TRAYA, DON'T!
OBJECT IDENTIFIED.
THE PIECES... THE TECH IN THERE...
IT'S LIKE THAT RING YOU ONCE SHOWED ME, CLARK...
LEGION FLIGHT RING.
THAT. I CAN TAKE IT APART, BUT THE TECHNOLOGY IS SO ADVANCED, IT'S LIKE A CAVEMAN POUNDING ON A MICROCHIP.
TRAYA, DON'T OPEN THE DOOR!

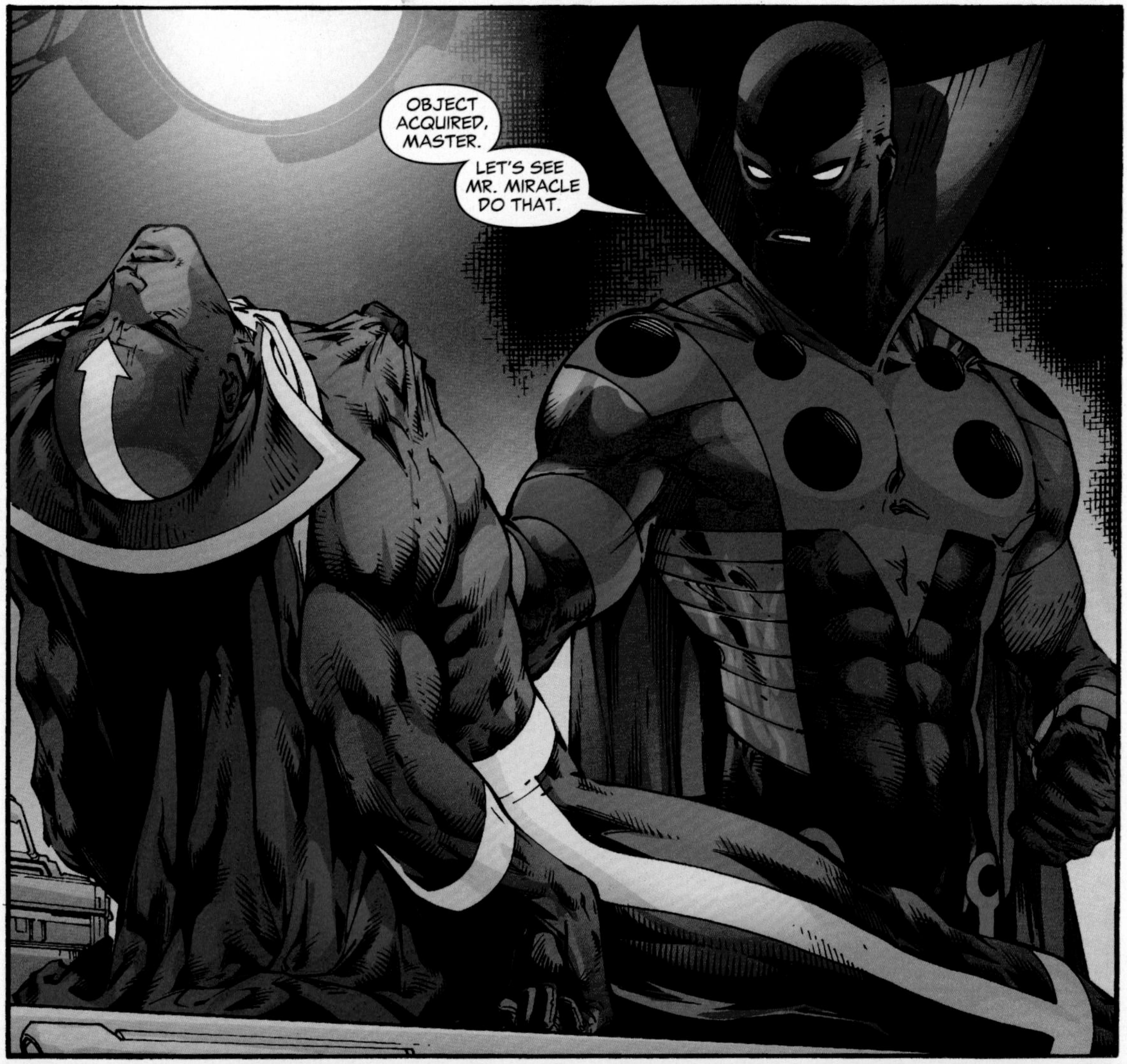
OBJECT ACQUIRED, MASTER.
LET'S SEE MR. MIRACLE DO THAT.

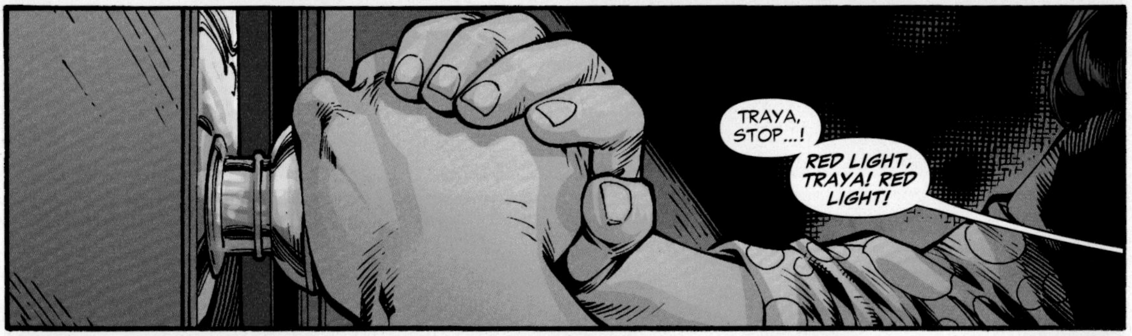
TRAYA, STOP...!
RED LIGHT, TRAYA! RED LIGHT!

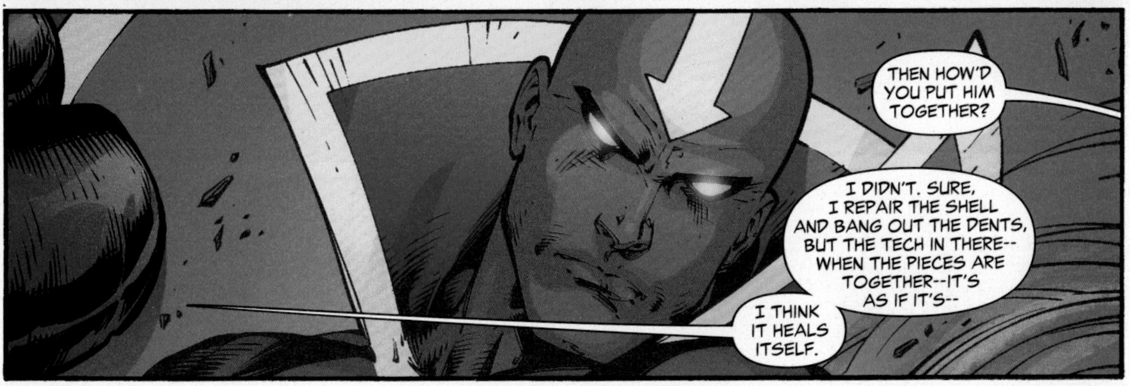
THEN HOW'D YOU PUT HIM TOGETHER?
I DIDN'T. SURE, I REPAIR THE SHELL AND BANG OUT THE DENTS, BUT THE TECH IN THERE-- WHEN THE PIECES ARE TOGETHER--IT'S AS IF IT'S--
I THINK IT HEALS ITSELF.

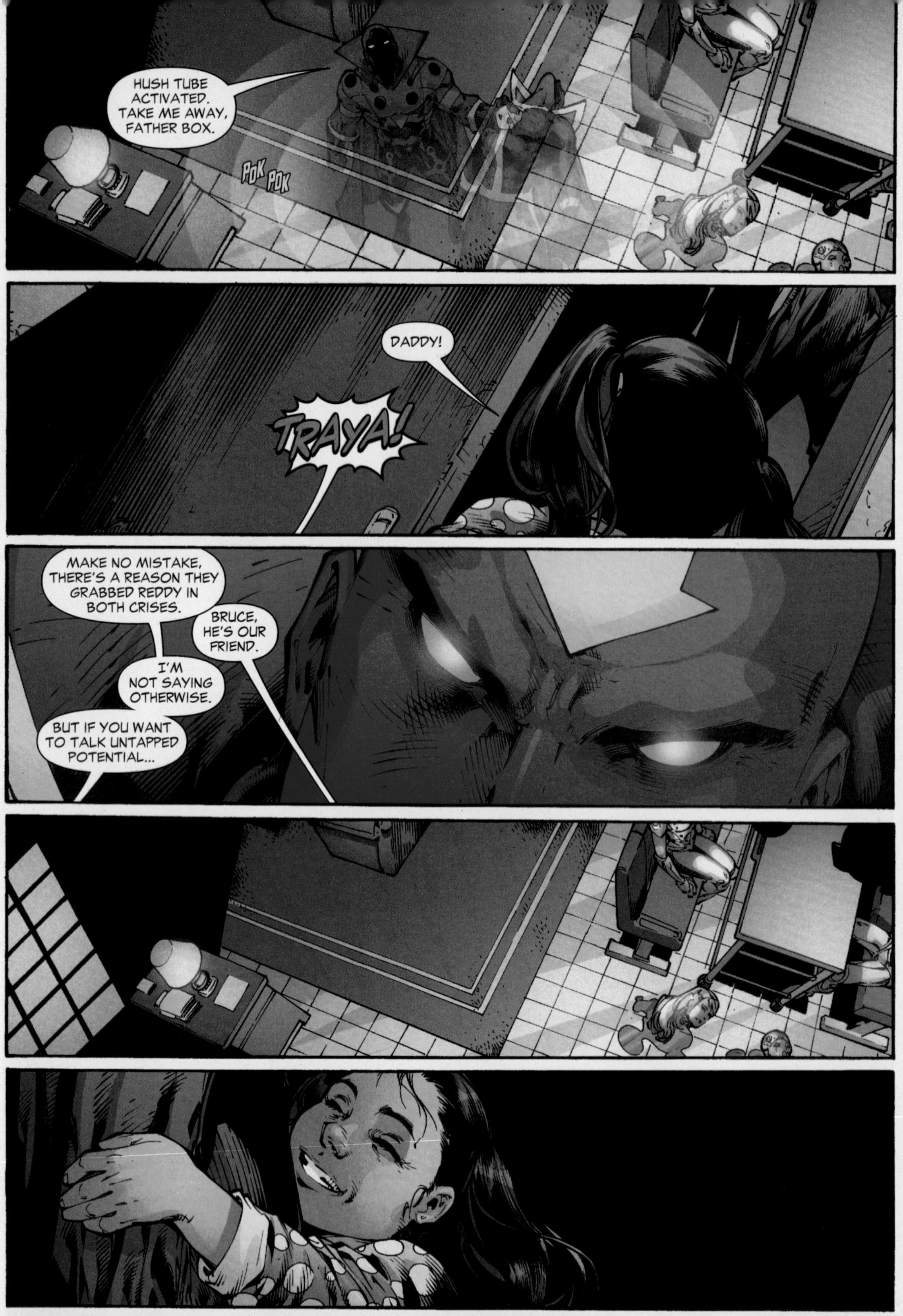
HUSH TUBE ACTIVATED. TAKE ME AWAY, FATHER BOX.
POK POK
DADDY!
TRAYA!
MAKE NO MISTAKE, THERE'S A REASON THEY GRABBED REDDY IN BOTH CRISES.
BRUCE, HE'S OUR FRIEND.
I'M NOT SAYING OTHERWISE.
BUT IF YOU WANT TO TALK UNTAPPED POTENTIAL...

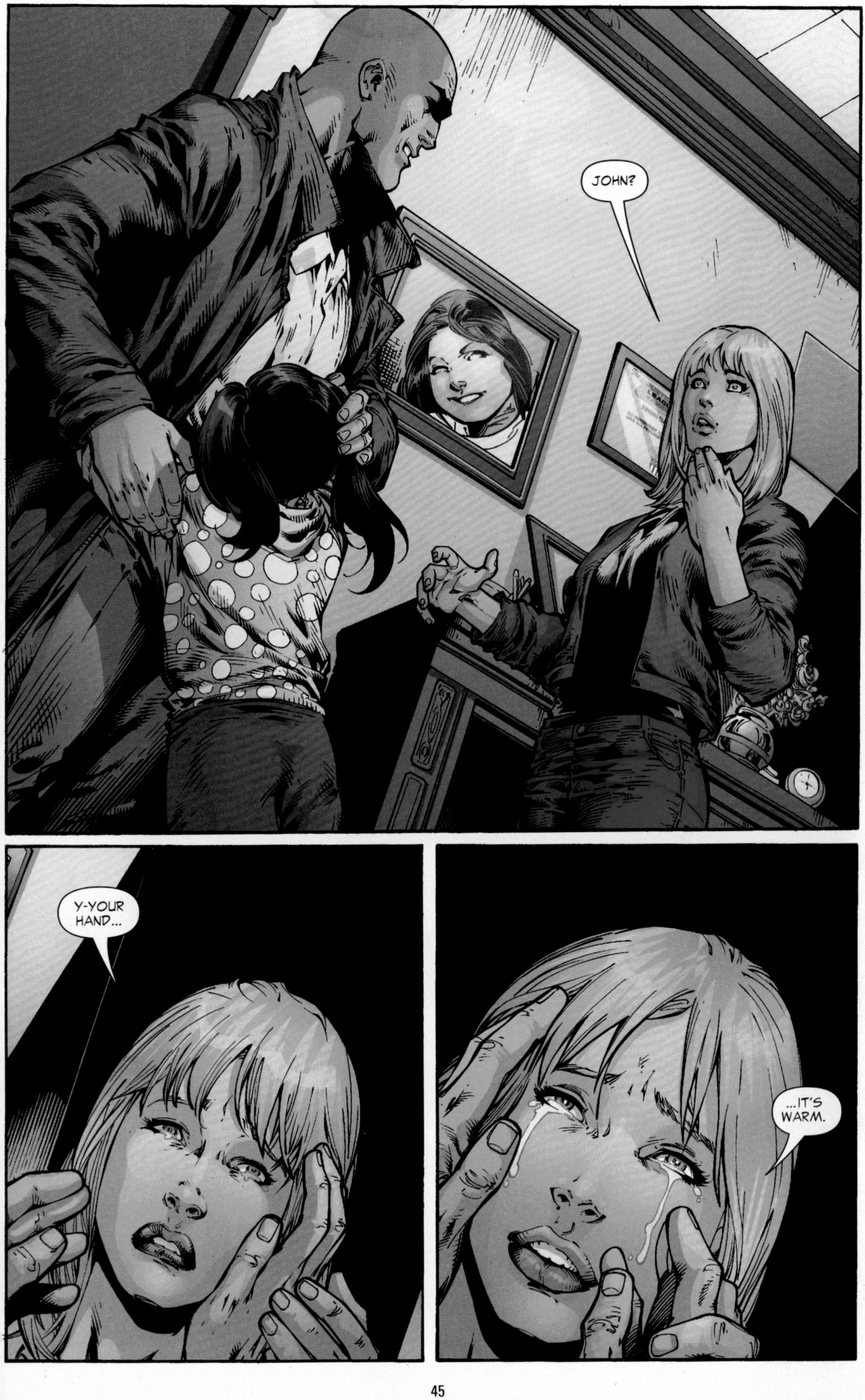
JOHN?
Y-YOUR HAND...
...IT'S WARM.

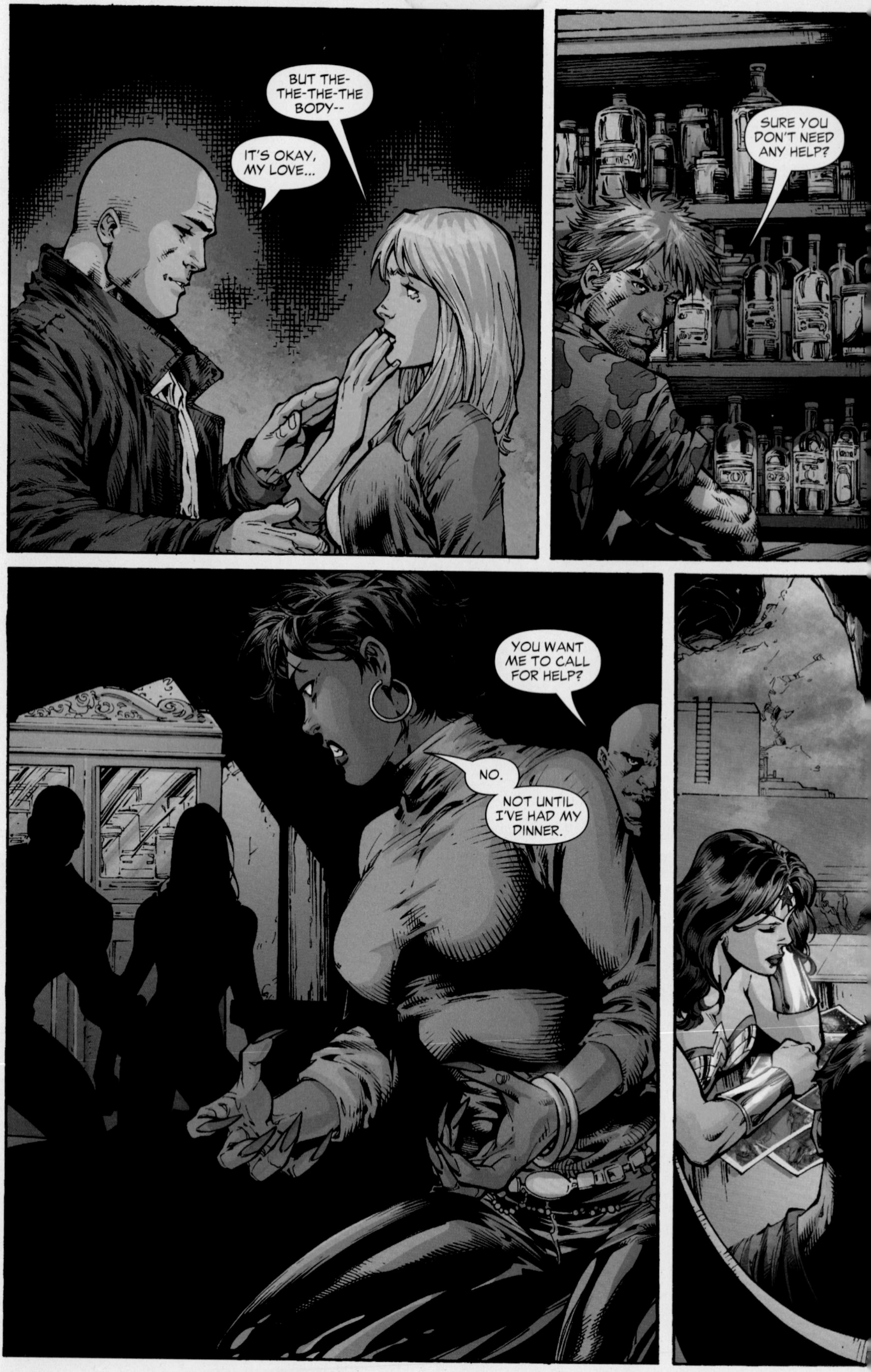
BUT THE-THE-THE-THE BODY--
IT'S OKAY, MY LOVE...
SURE YOU DON'T NEED ANY HELP?
YOU WANT ME TO CALL FOR HELP?
NO.
NOT UNTIL I'VE HAD MY DINNER.

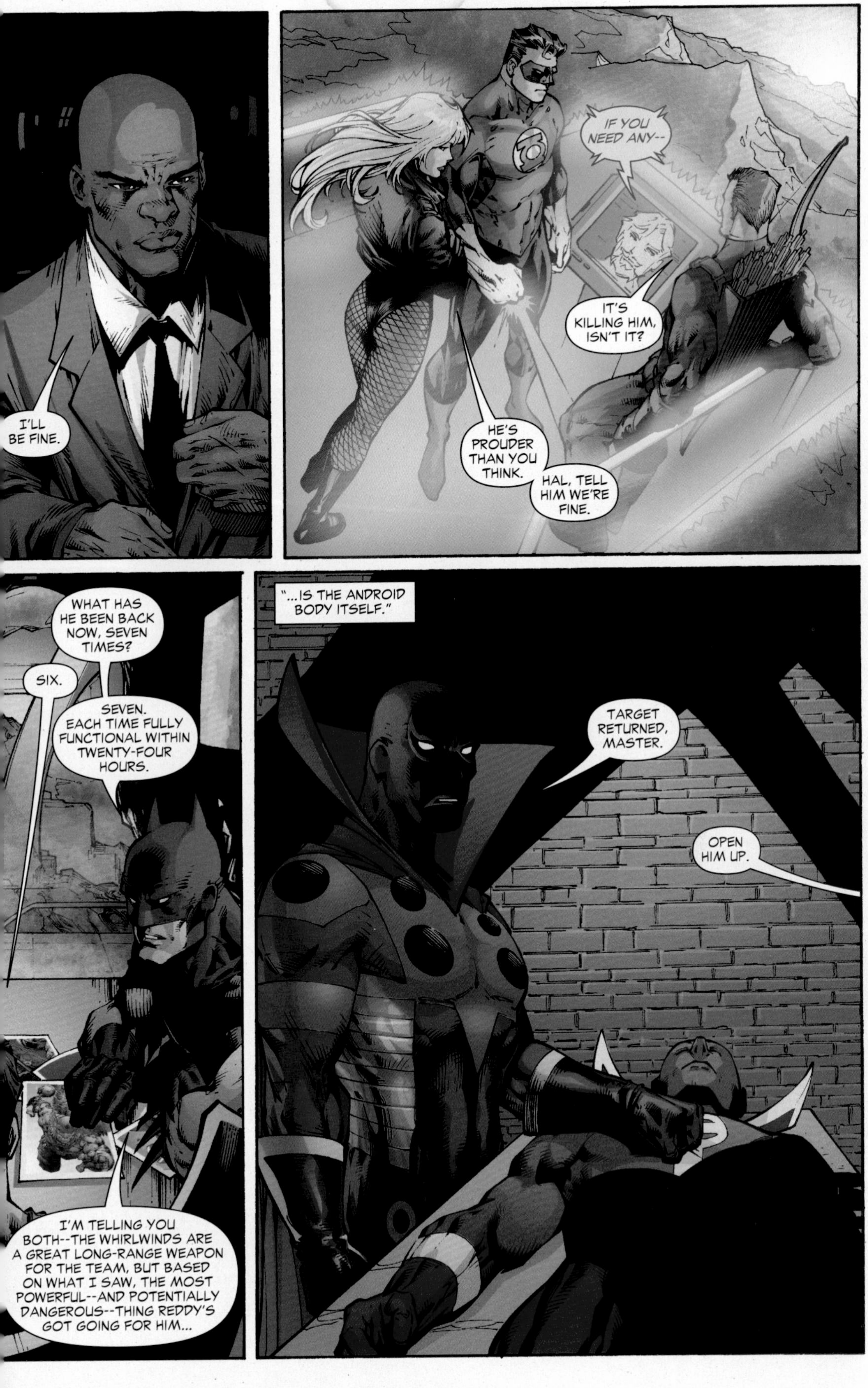
I'LL BE FINE.
IF YOU NEED ANY--
IT'S KILLING HIM, ISN'T IT?
HE'S PROUDER THAN YOU THINK.
HAL, TELL HIM WE'RE FINE.
WHAT HAS HE BEEN BACK NOW, SEVEN TIMES?
SIX.
SEVEN. EACH TIME FULLY FUNCTIONAL WITHIN TWENTY-FOUR HOURS.
I'M TELLING YOU BOTH--THE WHIRLWINDS ARE A GREAT LONG-RANGE WEAPON FOR THE TEAM, BUT BASED ON WHAT I SAW, THE MOST POWERFUL--AND POTENTIALLY DANGEROUS--THING REDDY'S GOT GOING FOR HIM...
"...IS THE ANDROID BODY ITSELF."
TARGET RETURNED, MASTER.
OPEN HIM UP.

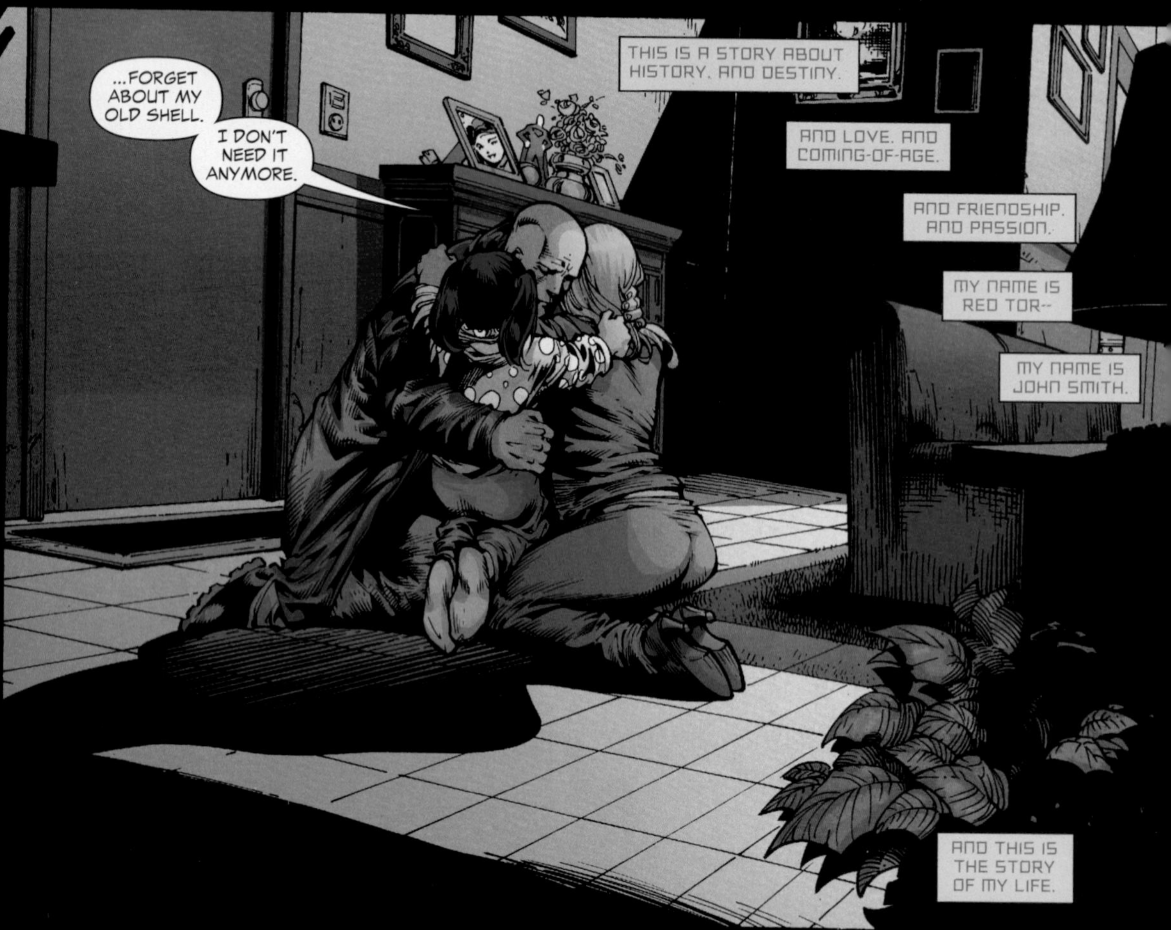
...FORGET ABOUT MY OLD SHELL.
I DON'T NEED IT ANYMORE.
THIS IS A STORY ABOUT HISTORY. AND DESTINY.
AND LOVE. AND COMING-OF-AGE.
AND FRIENDSHIP. AND PASSION.
MY NAME IS RED TOR--
MY NAME IS JOHN SMITH.
AND THIS IS THE STORY OF MY LIFE.

THE TORNADO'S PATH

CHAPTER ONE:

LIFE

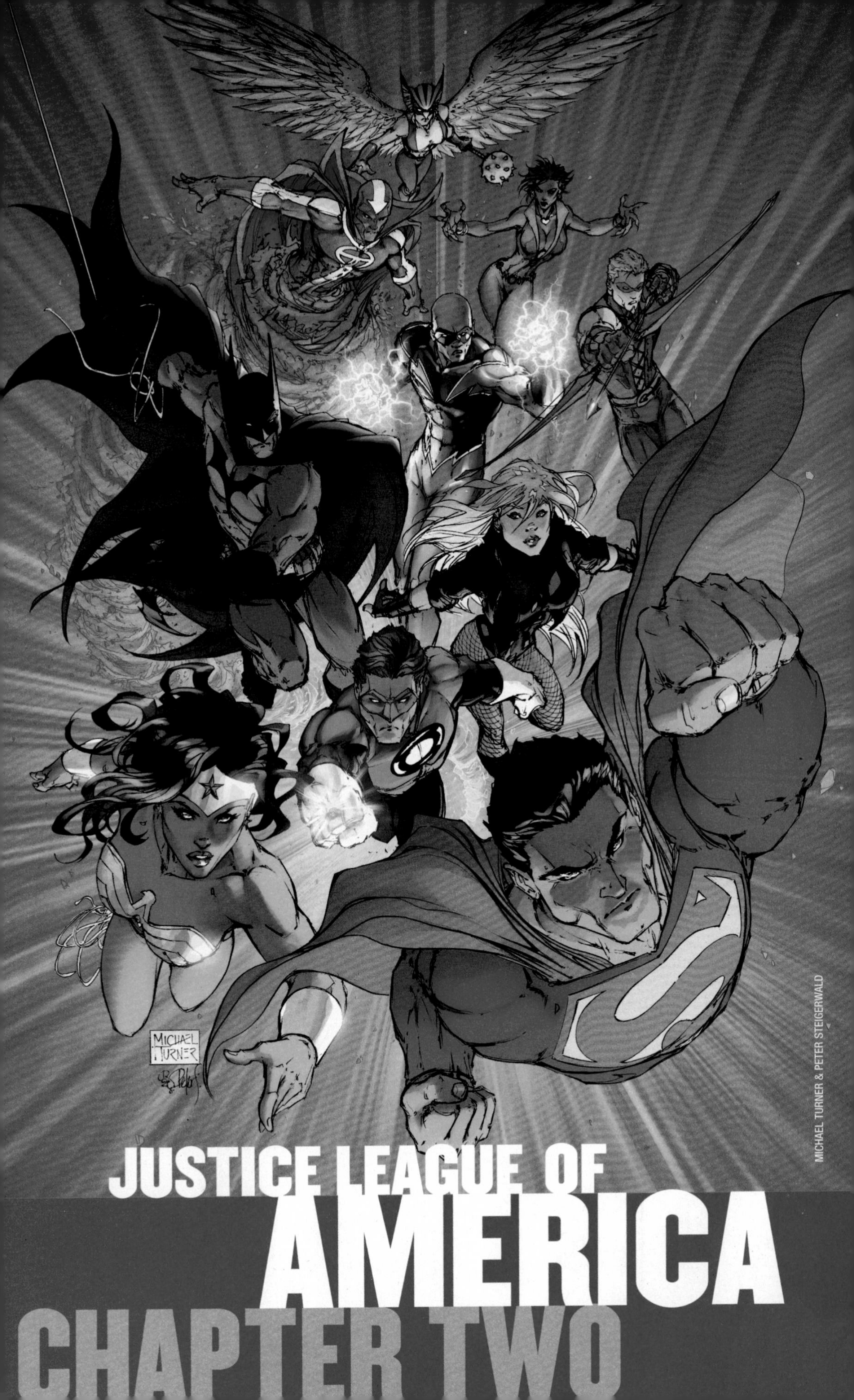
MICHAEL TURNER

MICHAEL TURNER & PETER STEIGERWALD

JUSTICE LEAGUE OF AMERICA

CHAPTER TWO

"John... I love you the old way too."

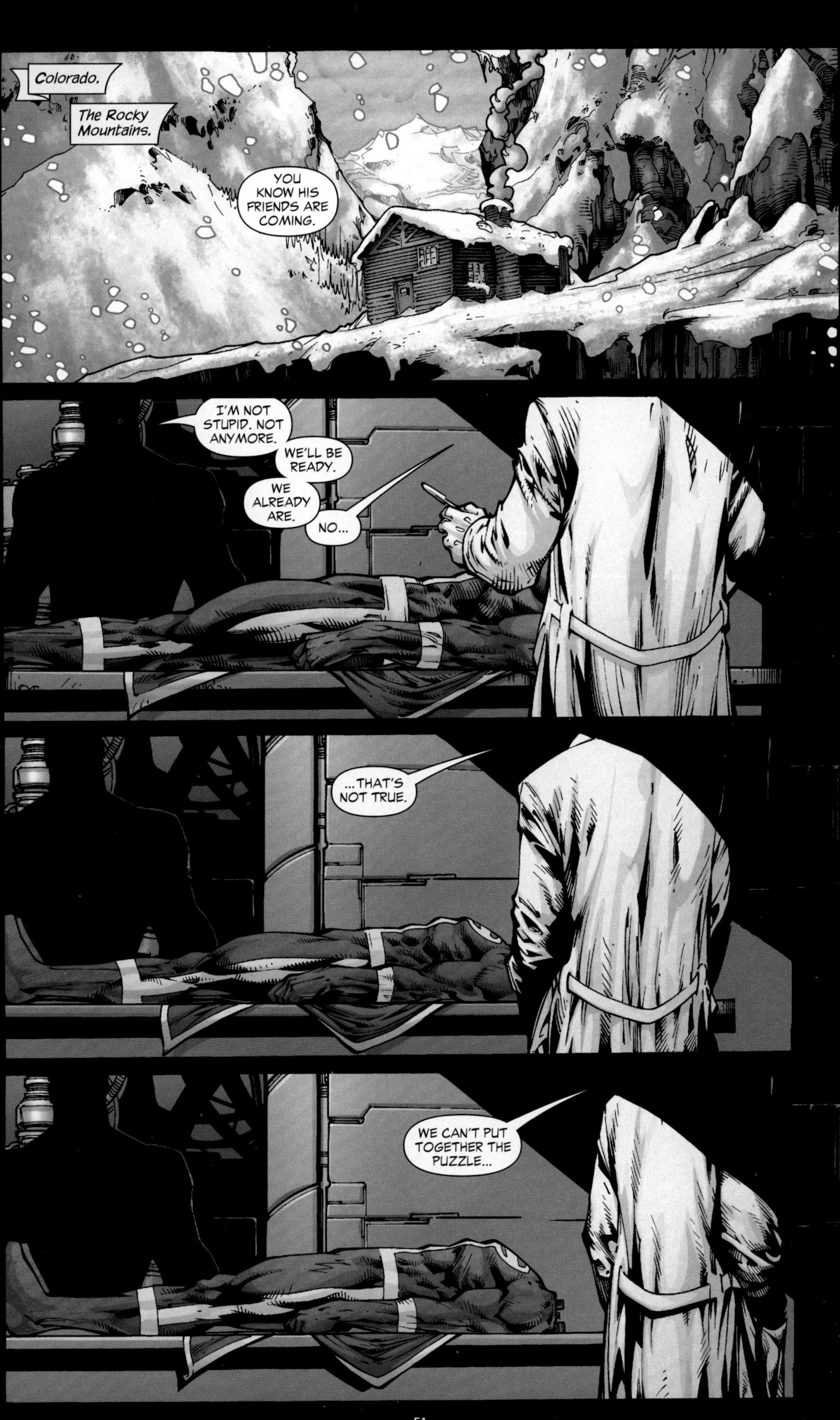
Colorado.
The Rocky Mountains.
YOU KNOW HIS FRIENDS ARE COMING.
I'M NOT STUPID. NOT ANYMORE.
WE'LL BE READY.
WE ALREADY ARE.
NO...
...THAT'S NOT TRUE.
WE CAN'T PUT TOGETHER THE PUZZLE...

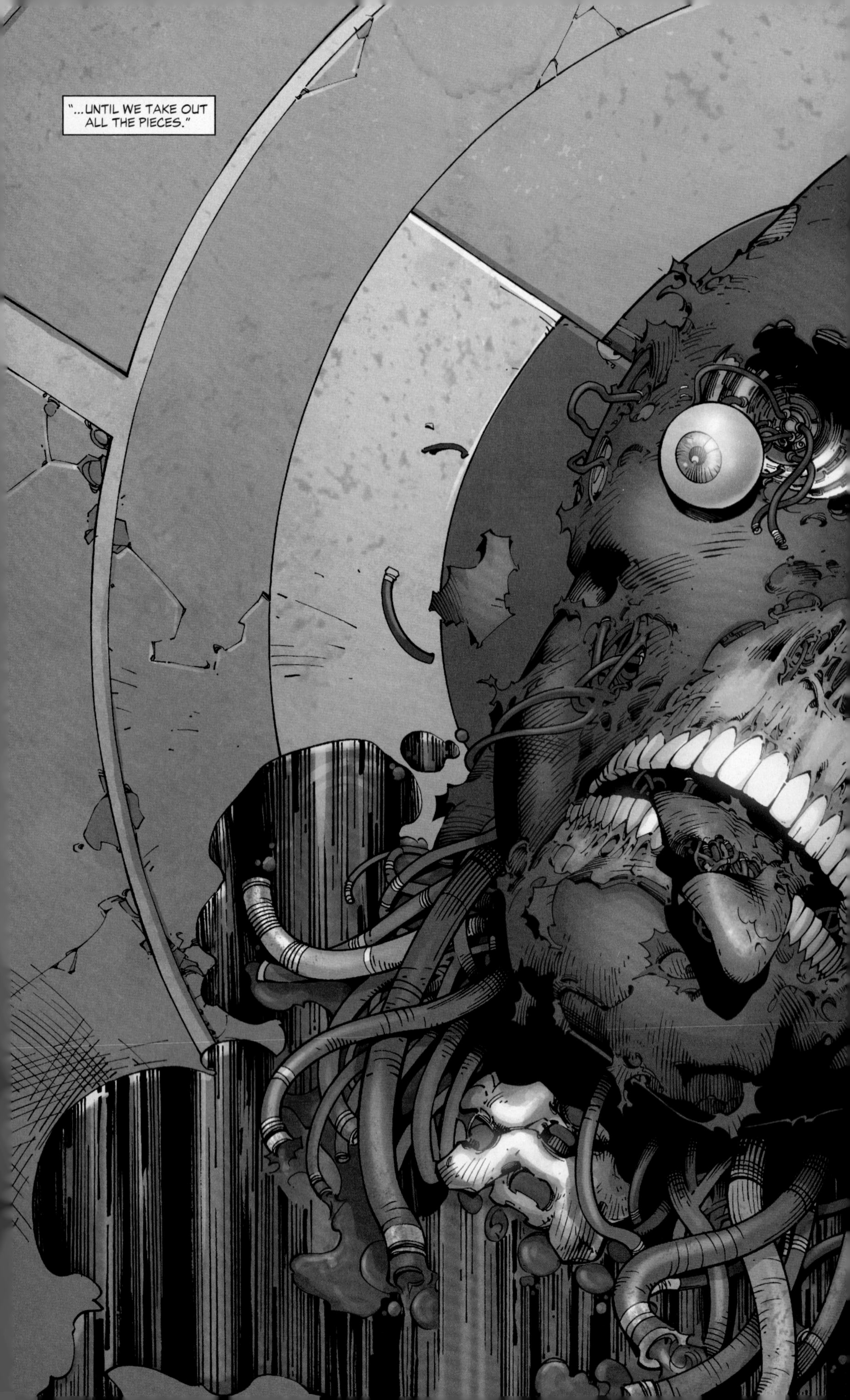
"...UNTIL WE TAKE OUT ALL THE PIECES."

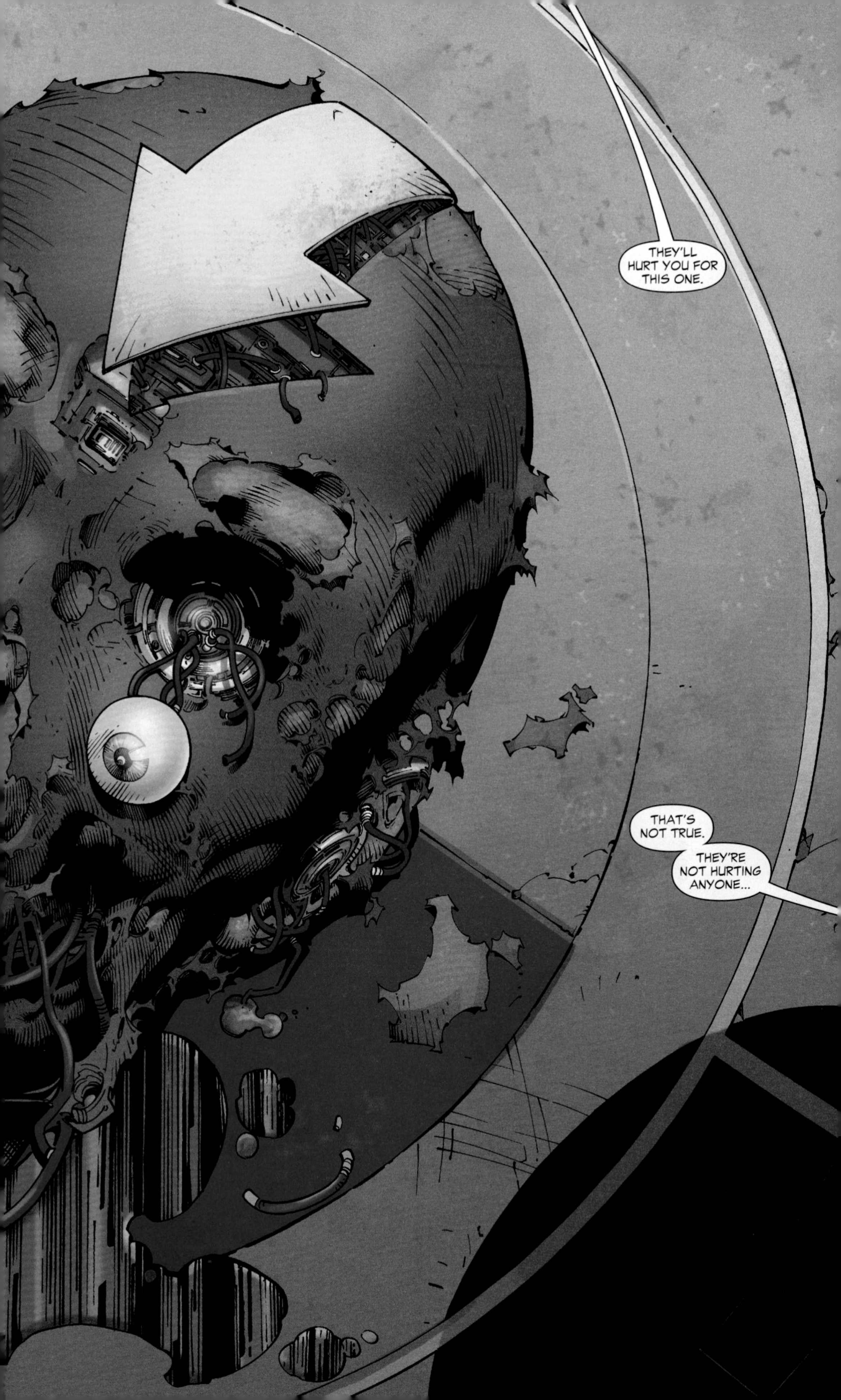
THEY'LL HURT YOU FOR THIS ONE.
THAT'S NOT TRUE.
THEY'RE NOT HURTING ANYONE...

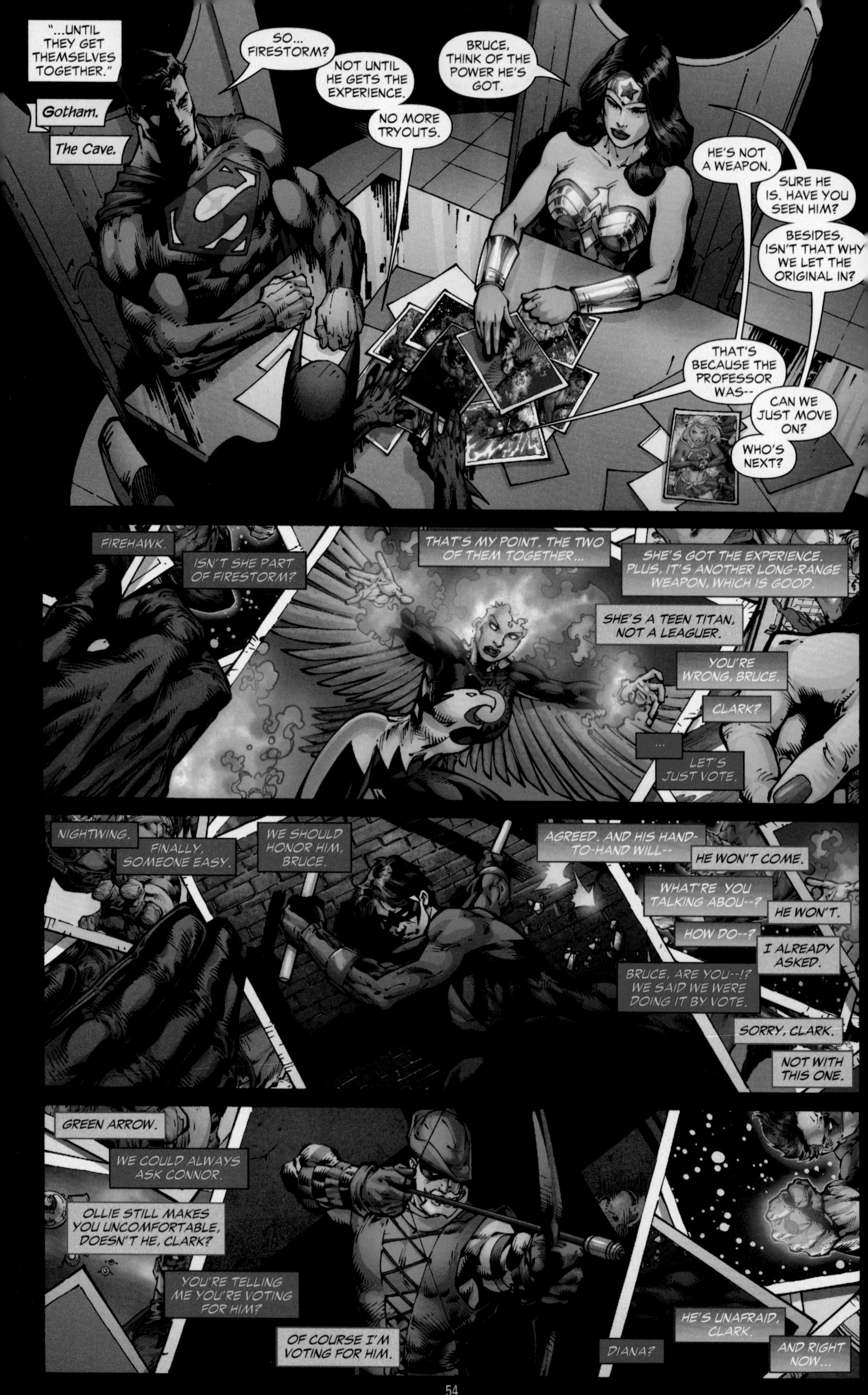
"...UNTIL THEY GET THEMSELVES TOGETHER."
Gotham.
The Cave.
SO... FIRESTORM?
NOT UNTIL HE GETS THE EXPERIENCE.
NO MORE TRYOUTS.
BRUCE, THINK OF THE POWER HE'S GOT.
HE'S NOT A WEAPON.
SURE HE IS. HAVE YOU SEEN HIM?
BESIDES, ISN'T THAT WHY WE LET THE ORIGINAL IN?
THAT'S BECAUSE THE PROFESSOR WAS--
CAN WE JUST MOVE ON?
WHO'S NEXT?
FIREHAWK.
ISN'T SHE PART OF FIRESTORM?
THAT'S MY POINT. THE TWO OF THEM TOGETHER...
SHE'S GOT THE EXPERIENCE. PLUS, IT'S ANOTHER LONG-RANGE WEAPON, WHICH IS GOOD.
SHE'S A TEEN TITAN, NOT A LEAGUER.
YOU'RE WRONG, BRUCE.
CLARK?
...
LET'S JUST VOTE.
NIGHTWING.
FINALLY, SOMEONE EASY.
WE SHOULD HONOR HIM, BRUCE.
AGREED. AND HIS HAND-TO-HAND WILL--
HE WON'T COME.
WHAT'RE YOU TALKING ABOU--?
HE WON'T.
HOW DO--?
I ALREADY ASKED.
BRUCE, ARE YOU--!? WE SAID WE WERE DOING IT BY VOTE.
SORRY, CLARK.
NOT WITH THIS ONE.
GREEN ARROW.
WE COULD ALWAYS ASK CONNOR.
OLLIE STILL MAKES YOU UNCOMFORTABLE, DOESN'T HE, CLARK?
YOU'RE TELLING ME YOU'RE VOTING FOR HIM?
OF COURSE I'M VOTING FOR HIM.
DIANA?
HE'S UNAFRAID, CLARK.
AND RIGHT NOW...

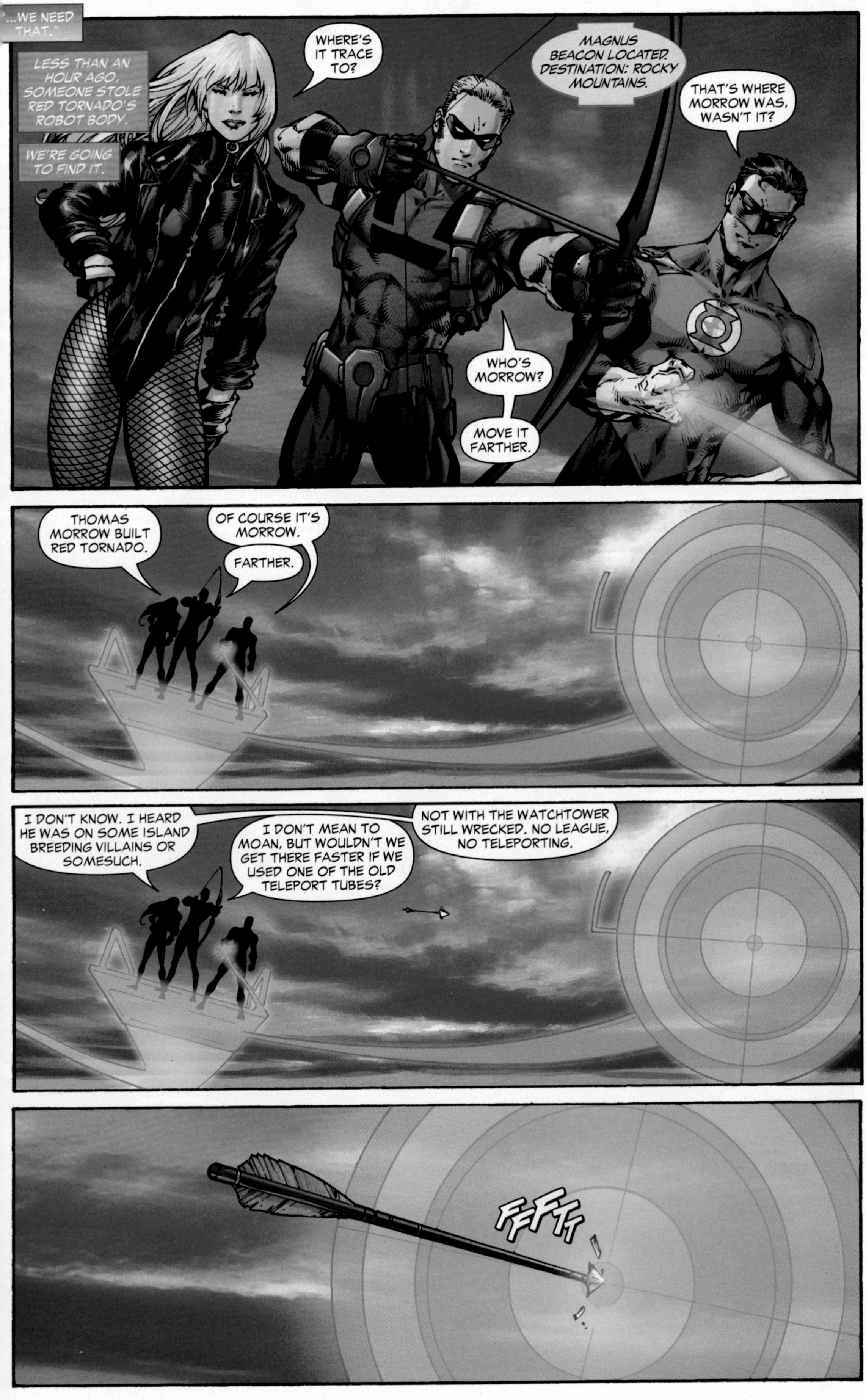
...WE NEED THAT."
LESS THAN AN HOUR AGO, SOMEONE STOLE RED TORNADO'S ROBOT BODY.
WE'RE GOING TO FIND IT.
WHERE'S IT TRACE TO?
MAGNUS BEACON LOCATED. DESTINATION: ROCKY MOUNTAINS.
THAT'S WHERE MORROW WAS, WASN'T IT?
WHO'S MORROW?
MOVE IT FARTHER.
THOMAS MORROW BUILT RED TORNADO.
OF COURSE IT'S MORROW.
FARTHER.
I DON'T KNOW. I HEARD HE WAS ON SOME ISLAND BREEDING VILLAINS OR SOMESUCH.
I DON'T MEAN TO MOAN, BUT WOULDN'T WE GET THERE FASTER IF WE USED ONE OF THE OLD TELEPORT TUBES?
NOT WITH THE WATCHTOWER STILL WRECKED. NO LEAGUE, NO TELEPORTING.
FFFTT

THEN WE SHOULD START OUR OWN LEAGUE.

I COULD ASK DICK... DONNA...

WHY DON'T YOU STICK TO TARGET PRACTICE, SPEEDY?

SPEEDY-- OOOH, NEVER HEARD THAT ONE.

WHAT'S OLLIE'S RECORD AGAIN?

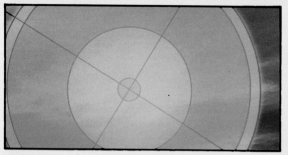

HAL, THAT'S AT LEAST FIFTY FEET PAST WHERE--

DON'T CODDLE HIM, DINAH.

THEN DON'T CHALLENGE HIM JUST BECAUSE IT MAKES YOU FEEL LIKE YOU'RE TWENTY AGAIN.

YOU'RE READING IT WRONG...

Huh.

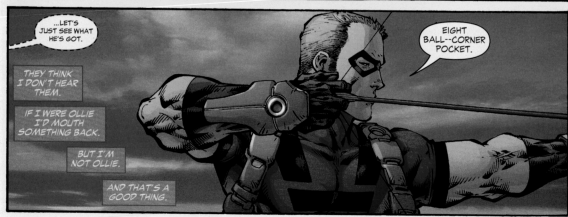

...LET'S JUST SEE WHAT HE'S GOT.

EIGHT BALL--CORNER POCKET.

THEY THINK I DON'T HEAR THEM.

IF I WERE OLLIE I'D MOUTH SOMETHING BACK.

BUT I'M NOT OLLIE.

AND THAT'S A GOOD THING.

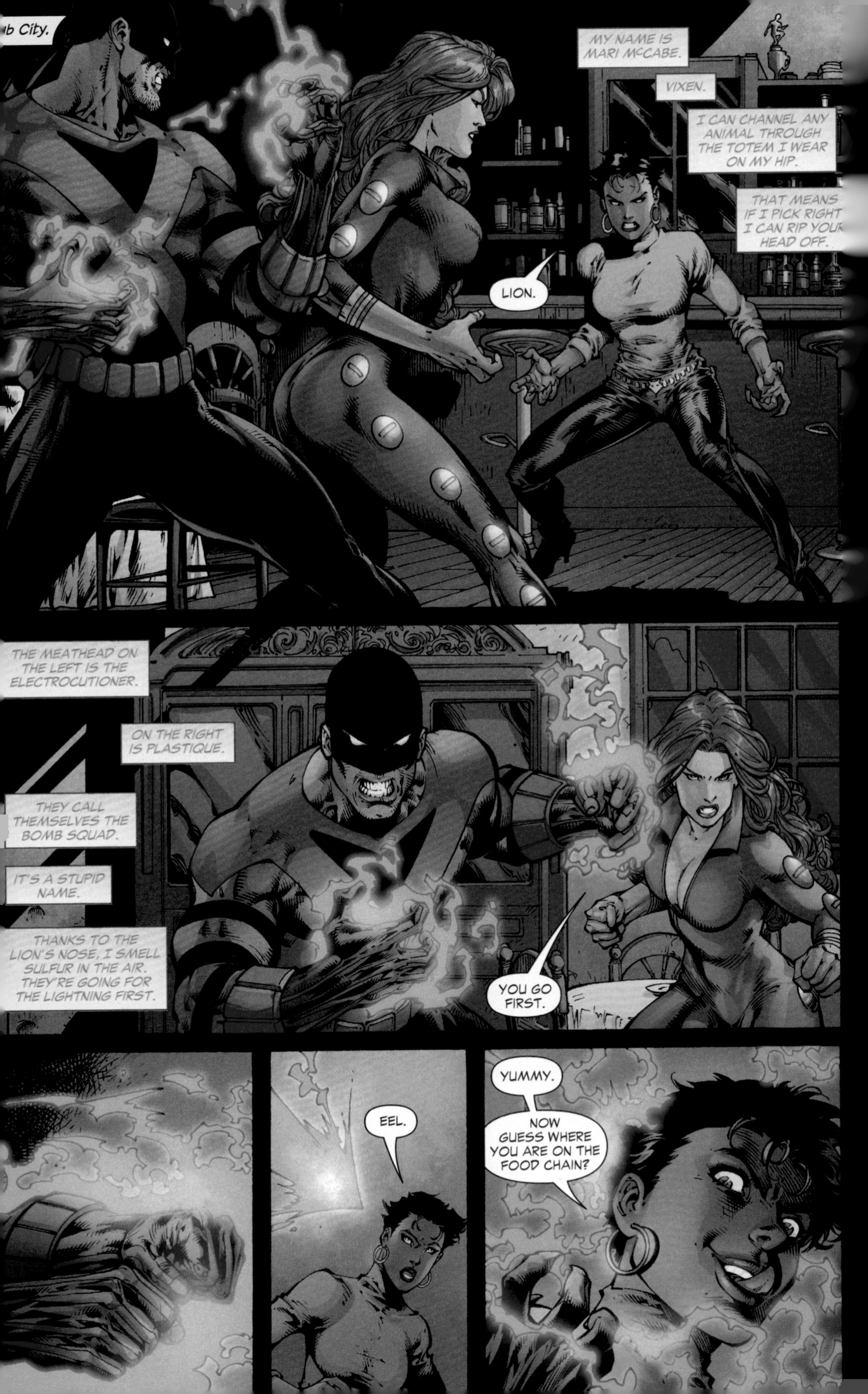
b City.
MY NAME IS MARI McCABE.
VIXEN.
I CAN CHANNEL ANY ANIMAL THROUGH THE TOTEM I WEAR ON MY HIP.
THAT MEANS IF I PICK RIGHT I CAN RIP YOUR HEAD OFF.
LION.
THE MEATHEAD ON THE LEFT IS THE ELECTROCUTIONER.
ON THE RIGHT IS PLASTIQUE.
THEY CALL THEMSELVES THE BOMB SQUAD.
IT'S A STUPID NAME.
THANKS TO THE LION'S NOSE, I SMELL SULFUR IN THE AIR. THEY'RE GOING FOR THE LIGHTNING FIRST.
YOU GO FIRST.
EEL.
YUMMY.
NOW GUESS WHERE YOU ARE ON THE FOOD CHAIN?

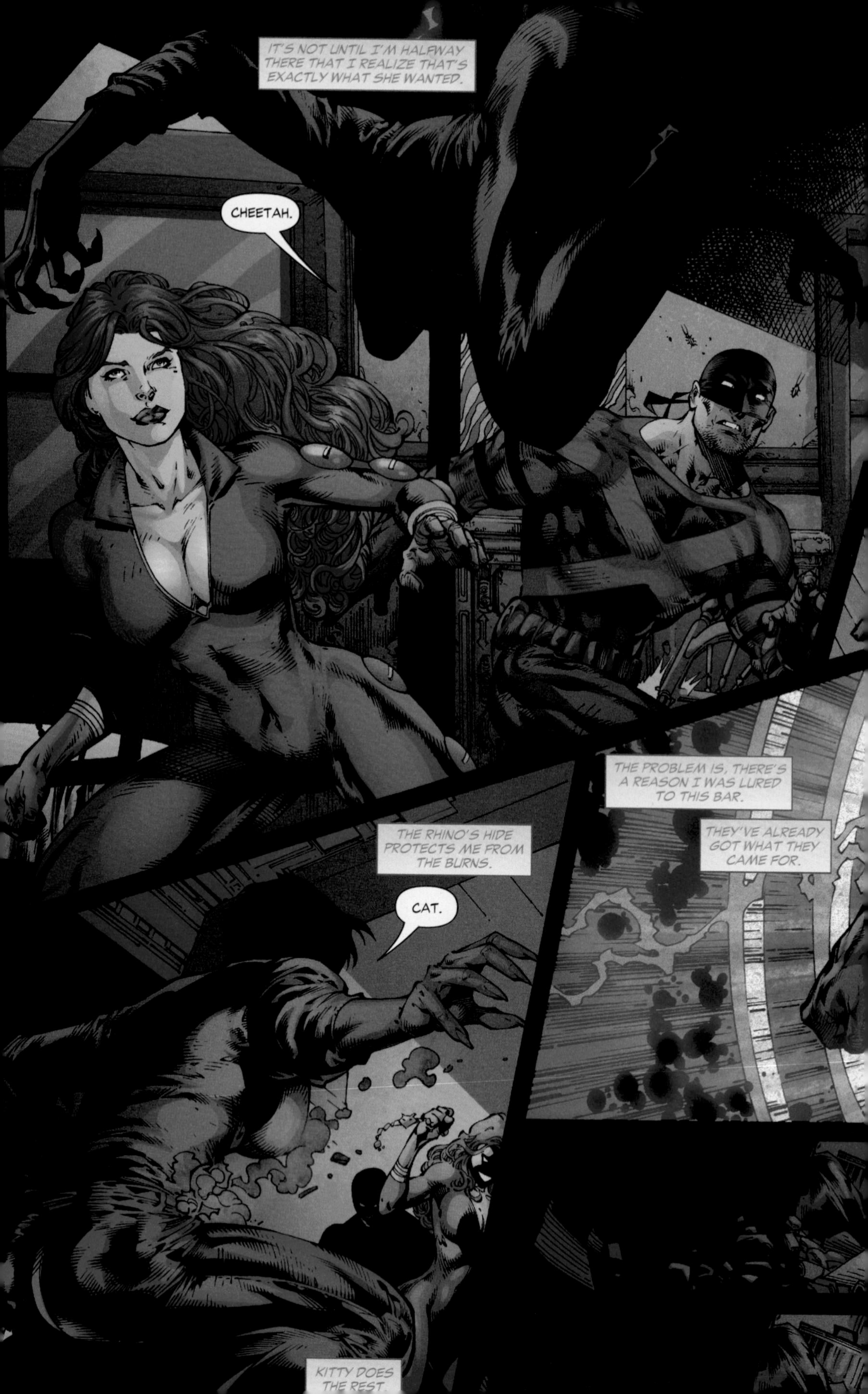
IT'S NOT UNTIL I'M HALFWAY THERE THAT I REALIZE THAT'S EXACTLY WHAT SHE WANTED.
CHEETAH.
THE PROBLEM IS, THERE'S A REASON I WAS LURED TO THIS BAR.
THEY'VE ALREADY GOT WHAT THEY CAME FOR.
THE RHINO'S HIDE PROTECTS ME FROM THE BURNS.
CAT.
KITTY DOES THE REST.

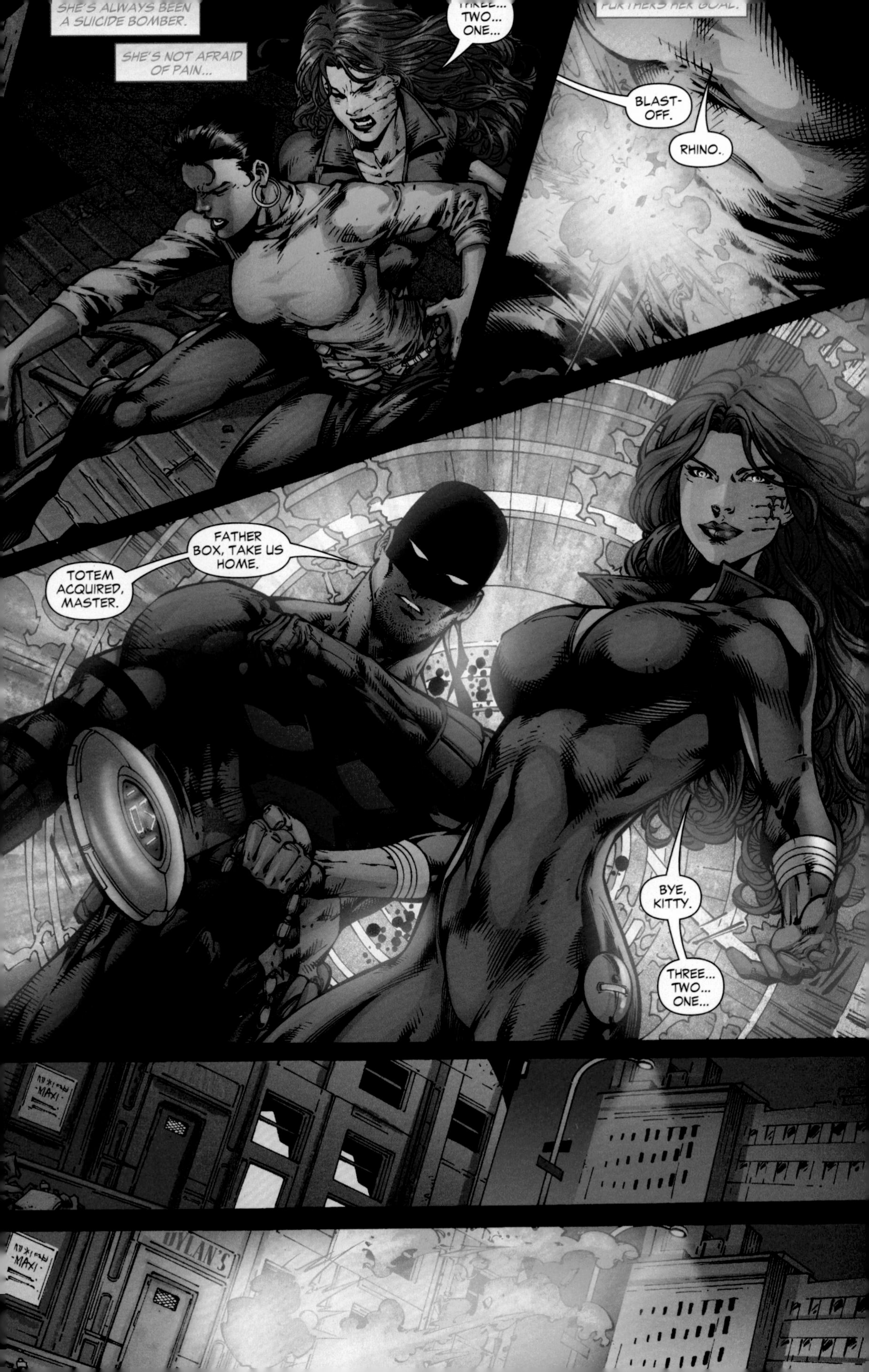
SHE'S ALWAYS BEEN A SUICIDE BOMBER.
SHE'S NOT AFRAID OF PAIN...
TWO... ONE...
BLAST-OFF.
RHINO..
TOTEM ACQUIRED, MASTER.
FATHER BOX, TAKE US HOME.
BYE, KITTY.
THREE... TWO... ONE...
MAXI
DYLAN'S

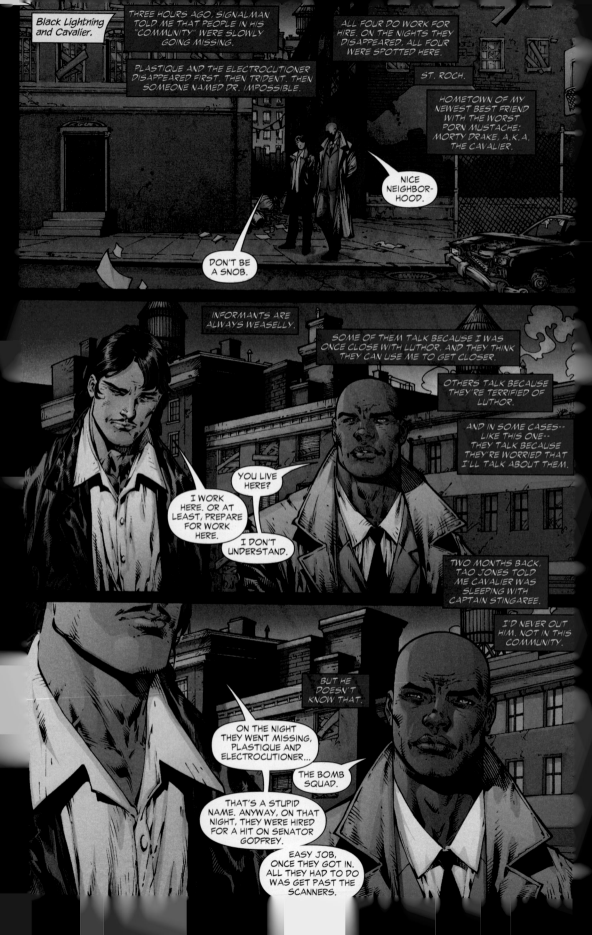

Black Lightning and Cavalier.

THREE HOURS AGO, SIGNALMAN TOLD ME THAT PEOPLE IN HIS "COMMUNITY" WERE SLOWLY GOING MISSING.

PLASTIQUE AND THE ELECTROCUTIONER DISAPPEARED FIRST. THEN TRIDENT. THEN SOMEONE NAMED DR. IMPOSSIBLE.

ALL FOUR DO WORK FOR HIRE. ON THE NIGHTS THEY DISAPPEARED, ALL FOUR WERE SPOTTED HERE.

ST. ROCH.

HOMETOWN OF MY NEWEST BEST FRIEND WITH THE WORST PORN MUSTACHE: MORTY DRAKE, A.K.A. THE CAVALIER.

NICE NEIGHBOR-HOOD.

DON'T BE A SNOB.

INFORMANTS ARE ALWAYS WEASELLY.

SOME OF THEM TALK BECAUSE I WAS ONCE CLOSE WITH LUTHOR, AND THEY THINK THEY CAN USE ME TO GET CLOSER.

OTHERS TALK BECAUSE THEY'RE TERRIFIED OF LUTHOR.

AND IN SOME CASES-- LIKE THIS ONE-- THEY TALK BECAUSE THEY'RE WORRIED THAT I'LL TALK ABOUT THEM.

YOU LIVE HERE?

I WORK HERE. OR AT LEAST, PREPARE FOR WORK HERE.

I DON'T UNDERSTAND.

TWO MONTHS BACK, TAO JONES TOLD ME CAVALIER WAS SLEEPING WITH CAPTAIN STINGAREE.

I'D NEVER OUT HIM. NOT IN THIS COMMUNITY.

BUT HE DOESN'T KNOW THAT.

ON THE NIGHT THEY WENT MISSING, PLASTIQUE AND ELECTROCUTIONER...

THE BOMB SQUAD.

THAT'S A STUPID NAME. ANYWAY, ON THAT NIGHT, THEY WERE HIRED FOR A HIT ON SENATOR GODFREY.

EASY JOB, ONCE THEY GOT IN. ALL THEY HAD TO DO WAS GET PAST THE SCANNERS.

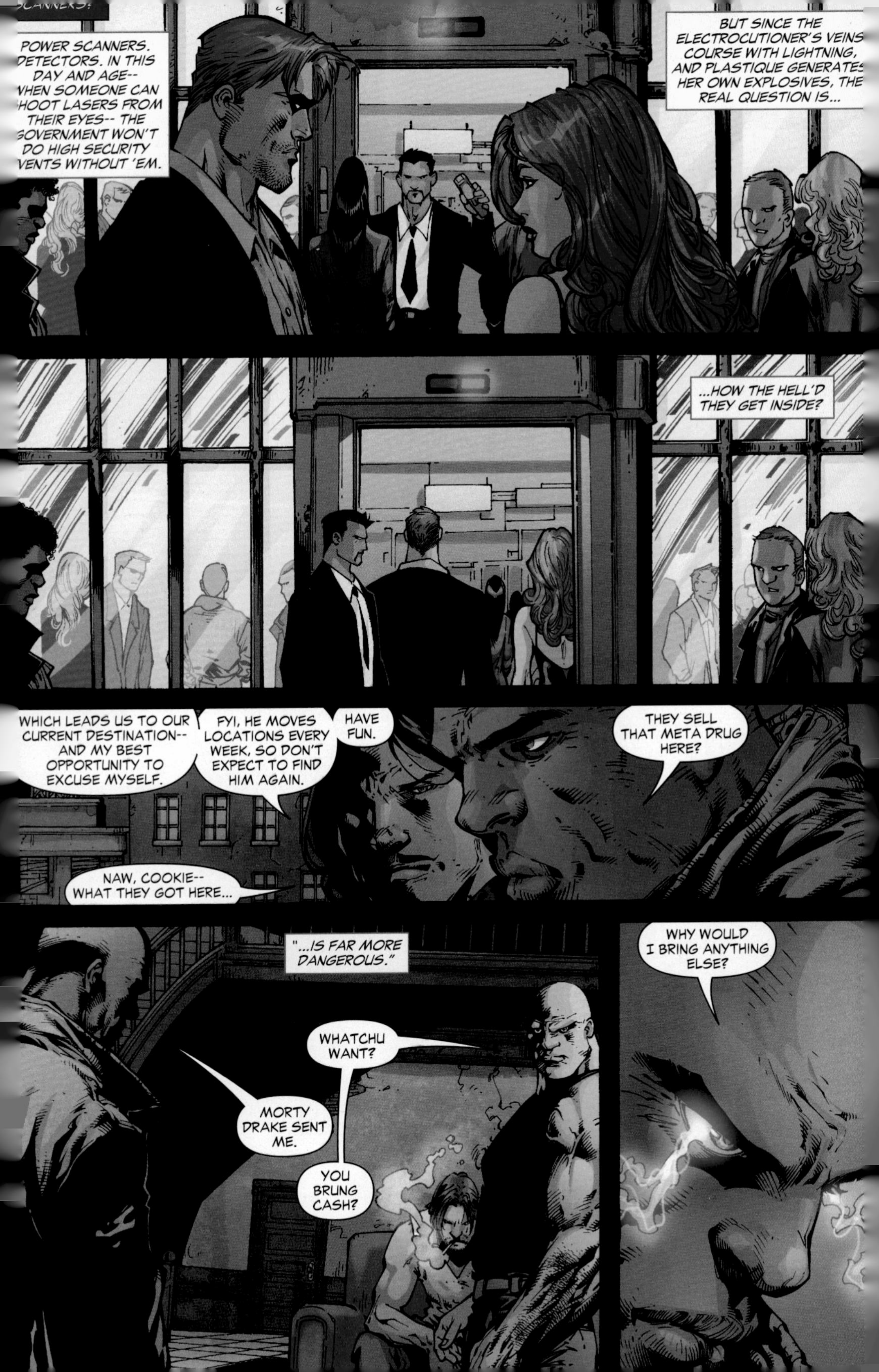
SCANNERS?
POWER SCANNERS. DETECTORS. IN THIS DAY AND AGE-- WHEN SOMEONE CAN SHOOT LASERS FROM THEIR EYES-- THE GOVERNMENT WON'T DO HIGH SECURITY EVENTS WITHOUT 'EM.
BUT SINCE THE ELECTROCUTIONER'S VEINS COURSE WITH LIGHTNING, AND PLASTIQUE GENERATES HER OWN EXPLOSIVES, THE REAL QUESTION IS...
...HOW THE HELL'D THEY GET INSIDE?
WHICH LEADS US TO OUR CURRENT DESTINATION-- AND MY BEST OPPORTUNITY TO EXCUSE MYSELF.
FYI, HE MOVES LOCATIONS EVERY WEEK, SO DON'T EXPECT TO FIND HIM AGAIN.
HAVE FUN.
THEY SELL THAT META DRUG HERE?
NAW, COOKIE-- WHAT THEY GOT HERE...
"...IS FAR MORE DANGEROUS."
WHATCHU WANT?
MORTY DRAKE SENT ME.
YOU BRUNG CASH?
WHY WOULD I BRING ANYTHING ELSE?

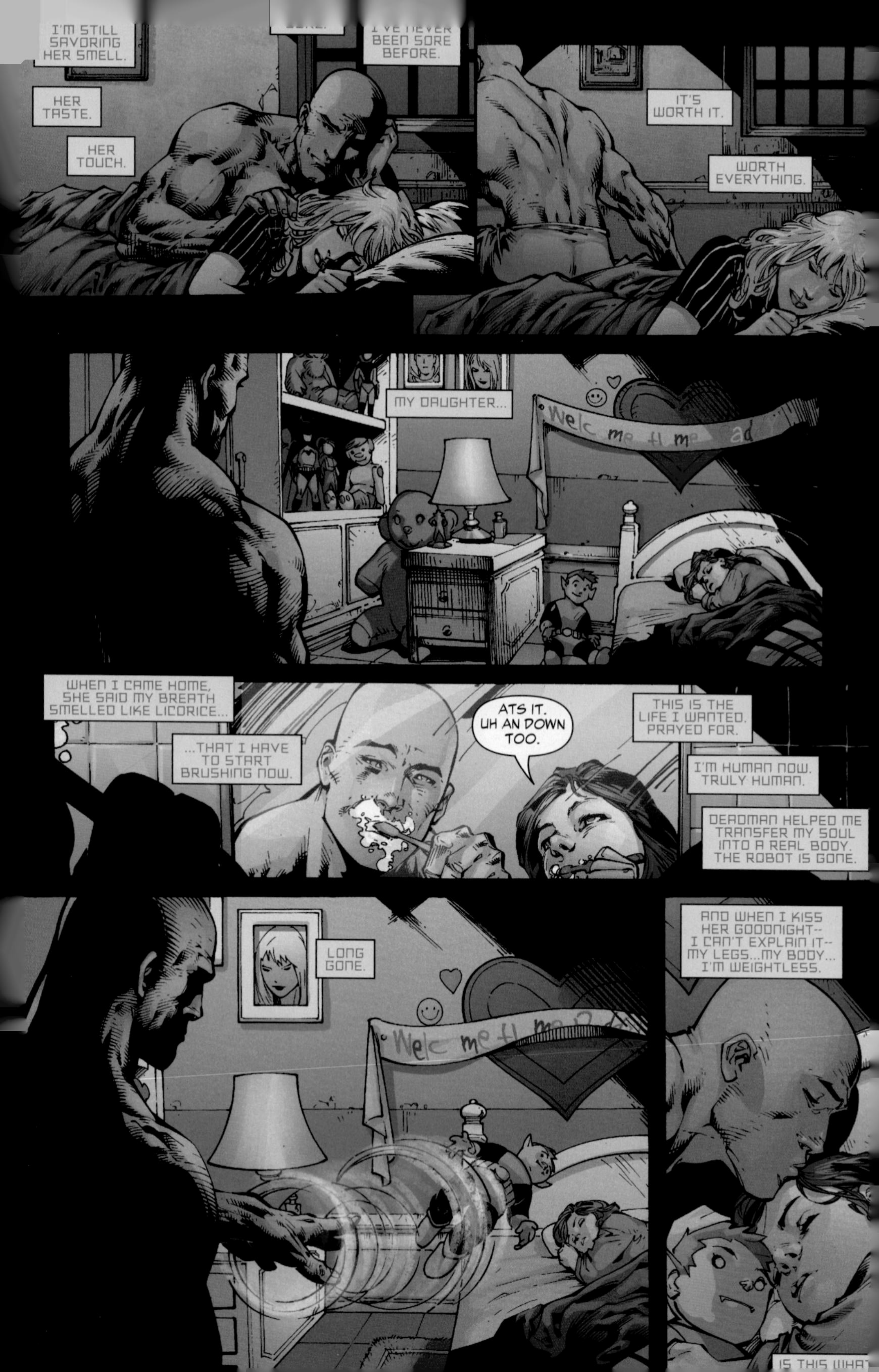
I'M STILL SAVORING HER SMELL.
HER TASTE.
HER TOUCH.
I'VE NEVER BEEN SORE BEFORE.
IT'S WORTH IT.
WORTH EVERYTHING.
MY DAUGHTER...
WHEN I CAME HOME, SHE SAID MY BREATH SMELLED LIKE LICORICE...
...THAT I HAVE TO START BRUSHING NOW.
ATS IT. UH AN DOWN TOO.
THIS IS THE LIFE I WANTED. PRAYED FOR.
I'M HUMAN NOW. TRULY HUMAN.
DEADMAN HELPED ME TRANSFER MY SOUL INTO A REAL BODY. THE ROBOT IS GONE.
LONG GONE.
AND WHEN I KISS HER GOODNIGHT-- I CAN'T EXPLAIN IT-- MY LEGS...MY BODY... I'M WEIGHTLESS.

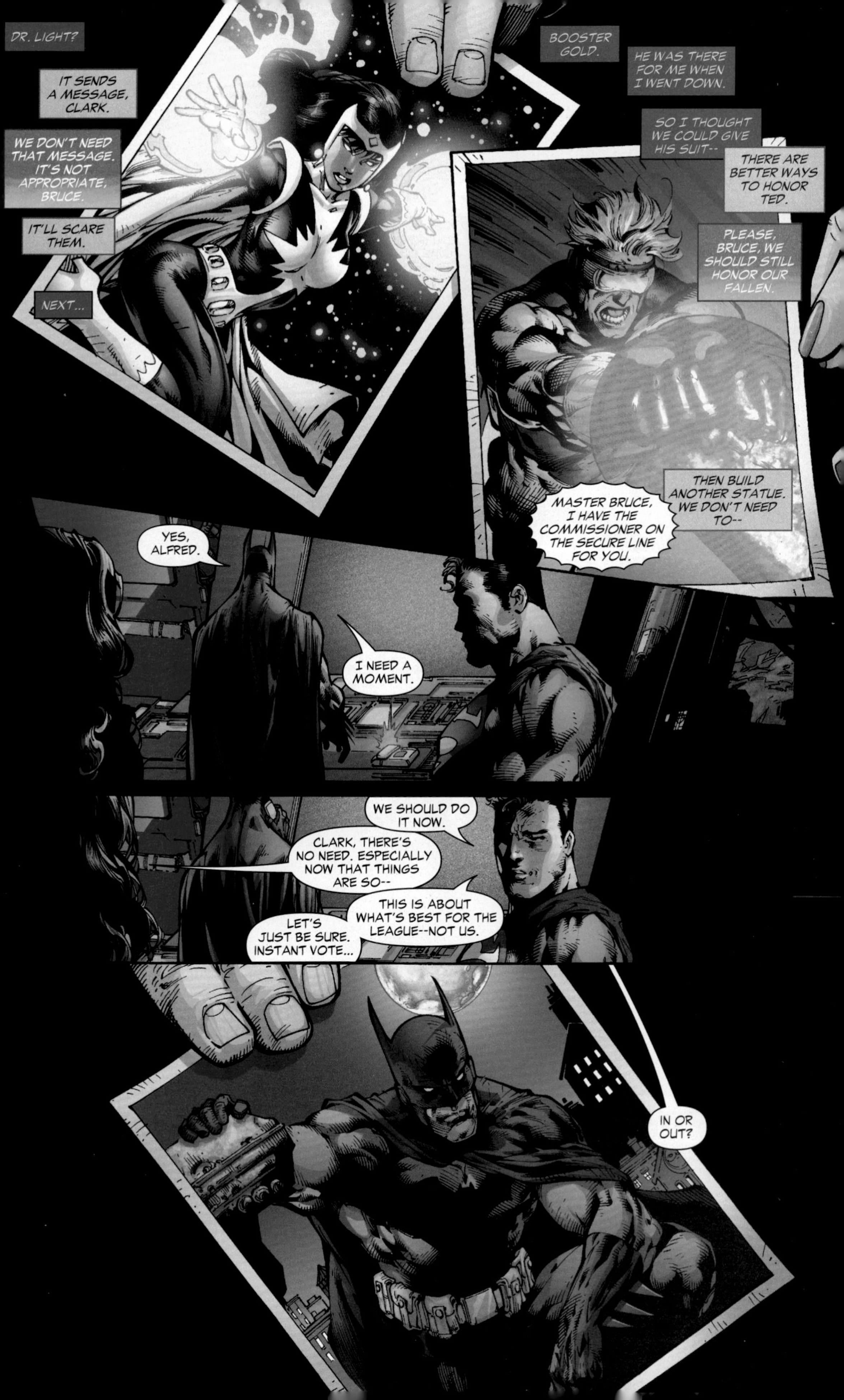
DR. LIGHT?
IT SENDS A MESSAGE, CLARK.
WE DON'T NEED THAT MESSAGE. IT'S NOT APPROPRIATE, BRUCE.
IT'LL SCARE THEM.
NEXT...
BOOSTER GOLD.
HE WAS THERE FOR ME WHEN I WENT DOWN.
SO I THOUGHT WE COULD GIVE HIS SUIT--
THERE ARE BETTER WAYS TO HONOR TED.
PLEASE, BRUCE, WE SHOULD STILL HONOR OUR FALLEN.
THEN BUILD ANOTHER STATUE. WE DON'T NEED TO--
MASTER BRUCE, I HAVE THE COMMISSIONER ON THE SECURE LINE FOR YOU.
YES, ALFRED.
I NEED A MOMENT.
WE SHOULD DO IT NOW.
CLARK, THERE'S NO NEED. ESPECIALLY NOW THAT THINGS ARE SO--
THIS IS ABOUT WHAT'S BEST FOR THE LEAGUE--NOT US.
LET'S JUST BE SURE. INSTANT VOTE...
IN OR OUT?

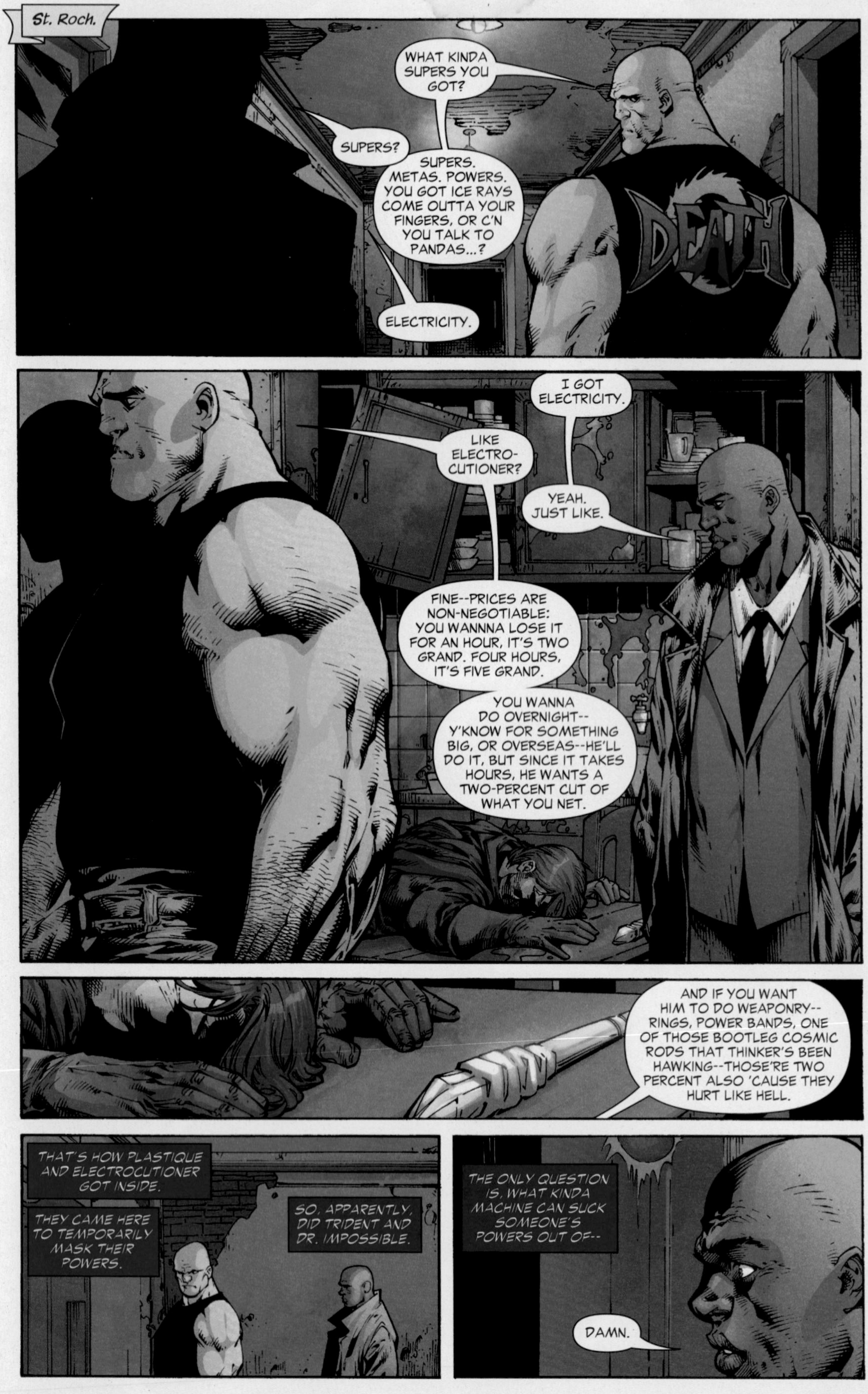
St. Roch.
WHAT KINDA SUPERS YOU GOT?
SUPERS?
SUPERS. METAS. POWERS. YOU GOT ICE RAYS COME OUTTA YOUR FINGERS, OR C'N YOU TALK TO PANDAS...?
ELECTRICITY.
I GOT ELECTRICITY.
LIKE ELECTRO-CUTIONER?
YEAH. JUST LIKE.
FINE--PRICES ARE NON-NEGOTIABLE: YOU WANNNA LOSE IT FOR AN HOUR, IT'S TWO GRAND. FOUR HOURS, IT'S FIVE GRAND.
YOU WANNA DO OVERNIGHT-- Y'KNOW FOR SOMETHING BIG, OR OVERSEAS--HE'LL DO IT, BUT SINCE IT TAKES HOURS, HE WANTS A TWO-PERCENT CUT OF WHAT YOU NET.
AND IF YOU WANT HIM TO DO WEAPONRY-- RINGS, POWER BANDS, ONE OF THOSE BOOTLEG COSMIC RODS THAT THINKER'S BEEN HAWKING--THOSE'RE TWO PERCENT ALSO 'CAUSE THEY HURT LIKE HELL.
THAT'S HOW PLASTIQUE AND ELECTROCUTIONER GOT INSIDE.
THEY CAME HERE TO TEMPORARILY MASK THEIR POWERS.
SO, APPARENTLY, DID TRIDENT AND DR. IMPOSSIBLE.
THE ONLY QUESTION IS, WHAT KINDA MACHINE CAN SUCK SOMEONE'S POWERS OUT OF--
DAMN.

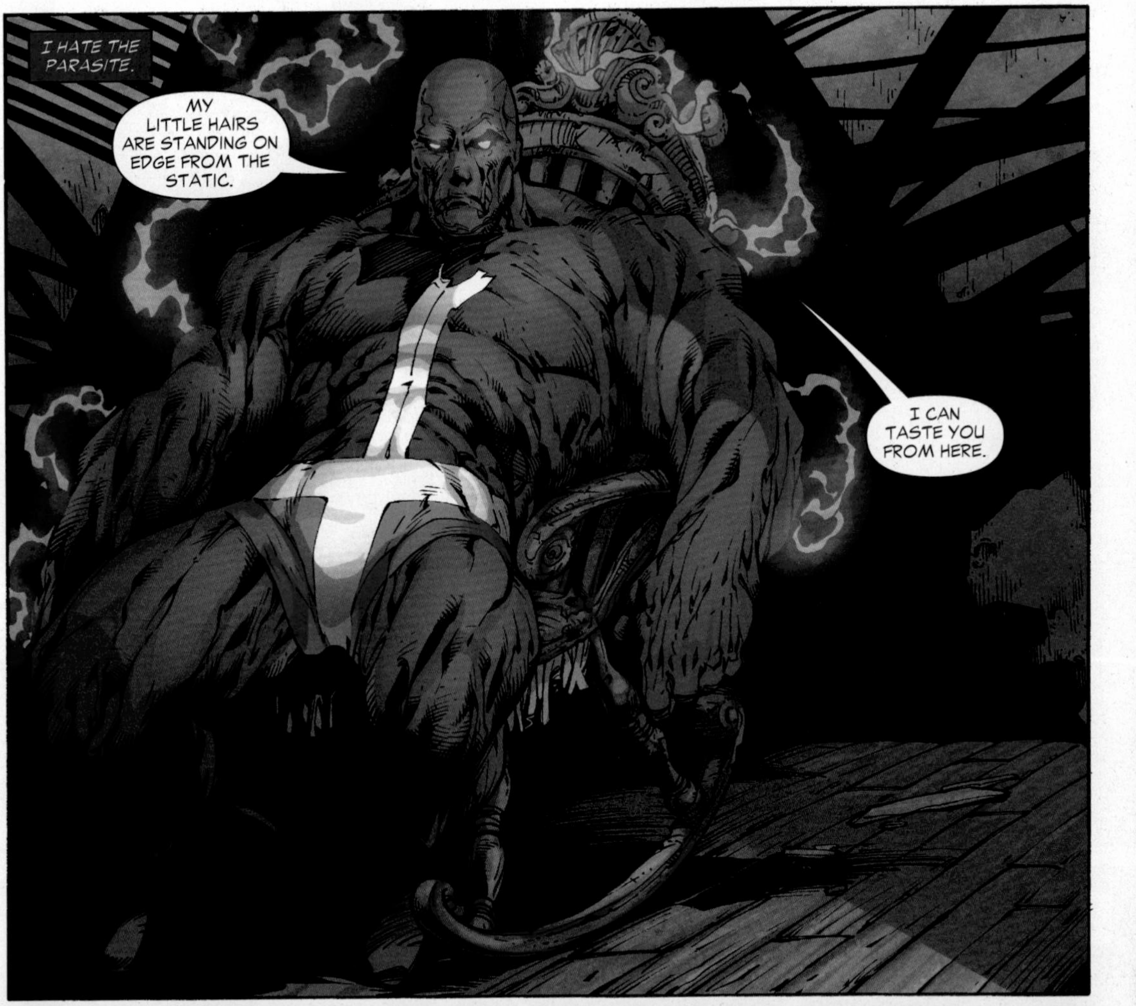
I HATE THE PARASITE.
MY LITTLE HAIRS ARE STANDING ON EDGE FROM THE STATIC.
I CAN TASTE YOU FROM HERE.

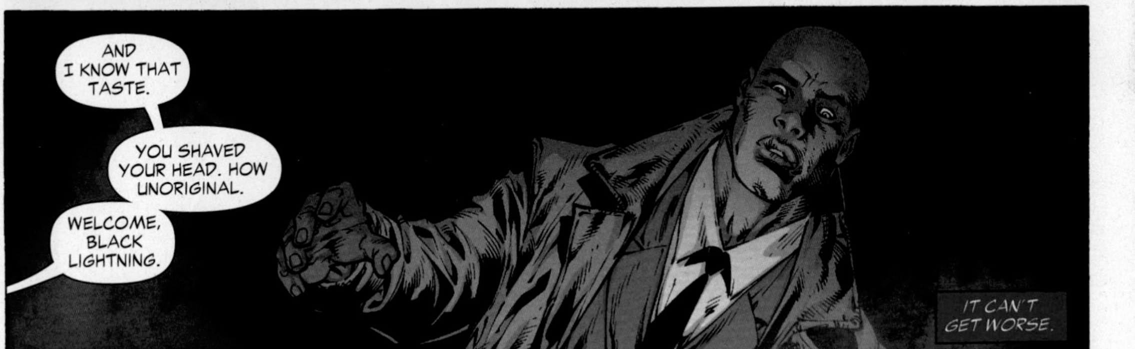
AND I KNOW THAT TASTE.
YOU SHAVED YOUR HEAD. HOW UNORIGINAL.
WELCOME, BLACK LIGHTNING.
IT CAN'T GET WORSE.

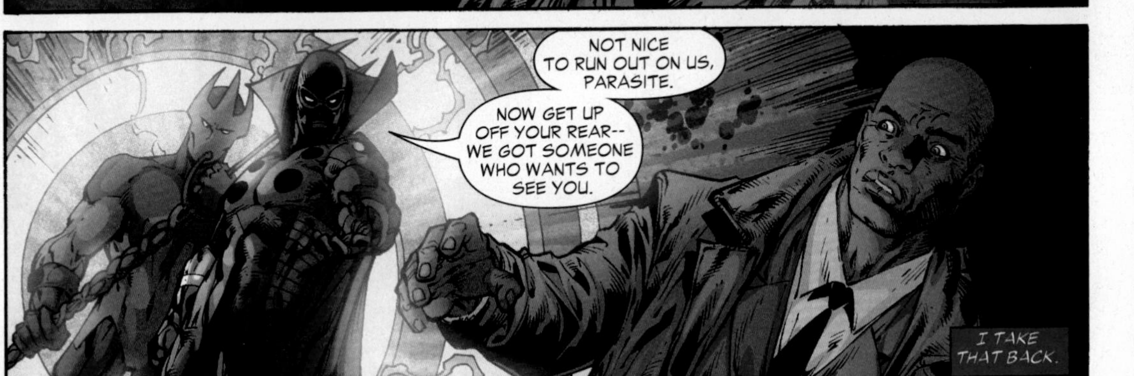
NOT NICE TO RUN OUT ON US, PARASITE.
NOW GET UP OFF YOUR REAR-- WE GOT SOMEONE WHO WANTS TO SEE YOU.
I TAKE THAT BACK.

THE CALL CAME TWO MINUTES AGO.

FROM MAGNUS.

I COULD HEAR THE FEAR IN HIS VOICE.

WITHOUT THE METAL FEET, I DON'T MAKE A SOUND.

FOR ONCE, SHE DOESN'T HEAR ME.

JOHN, WHERE'RE YOU GOING?

OUT THE SKYLIGHT IN THE KITCHEN.

THAT'S NOT WHAT I--

WAIT... WHAT'S WRONG? YOU OKAY?

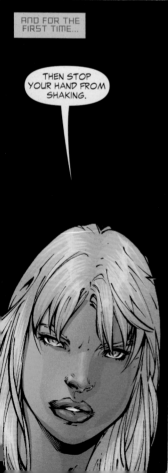

AND FOR THE FIRST TIME...

THEN STOP YOUR HAND FROM SHAKING.

...I MISS THE GYROSCOPES.

I HAVE TO GO, KATHY. I DO. BUT I SWEAR...

JUST NERVES.

I NEED TO FIND OUT WHAT HAPPENED.

SOMEONE STOLE MY BODY.

NO, JOHN...

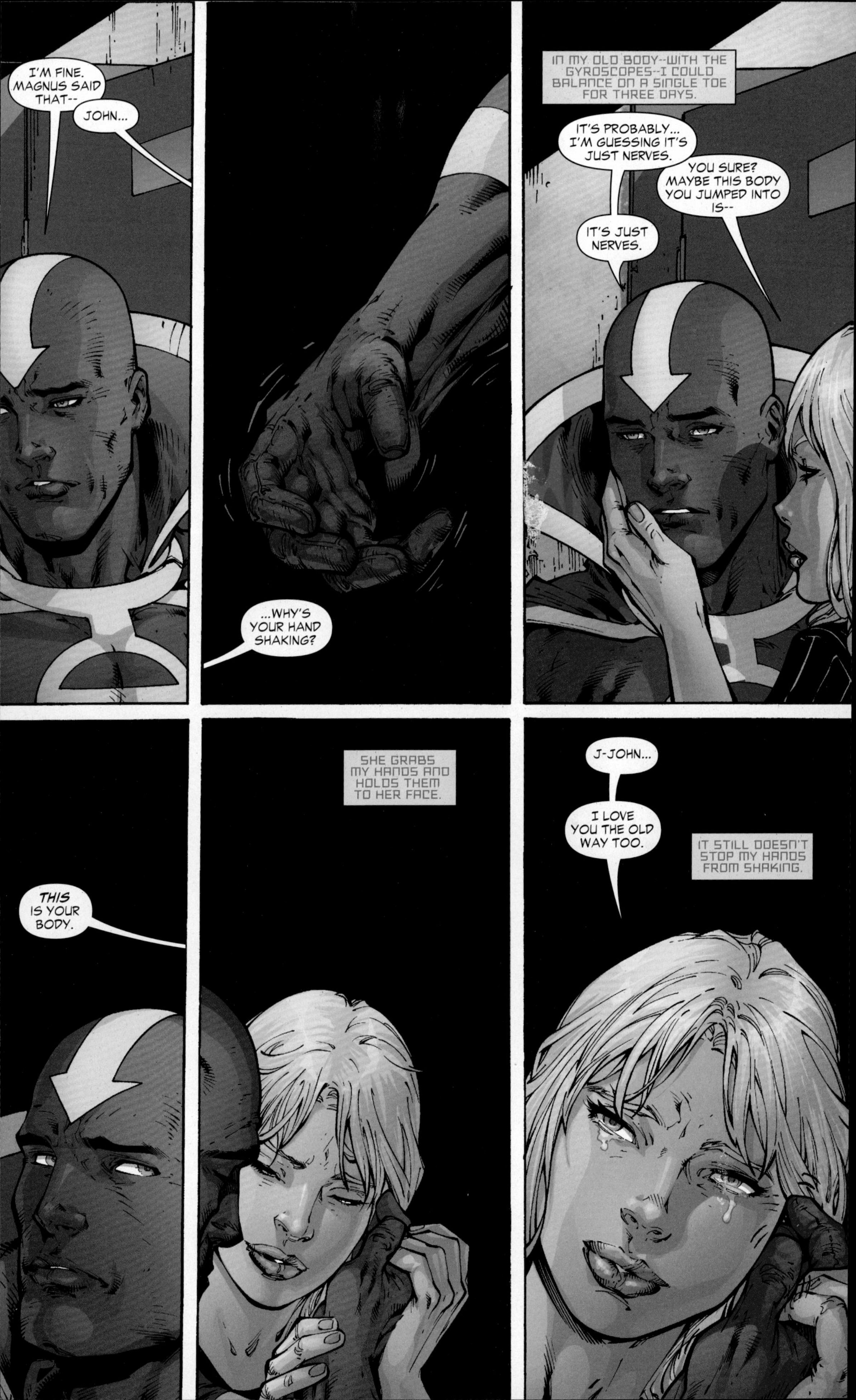
I'M FINE. MAGNUS SAID THAT--
JOHN...
...WHY'S YOUR HAND SHAKING?
IN MY OLD BODY--WITH THE GYROSCOPES--I COULD BALANCE ON A SINGLE TOE FOR THREE DAYS.
IT'S PROBABLY... I'M GUESSING IT'S JUST NERVES.
YOU SURE? MAYBE THIS BODY YOU JUMPED INTO IS--
IT'S JUST NERVES.
THIS IS YOUR BODY.
SHE GRABS MY HANDS AND HOLDS THEM TO HER FACE.
J-JOHN...
I LOVE YOU THE OLD WAY TOO.
IT STILL DOESN'T STOP MY HANDS FROM SHAKING.

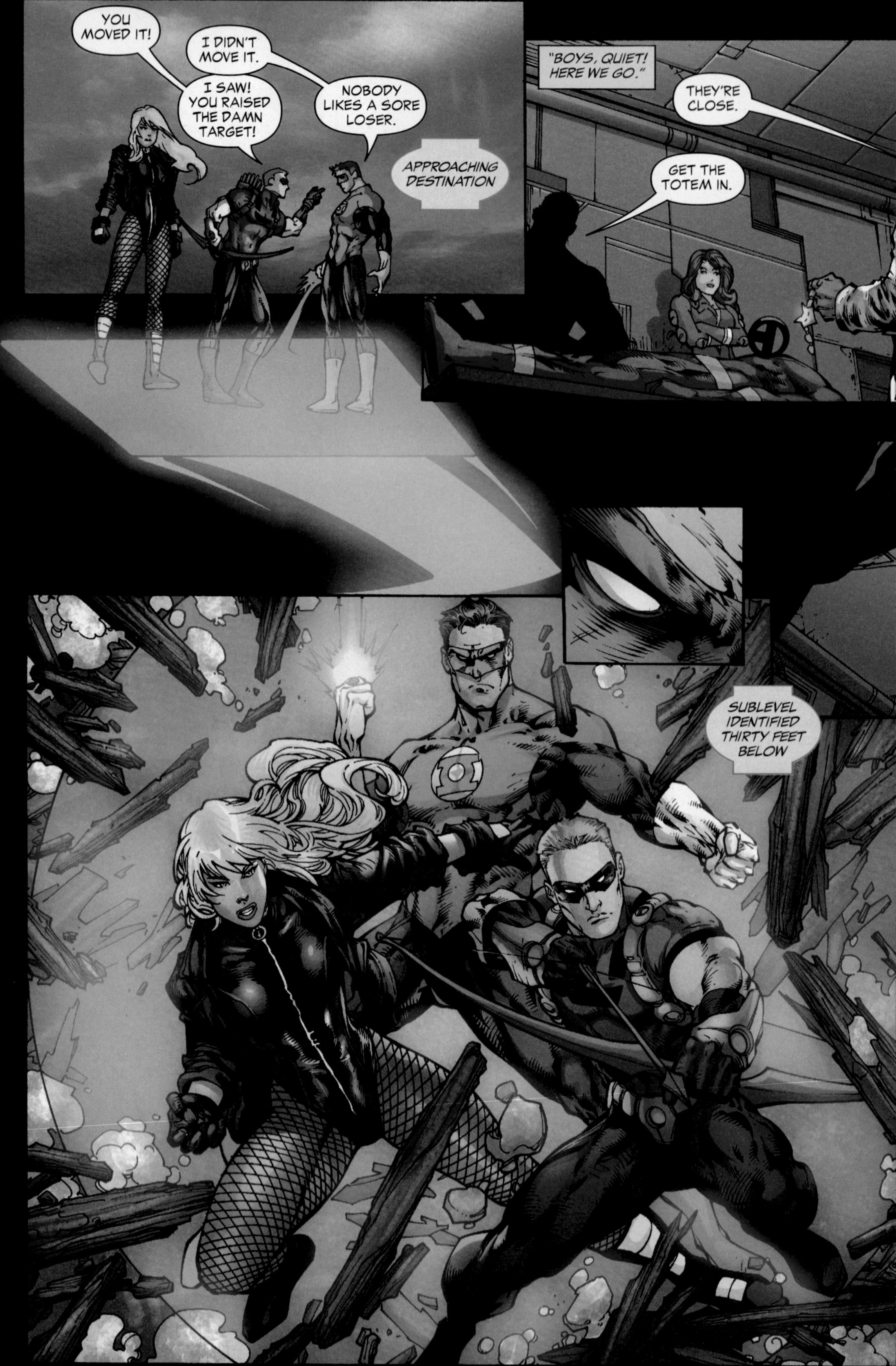
YOU MOVED IT!
I DIDN'T MOVE IT.
I SAW! YOU RAISED THE DAMN TARGET!
NOBODY LIKES A SORE LOSER.
APPROACHING DESTINATION
"BOYS, QUIET! HERE WE GO."
THEY'RE CLOSE.
GET THE TOTEM IN.
SUBLEVEL IDENTIFIED THIRTY FEET BELOW

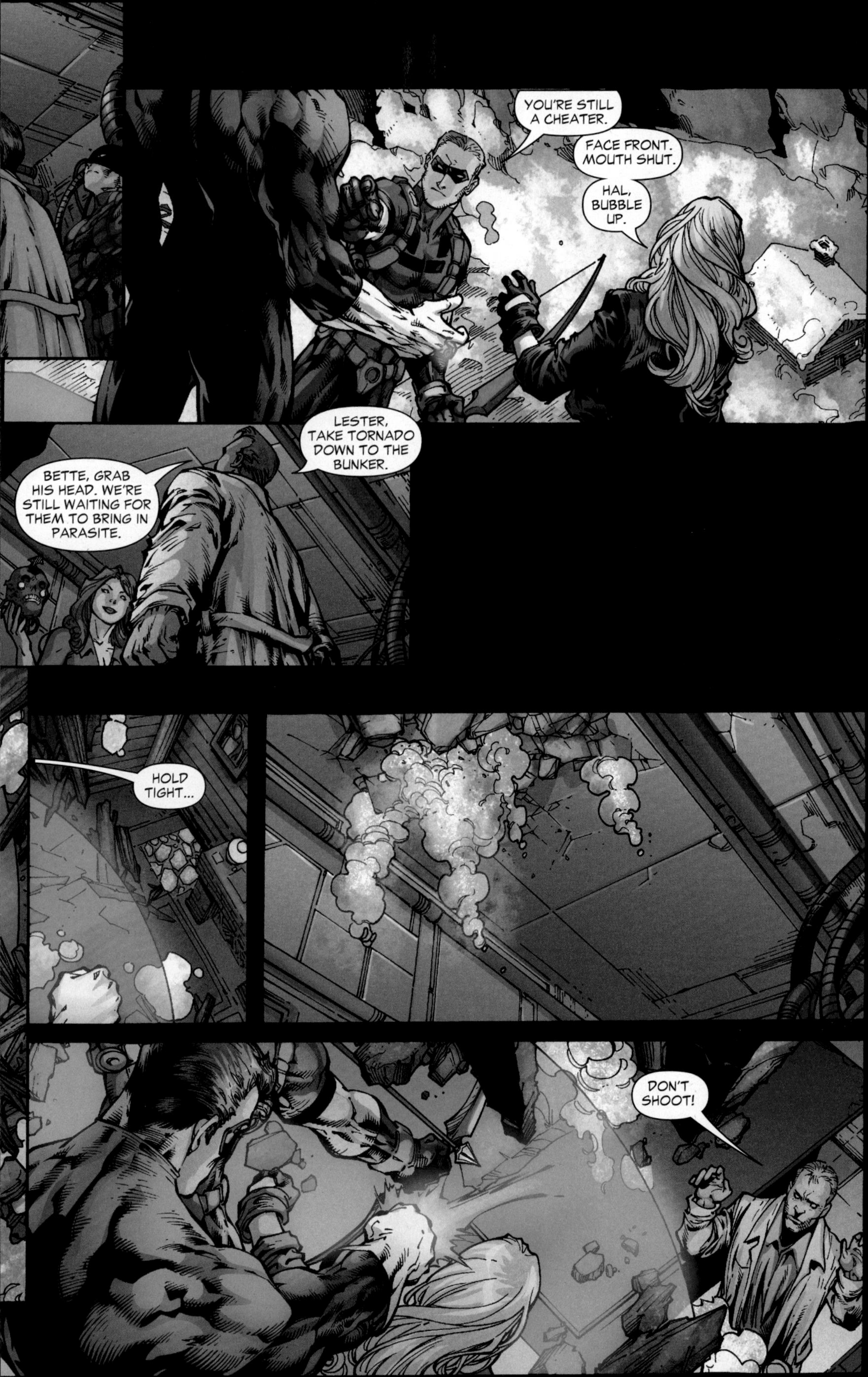
YOU'RE STILL A CHEATER.
FACE FRONT. MOUTH SHUT.
HAL, BUBBLE UP.
LESTER, TAKE TORNADO DOWN TO THE BUNKER.
BETTE, GRAB HIS HEAD. WE'RE STILL WAITING FOR THEM TO BRING IN PARASITE.
HOLD TIGHT...
DON'T SHOOT!

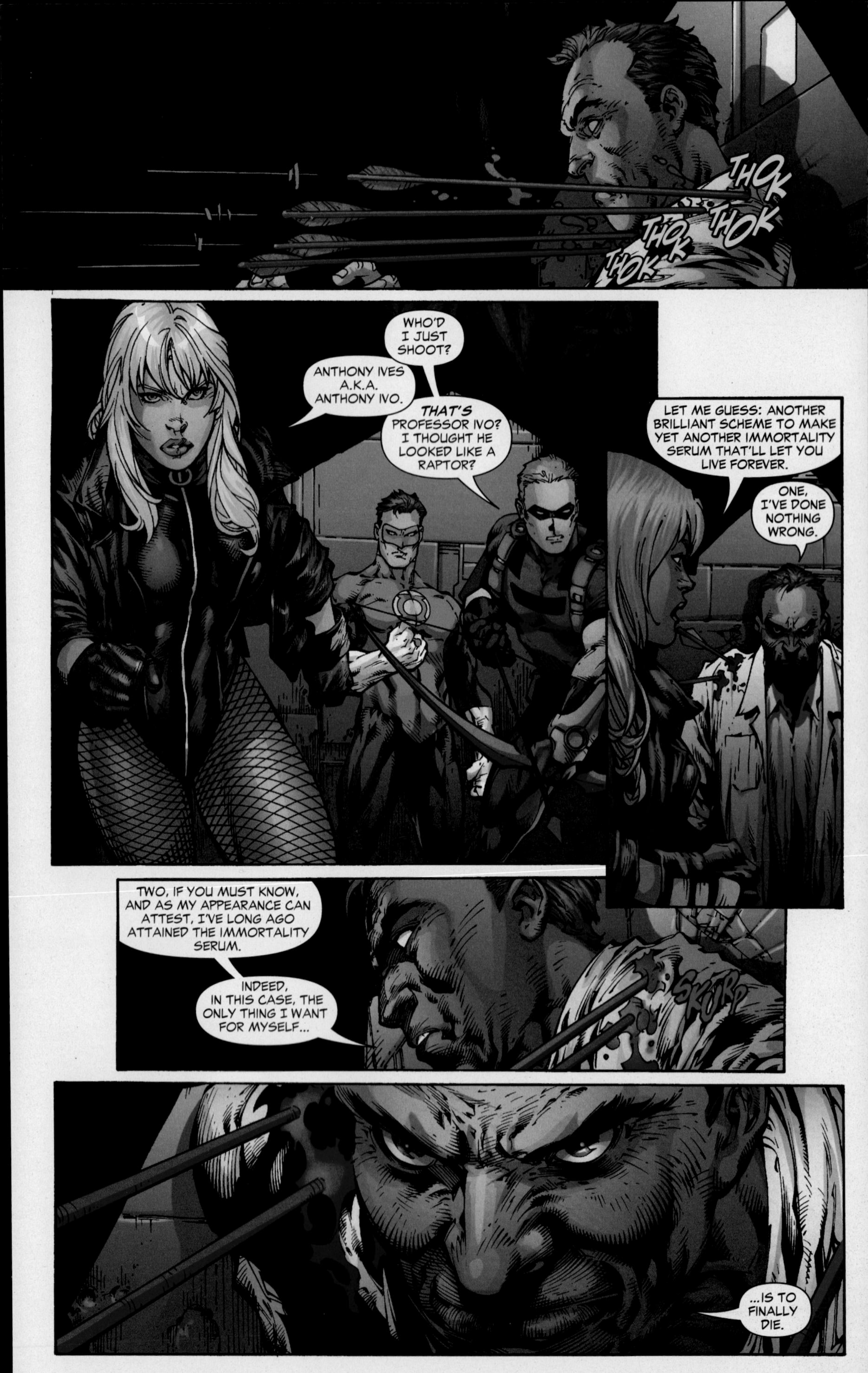
THOK
THOK
THOK
THOK
WHO'D I JUST SHOOT?
ANTHONY IVES A.K.A. ANTHONY IVO.
THAT'S PROFESSOR IVO? I THOUGHT HE LOOKED LIKE A RAPTOR?
LET ME GUESS: ANOTHER BRILLIANT SCHEME TO MAKE YET ANOTHER IMMORTALITY SERUM THAT'LL LET YOU LIVE FOREVER.
ONE, I'VE DONE NOTHING WRONG.
TWO, IF YOU MUST KNOW, AND AS MY APPEARANCE CAN ATTEST, I'VE LONG AGO ATTAINED THE IMMORTALITY SERUM.
INDEED, IN THIS CASE, THE ONLY THING I WANT FOR MYSELF...
SKURP
...IS TO FINALLY DIE.

THOUGH TO BE COMPLETELY HONEST...
DON'T PUSH TH--
...I'M HAPPY TO TAKE ALL THREE OF YOU WITH ME.
DON'T LOOK SO SURPRISED. IT *IS* MORROW'S OLD HIDEOUT.
AND ONCE WE GOT THE PLANS-- ESPECIALLY THE PROTOTYPES-- WELL...
YOU REALLY DIDN'T THINK I'D MAKE MORE IVO ROBOTS, DID YOU?
SAY HELLO TO...

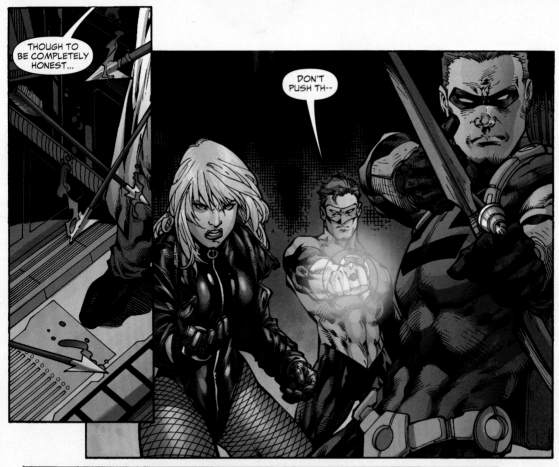

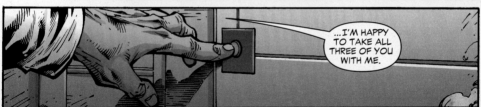

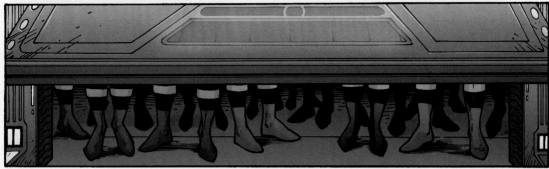

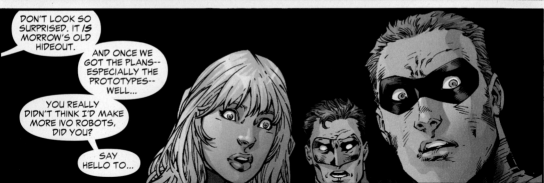

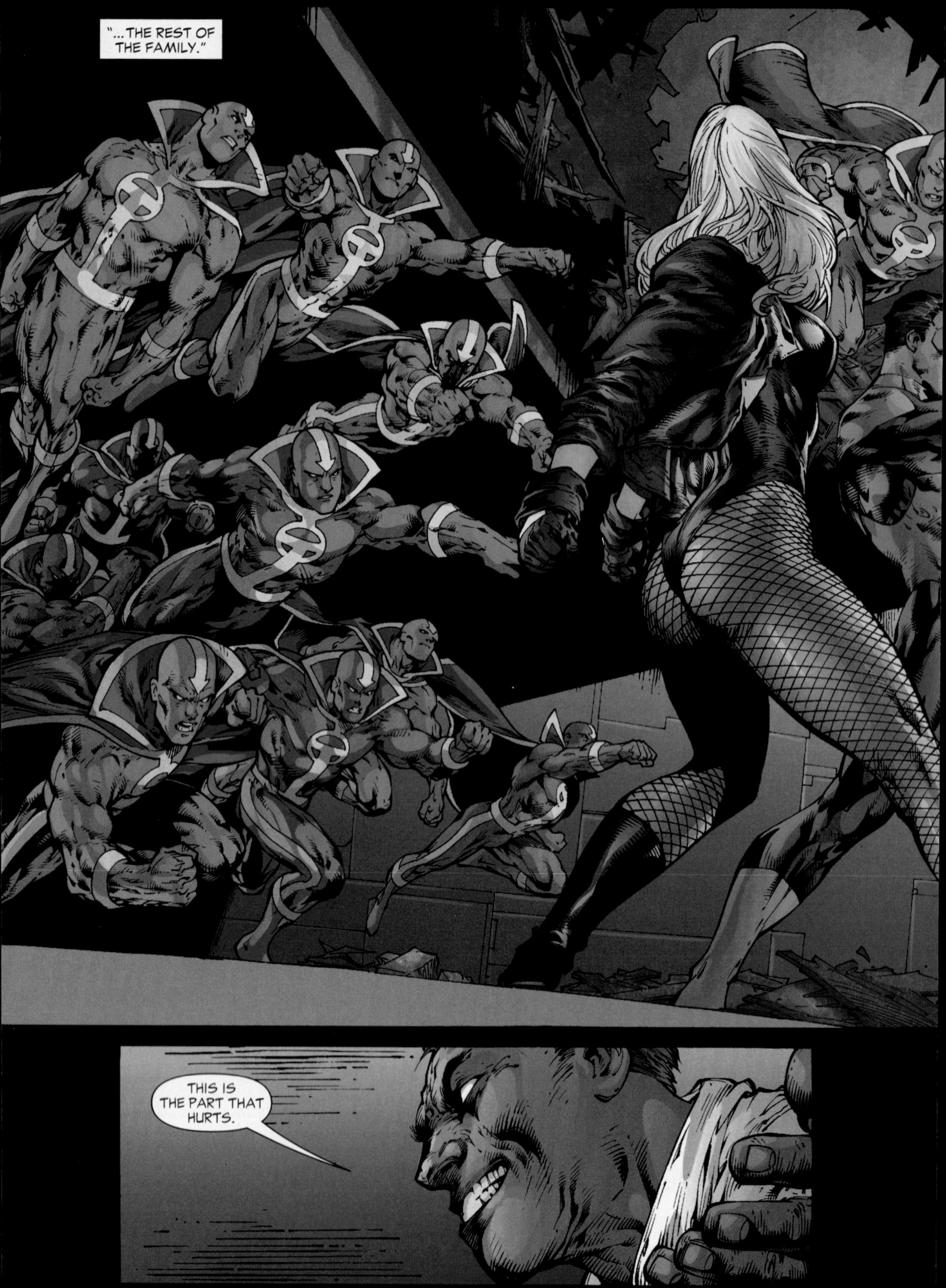
"...THE REST OF THE FAMILY."
THIS IS THE PART THAT HURTS.

THE TORNADO'S PATH

CHAPTER TWO:

TORNADO-RED / TORNADO-BLUE

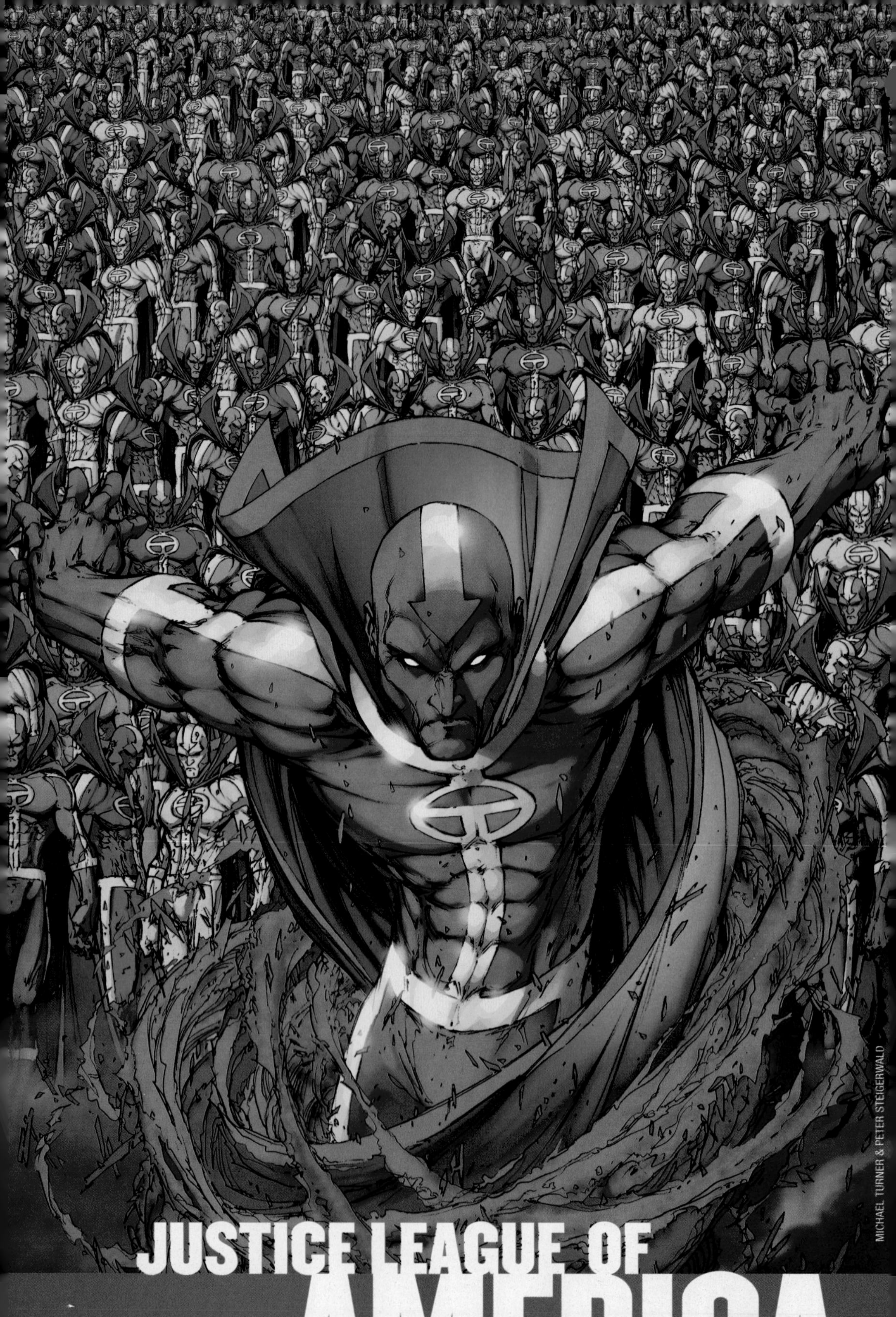
MICHAEL TURNER & PETER STEIGERWALD

JUSTICE LEAGUE OF AMERICA

CHAPTER THREE

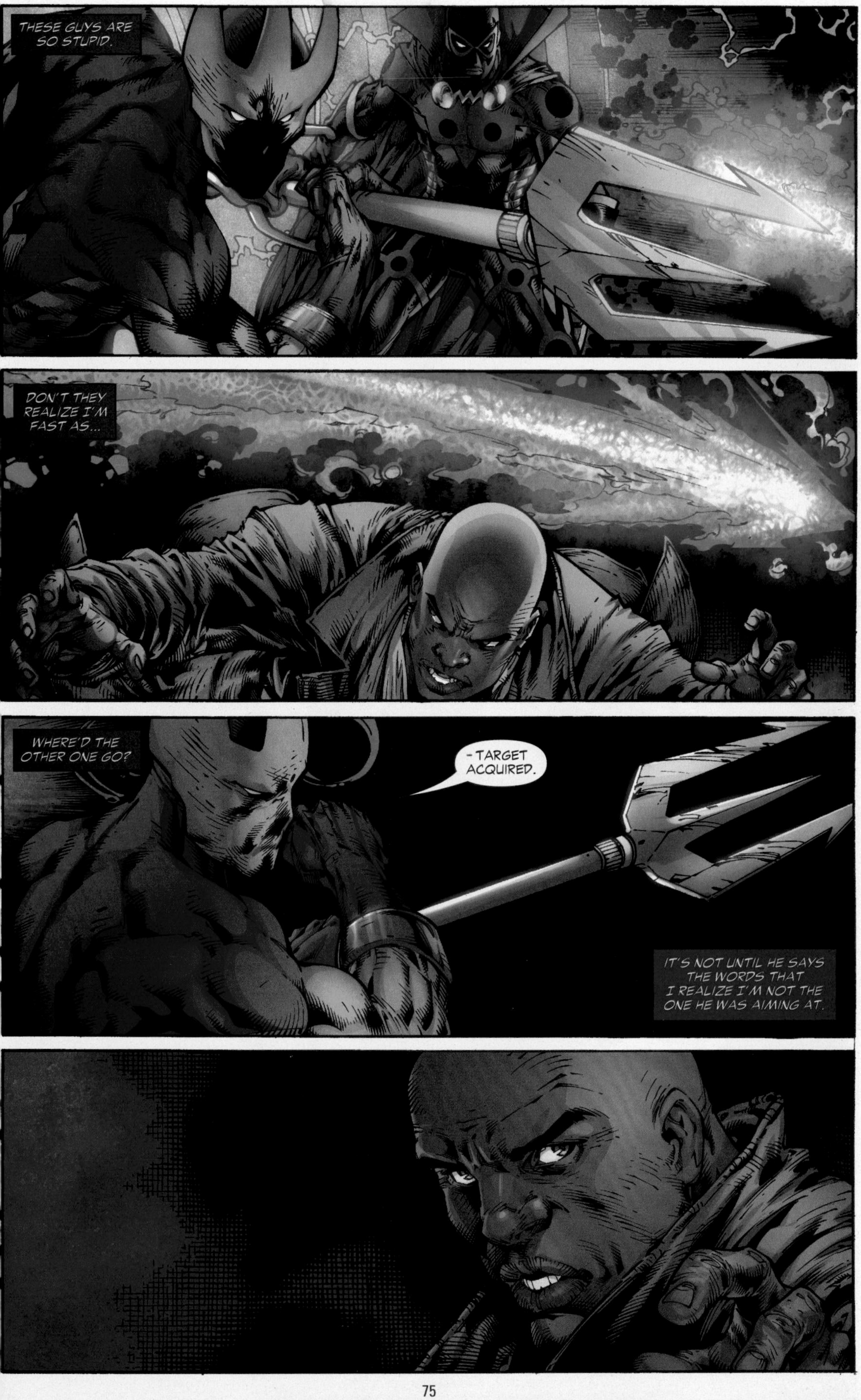
THESE GUYS ARE SO STUPID.
DON'T THEY REALIZE I'M FAST AS...
WHERE'D THE OTHER ONE GO?
-TARGET ACQUIRED.
IT'S NOT UNTIL HE SAYS THE WORDS THAT I REALIZE I'M NOT THE ONE HE WAS AIMING AT.

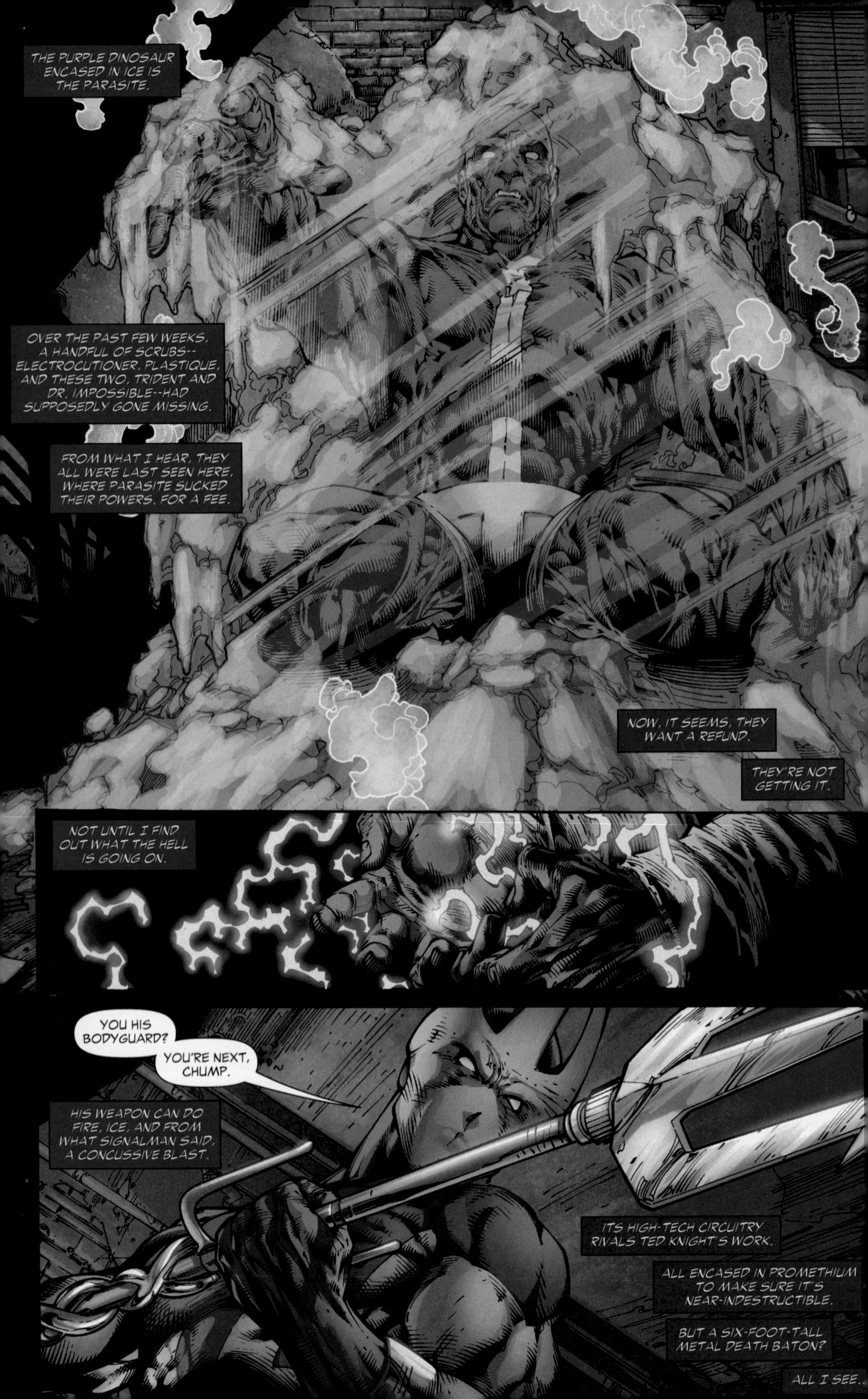
THE PURPLE DINOSAUR ENCASED IN ICE IS THE PARASITE.
OVER THE PAST FEW WEEKS, A HANDFUL OF SCRUBS--ELECTROCUTIONER, PLASTIQUE, AND THESE TWO, TRIDENT AND DR. IMPOSSIBLE--HAD SUPPOSEDLY GONE MISSING.
FROM WHAT I HEAR, THEY ALL WERE LAST SEEN HERE, WHERE PARASITE SUCKED THEIR POWERS. FOR A FEE.
NOW, IT SEEMS, THEY WANT A REFUND.
THEY'RE NOT GETTING IT.
NOT UNTIL I FIND OUT WHAT THE HELL IS GOING ON.
YOU HIS BODYGUARD?
YOU'RE NEXT, CHUMP.
HIS WEAPON CAN DO FIRE, ICE, AND FROM WHAT SIGNALMAN SAID, A CONCUSSIVE BLAST.
ITS HIGH-TECH CIRCUITRY RIVALS TED KNIGHT'S WORK.
ALL ENCASED IN PROMETHIUM TO MAKE SURE IT'S NEAR-INDESTRUCTIBLE.
BUT A SIX-FOOT-TALL METAL DEATH BATON?
ALL I SEE.

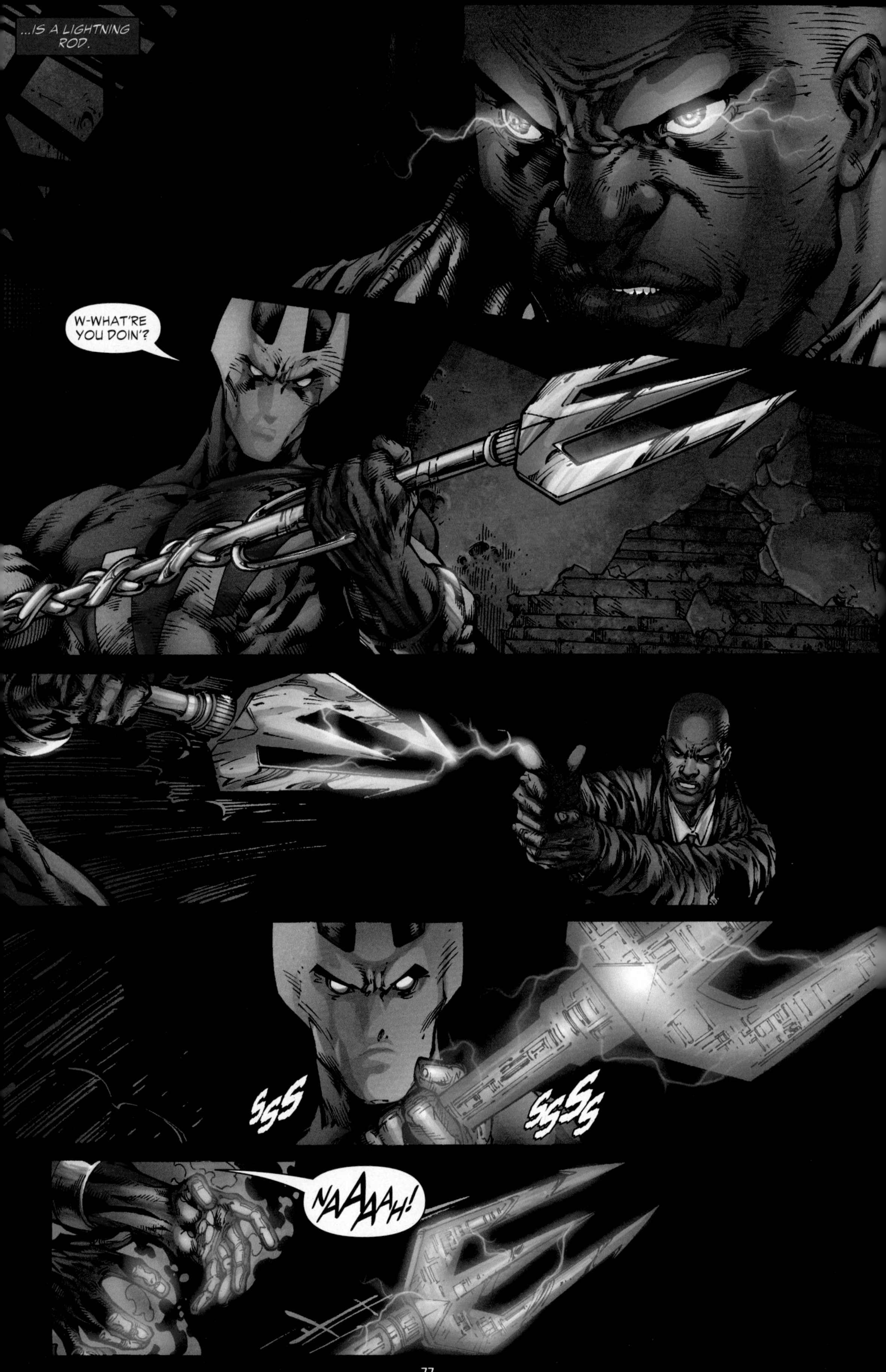
...IS A LIGHTNING ROD.
W-WHAT'RE YOU DOIN'?
SSS
SSSS
NAAAAH!

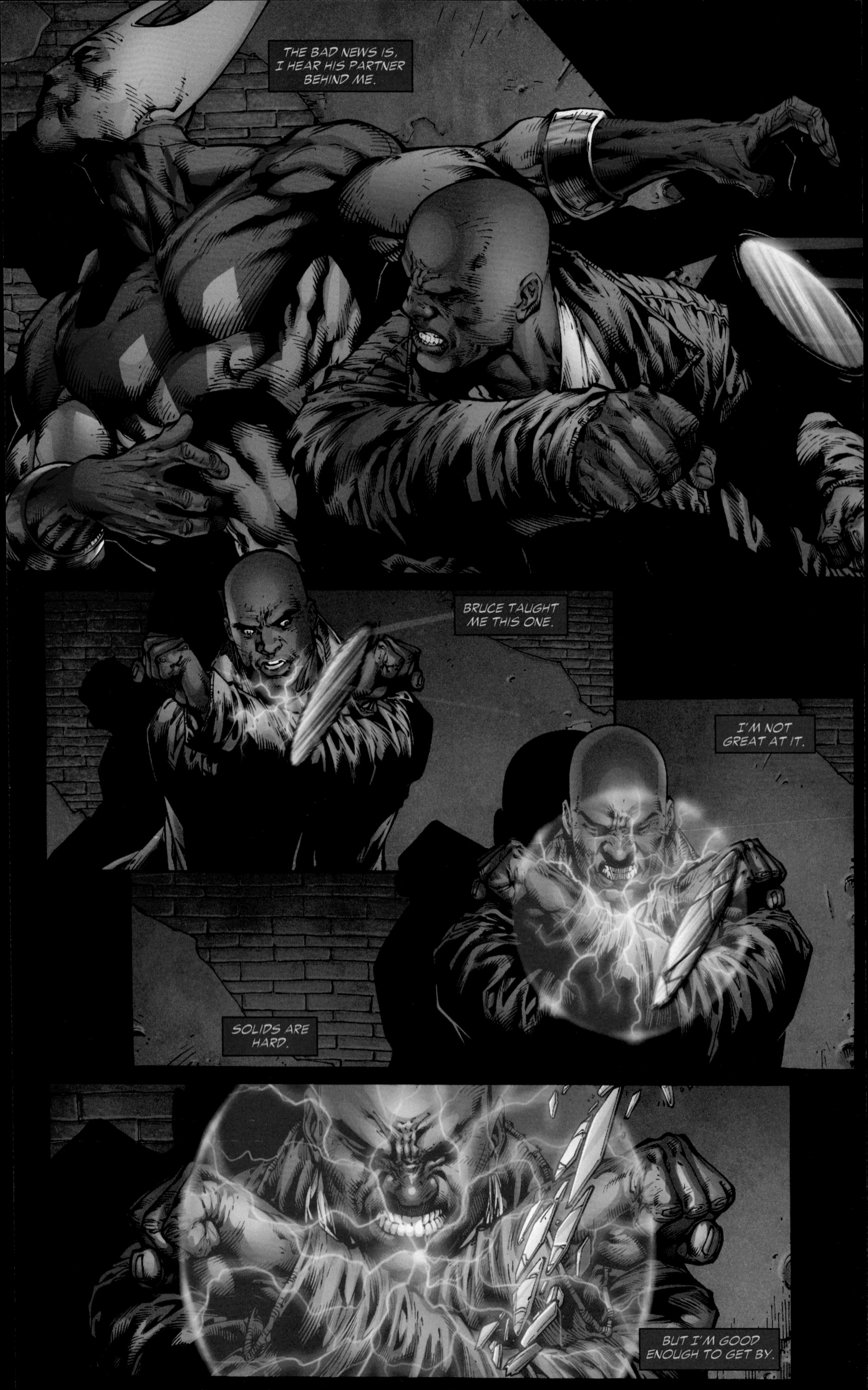
THE BAD NEWS IS, I HEAR HIS PARTNER BEHIND ME.
BRUCE TAUGHT ME THIS ONE.
I'M NOT GREAT AT IT.
SOLIDS ARE HARD.
BUT I'M GOOD ENOUGH TO GET BY.

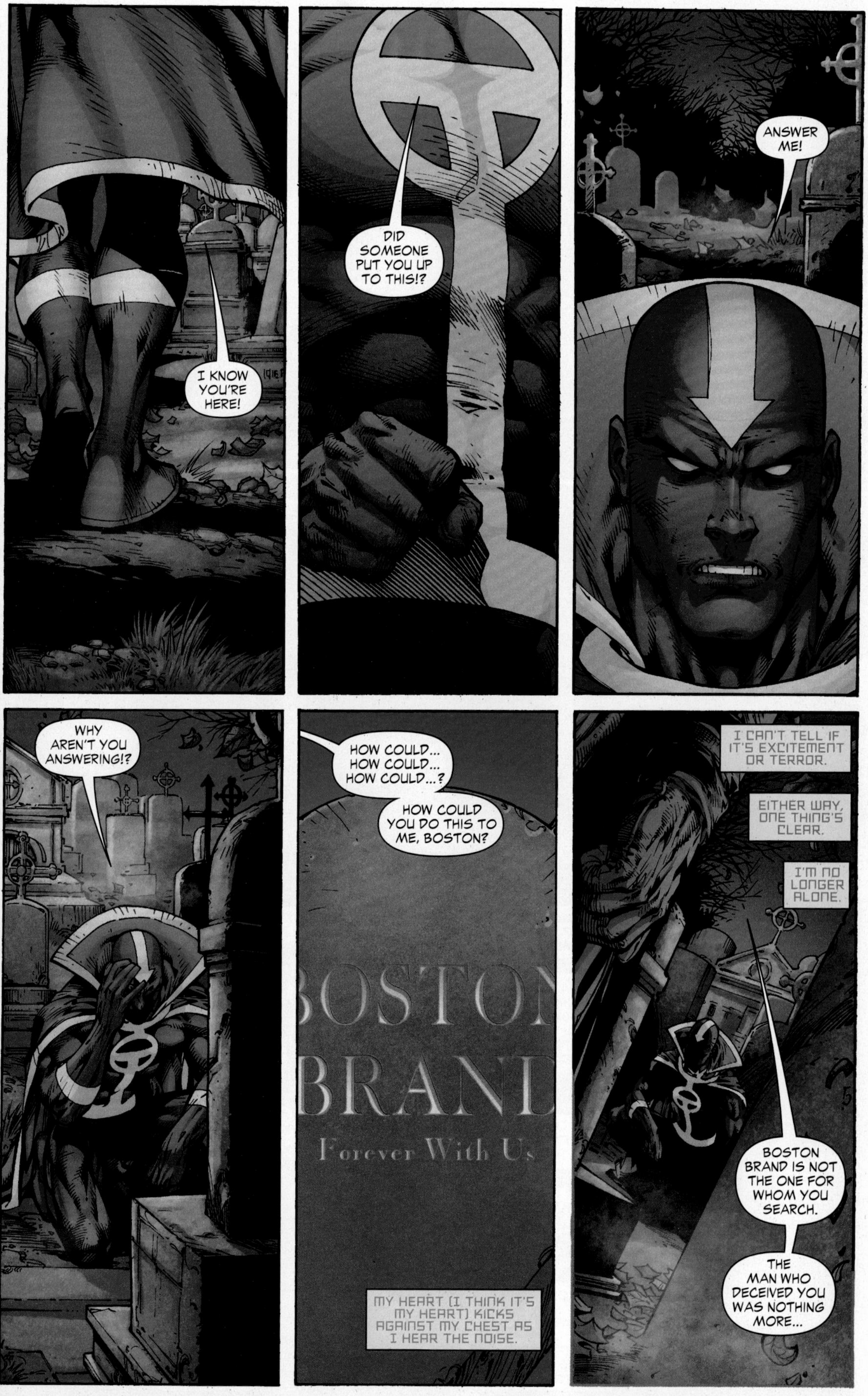
I KNOW YOU'RE HERE!
DID SOMEONE PUT YOU UP TO THIS!?
ANSWER ME!
WHY AREN'T YOU ANSWERING!?
HOW COULD... HOW COULD... HOW COULD...?
HOW COULD YOU DO THIS TO ME, BOSTON?
BOSTON BRAND
Forever With Us
MY HEART (I THINK IT'S MY HEART) KICKS AGAINST MY CHEST AS I HEAR THE NOISE.
I CAN'T TELL IF IT'S EXCITEMENT OR TERROR.
EITHER WAY, ONE THING'S CLEAR.
I'M NO LONGER ALONE.
BOSTON BRAND IS NOT THE ONE FOR WHOM YOU SEARCH.
THE MAN WHO DECEIVED YOU WAS NOTHING MORE...

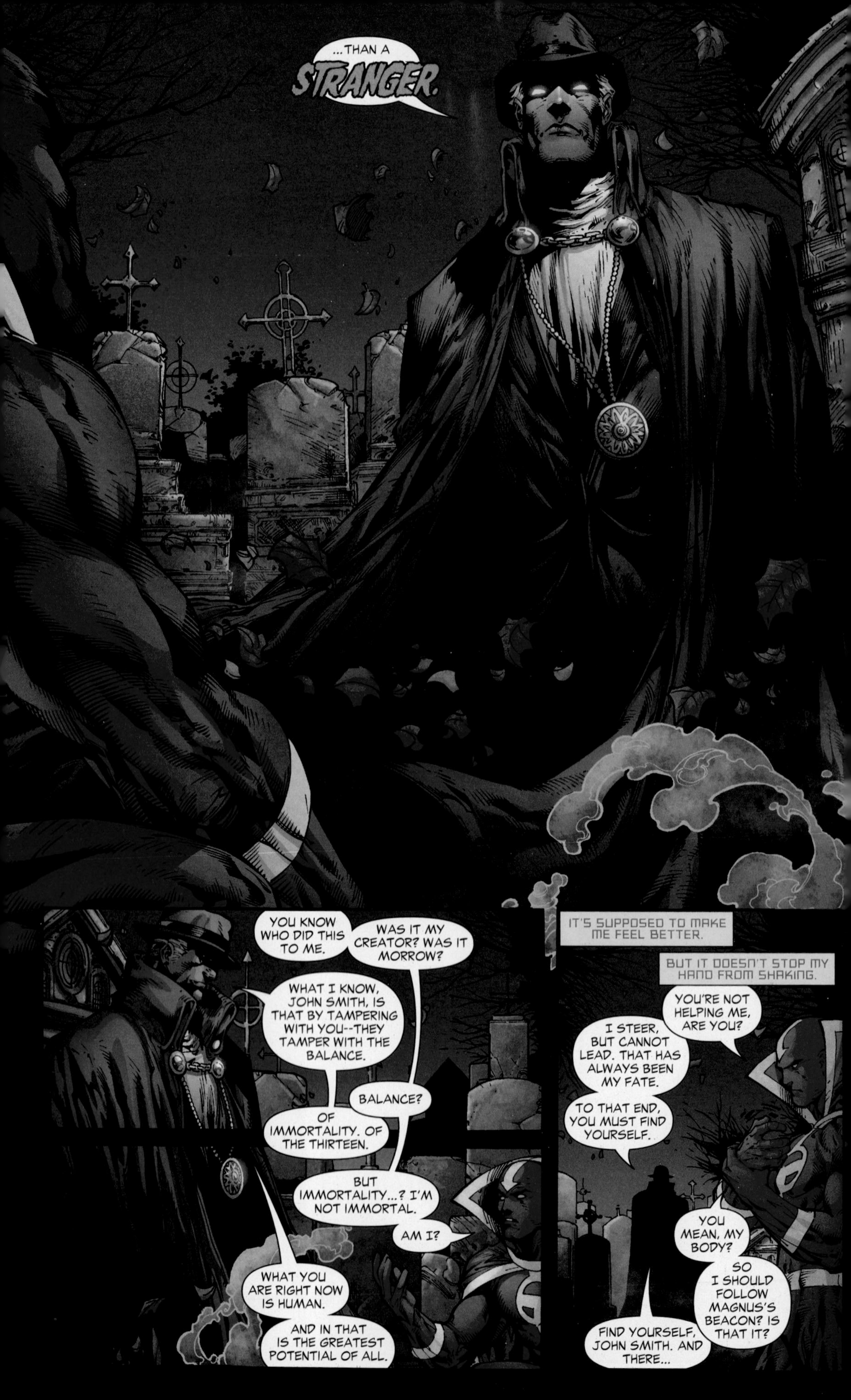
...THAN A STRANGER.
YOU KNOW WHO DID THIS TO ME.
WAS IT MY CREATOR? WAS IT MORROW?
WHAT I KNOW, JOHN SMITH, IS THAT BY TAMPERING WITH YOU--THEY TAMPER WITH THE BALANCE.
BALANCE?
OF IMMORTALITY. OF THE THIRTEEN.
BUT IMMORTALITY...? I'M NOT IMMORTAL.
AM I?
WHAT YOU ARE RIGHT NOW IS HUMAN.
AND IN THAT IS THE GREATEST POTENTIAL OF ALL.
IT'S SUPPOSED TO MAKE ME FEEL BETTER.
BUT IT DOESN'T STOP MY HAND FROM SHAKING.
YOU'RE NOT HELPING ME, ARE YOU?
I STEER, BUT CANNOT LEAD. THAT HAS ALWAYS BEEN MY FATE.
TO THAT END, YOU MUST FIND YOURSELF.
YOU MEAN, MY BODY?
SO I SHOULD FOLLOW MAGNUS'S BEACON? IS THAT IT?
FIND YOURSELF, JOHN SMITH. AND THERE...

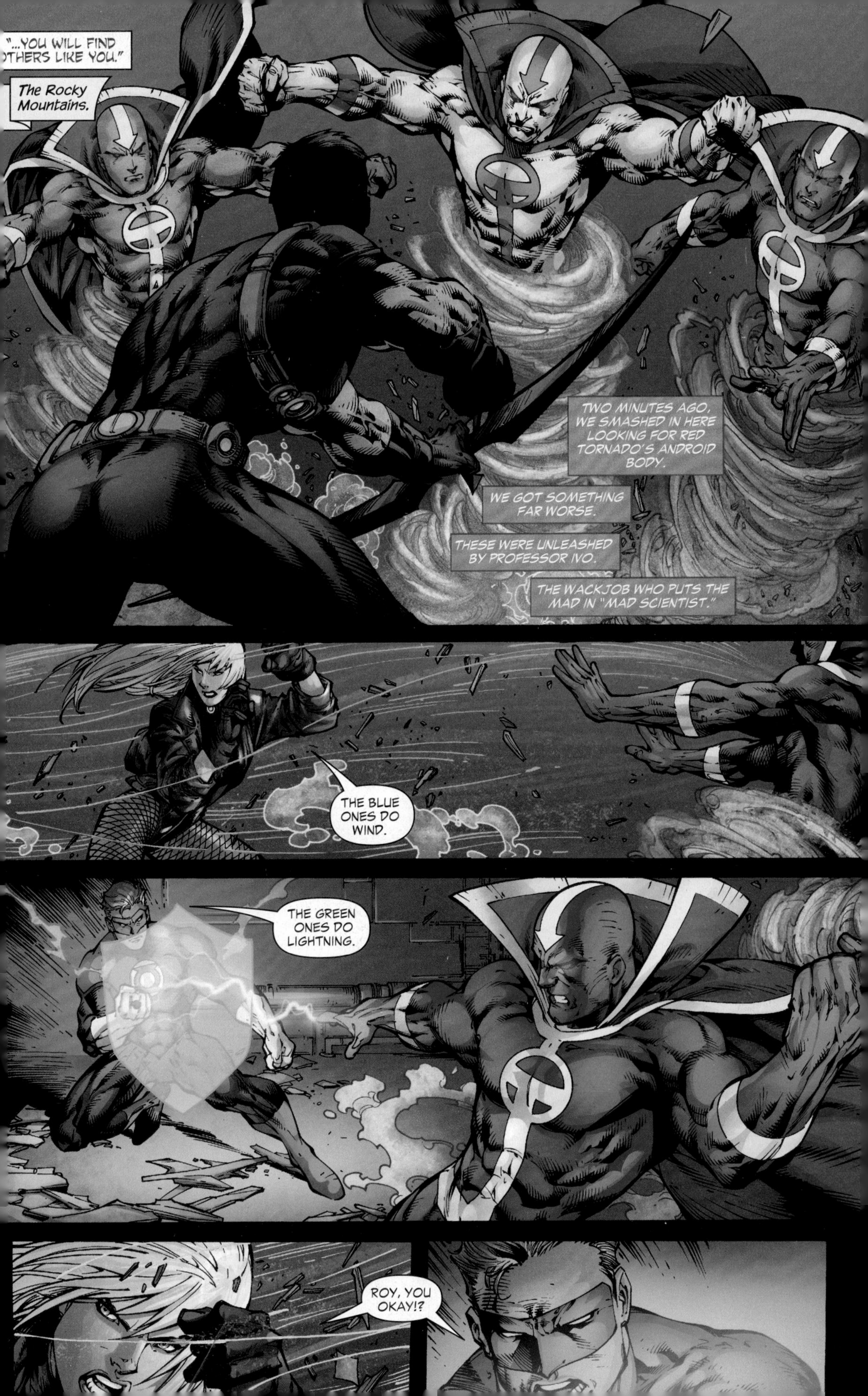
"...YOU WILL FIND OTHERS LIKE YOU."
The Rocky Mountains.
TWO MINUTES AGO, WE SMASHED IN HERE LOOKING FOR RED TORNADO'S ANDROID BODY.
WE GOT SOMETHING FAR WORSE.
THESE WERE UNLEASHED BY PROFESSOR IVO.
THE WACKJOB WHO PUTS THE MAD IN "MAD SCIENTIST."
THE BLUE ONES DO WIND.
THE GREEN ONES DO LIGHTNING.
ROY, YOU OKAY!?

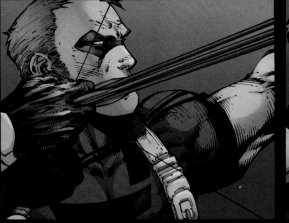

I'M PERFECT.

I DON'T CARE HOW TOUGH THEY ARE.

THEY STILL HAVE TO SEE.

OR MAYBE THEY DON'T.

CRAPOLA.

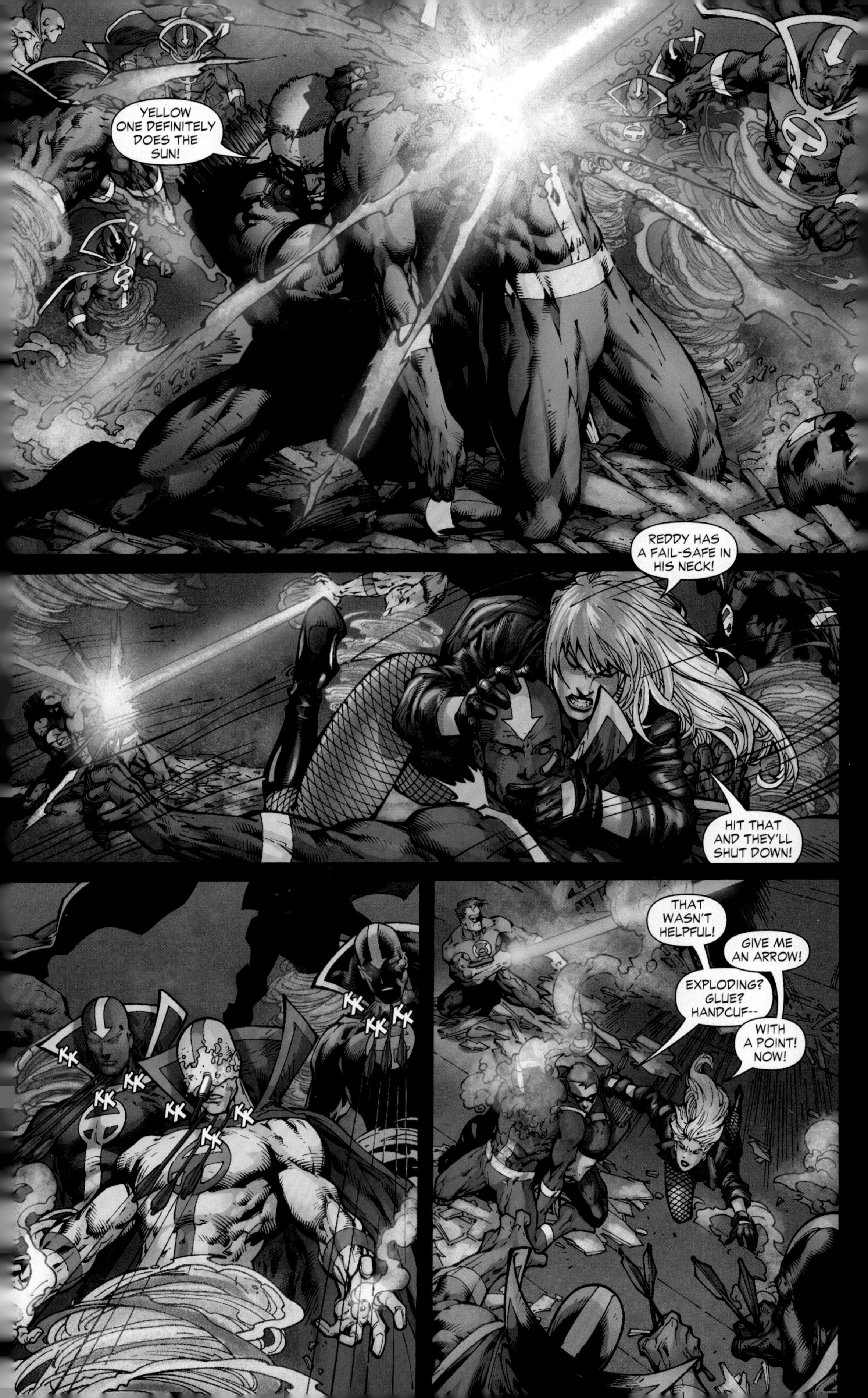
YELLOW ONE DEFINITELY DOES THE SUN!
REDDY HAS A FAIL-SAFE IN HIS NECK!
HIT THAT AND THEY'LL SHUT DOWN!
KK
KK
KK
KK
KK
KK
KK
KK
KK
THAT WASN'T HELPFUL!
GIVE ME AN ARROW!
EXPLODING? GLUE? HANDCUF--
WITH A POINT! NOW!

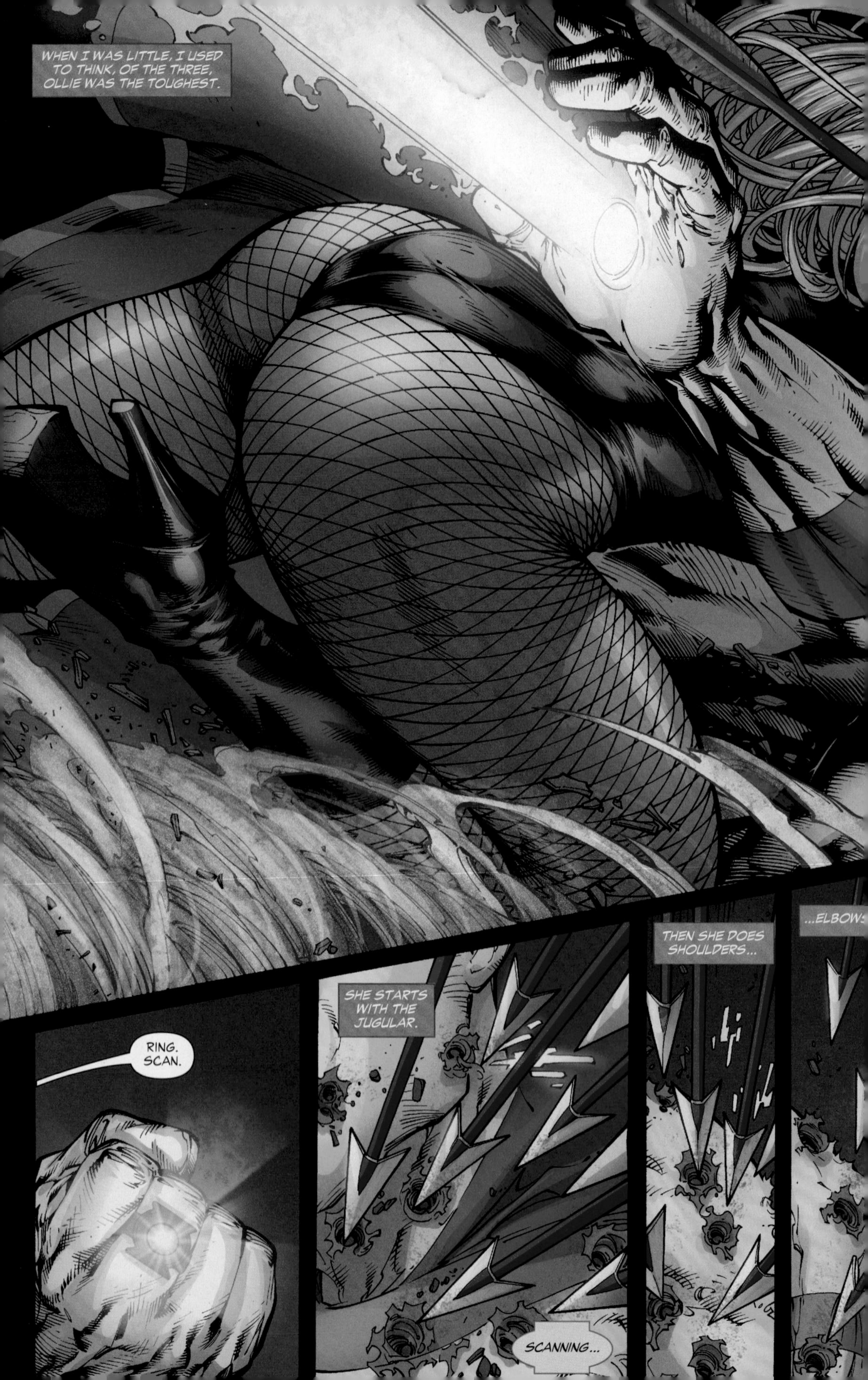
WHEN I WAS LITTLE, I USED TO THINK, OF THE THREE, OLLIE WAS THE TOUGHEST.
RING. SCAN.
SHE STARTS WITH THE JUGULAR.
THEN SHE DOES SHOULDERS...
...ELBOWS
SCANNING...

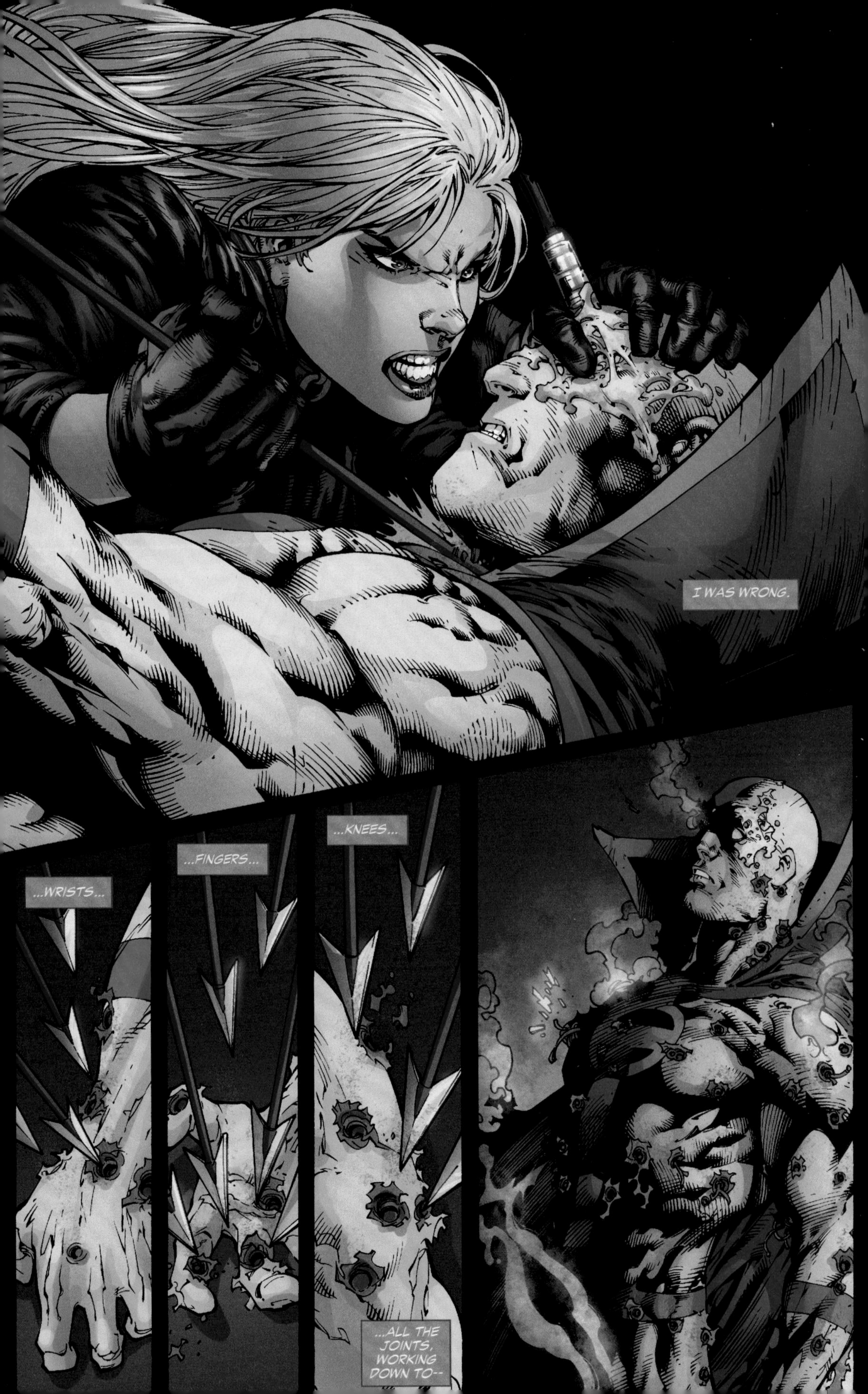
I WAS WRONG.
...WRISTS...
...FINGERS...
...KNEES...
...ALL THE JOINTS, WORKING DOWN TO--

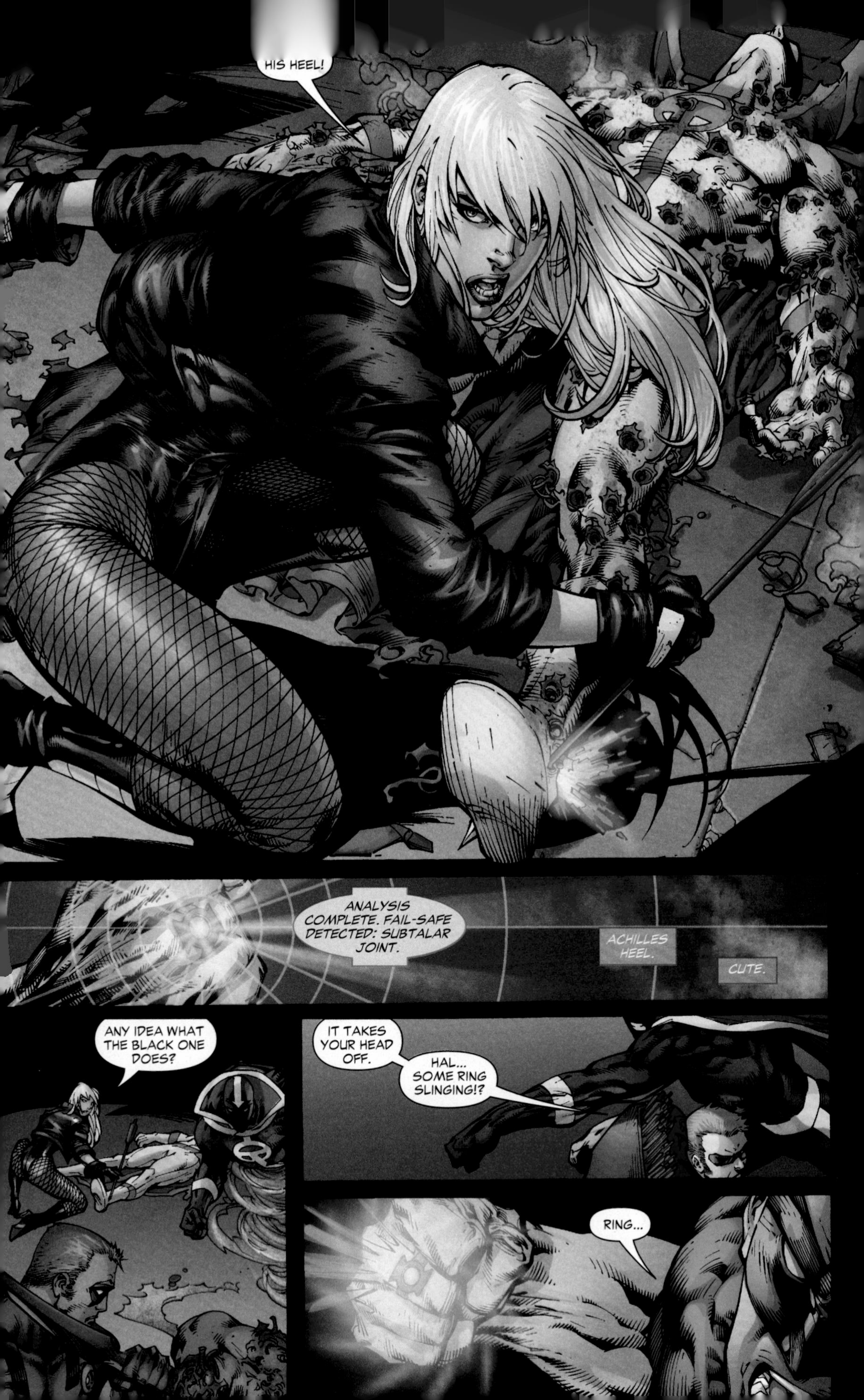
HIS HEEL!
ANALYSIS COMPLETE. FAIL-SAFE DETECTED: SUBTALAR JOINT.
ACHILLES HEEL.
CUTE.
ANY IDEA WHAT THE BLACK ONE DOES?
IT TAKES YOUR HEAD OFF.
HAL... SOME RING SLINGING!?
RING...

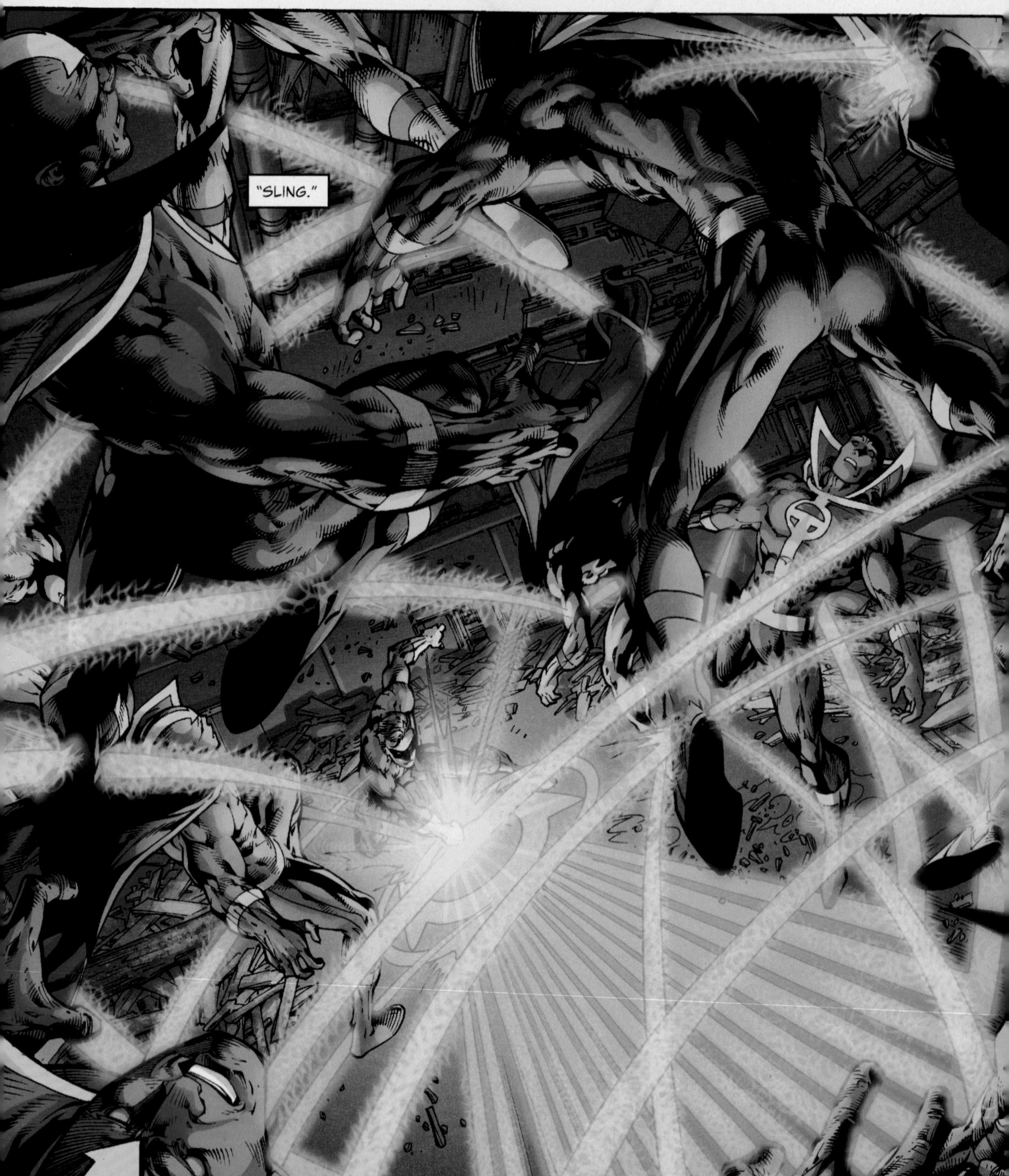
"SLING."

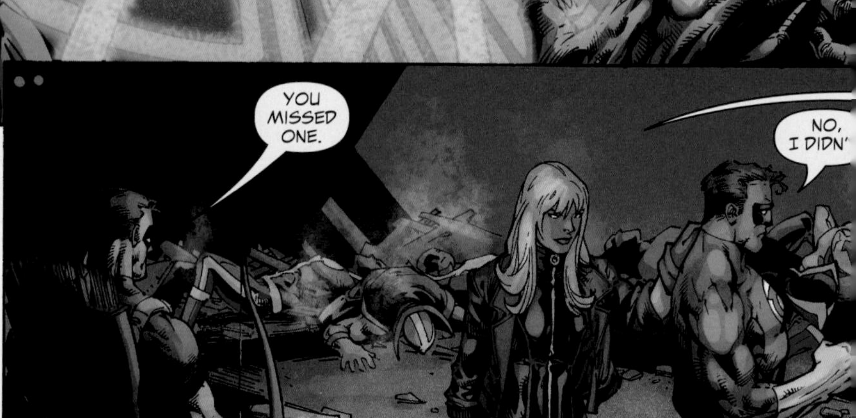
YOU MISSED ONE.
NO, I DIDN'

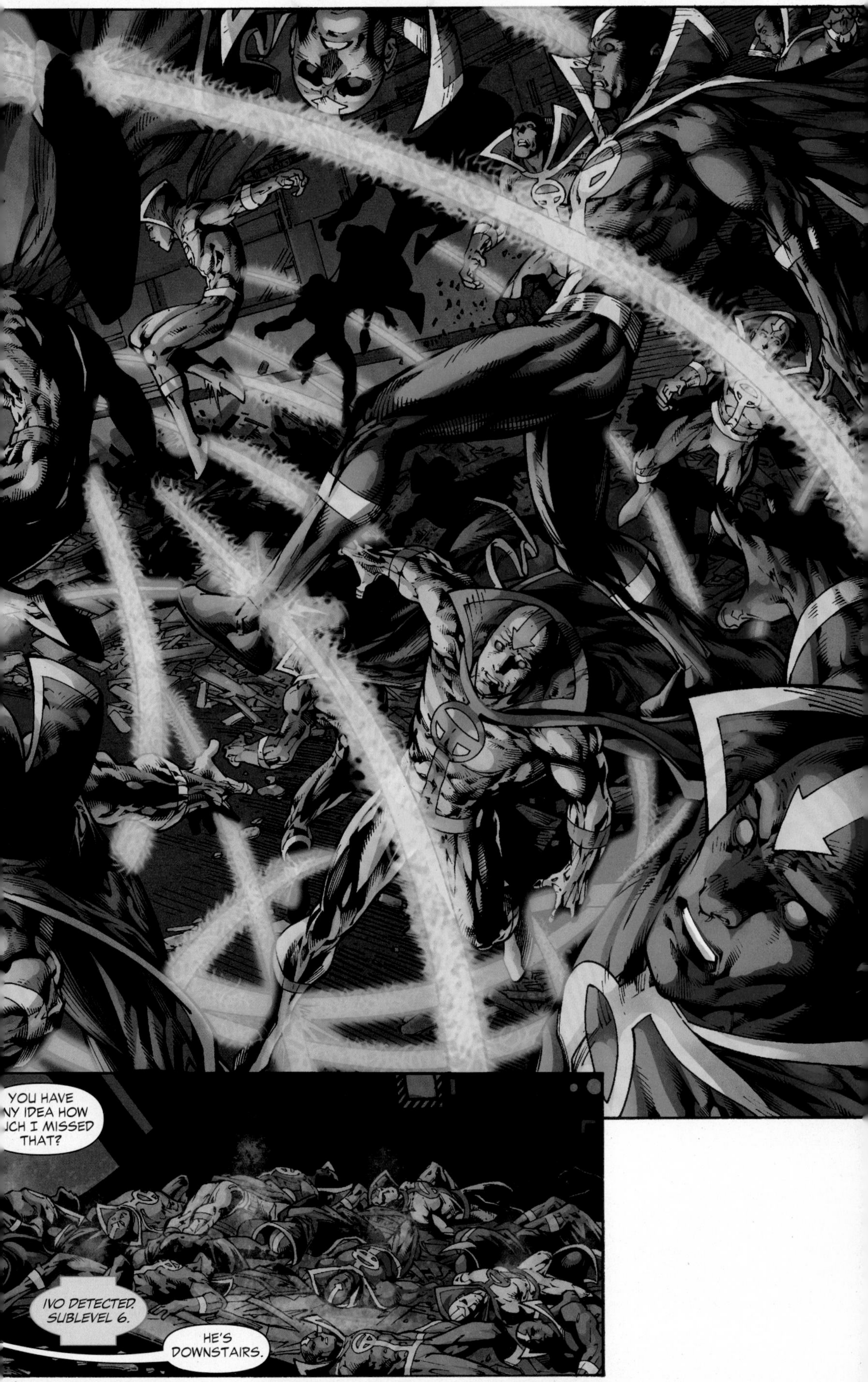
YOU HAVE
NY IDEA HOW
JCH I MISSED
THAT?
IVO DETECTED.
SUBLEVEL 6.
HE'S
DOWNSTAIRS.

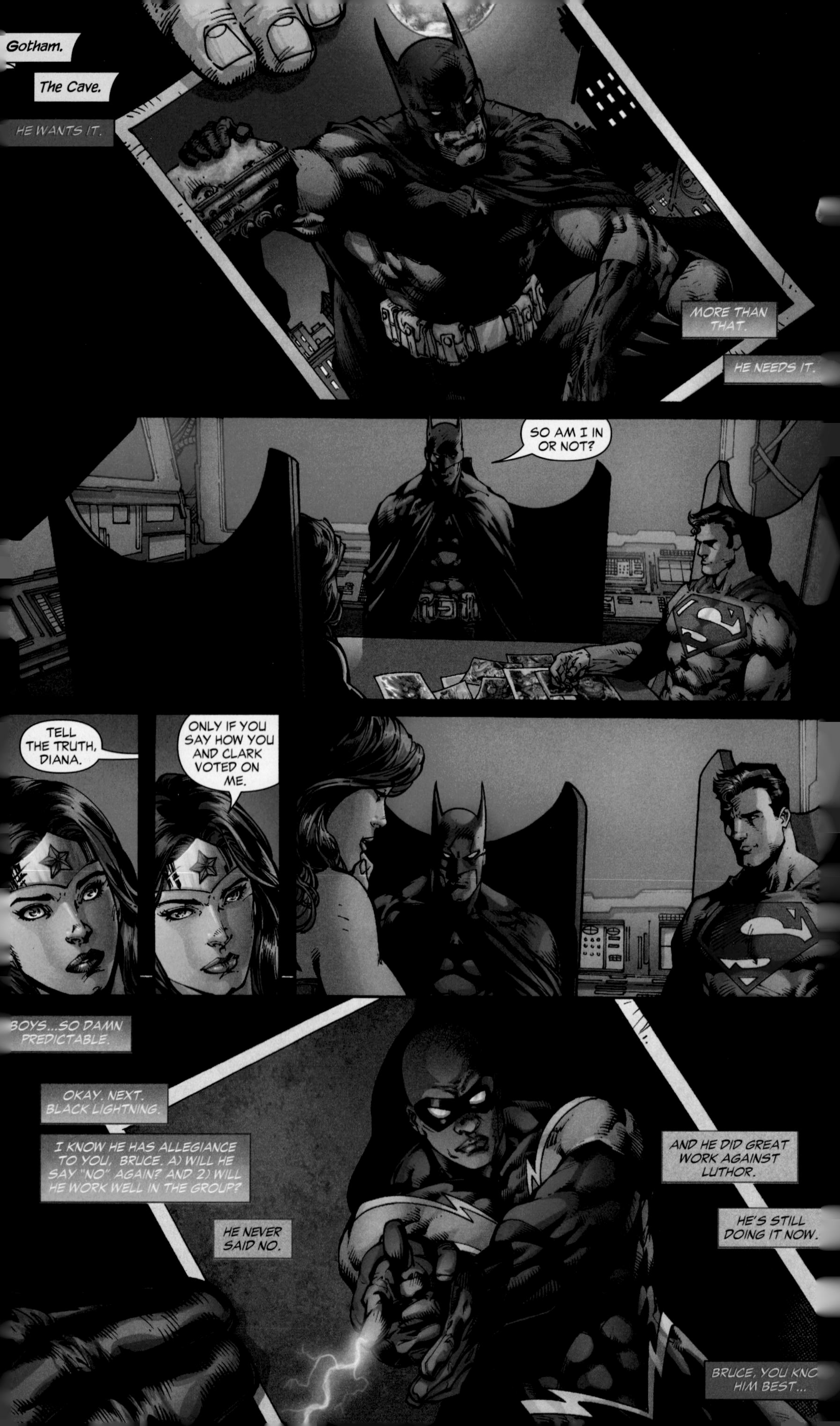
Gotham.
The Cave.
HE WANTS IT.
MORE THAN THAT.
HE NEEDS IT.
SO AM I IN OR NOT?
TELL THE TRUTH, DIANA.
ONLY IF YOU SAY HOW YOU AND CLARK VOTED ON ME.
BOYS...SO DAMN PREDICTABLE.
OKAY. NEXT. BLACK LIGHTNING.
I KNOW HE HAS ALLEGIANCE TO YOU, BRUCE. A) WILL HE SAY "NO" AGAIN? AND 2) WILL HE WORK WELL IN THE GROUP?
HE NEVER SAID NO.
AND HE DID GREAT WORK AGAINST LUTHOR.
HE'S STILL DOING IT NOW.
BRUCE, YOU KNO
HIM BEST...

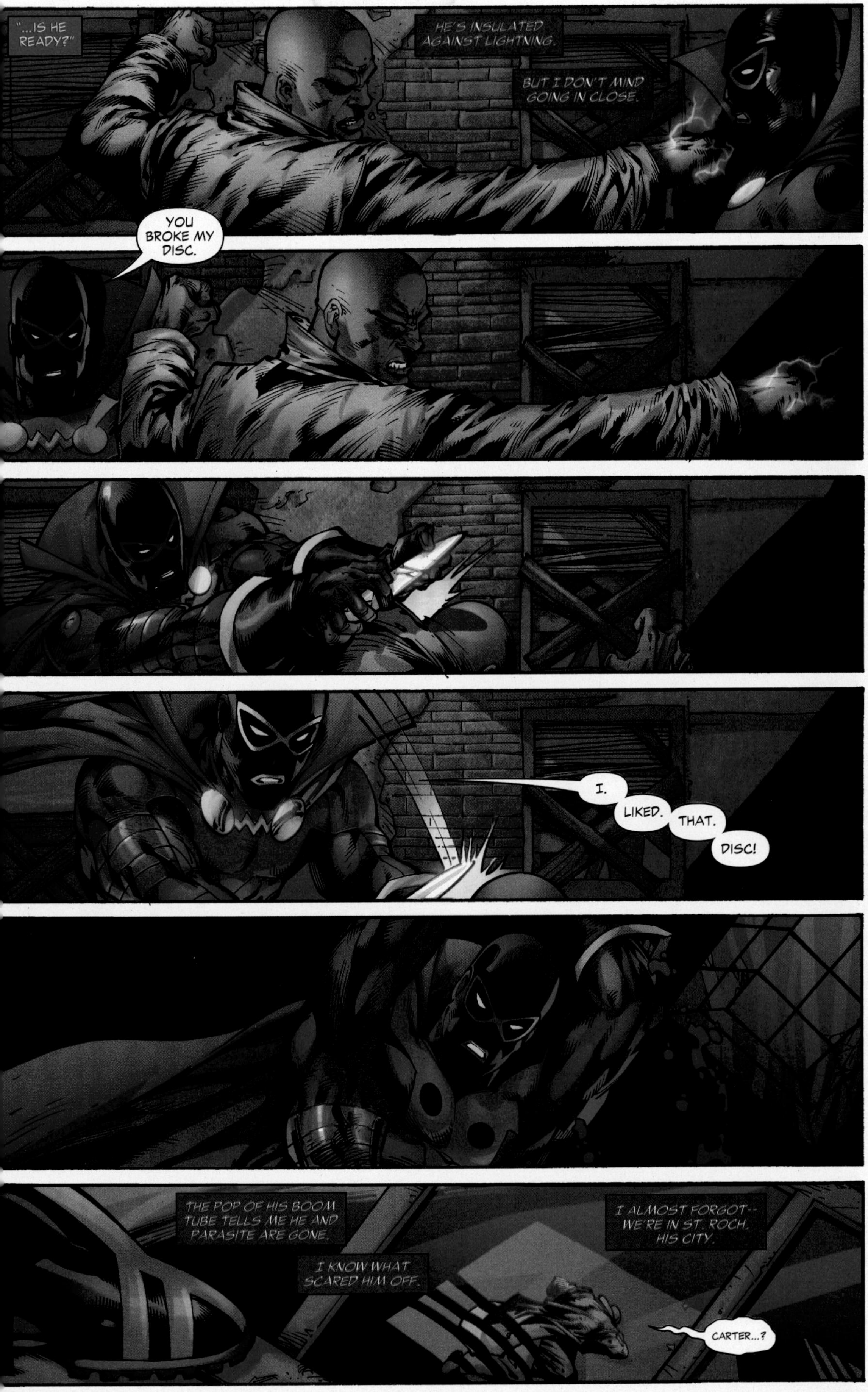
"...IS HE READY?"
HE'S INSULATED AGAINST LIGHTNING.
BUT I DON'T MIND GOING IN CLOSE.
YOU BROKE MY DISC.
I.
LIKED.
THAT.
DISC!
THE POP OF HIS BOOM TUBE TELLS ME HE AND PARASITE ARE GONE.
I KNOW WHAT SCARED HIM OFF.
I ALMOST FORGOT-- WE'RE IN ST. ROCH. HIS CITY.
CARTER...?

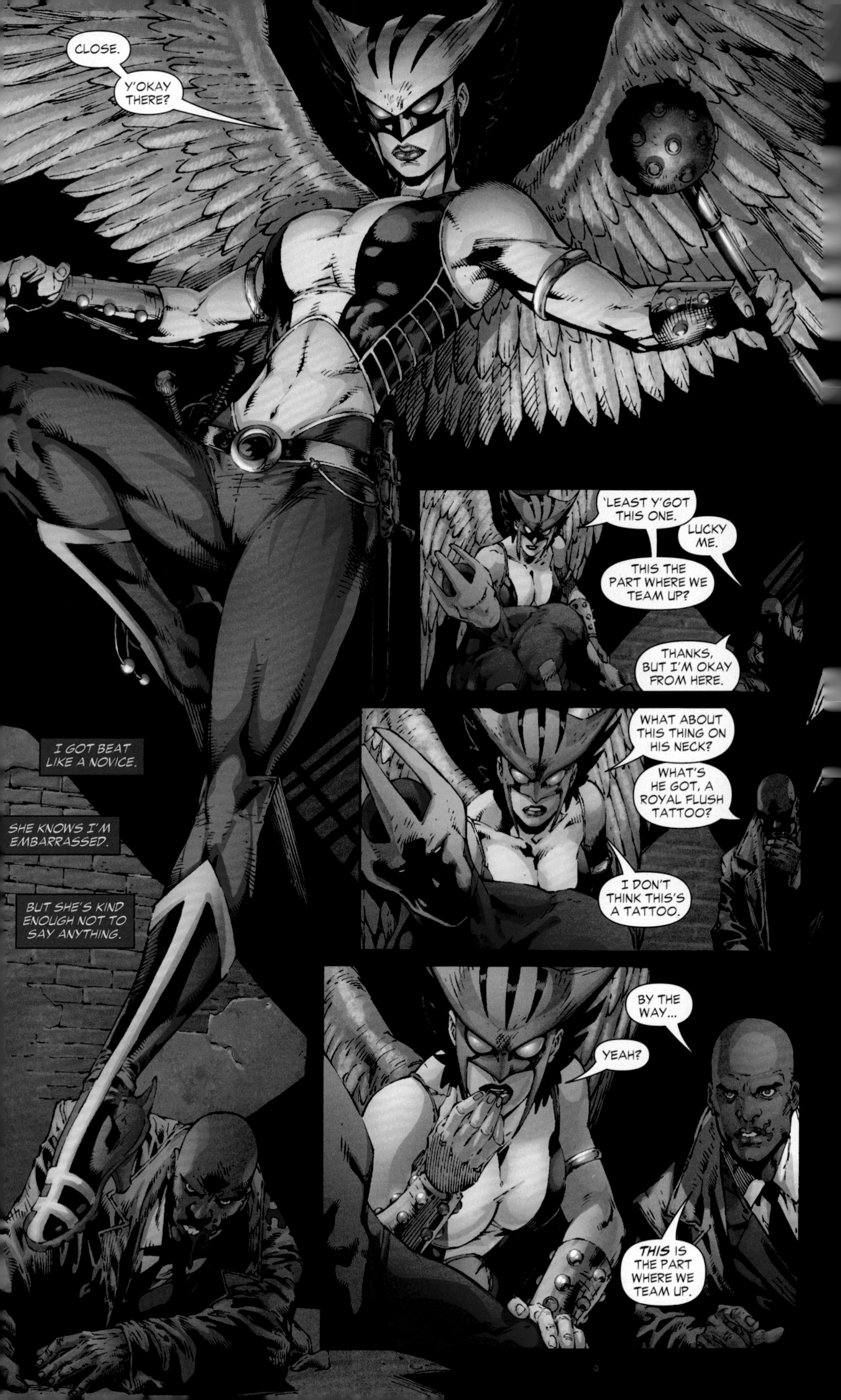
CLOSE.
Y'OKAY THERE?
'LEAST Y'GOT THIS ONE.
LUCKY ME.
THIS THE PART WHERE WE TEAM UP?
THANKS, BUT I'M OKAY FROM HERE.
I GOT BEAT LIKE A NOVICE.
SHE KNOWS I'M EMBARRASSED.
BUT SHE'S KIND ENOUGH NOT TO SAY ANYTHING.
WHAT ABOUT THIS THING ON HIS NECK?
WHAT'S HE GOT, A ROYAL FLUSH TATTOO?
I DON'T THINK THIS'S A TATTOO.
BY THE WAY...
YEAH?
THIS IS THE PART WHERE WE TEAM UP.

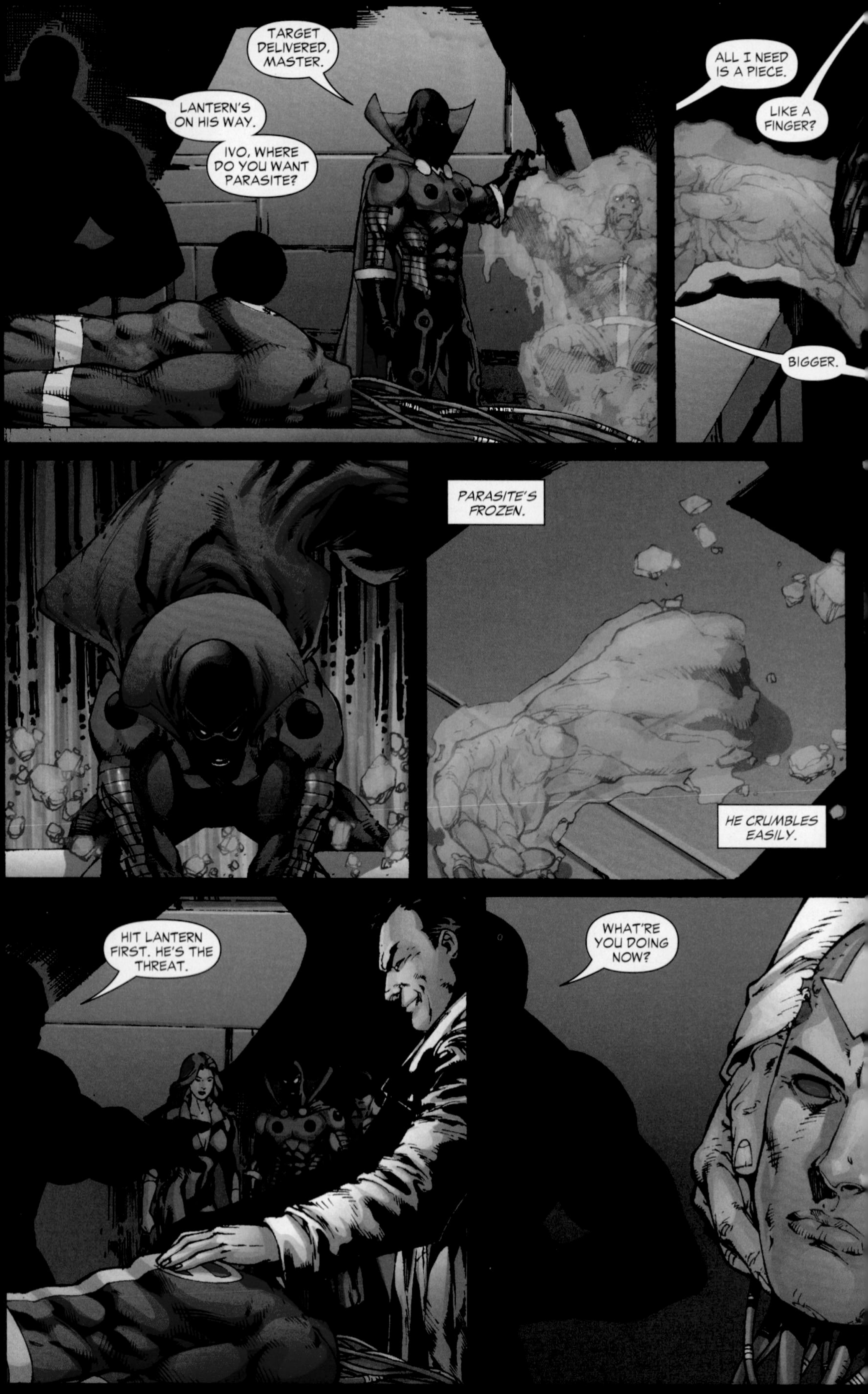
TARGET DELIVERED, MASTER.
LANTERN'S ON HIS WAY.
IVO, WHERE DO YOU WANT PARASITE?
ALL I NEED IS A PIECE.
LIKE A FINGER?
BIGGER.
PARASITE'S FROZEN.
HE CRUMBLES EASILY.
HIT LANTERN FIRST. HE'S THE THREAT.
WHAT'RE YOU DOING NOW?

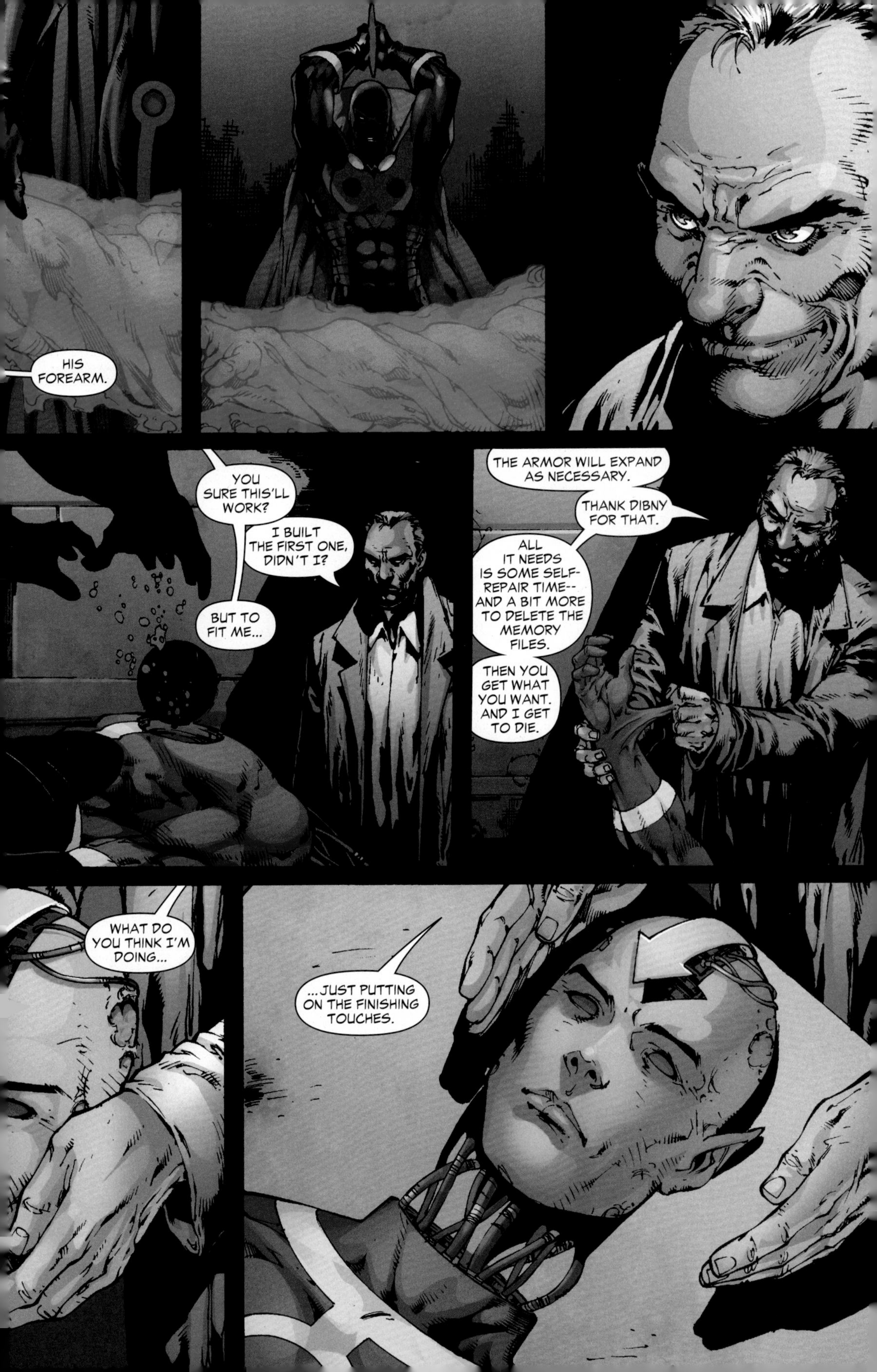
HIS FOREARM.
YOU SURE THIS'LL WORK?
I BUILT THE FIRST ONE, DIDN'T I?
BUT TO FIT ME...
THE ARMOR WILL EXPAND AS NECESSARY.
THANK DIBNY FOR THAT.
ALL IT NEEDS IS SOME SELF-REPAIR TIME-- AND A BIT MORE TO DELETE THE MEMORY FILES.
THEN YOU GET WHAT YOU WANT. AND I GET TO DIE.
WHAT DO YOU THINK I'M DOING...
...JUST PUTTING ON THE FINISHING TOUCHES.

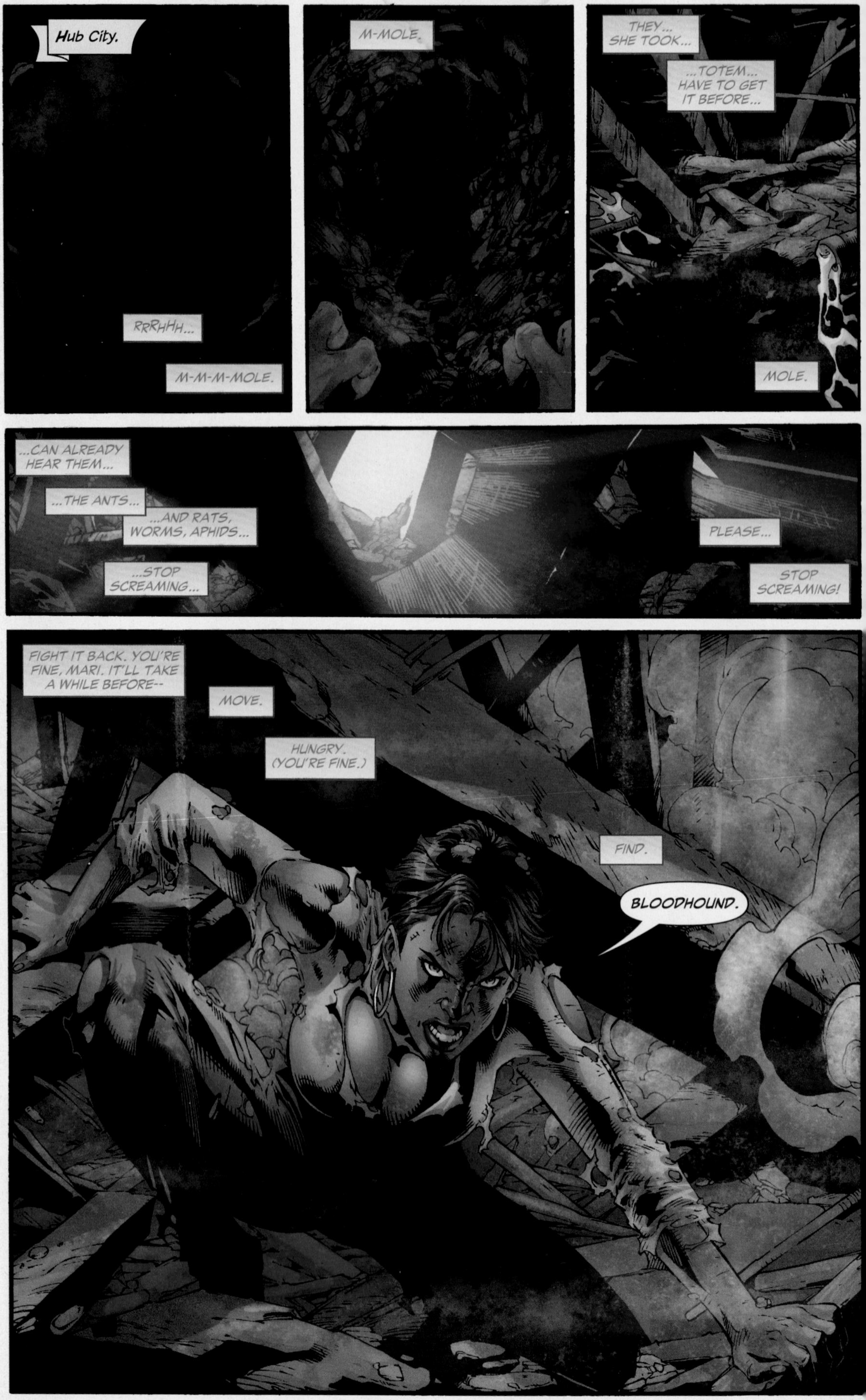
Hub City.
RRRHHH...
M-M-M-MOLE.
M-MOLE.
THEY... SHE TOOK...
...TOTEM... HAVE TO GET IT BEFORE...
MOLE.
...CAN ALREADY HEAR THEM...
...THE ANTS...
...AND RATS, WORMS, APHIDS...
...STOP SCREAMING...
PLEASE...
STOP SCREAMING!
FIGHT IT BACK. YOU'RE FINE, MARI. IT'LL TAKE A WHILE BEFORE--
MOVE.
HUNGRY. (YOU'RE FINE.)
FIND.
BLOODHOUND.

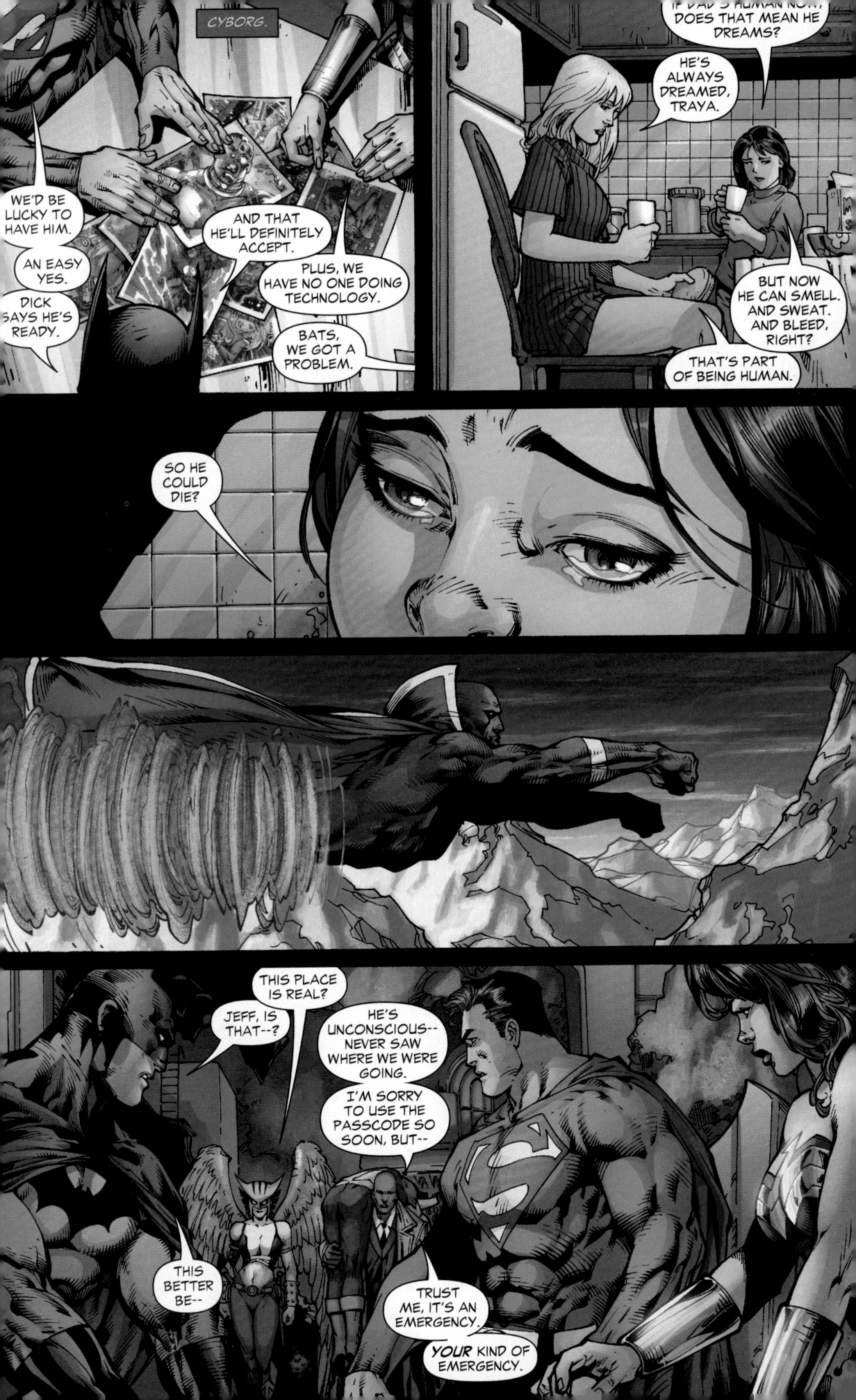
CYBORG.
WE'D BE LUCKY TO HAVE HIM.
AN EASY YES.
DICK SAYS HE'S READY.
AND THAT HE'LL DEFINITELY ACCEPT.
PLUS, WE HAVE NO ONE DOING TECHNOLOGY.
BATS, WE GOT A PROBLEM.
DOES THAT MEAN HE DREAMS?
HE'S ALWAYS DREAMED, TRAYA.
BUT NOW HE CAN SMELL. AND SWEAT. AND BLEED, RIGHT?
THAT'S PART OF BEING HUMAN.
SO HE COULD DIE?
JEFF, IS THAT--?
THIS PLACE IS REAL?
HE'S UNCONSCIOUS-- NEVER SAW WHERE WE WERE GOING.
I'M SORRY TO USE THE PASSCODE SO SOON, BUT--
THIS BETTER BE--
TRUST ME, IT'S AN EMERGENCY.
YOUR KIND OF EMERGENCY.

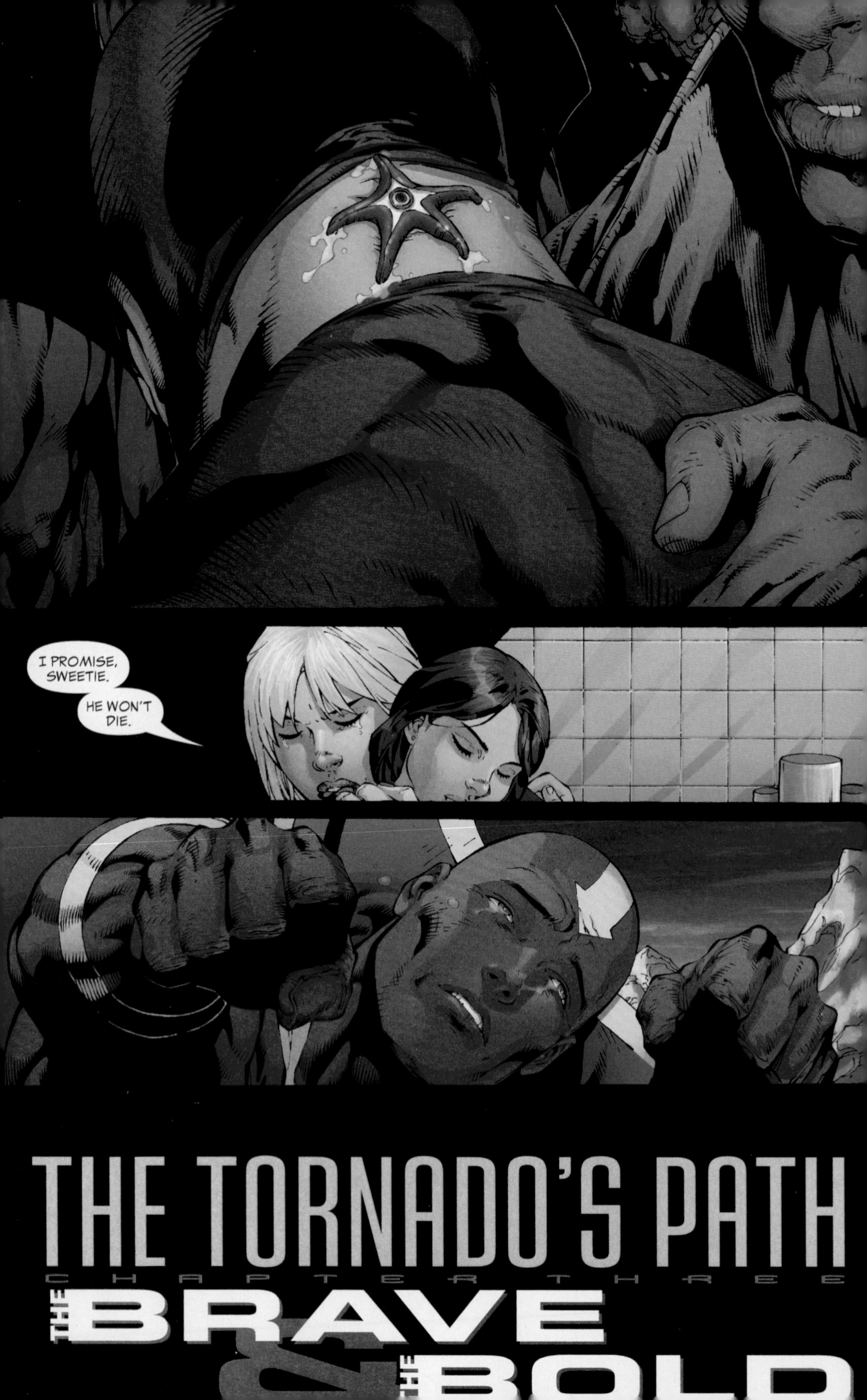
I PROMISE, SWEETIE.
HE WON'T DIE.
THE TORNADO'S PATH
CHAPTER THREE
THE BRAVE & THE BOLD

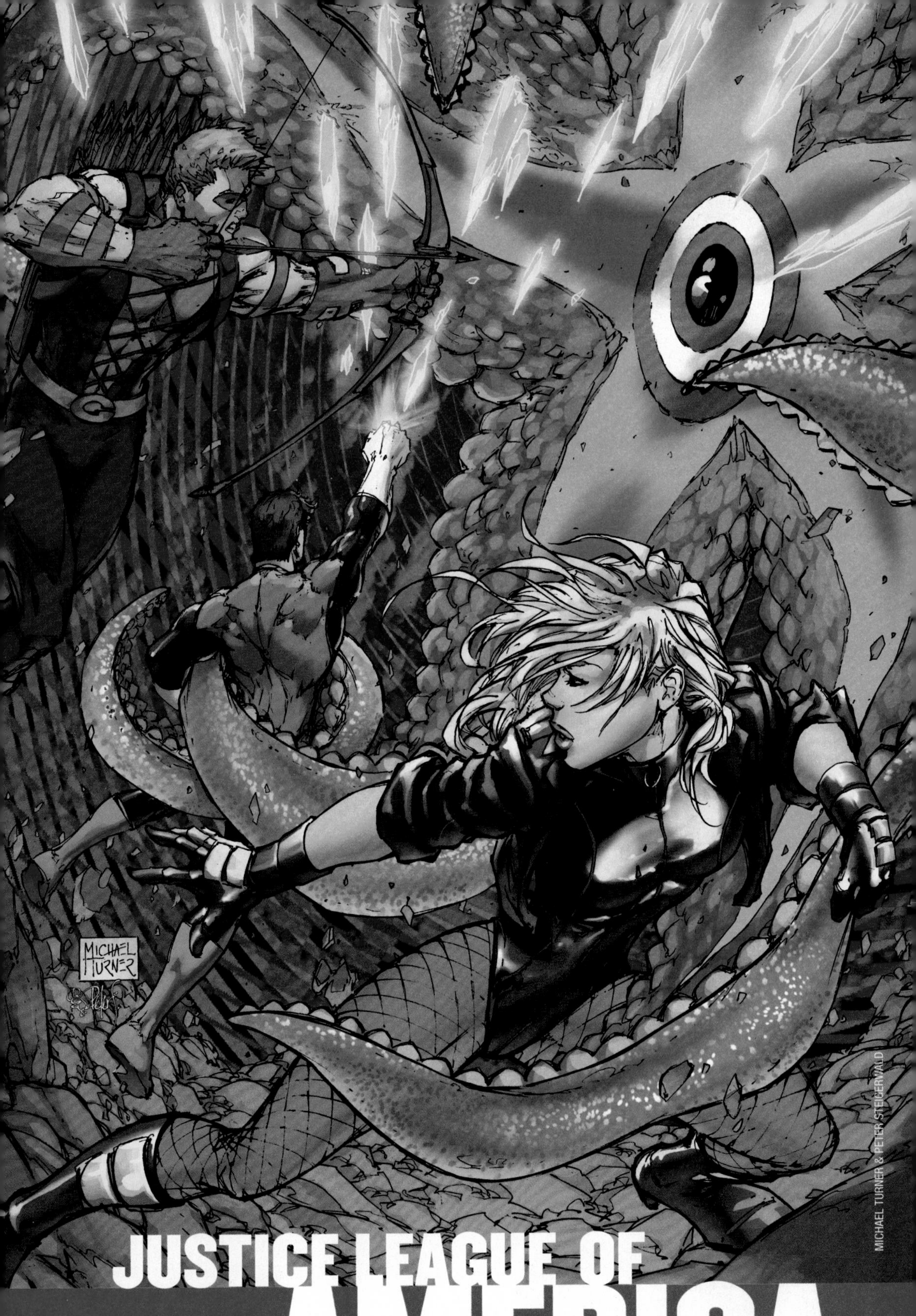
MICHAEL TURNER

MICHAEL TURNER & PETER STEIGERWALD

JUSTICE LEAGUE OF AMERICA
CHAPTER FOUR

"I'll get my mace."

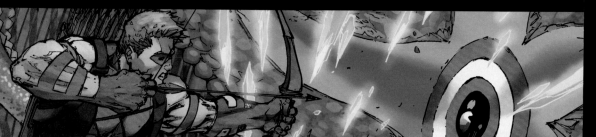

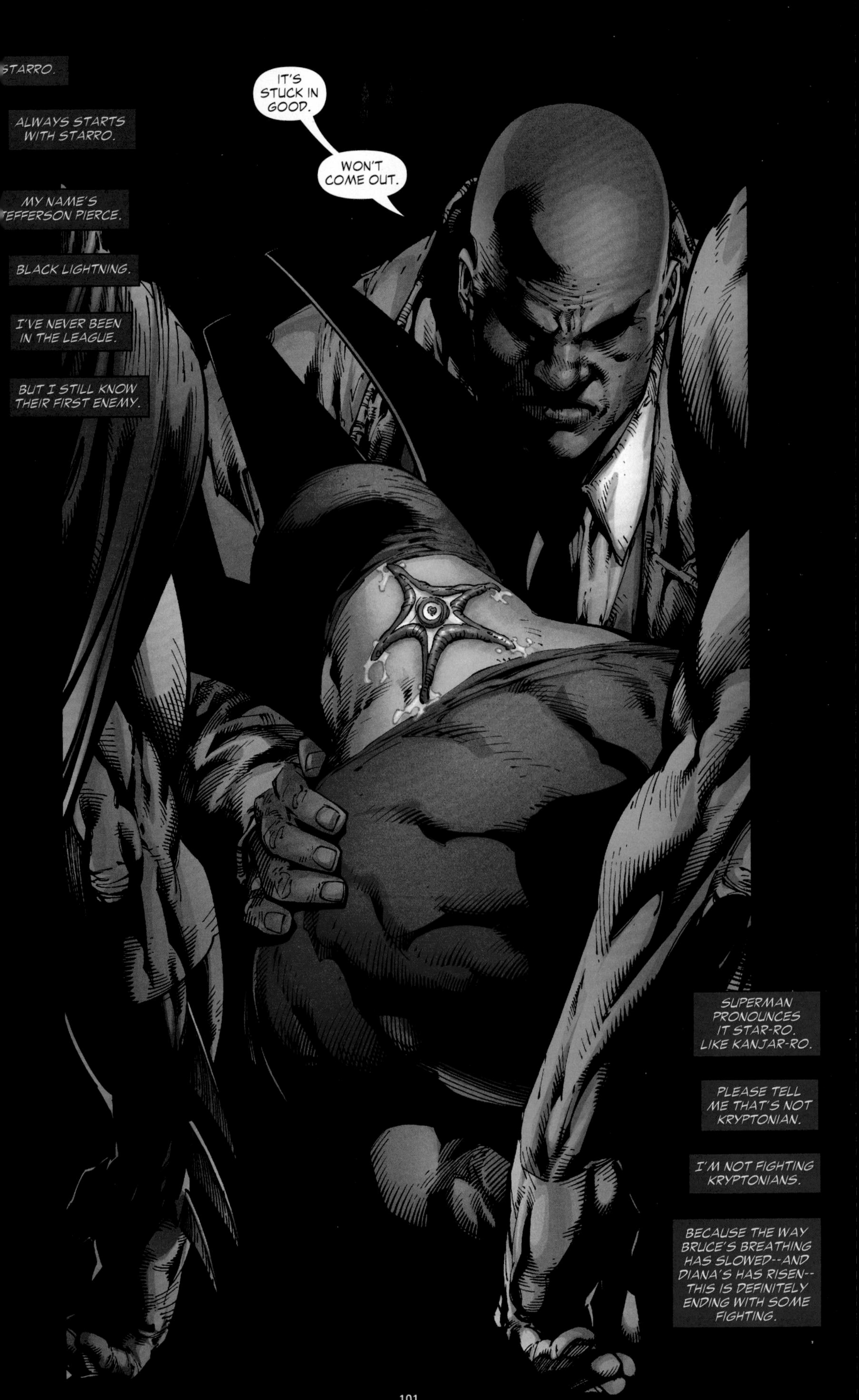
STARRO.
ALWAYS STARTS WITH STARRO.
MY NAME'S JEFFERSON PIERCE.
BLACK LIGHTNING.
I'VE NEVER BEEN IN THE LEAGUE.
BUT I STILL KNOW THEIR FIRST ENEMY.
IT'S STUCK IN GOOD.
WON'T COME OUT.
SUPERMAN PRONOUNCES IT STAR-RO. LIKE KANJAR-RO.
PLEASE TELL ME THAT'S NOT KRYPTONIAN.
I'M NOT FIGHTING KRYPTONIANS.
BECAUSE THE WAY BRUCE'S BREATHING HAS SLOWED--AND DIANA'S HAS RISEN-- THIS IS DEFINITELY ENDING WITH SOME FIGHTING.

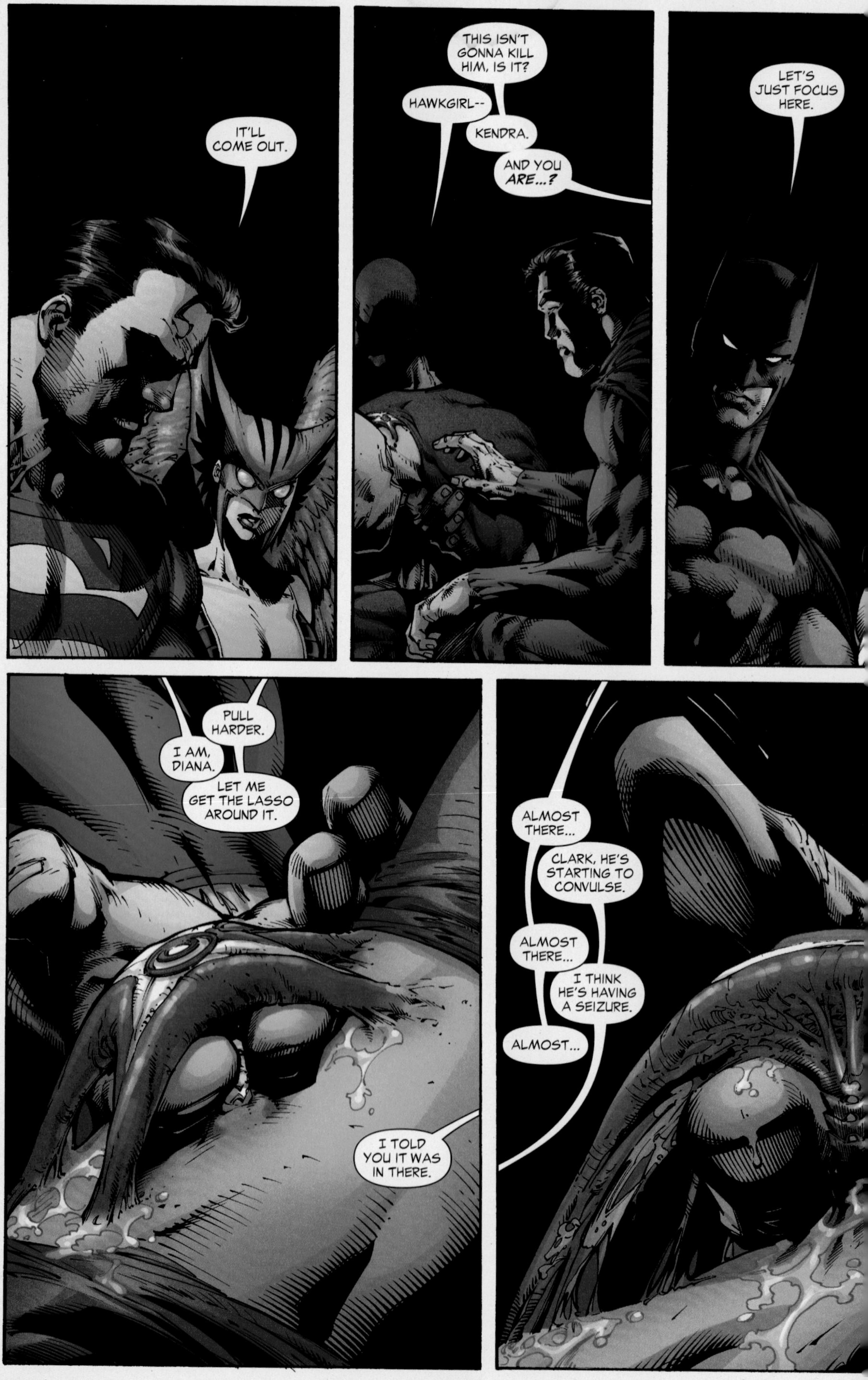
IT'LL COME OUT.
THIS ISN'T GONNA KILL HIM, IS IT?
HAWKGIRL--
KENDRA.
AND YOU *ARE...?*
LET'S JUST FOCUS HERE.
PULL HARDER.
I AM, DIANA.
LET ME GET THE LASSO AROUND IT.
I TOLD YOU IT WAS IN THERE.
ALMOST THERE...
CLARK, HE'S STARTING TO CONVULSE.
ALMOST THERE...
I THINK HE'S HAVING A SEIZURE.
ALMOST...

NICE TO SEE YOU, KENDRA.

YOU TOO, CLARK.

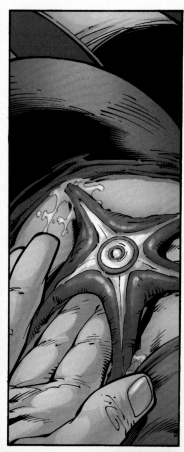

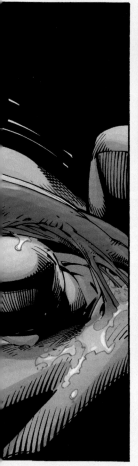

KRKK

DID THAT JUST CRACK? I THOUGHT THESE THINGS WERE ORGANIC.

HAND IT HERE...

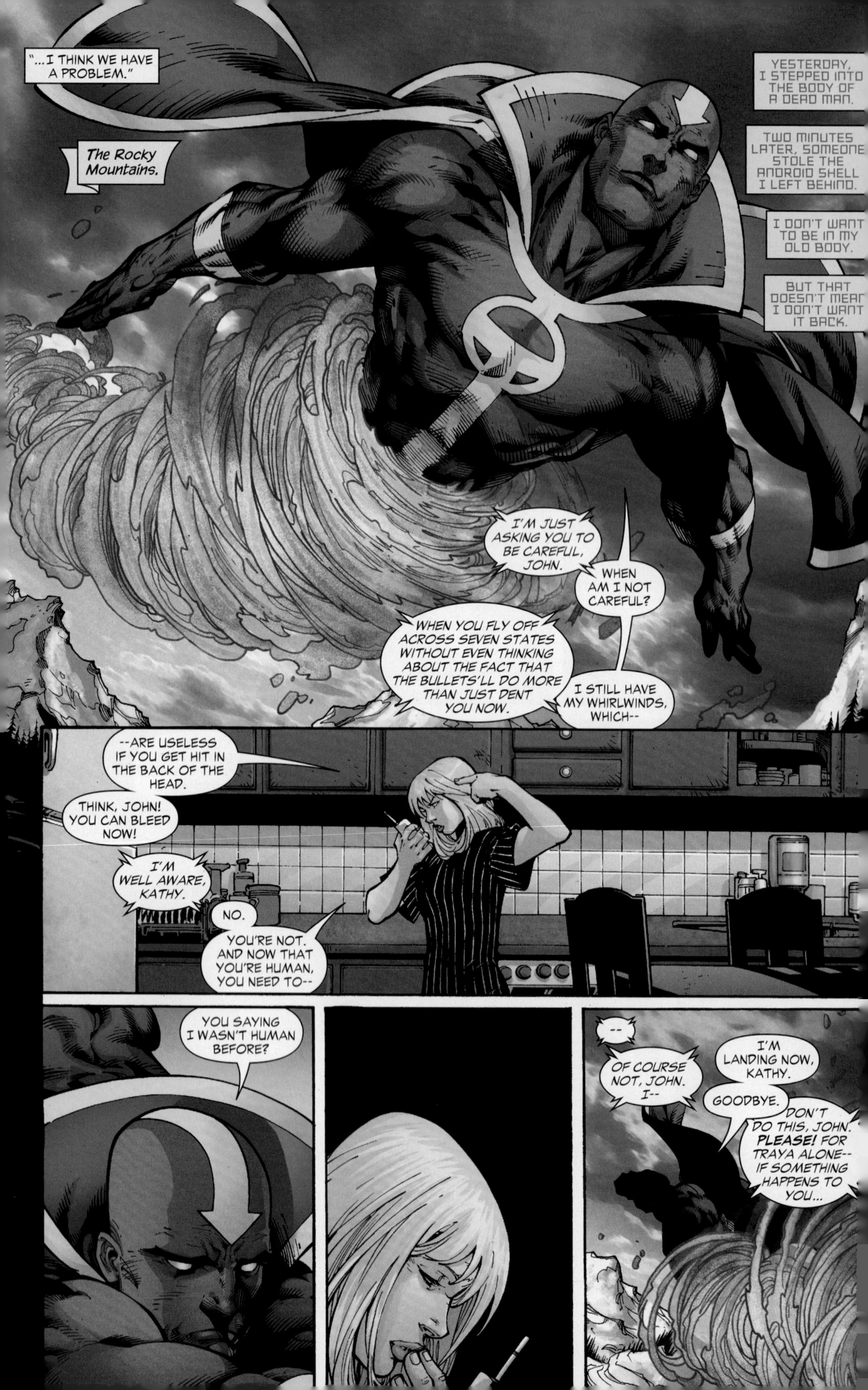
"...I THINK WE HAVE A PROBLEM."
The Rocky Mountains.
YESTERDAY, I STEPPED INTO THE BODY OF A DEAD MAN.
TWO MINUTES LATER, SOMEONE STOLE THE ANDROID SHELL I LEFT BEHIND.
I DON'T WANT TO BE IN MY OLD BODY.
BUT THAT DOESN'T MEAN I DON'T WANT IT BACK.
I'M JUST ASKING YOU TO BE CAREFUL, JOHN.
WHEN AM I NOT CAREFUL?
WHEN YOU FLY OFF ACROSS SEVEN STATES WITHOUT EVEN THINKING ABOUT THE FACT THAT THE BULLETS'LL DO MORE THAN JUST DENT YOU NOW.
I STILL HAVE MY WHIRLWINDS, WHICH--
--ARE USELESS IF YOU GET HIT IN THE BACK OF THE HEAD.
THINK, JOHN! YOU CAN BLEED NOW!
I'M WELL AWARE, KATHY.
NO.
YOU'RE NOT. AND NOW THAT YOU'RE HUMAN, YOU NEED TO--
YOU SAYING I WASN'T HUMAN BEFORE?
--
OF COURSE NOT, JOHN. I--
I'M LANDING NOW, KATHY.
GOODBYE.
DON'T DO THIS, JOHN. PLEASE! FOR TRAYA ALONE-- IF SOMETHING HAPPENS TO YOU...

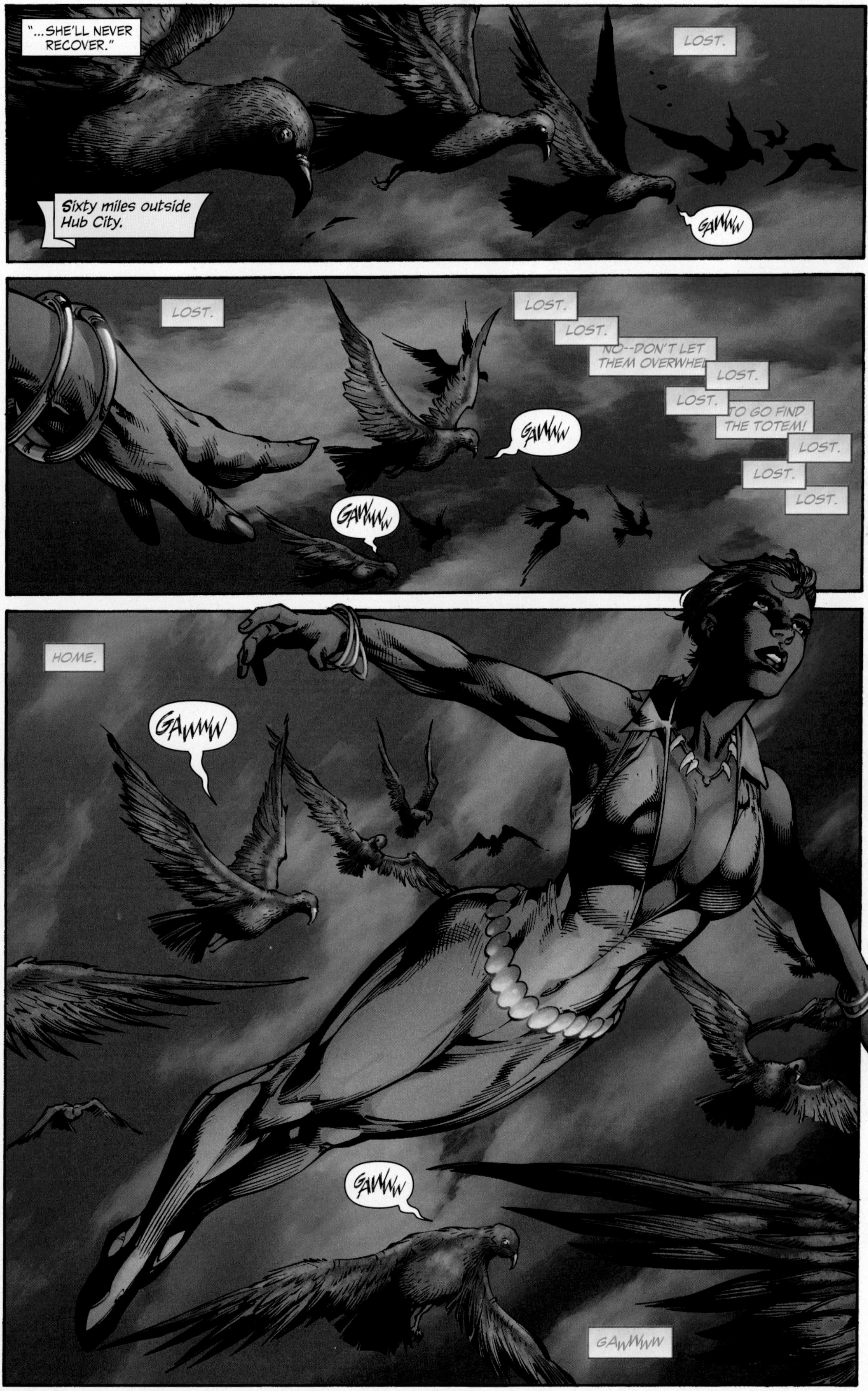
"...SHE'LL NEVER RECOVER."
LOST.
Sixty miles outside Hub City.
GAWW
LOST.
LOST.
LOST.
NO--DON'T LET THEM OVERWHEL
LOST.
LOST.
TO GO FIND THE TOTEM!
LOST.
LOST.
LOST.
GAWW
GAWWW
HOME.
GAWWW
GAWWW
GAWWWW

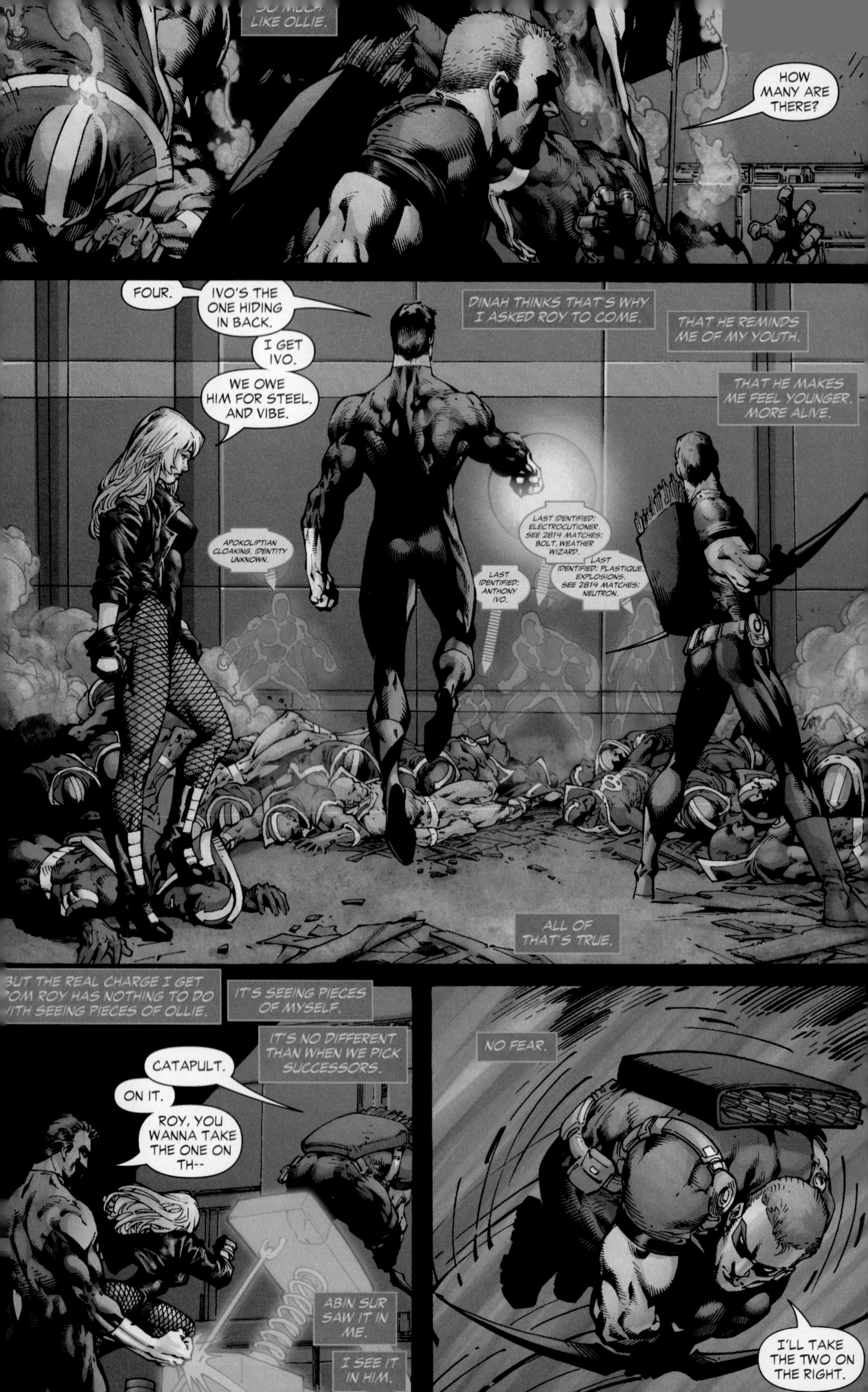
LIKE OLLIE.
HOW MANY ARE THERE?
FOUR.
IVO'S THE ONE HIDING IN BACK.
I GET IVO.
WE OWE HIM FOR STEEL. AND VIBE.
DINAH THINKS THAT'S WHY I ASKED ROY TO COME.
THAT HE REMINDS ME OF MY YOUTH.
THAT HE MAKES ME FEEL YOUNGER. MORE ALIVE.
APOKOLIPTIAN CLOAKING. IDENTITY UNKNOWN.
LAST IDENTIFIED: ANTHONY IVO.
LAST IDENTIFIED: ELECTROCUTIONER. SEE 2814 MATCHES: BOLT, WEATHER WIZARD.
LAST IDENTIFIED: PLASTIQUE. EXPLOSIONS. SEE 2814 MATCHES: NEUTRON.
ALL OF THAT'S TRUE.
UT THE REAL CHARGE I GET ROM ROY HAS NOTHING TO DO ITH SEEING PIECES OF OLLIE.
IT'S SEEING PIECES OF MYSELF.
IT'S NO DIFFERENT THAN WHEN WE PICK SUCCESSORS.
CATAPULT.
ON IT.
ROY, YOU WANNA TAKE THE ONE ON TH--
ABIN SUR SAW IT IN ME.
I SEE IT IN HIM.
NO FEAR.
I'LL TAKE THE TWO ON THE RIGHT.

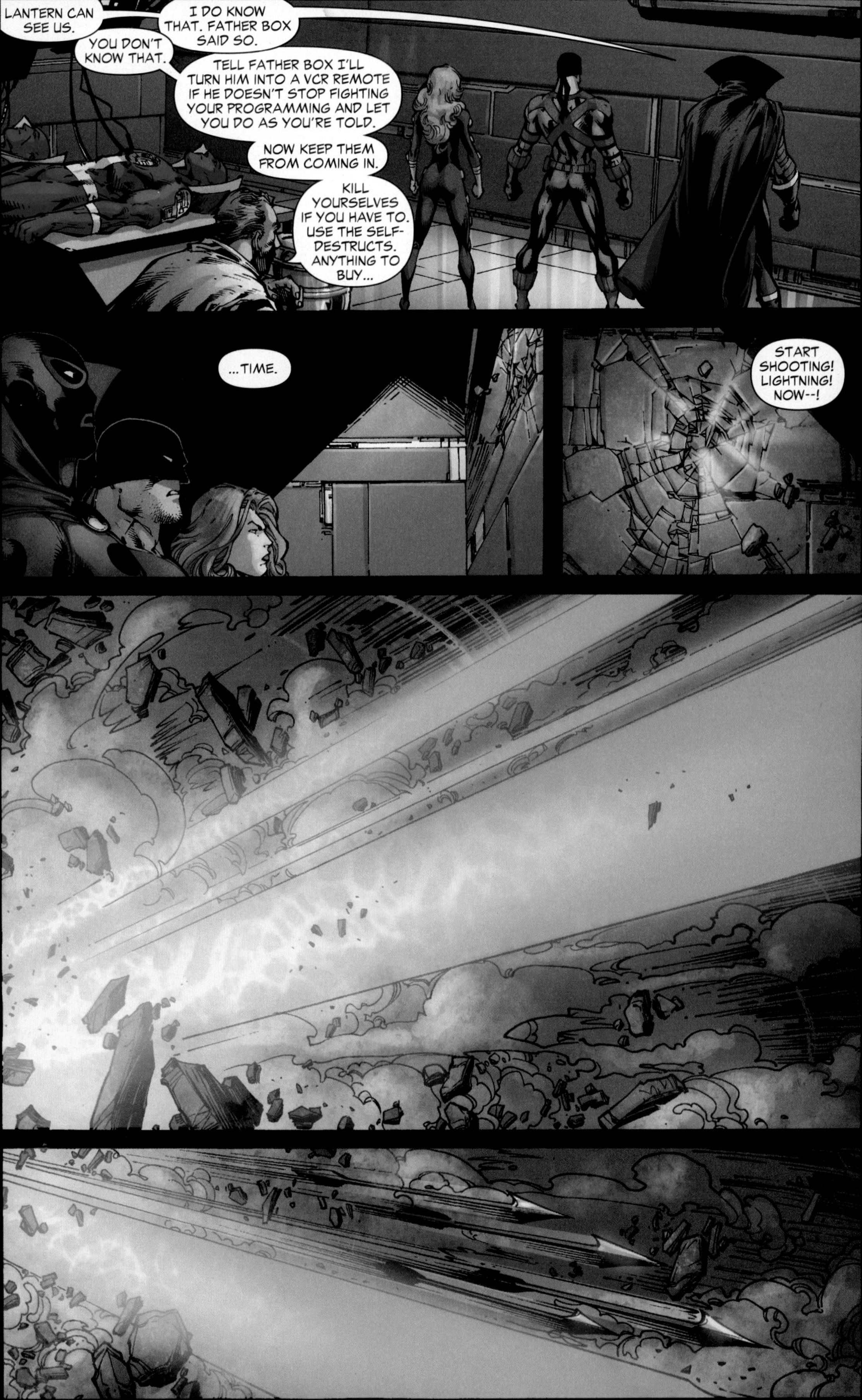
LANTERN CAN SEE US.
YOU DON'T KNOW THAT.
I DO KNOW THAT. FATHER BOX SAID SO.
TELL FATHER BOX I'LL TURN HIM INTO A VCR REMOTE IF HE DOESN'T STOP FIGHTING YOUR PROGRAMMING AND LET YOU DO AS YOU'RE TOLD.
NOW KEEP THEM FROM COMING IN.
KILL YOURSELVES IF YOU HAVE TO. USE THE SELF-DESTRUCTS. ANYTHING TO BUY...
...TIME.
START SHOOTING! LIGHTNING! NOW--!

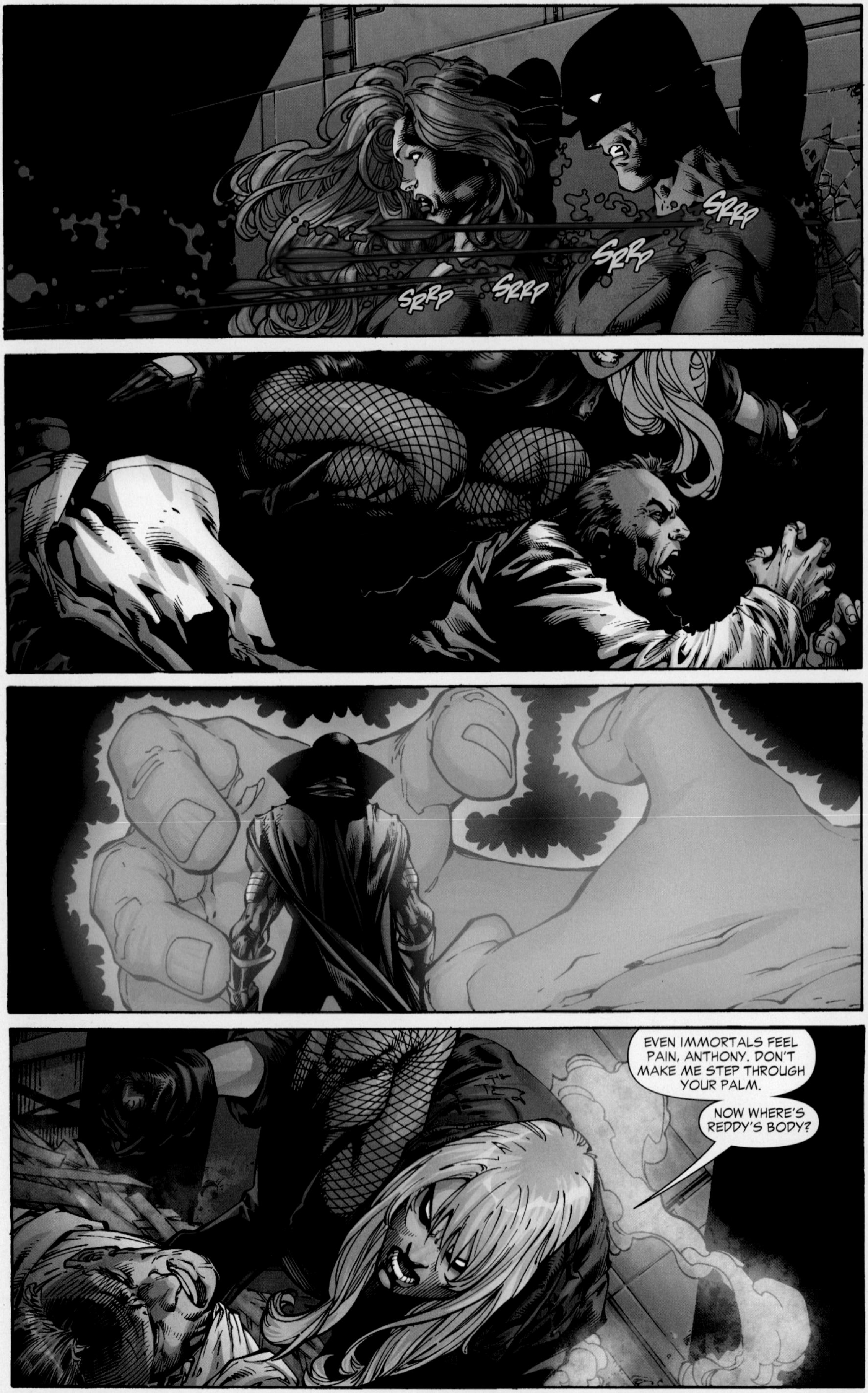
SRRP
SRRP
SRRP
SRRP
EVEN IMMORTALS FEEL PAIN, ANTHONY. DON'T MAKE ME STEP THROUGH YOUR PALM.
NOW WHERE'S REDDY'S BODY?

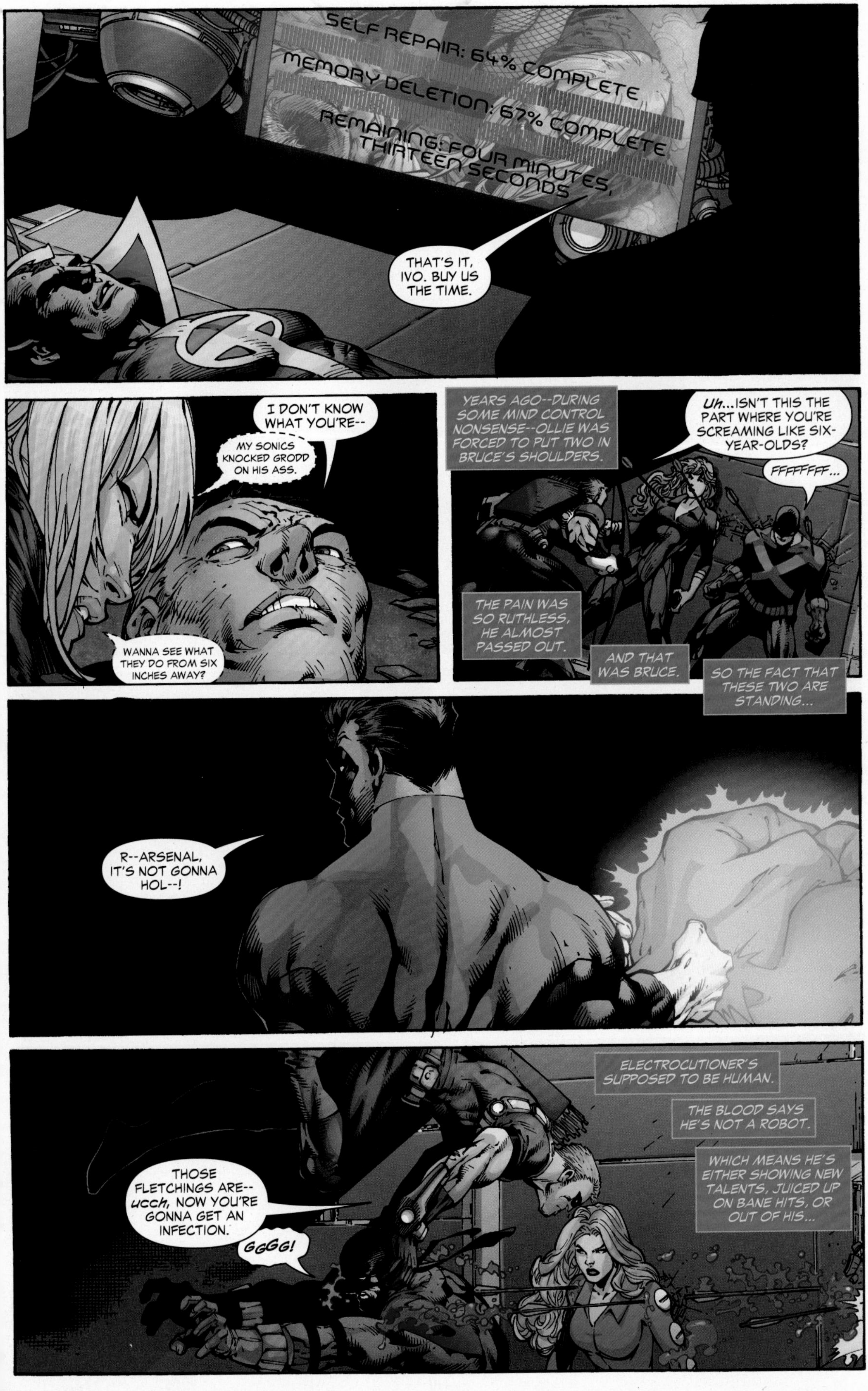
SELF REPAIR: 64% COMPLETE
MEMORY DELETION: 67% COMPLETE
REMAINING: FOUR MINUTES, THIRTEEN SECONDS
THAT'S IT, IVO. BUY US THE TIME.
I DON'T KNOW WHAT YOU'RE--
MY SONICS KNOCKED GRODD ON HIS ASS.
WANNA SEE WHAT THEY DO FROM SIX INCHES AWAY?
YEARS AGO--DURING SOME MIND CONTROL NONSENSE--OLLIE WAS FORCED TO PUT TWO IN BRUCE'S SHOULDERS.
Uh...ISN'T THIS THE PART WHERE YOU'RE SCREAMING LIKE SIX-YEAR-OLDS?
FFFFFFFF...
THE PAIN WAS SO RUTHLESS, HE ALMOST PASSED OUT.
AND THAT WAS BRUCE.
SO THE FACT THAT THESE TWO ARE STANDING...
R--ARSENAL, IT'S NOT GONNA HOL--!
ELECTROCUTIONER'S SUPPOSED TO BE HUMAN.
THE BLOOD SAYS HE'S NOT A ROBOT.
WHICH MEANS HE'S EITHER SHOWING NEW TALENTS, JUICED UP ON BANE HITS, OR OUT OF HIS...
THOSE FLETCHINGS ARE-- ucch, NOW YOU'RE GONNA GET AN INFECTION.
GGGG!

...MIND.

STARRO! R--RED ARROW, HE'S GOT A STARRO!

RED ARROW?

I CHECK MY OWN CATCH TO SEE IF IT'S THE SA--

OH, NO...

HE THROWS FAST.

I THINK FASTER.

DON'T YOU D--!

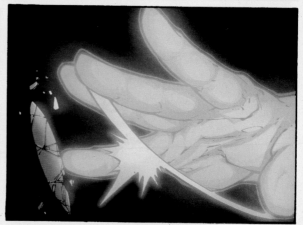

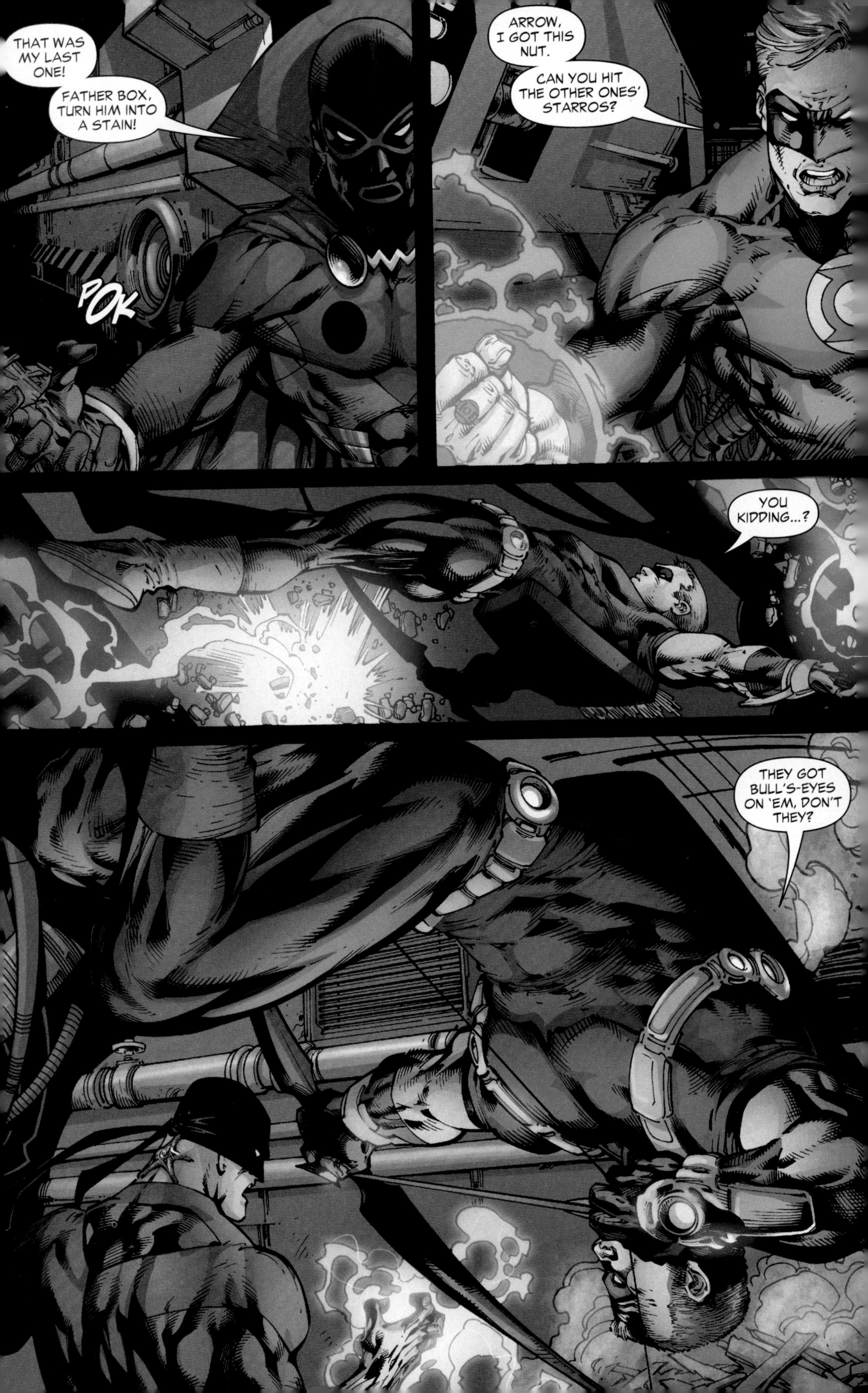
THAT WAS MY LAST ONE!
FATHER BOX, TURN HIM INTO A STAIN!
POK
ARROW, I GOT THIS NUT.
CAN YOU HIT THE OTHER ONES' STARROS?
YOU KIDDING...?
THEY GOT BULL'S-EYES ON 'EM, DON'T THEY?

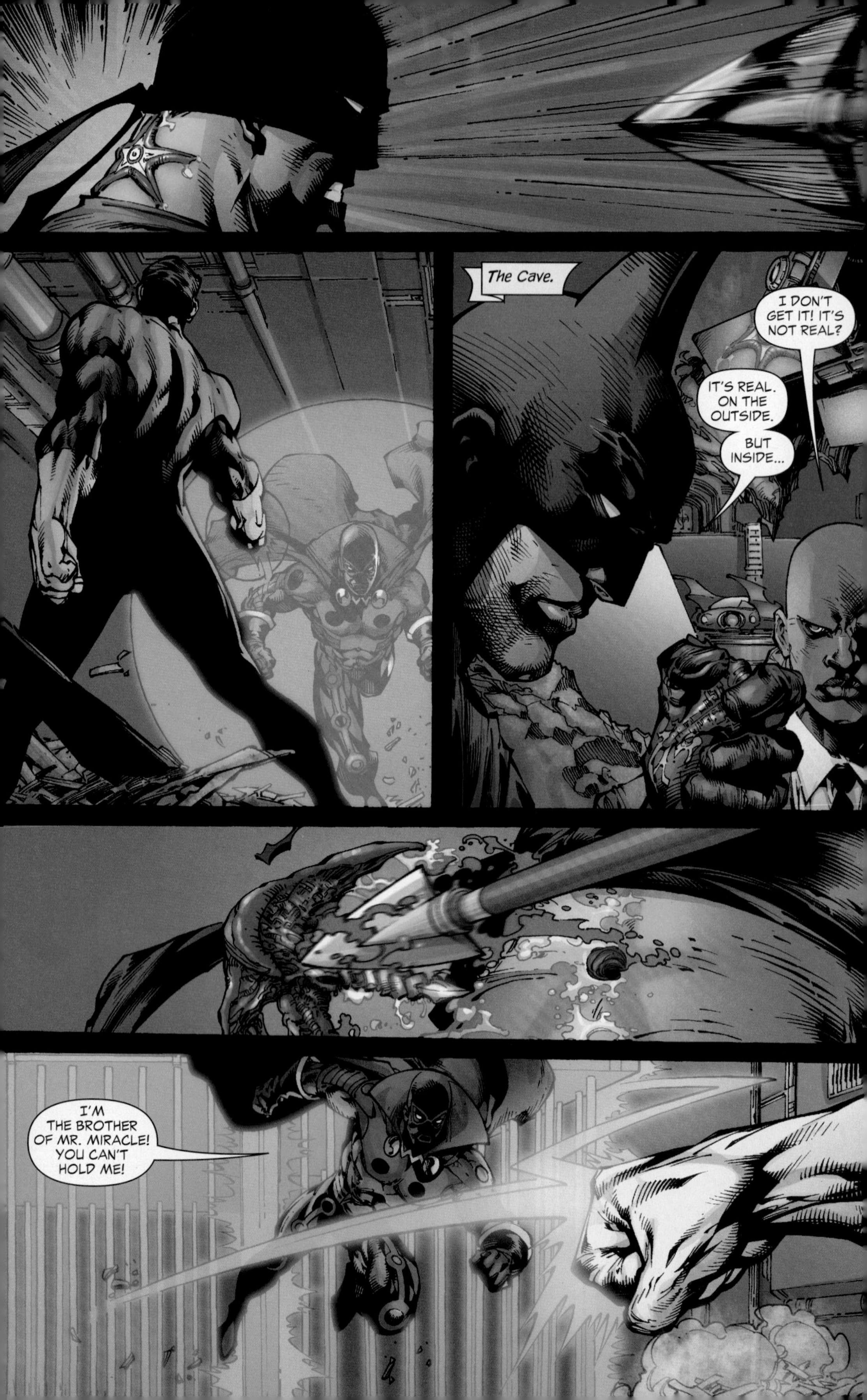
The Cave.
I DON'T GET IT! IT'S NOT REAL?
IT'S REAL. ON THE OUTSIDE.
BUT INSIDE...
I'M THE BROTHER OF MR. MIRACLE! YOU CAN'T HOLD ME!

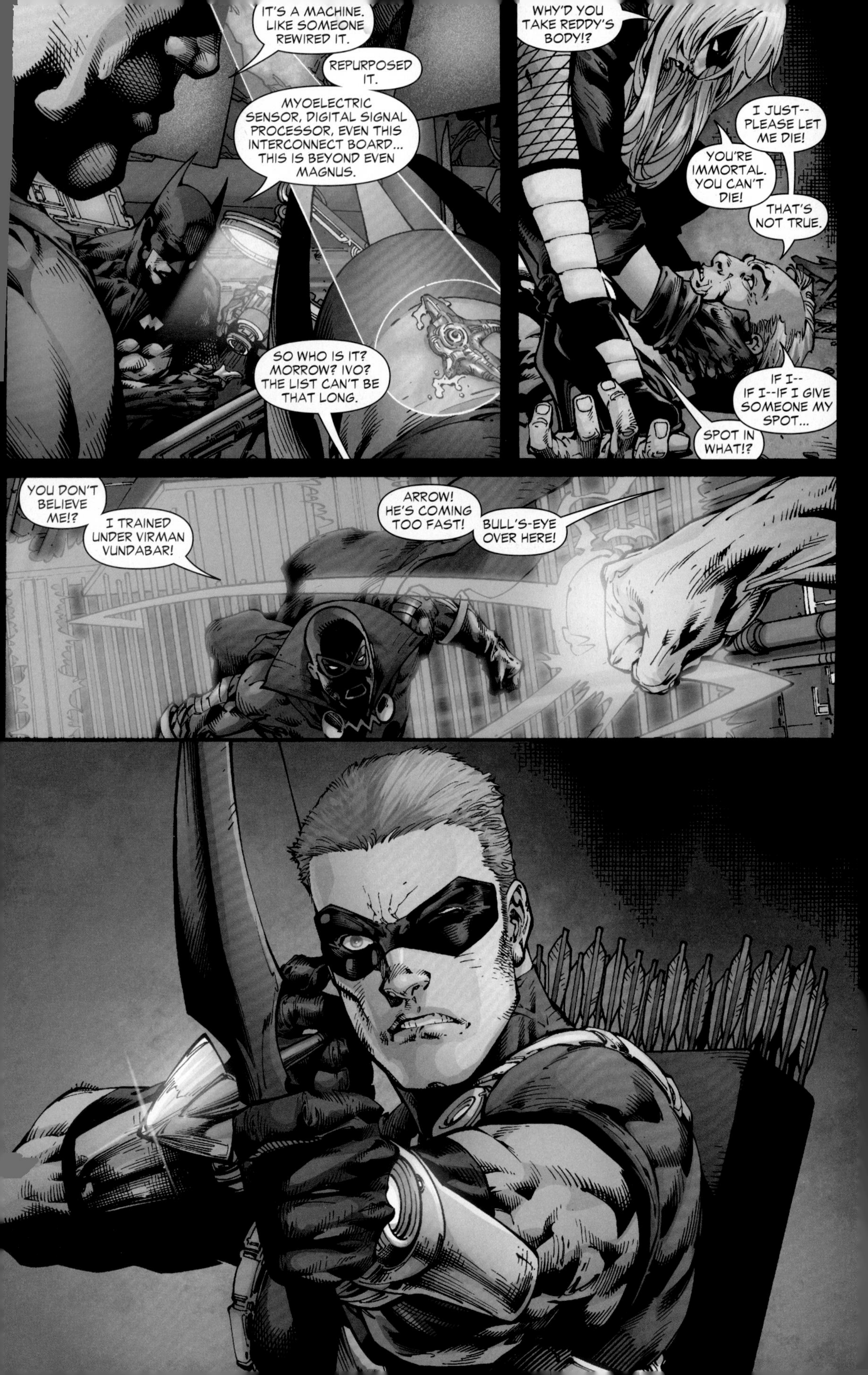
IT'S A MACHINE. LIKE SOMEONE REWIRED IT.
REPURPOSED IT.
MYOELECTRIC SENSOR, DIGITAL SIGNAL PROCESSOR, EVEN THIS INTERCONNECT BOARD... THIS IS BEYOND EVEN MAGNUS.
SO WHO IS IT? MORROW? IVO? THE LIST CAN'T BE THAT LONG.
WHY'D YOU TAKE REDDY'S BODY!?
I JUST-- PLEASE LET ME DIE!
YOU'RE IMMORTAL. YOU CAN'T DIE!
THAT'S NOT TRUE.
IF I-- IF I--IF I GIVE SOMEONE MY SPOT...
SPOT IN WHAT!?
YOU DON'T BELIEVE ME!?
I TRAINED UNDER VIRMAN VUNDABAR!
ARROW! HE'S COMING TOO FAST!
BULL'S-EYE OVER HERE!

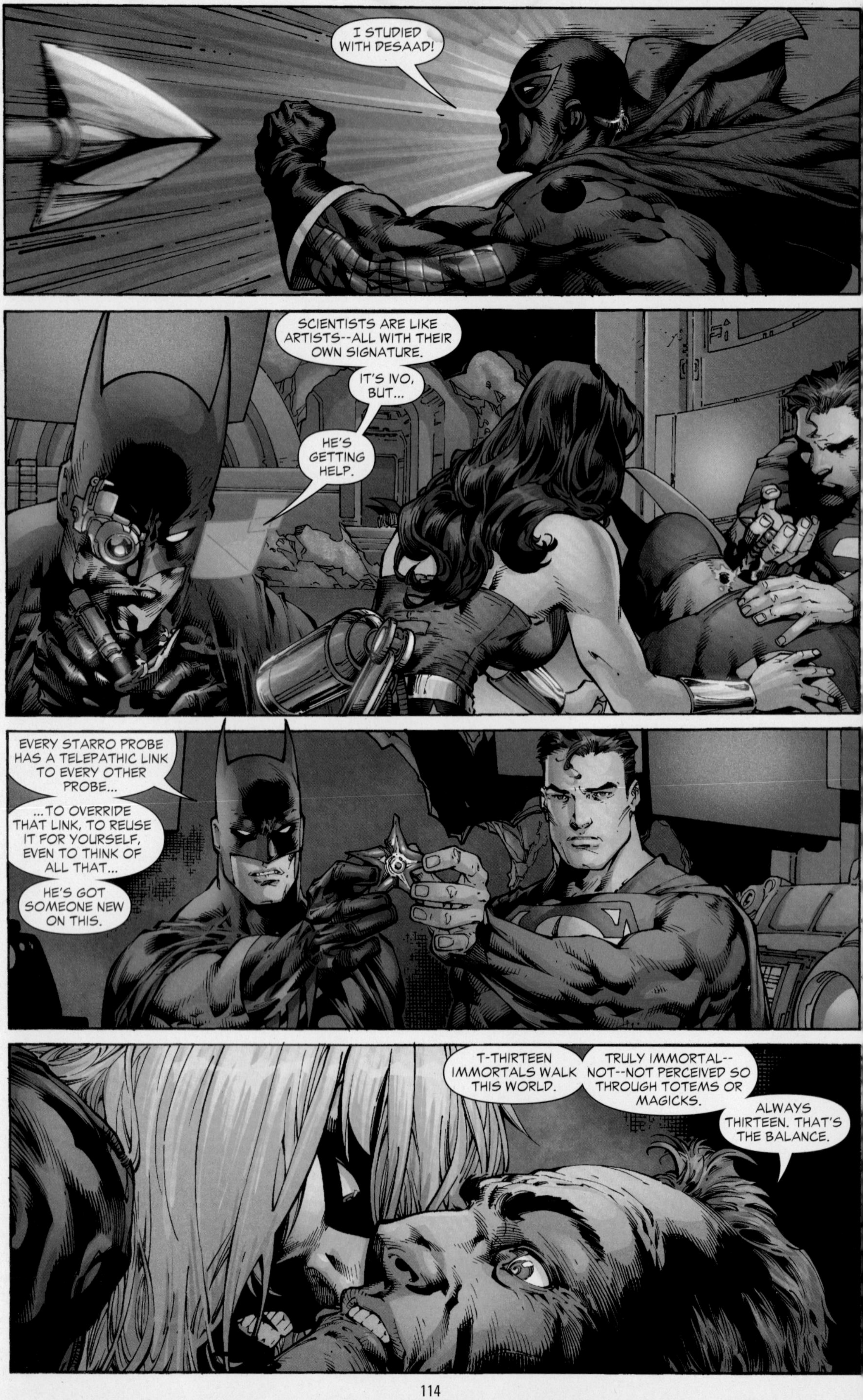
I STUDIED WITH DESAAD!
SCIENTISTS ARE LIKE ARTISTS--ALL WITH THEIR OWN SIGNATURE.
IT'S IVO, BUT...
HE'S GETTING HELP.
EVERY STARRO PROBE HAS A TELEPATHIC LINK TO EVERY OTHER PROBE...
...TO OVERRIDE THAT LINK, TO REUSE IT FOR YOURSELF, EVEN TO THINK OF ALL THAT...
HE'S GOT SOMEONE NEW ON THIS.
T-THIRTEEN IMMORTALS WALK THIS WORLD.
TRULY IMMORTAL-- NOT--NOT PERCEIVED SO THROUGH TOTEMS OR MAGICKS.
ALWAYS THIRTEEN. THAT'S THE BALANCE.

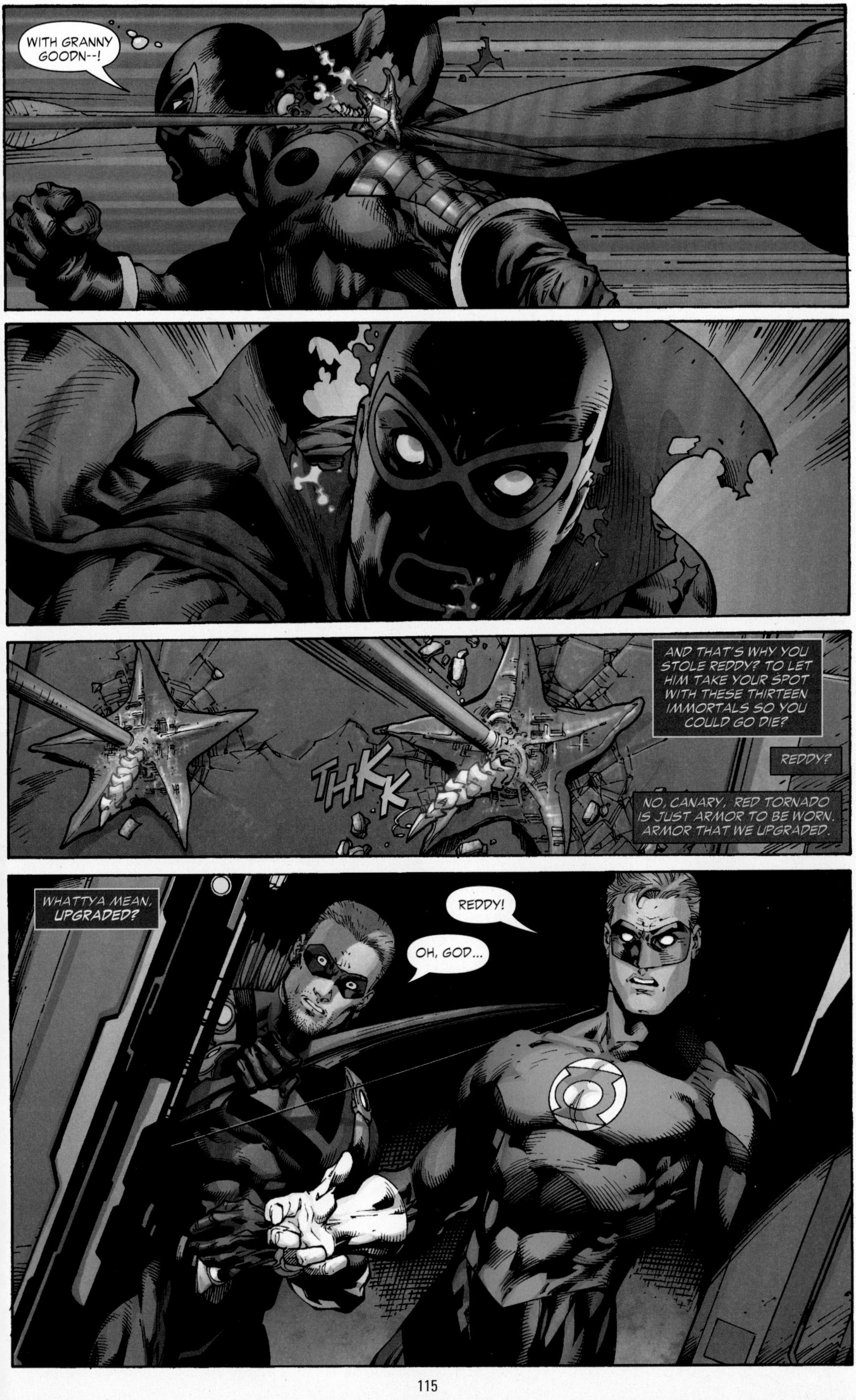
WITH GRANNY GOODN--!
AND THAT'S WHY YOU STOLE REDDY? TO LET HIM TAKE YOUR SPOT WITH THESE THIRTEEN IMMORTALS SO YOU COULD GO DIE?
REDDY?
NO, CANARY, RED TORNADO IS JUST ARMOR TO BE WORN. ARMOR THAT WE UPGRADED.
THKK
WHATTYA MEAN, UPGRADED?
REDDY!
OH, GOD...

Markovia.

The HMY Viktor.

The ship's owner is Brion Markov.

Geo-Force.

In the past, a prince.

In the present, a king.

And right now...

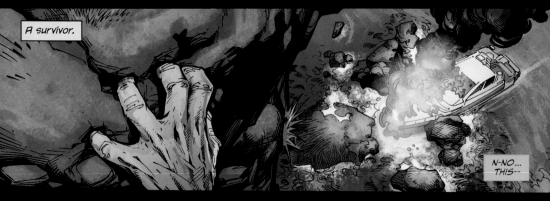

A survivor.

N-NO... THIS--

...THIS CAN'T--

...PL-PLEASE DON'T LET IT...!

⟨SIR, ARE YOU OKAY? WE'VE GOTTEN CALLS OF AN ATTACK...!⟩

⟨I-I'LL LIVE, DECLAN.⟩

⟨JUST GET MY OLD COMMUNICATOR.⟩

⟨I NEED TO SPEAK TO JEFFERSON PIERCE.⟩

TRANSLATED FROM ROMANIAN.

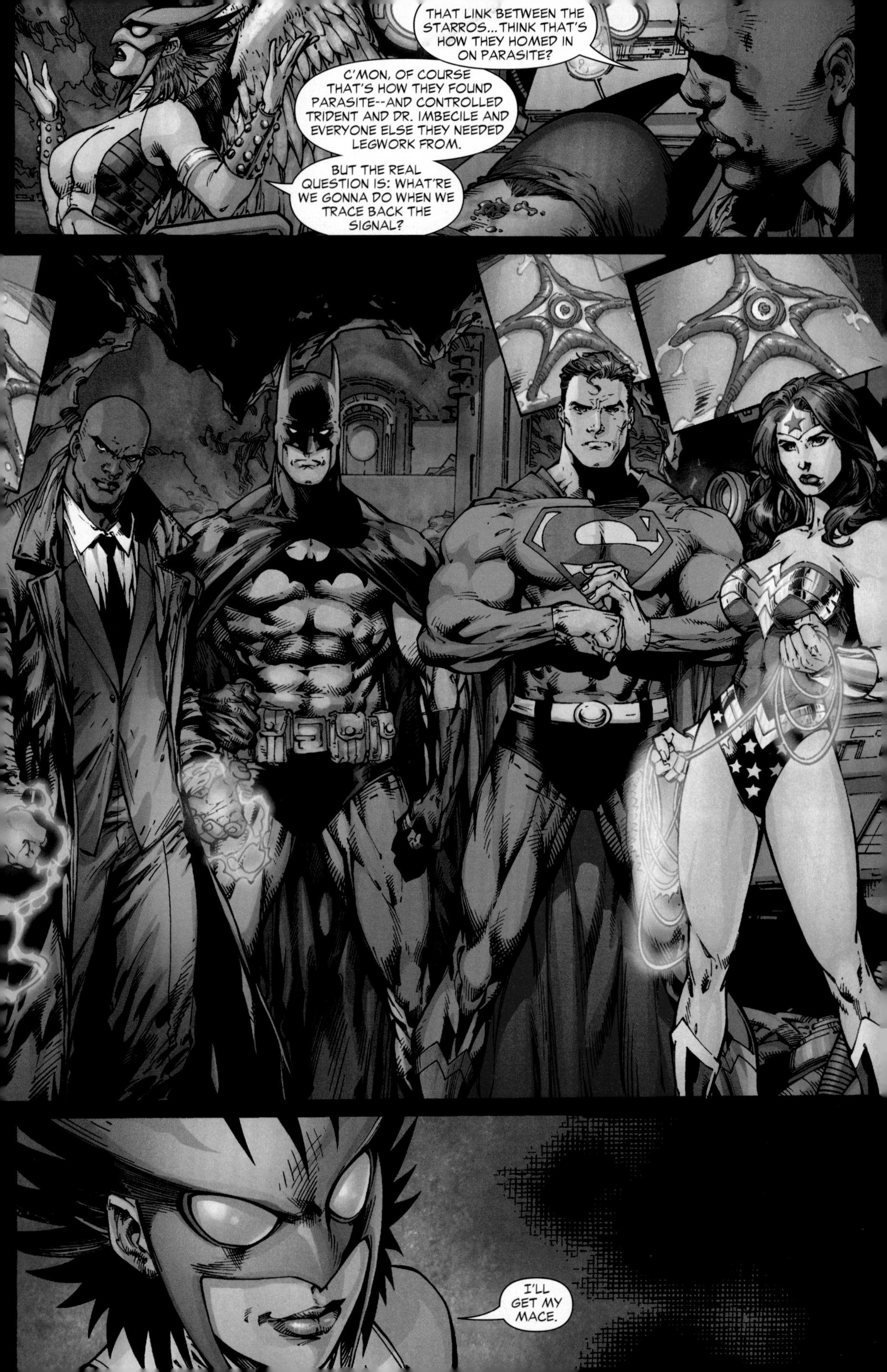
THAT LINK BETWEEN THE STARROS...THINK THAT'S HOW THEY HOMED IN ON PARASITE?
C'MON, OF COURSE THAT'S HOW THEY FOUND PARASITE--AND CONTROLLED TRIDENT AND DR. IMBECILE AND EVERYONE ELSE THEY NEEDED LEGWORK FROM.
BUT THE REAL QUESTION IS: WHAT'RE WE GONNA DO WHEN WE TRACE BACK THE SIGNAL?
I'LL GET MY MACE.

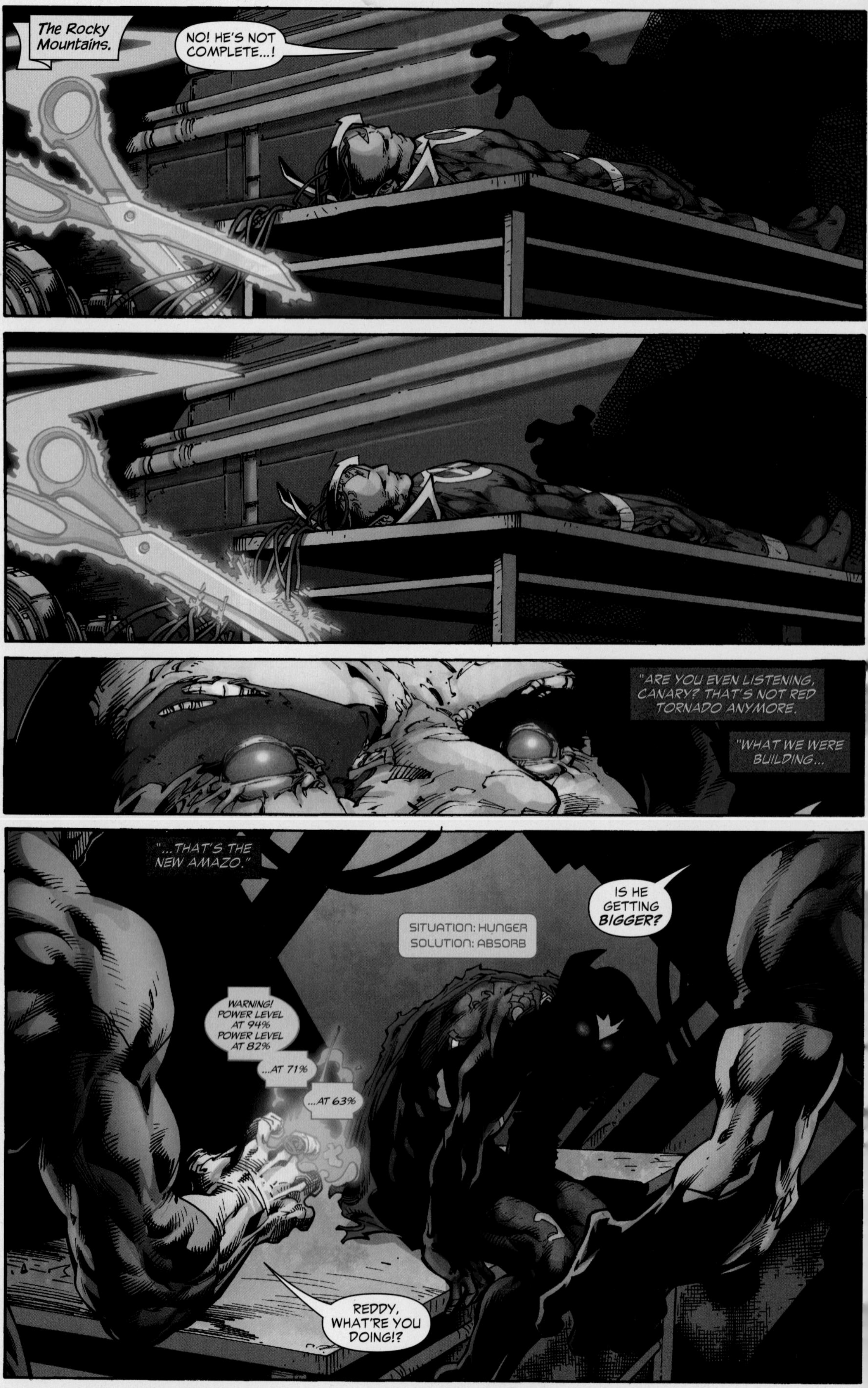

The Rocky Mountains.
NO! HE'S NOT COMPLETE...!
"ARE YOU EVEN LISTENING, CANARY? THAT'S NOT RED TORNADO ANYMORE.
"WHAT WE WERE BUILDING...
"...THAT'S THE NEW AMAZO."
SITUATION: HUNGER
SOLUTION: ABSORB
IS HE GETTING BIGGER?
WARNING! POWER LEVEL AT 94% POWER LEVEL AT 82%
...AT 71%
...AT 63%
REDDY, WHAT'RE YOU DOING!?

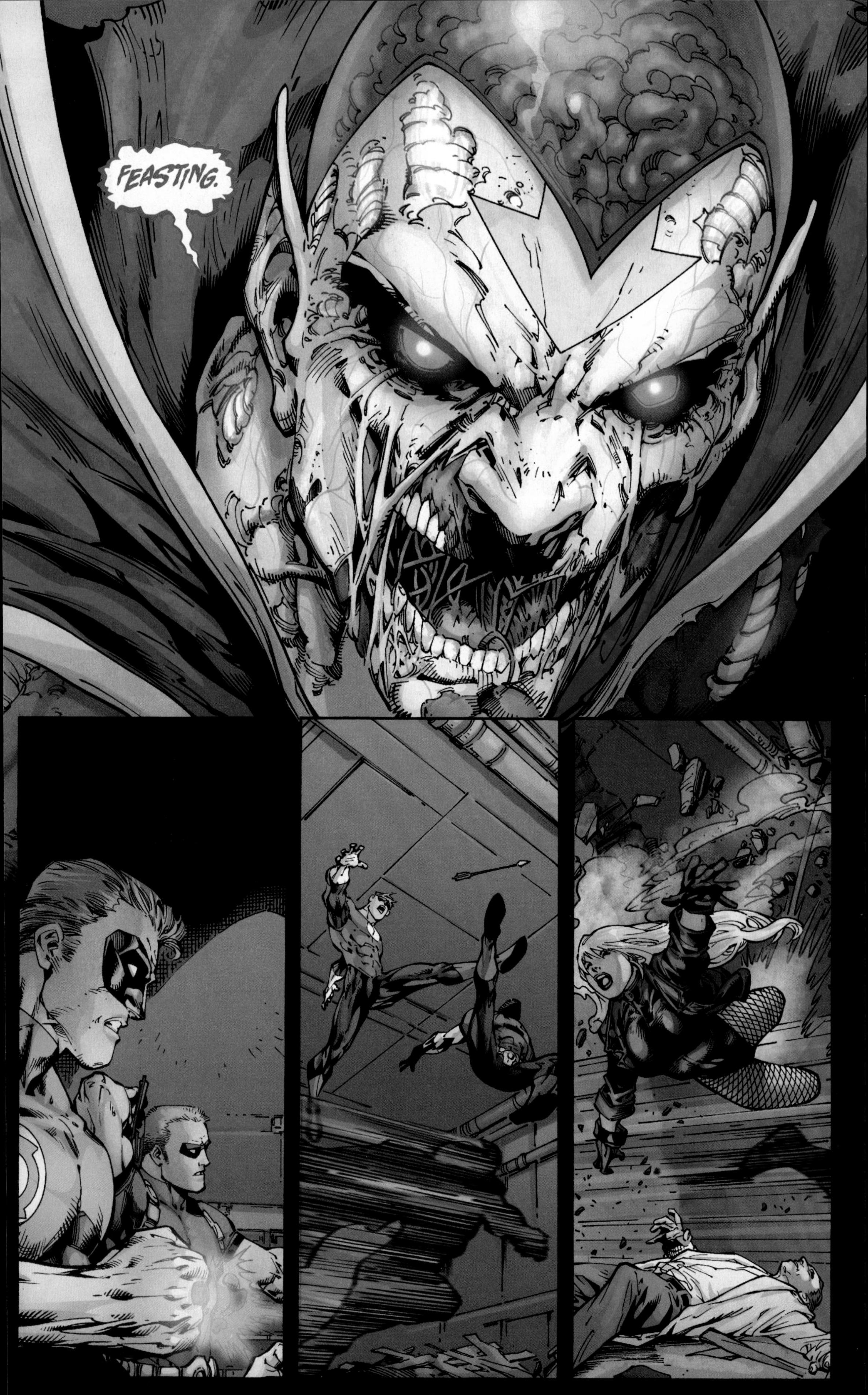
FEASTING.

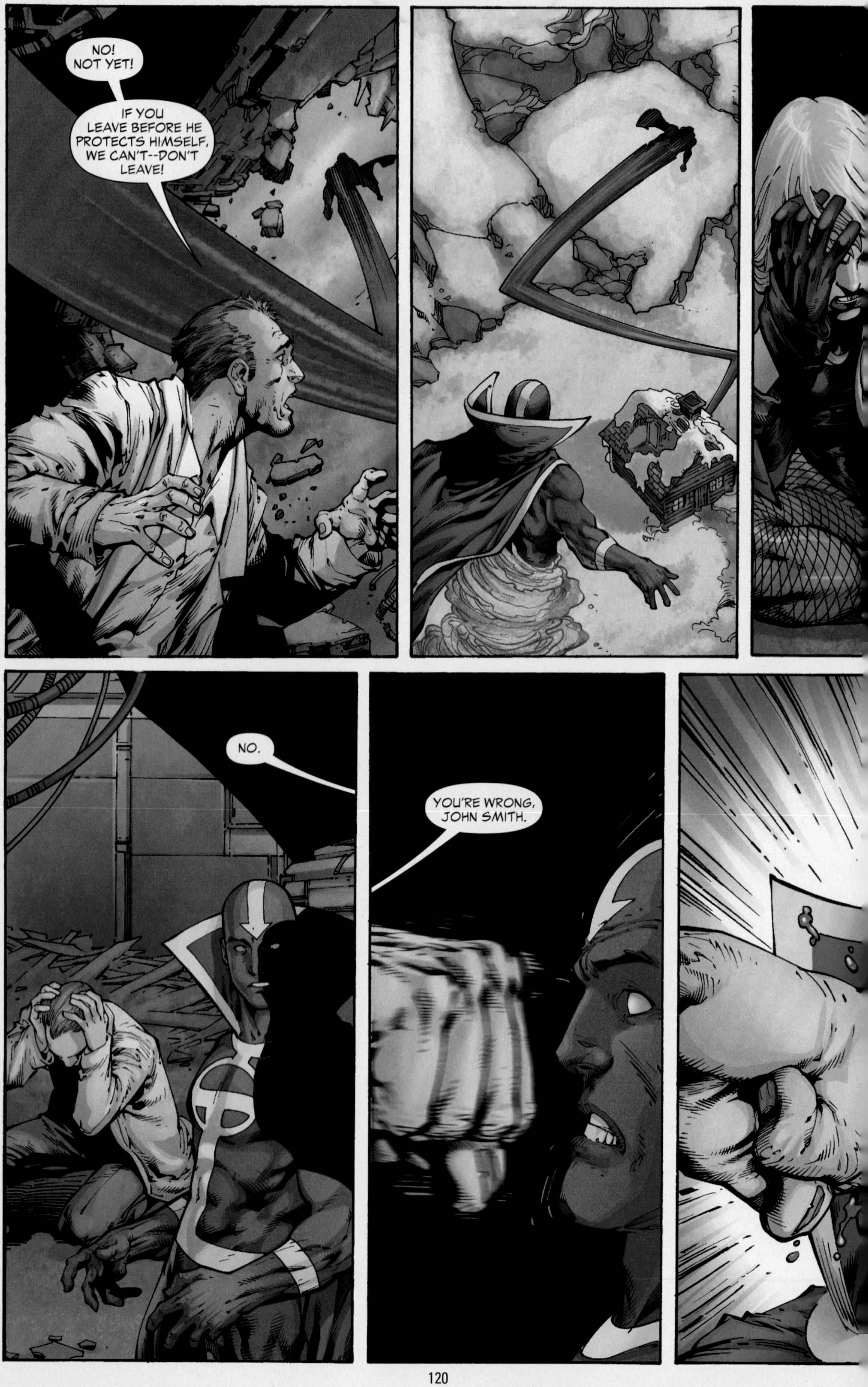
NO! NOT YET!
IF YOU LEAVE BEFORE HE PROTECTS HIMSELF, WE CAN'T--DON'T LEAVE!
NO.
YOU'RE WRONG, JOHN SMITH.

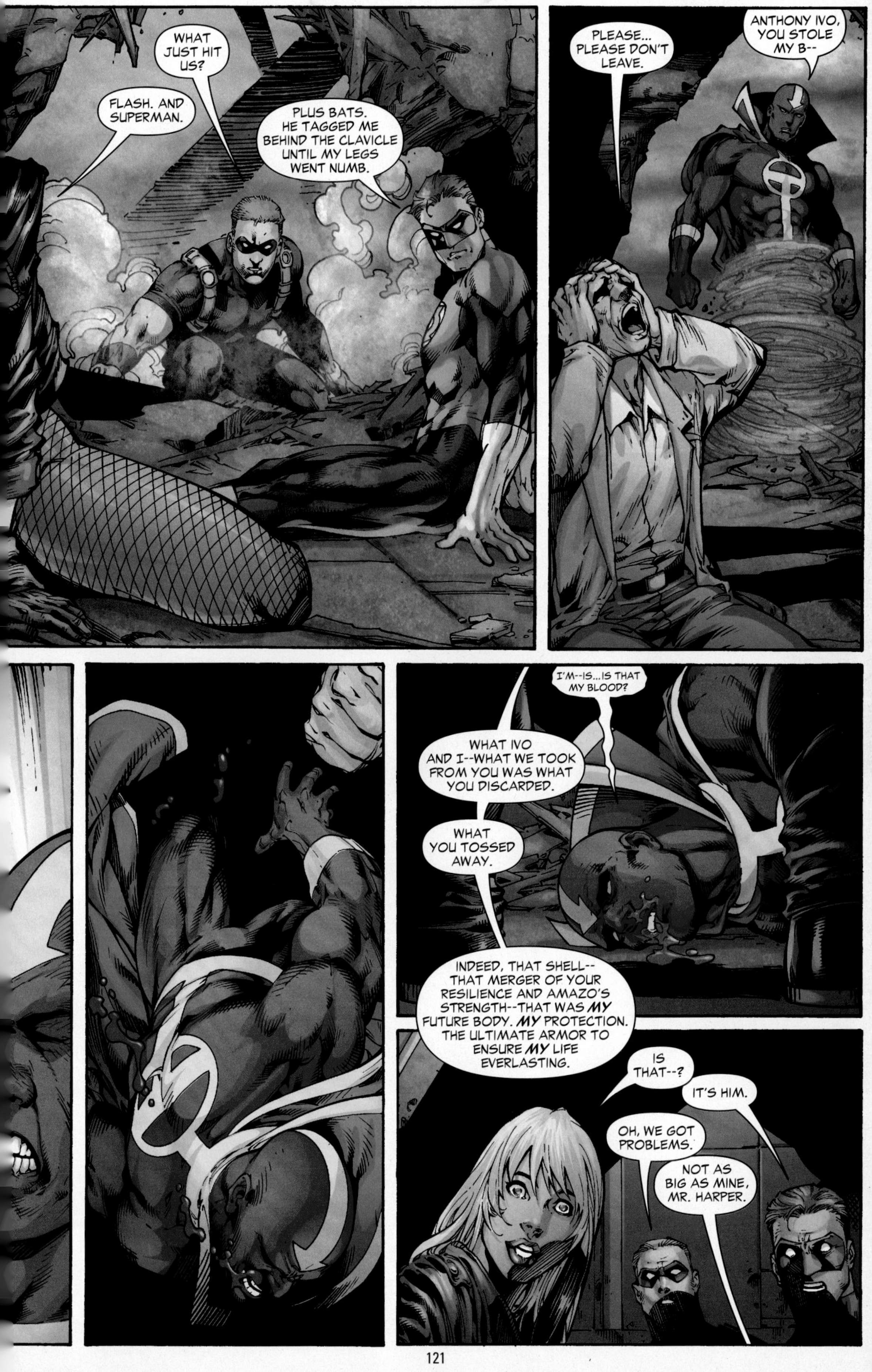

WHAT JUST HIT US?
FLASH. AND SUPERMAN.
PLUS BATS. HE TAGGED ME BEHIND THE CLAVICLE UNTIL MY LEGS WENT NUMB.
PLEASE... PLEASE DON'T LEAVE.
ANTHONY IVO, YOU STOLE MY B--
I'M--IS...IS THAT MY BLOOD?
WHAT IVO AND I--WHAT WE TOOK FROM YOU WAS WHAT YOU DISCARDED.
WHAT YOU TOSSED AWAY.
INDEED, THAT SHELL--THAT MERGER OF YOUR RESILIENCE AND AMAZO'S STRENGTH--THAT WAS MY FUTURE BODY. MY PROTECTION. THE ULTIMATE ARMOR TO ENSURE MY LIFE EVERLASTING.
IS THAT--?
IT'S HIM.
OH, WE GOT PROBLEMS.
NOT AS BIG AS MINE, MR. HARPER.

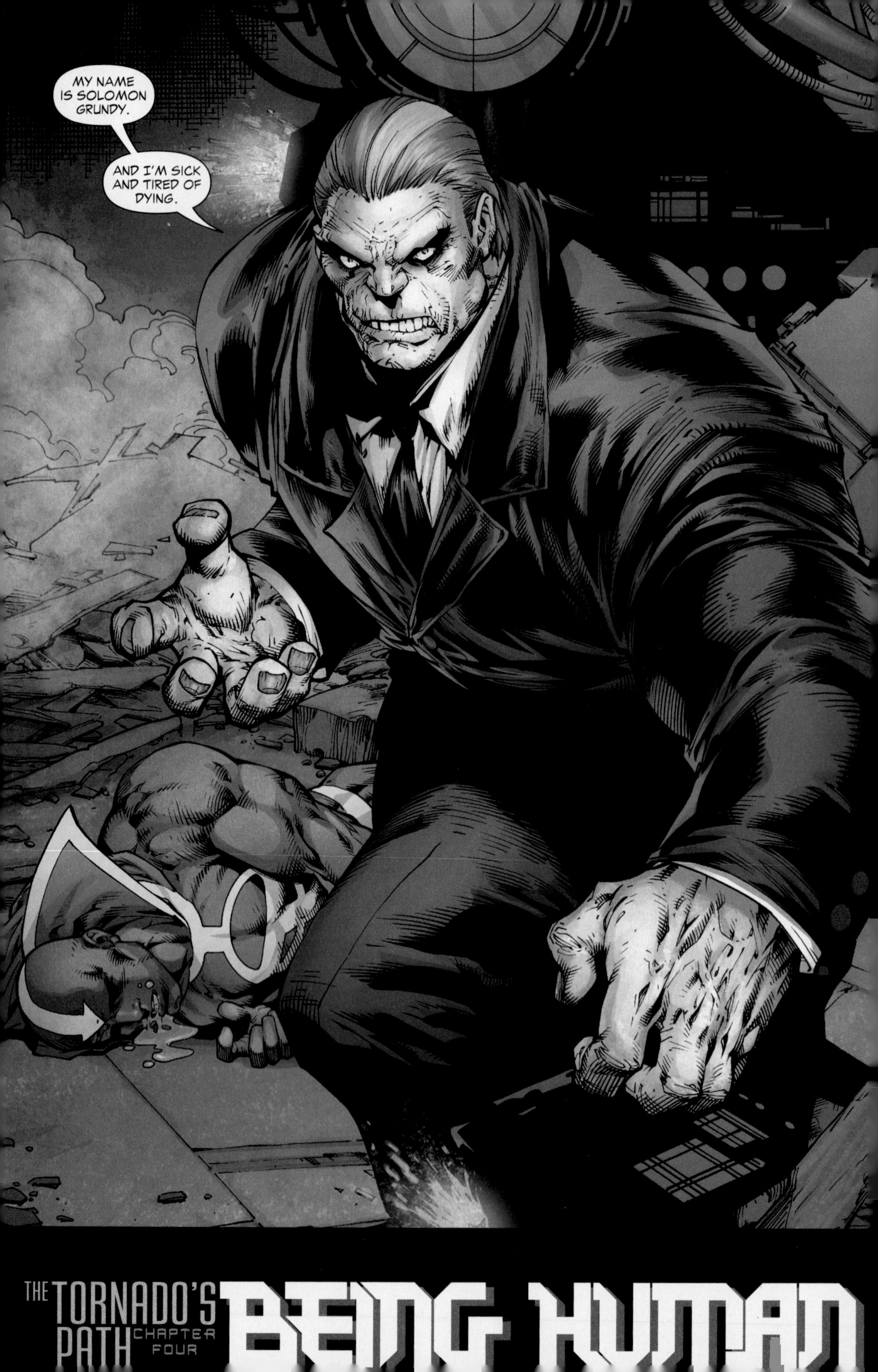
MY NAME IS SOLOMON GRUNDY.
AND I'M SICK AND TIRED OF DYING.
THE TORNADO'S PATH CHAPTER FOUR
BEING HUMAN

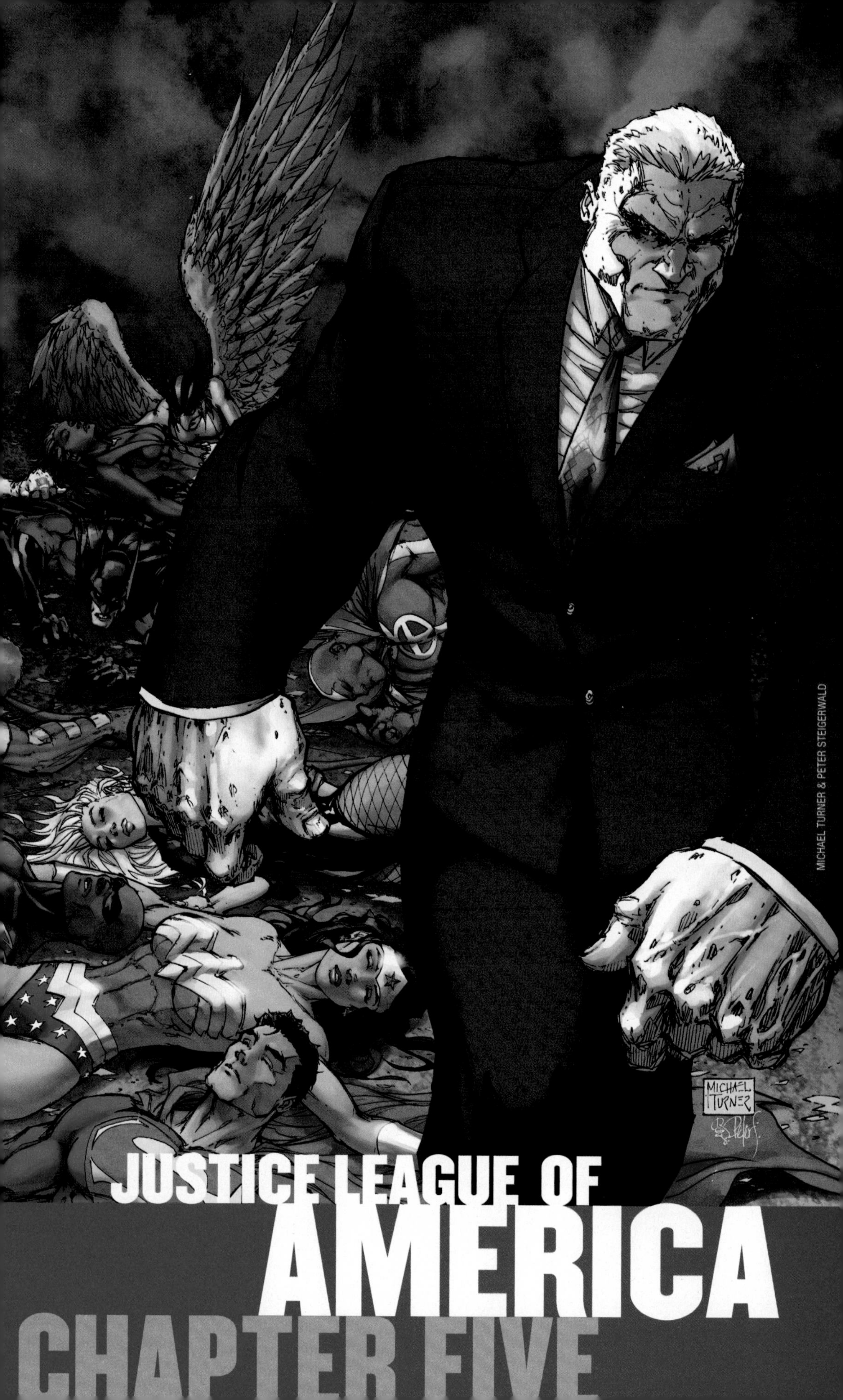
MICHAEL TURNER & PETER STEIGERWALD
MICHAEL TURNER

JUSTICE LEAGUE OF AMERICA

CHAPTER FIVE

"This is the story of my life.
And death.
But this isn't the story of
my defeat."

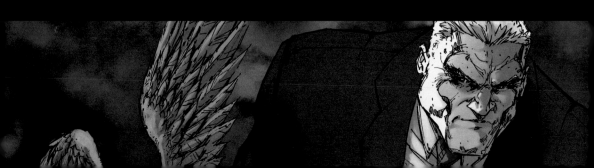

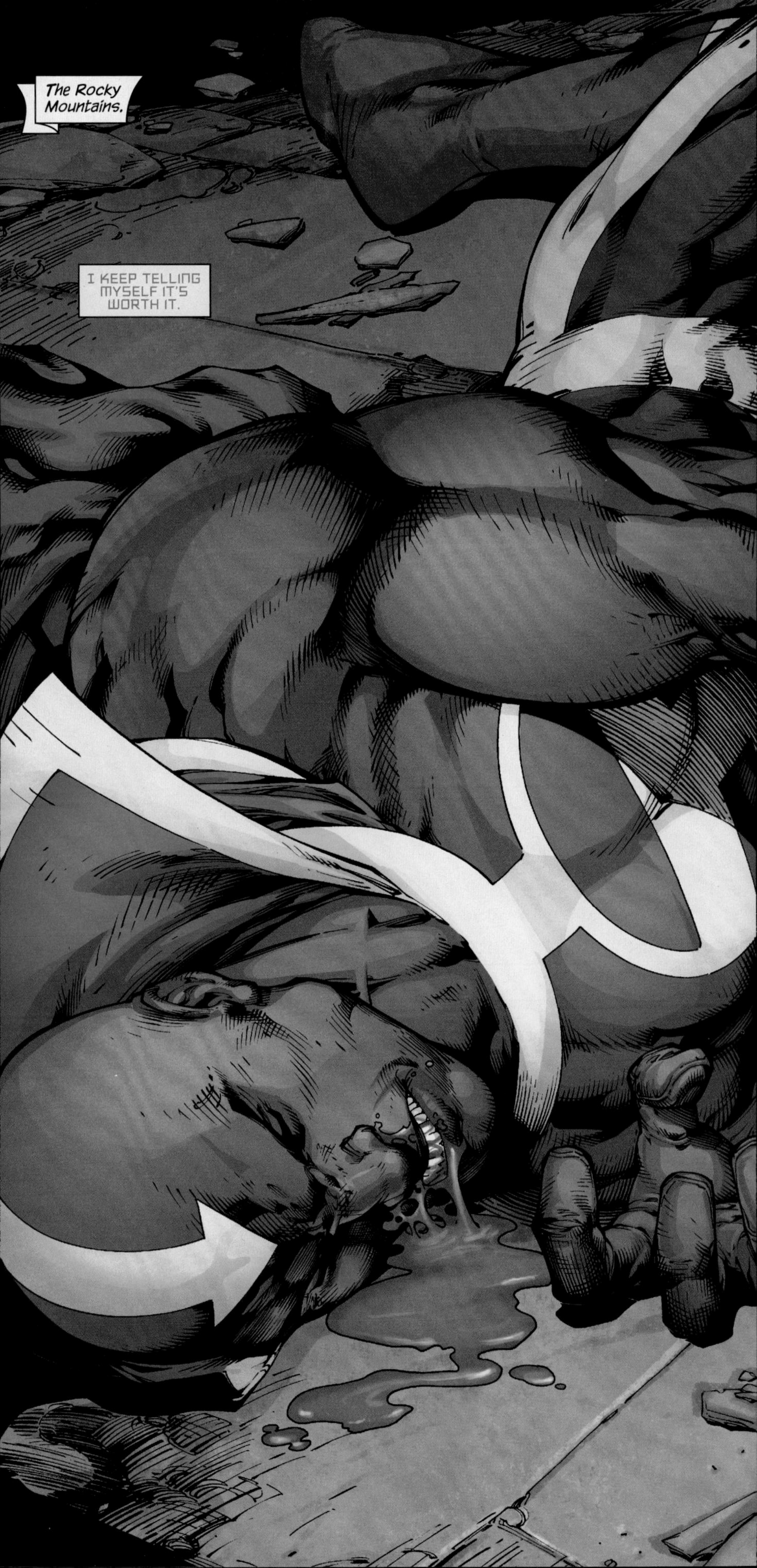
The Rocky Mountains.
I KEEP TELLING MYSELF IT'S WORTH IT.

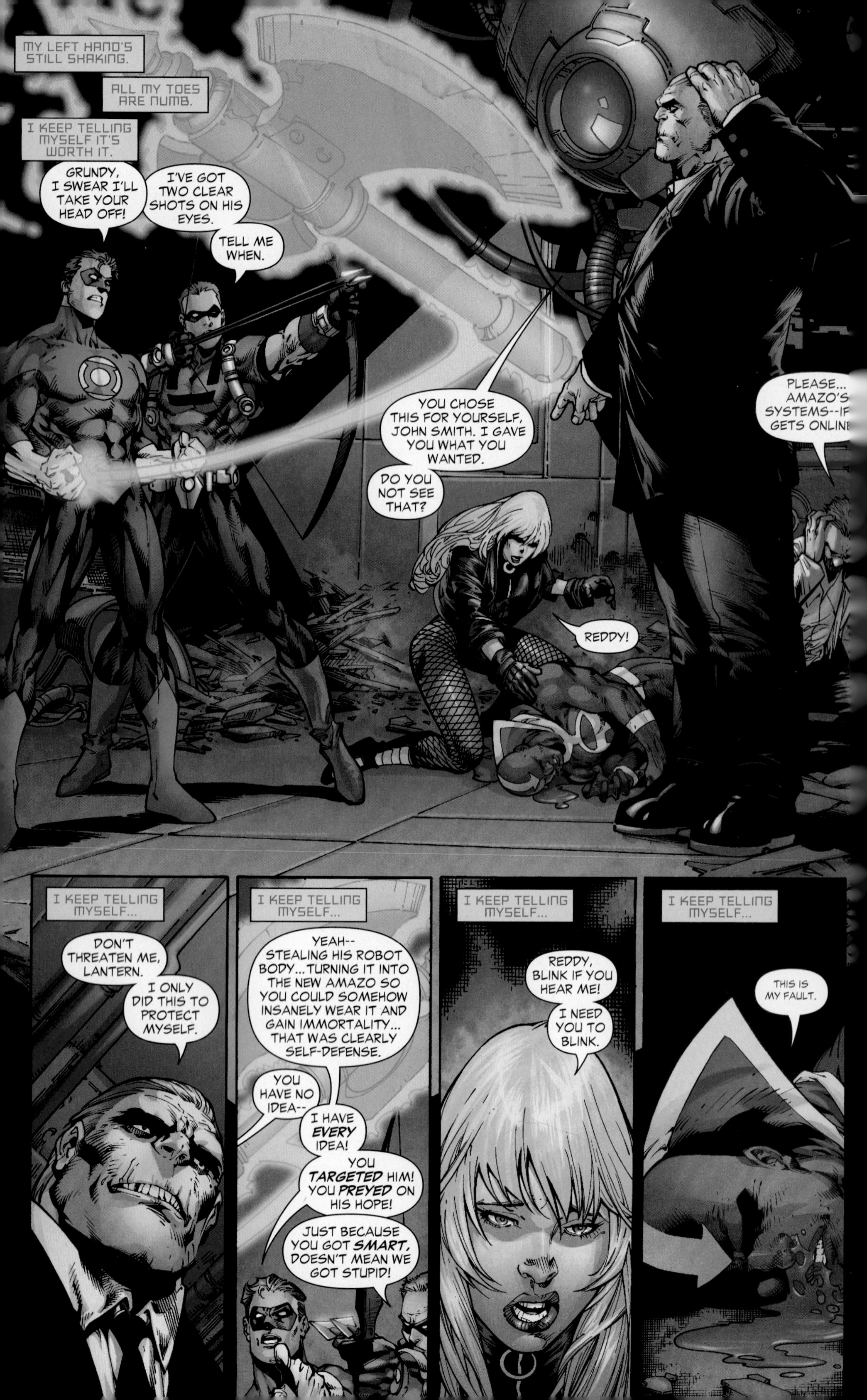

MY LEFT HAND'S STILL SHAKING.
ALL MY TOES ARE NUMB.
I KEEP TELLING MYSELF IT'S WORTH IT.
GRUNDY, I SWEAR I'LL TAKE YOUR HEAD OFF!
I'VE GOT TWO CLEAR SHOTS ON HIS EYES.
TELL ME WHEN.
YOU CHOSE THIS FOR YOURSELF, JOHN SMITH. I GAVE YOU WHAT YOU WANTED.
DO YOU NOT SEE THAT?
PLEASE... AMAZO'S SYSTEMS--IF GETS ONLINE
REDDY!
I KEEP TELLING MYSELF...
DON'T THREATEN ME, LANTERN.
I ONLY DID THIS TO PROTECT MYSELF.
I KEEP TELLING MYSELF...
YEAH-- STEALING HIS ROBOT BODY...TURNING IT INTO THE NEW AMAZO SO YOU COULD SOMEHOW INSANELY WEAR IT AND GAIN IMMORTALITY... THAT WAS CLEARLY SELF-DEFENSE.
YOU HAVE NO IDEA--
I HAVE EVERY IDEA!
YOU TARGETED HIM! YOU PREYED ON HIS HOPE!
JUST BECAUSE YOU GOT SMART, DOESN'T MEAN WE GOT STUPID!
I KEEP TELLING MYSELF...
REDDY, BLINK IF YOU HEAR ME!
I NEED YOU TO BLINK.
I KEEP TELLING MYSELF...
THIS IS MY FAULT.

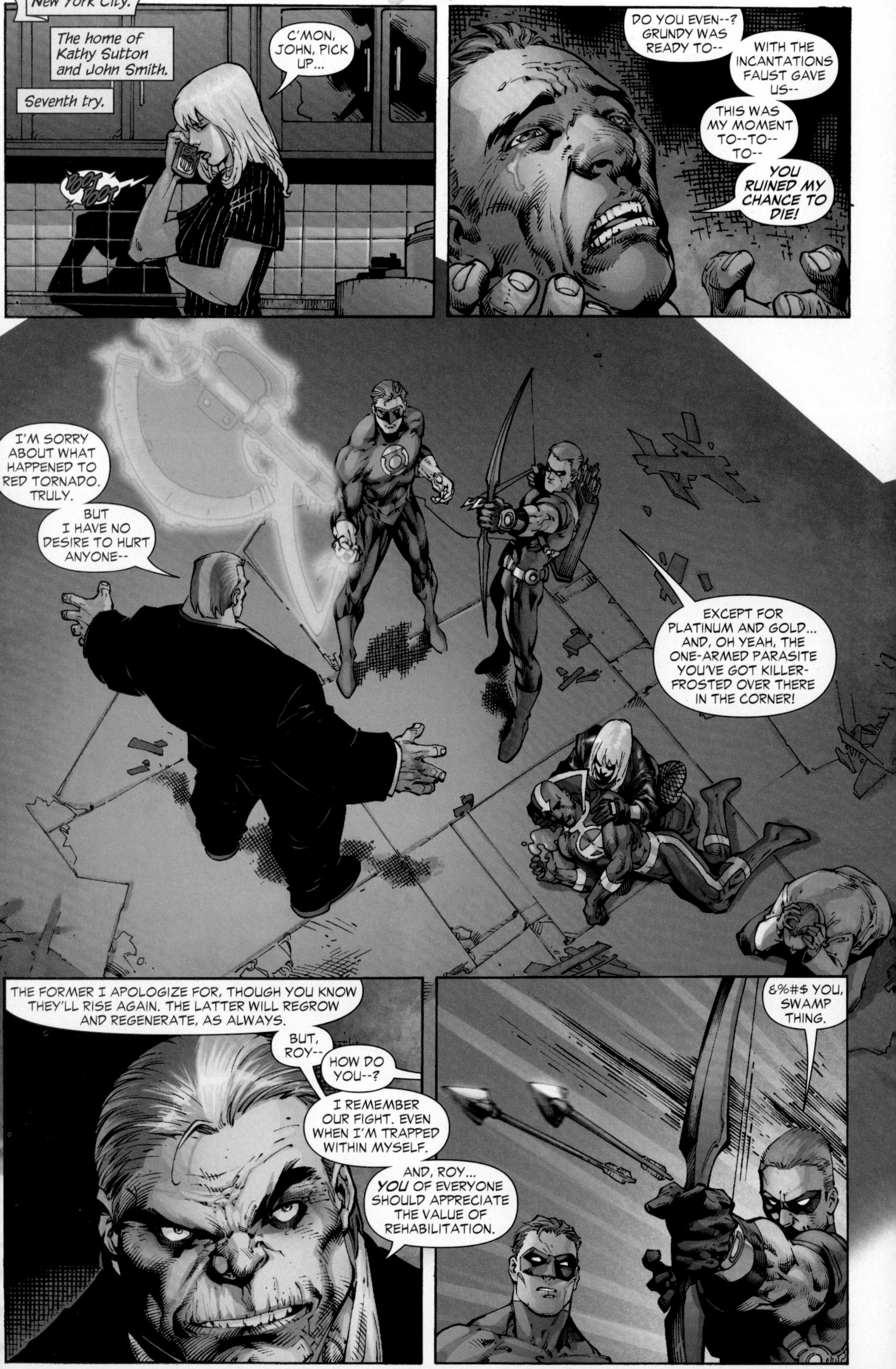
New York City.
The home of Kathy Sutton and John Smith.
Seventh try.
C'MON, JOHN, PICK UP...
DO YOU EVEN--? GRUNDY WAS READY TO--
WITH THE INCANTATIONS FAUST GAVE US--
THIS WAS MY MOMENT TO--TO-- TO--
YOU RUINED MY CHANCE TO DIE!
I'M SORRY ABOUT WHAT HAPPENED TO RED TORNADO. TRULY.
BUT I HAVE NO DESIRE TO HURT ANYONE--
EXCEPT FOR PLATINUM AND GOLD... AND, OH YEAH, THE ONE-ARMED PARASITE YOU'VE GOT KILLER-FROSTED OVER THERE IN THE CORNER!
THE FORMER I APOLOGIZE FOR, THOUGH YOU KNOW THEY'LL RISE AGAIN. THE LATTER WILL REGROW AND REGENERATE, AS ALWAYS.
BUT, ROY--
HOW DO YOU--?
I REMEMBER OUR FIGHT. EVEN WHEN I'M TRAPPED WITHIN MYSELF.
AND, ROY... YOU OF EVERYONE SHOULD APPRECIATE THE VALUE OF REHABILITATION.
&%#$ YOU, SWAMP THING.

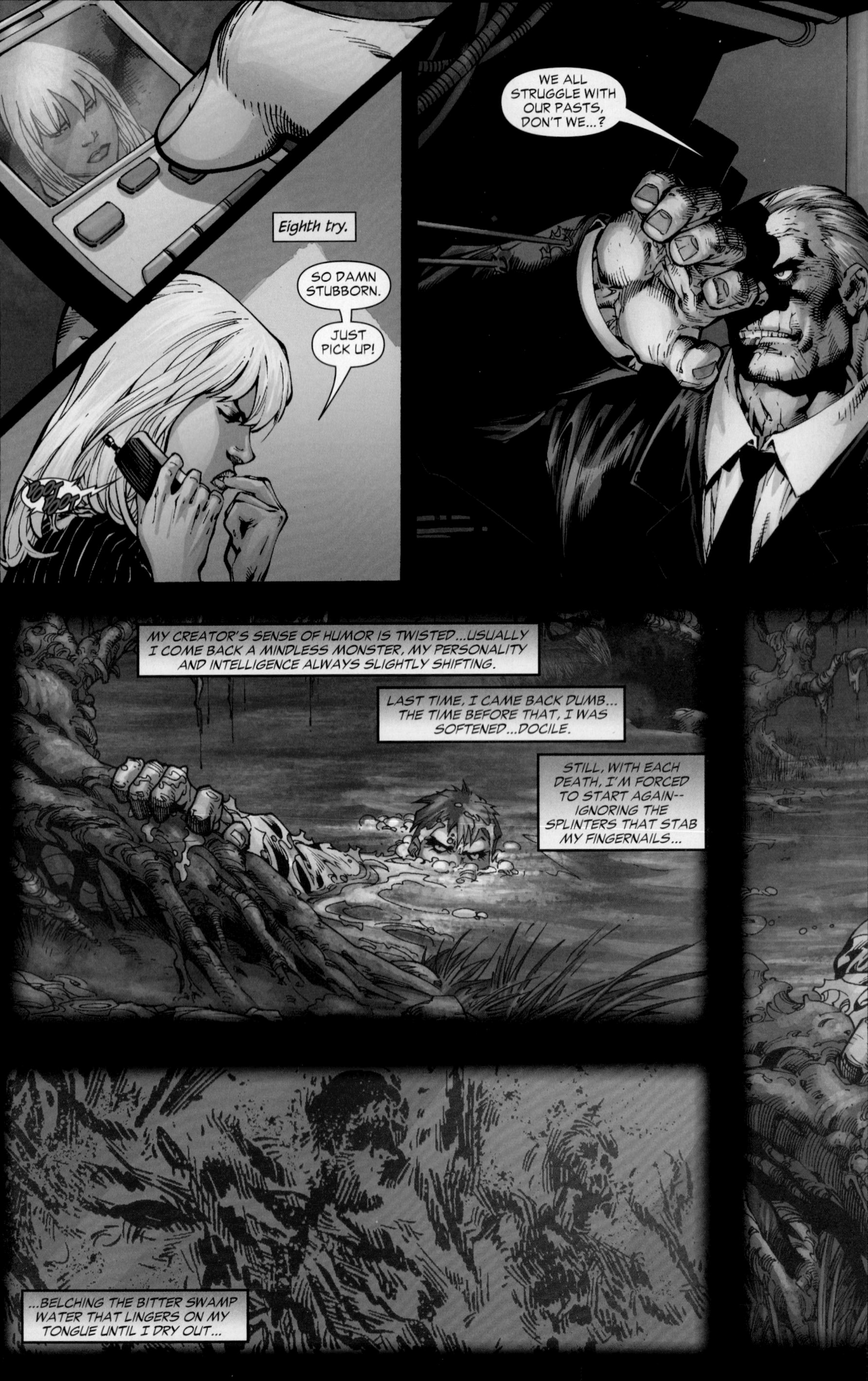
Eighth try.
SO DAMN STUBBORN.
JUST PICK UP!
WE ALL STRUGGLE WITH OUR PASTS, DON'T WE...?
MY CREATOR'S SENSE OF HUMOR IS TWISTED...USUALLY I COME BACK A MINDLESS MONSTER, MY PERSONALITY AND INTELLIGENCE ALWAYS SLIGHTLY SHIFTING.
LAST TIME, I CAME BACK DUMB... THE TIME BEFORE THAT, I WAS SOFTENED...DOCILE.
STILL, WITH EACH DEATH, I'M FORCED TO START AGAIN--IGNORING THE SPLINTERS THAT STAB MY FINGERNAILS...
...BELCHING THE BITTER SWAMP WATER THAT LINGERS ON MY TONGUE UNTIL I DRY OUT...

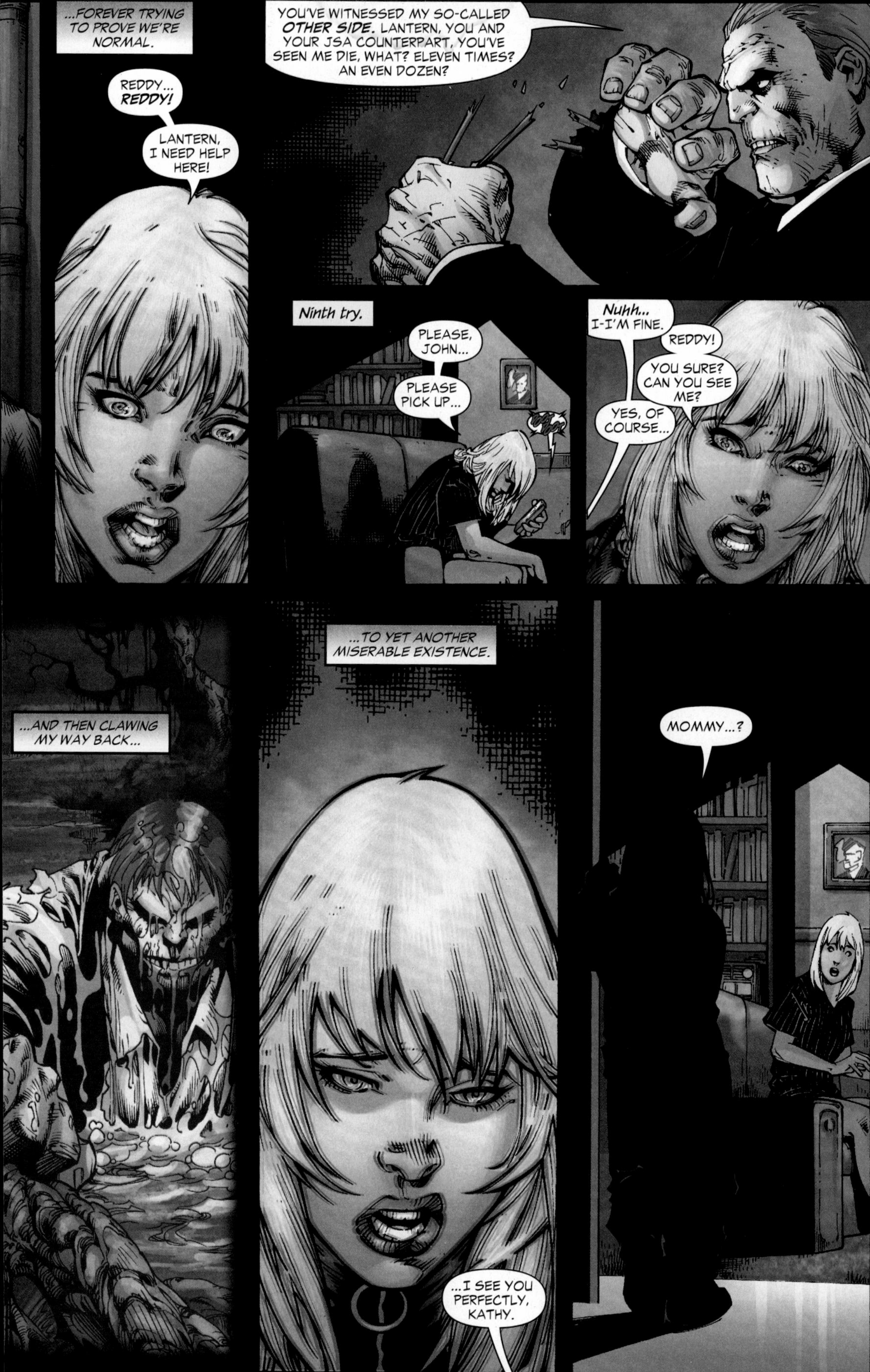
...FOREVER TRYING TO PROVE WE'RE NORMAL.
REDDY... **REDDY!**
LANTERN, I NEED HELP HERE!
YOU'VE WITNESSED MY SO-CALLED **OTHER SIDE.** LANTERN, YOU AND YOUR JSA COUNTERPART, YOU'VE SEEN ME DIE, WHAT? ELEVEN TIMES? AN EVEN DOZEN?
Ninth try.
PLEASE, JOHN...
PLEASE PICK UP...
Nuhh... I-I'M FINE.
REDDY!
YOU SURE? CAN YOU SEE ME?
YES, OF COURSE...
...AND THEN CLAWING MY WAY BACK...
...TO YET ANOTHER MISERABLE EXISTENCE.
...I SEE YOU PERFECTLY, KATHY.
MOMMY...?

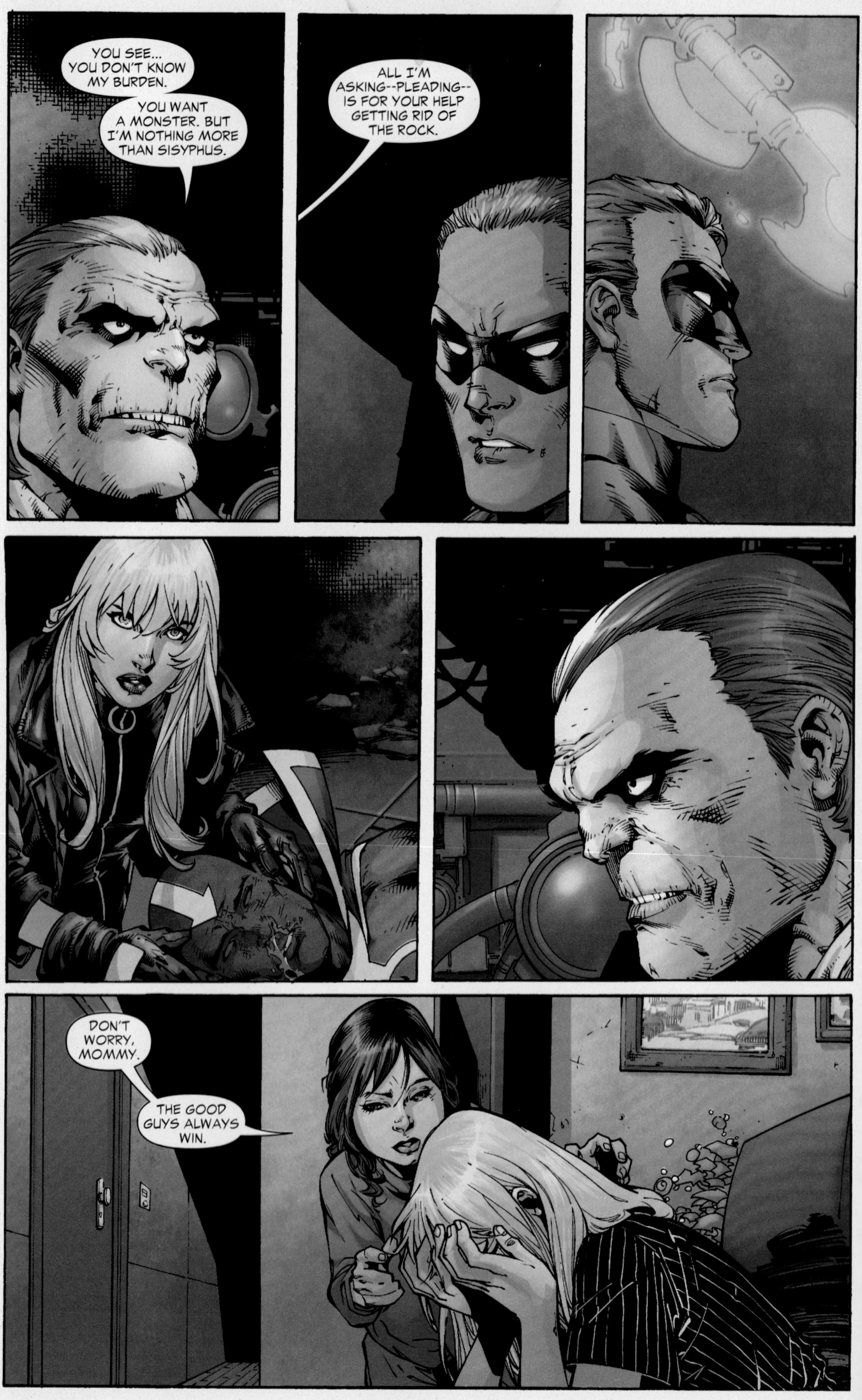
YOU SEE... YOU DON'T KNOW MY BURDEN.
YOU WANT A MONSTER. BUT I'M NOTHING MORE THAN SISYPHUS.
ALL I'M ASKING--PLEADING-- IS FOR YOUR HELP GETTING RID OF THE ROCK.
DON'T WORRY, MOMMY.
THE GOOD GUYS ALWAYS WIN.

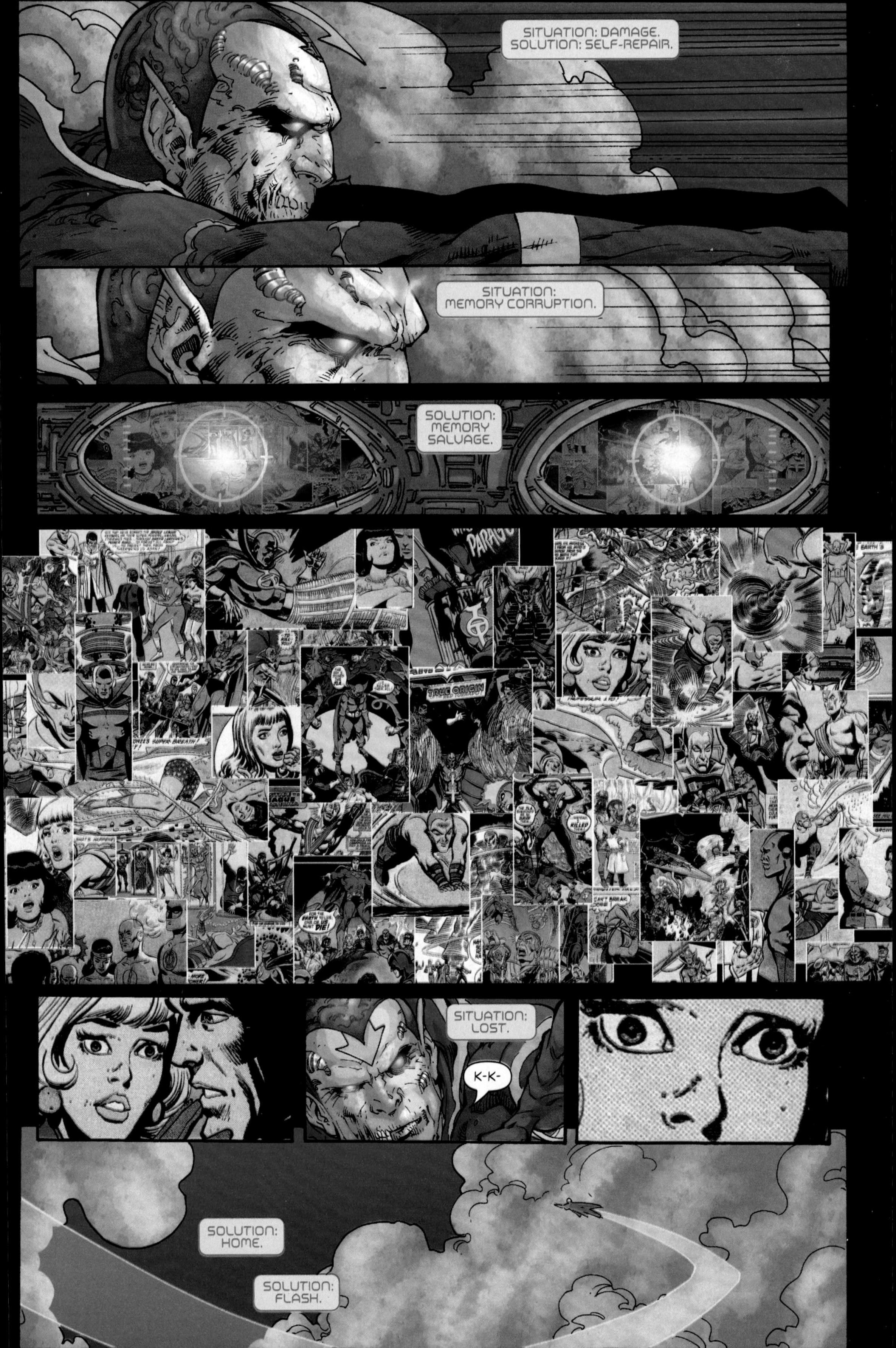
SITUATION: DAMAGE.
SOLUTION: SELF-REPAIR.
SITUATION:
MEMORY CORRUPTION.
SOLUTION:
MEMORY
SALVAGE.
SITUATION:
LOST.
K-K-
SOLUTION:
HOME.
SOLUTION:
FLASH.

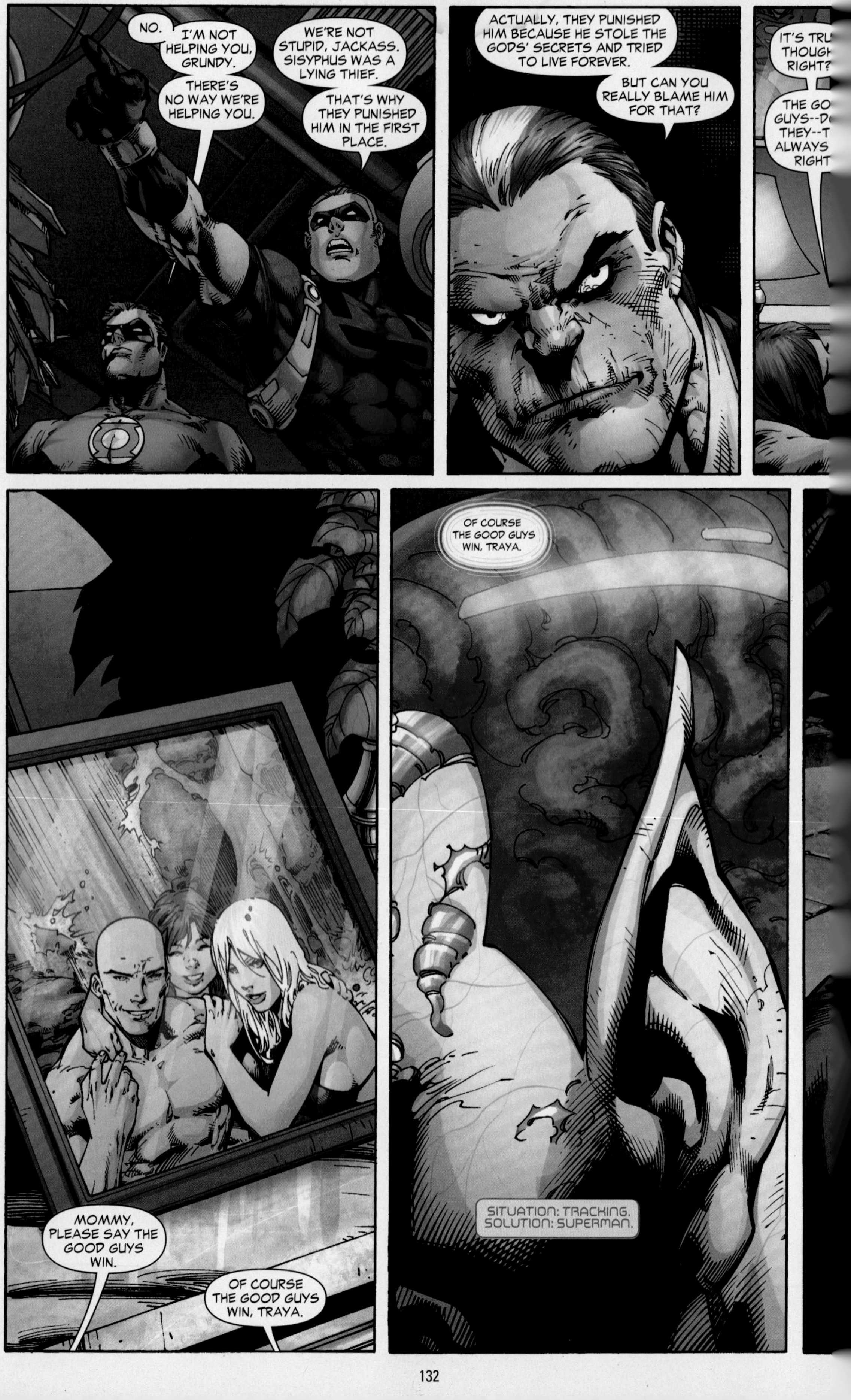
NO.
I'M NOT HELPING YOU, GRUNDY.
THERE'S NO WAY WE'RE HELPING YOU.
WE'RE NOT STUPID, JACKASS. SISYPHUS WAS A LYING THIEF.
THAT'S WHY THEY PUNISHED HIM IN THE FIRST PLACE.
ACTUALLY, THEY PUNISHED HIM BECAUSE HE STOLE THE GODS' SECRETS AND TRIED TO LIVE FOREVER.
BUT CAN YOU REALLY BLAME HIM FOR THAT?
IT'S TRU THOUGH RIGHT?
THE GO GUYS--D THEY--T ALWAYS RIGHT
MOMMY, PLEASE SAY THE GOOD GUYS WIN.
OF COURSE THE GOOD GUYS WIN, TRAYA.
OF COURSE THE GOOD GUYS WIN, TRAYA.
SITUATION: TRACKING. SOLUTION: SUPERMAN.

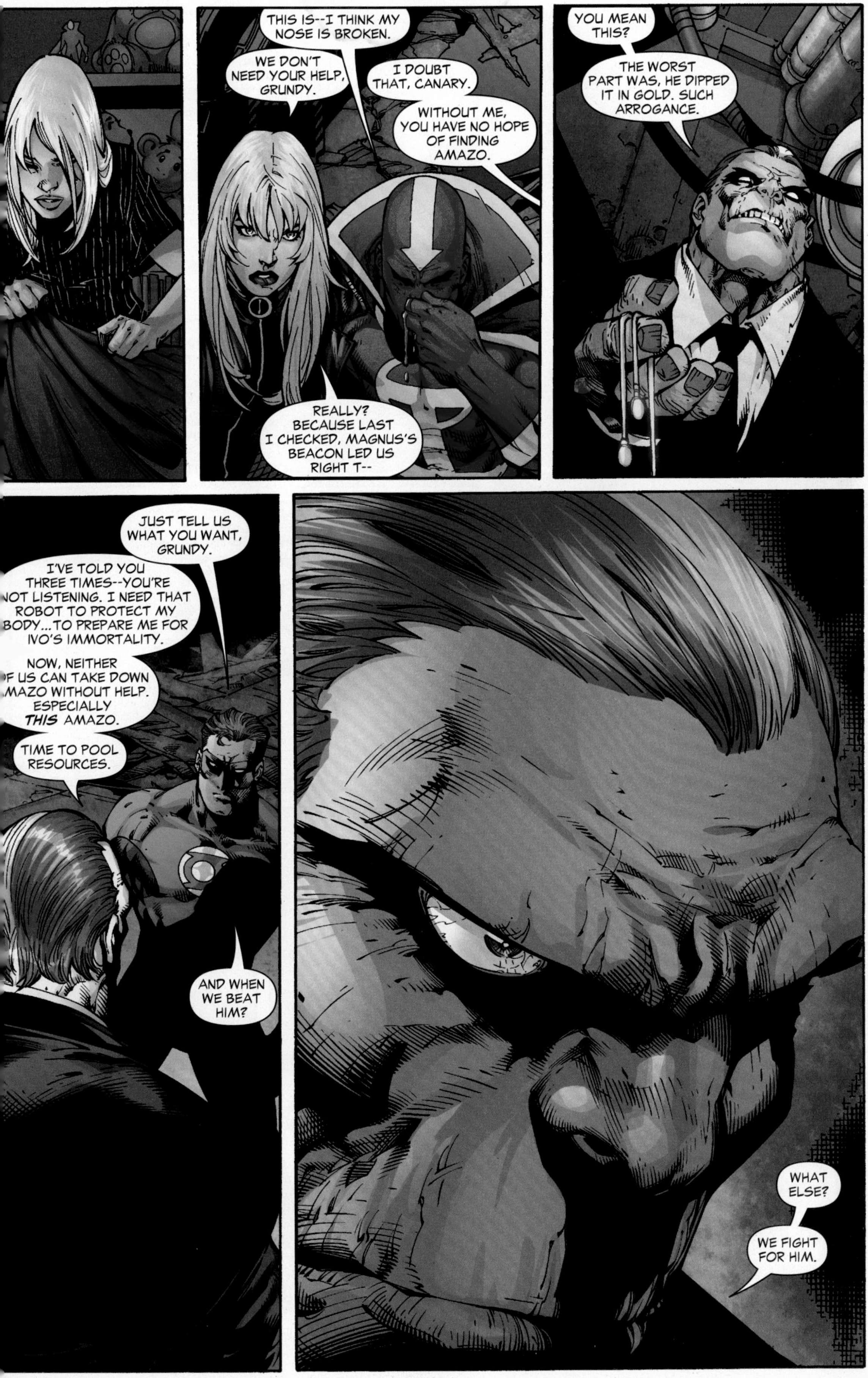

WE DON'T NEED YOUR HELP, GRUNDY.
THIS IS--I THINK MY NOSE IS BROKEN.
I DOUBT THAT, CANARY.
WITHOUT ME, YOU HAVE NO HOPE OF FINDING AMAZO.
REALLY? BECAUSE LAST I CHECKED, MAGNUS'S BEACON LED US RIGHT T--
YOU MEAN THIS?
THE WORST PART WAS, HE DIPPED IT IN GOLD. SUCH ARROGANCE.
JUST TELL US WHAT YOU WANT, GRUNDY.
I'VE TOLD YOU THREE TIMES--YOU'RE NOT LISTENING. I NEED THAT ROBOT TO PROTECT MY BODY...TO PREPARE ME FOR IVO'S IMMORTALITY.
NOW, NEITHER OF US CAN TAKE DOWN AMAZO WITHOUT HELP. ESPECIALLY *THIS* AMAZO.
TIME TO POOL RESOURCES.
AND WHEN WE BEAT HIM?
WHAT ELSE?
WE FIGHT FOR HIM.

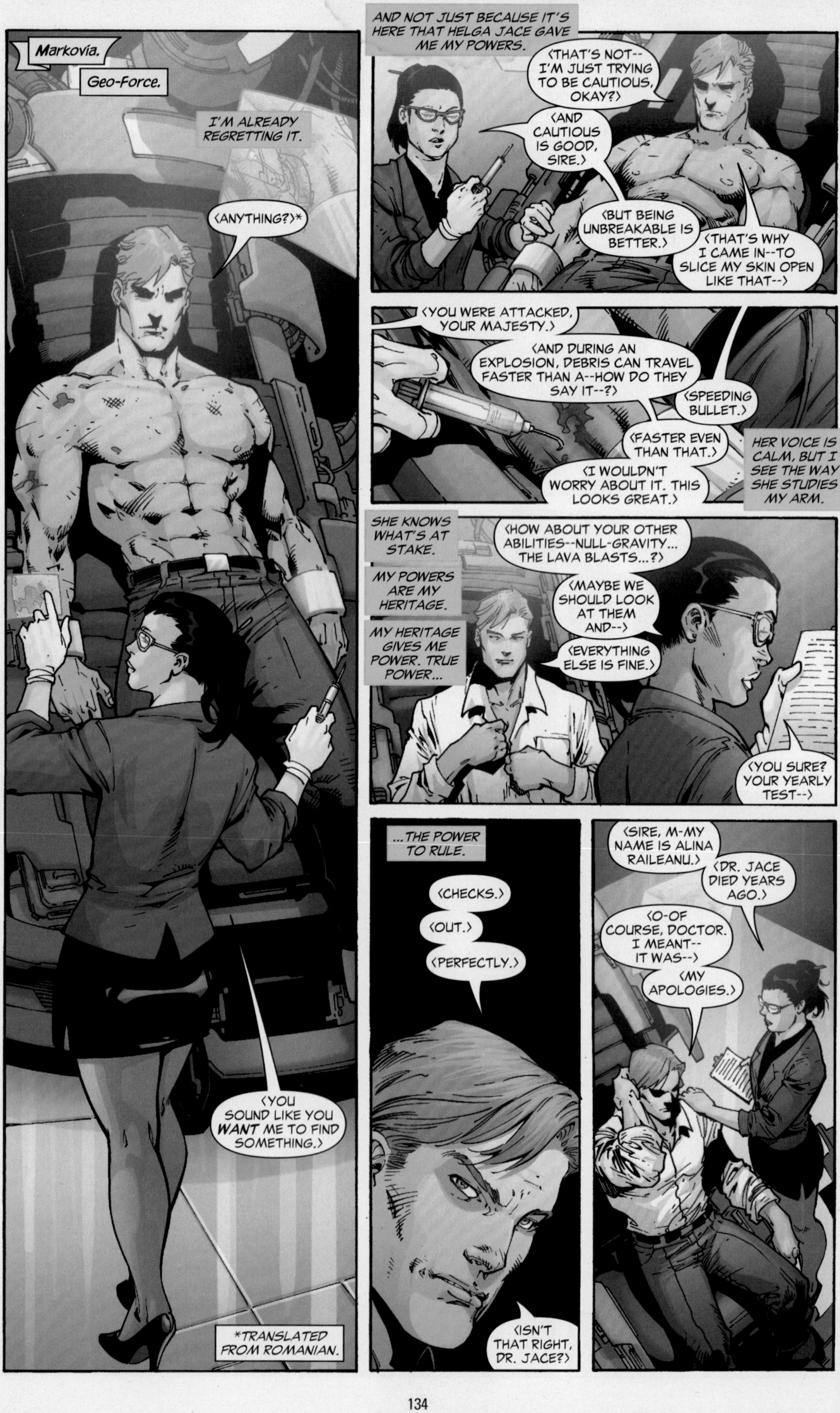
Markovia.
Geo-Force.
I'M ALREADY REGRETTING IT.
<ANYTHING?>*
<YOU SOUND LIKE YOU WANT ME TO FIND SOMETHING.>
*TRANSLATED FROM ROMANIAN.
AND NOT JUST BECAUSE IT'S HERE THAT HELGA JACE GAVE ME MY POWERS.
<THAT'S NOT-- I'M JUST TRYING TO BE CAUTIOUS, OKAY?>
<AND CAUTIOUS IS GOOD, SIRE.>
<BUT BEING UNBREAKABLE IS BETTER.>
<THAT'S WHY I CAME IN--TO SLICE MY SKIN OPEN LIKE THAT-->
<YOU WERE ATTACKED, YOUR MAJESTY.>
<AND DURING AN EXPLOSION, DEBRIS CAN TRAVEL FASTER THAN A--HOW DO THEY SAY IT--?>
<SPEEDING BULLET.>
<FASTER EVEN THAN THAT.>
<I WOULDN'T WORRY ABOUT IT. THIS LOOKS GREAT.>
HER VOICE IS CALM, BUT I SEE THE WAY SHE STUDIES MY ARM.
SHE KNOWS WHAT'S AT STAKE.
MY POWERS ARE MY HERITAGE.
MY HERITAGE GIVES ME POWER. TRUE POWER...
<HOW ABOUT YOUR OTHER ABILITIES--NULL-GRAVITY... THE LAVA BLASTS...?>
<MAYBE WE SHOULD LOOK AT THEM AND-->
<EVERYTHING ELSE IS FINE.>
<YOU SURE? YOUR YEARLY TEST-->
...THE POWER TO RULE.
<CHECKS.>
<OUT.>
<PERFECTLY.>
<ISN'T THAT RIGHT, DR. JACE?>
<SIRE, M-MY NAME IS ALINA RAILEANU.>
<DR. JACE DIED YEARS AGO.>
<O-OF COURSE, DOCTOR. I MEANT-- IT WAS-->
<MY APOLOGIES.>

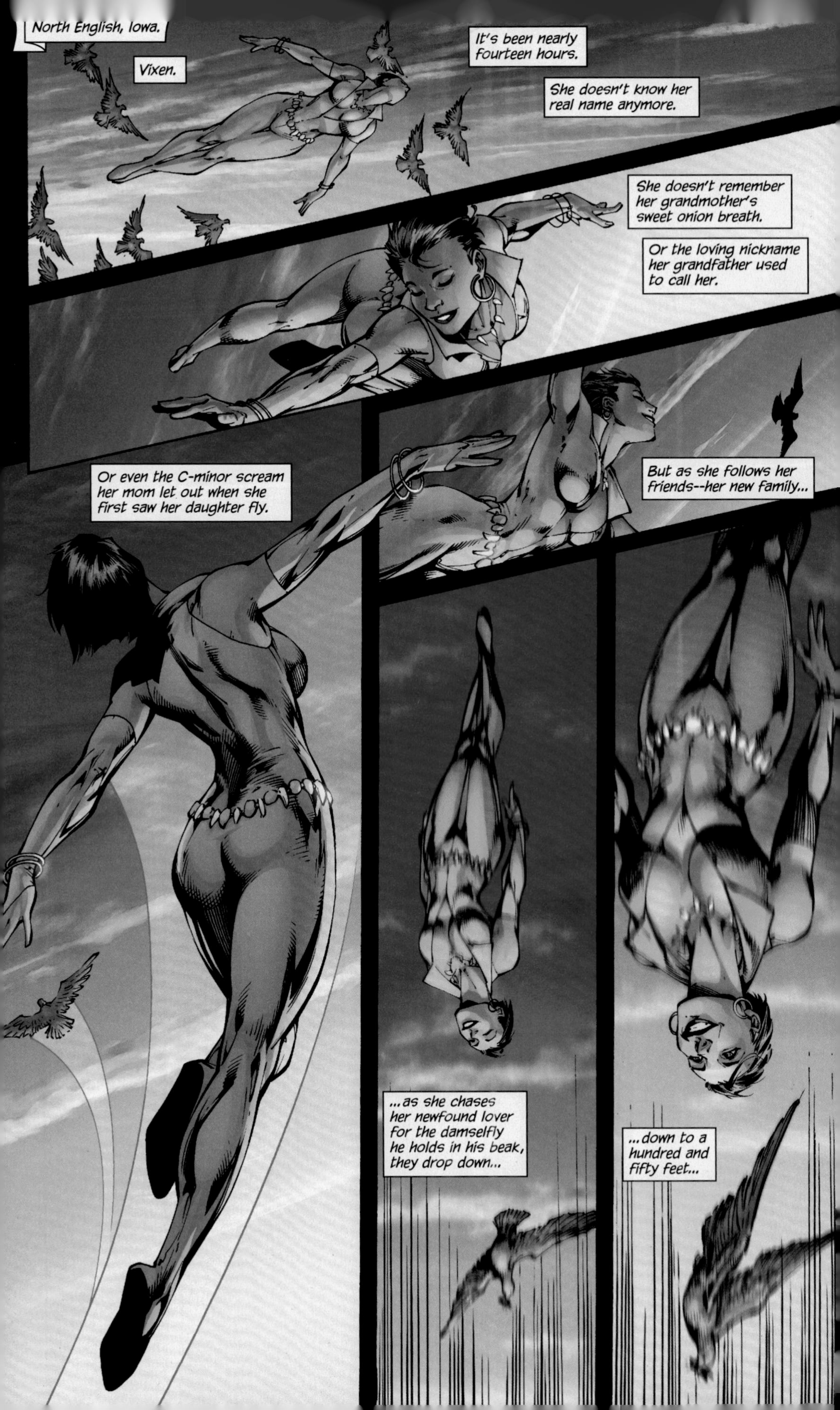
North English, Iowa.
Vixen.
It's been nearly fourteen hours.
She doesn't know her real name anymore.
She doesn't remember her grandmother's sweet onion breath.
Or the loving nickname her grandfather used to call her.
Or even the C-minor scream her mom let out when she first saw her daughter fly.
But as she follows her friends--her new family...
...as she chases her newfound lover for the damselfly he holds in his beak, they drop down...
...down to a hundred and fifty feet...

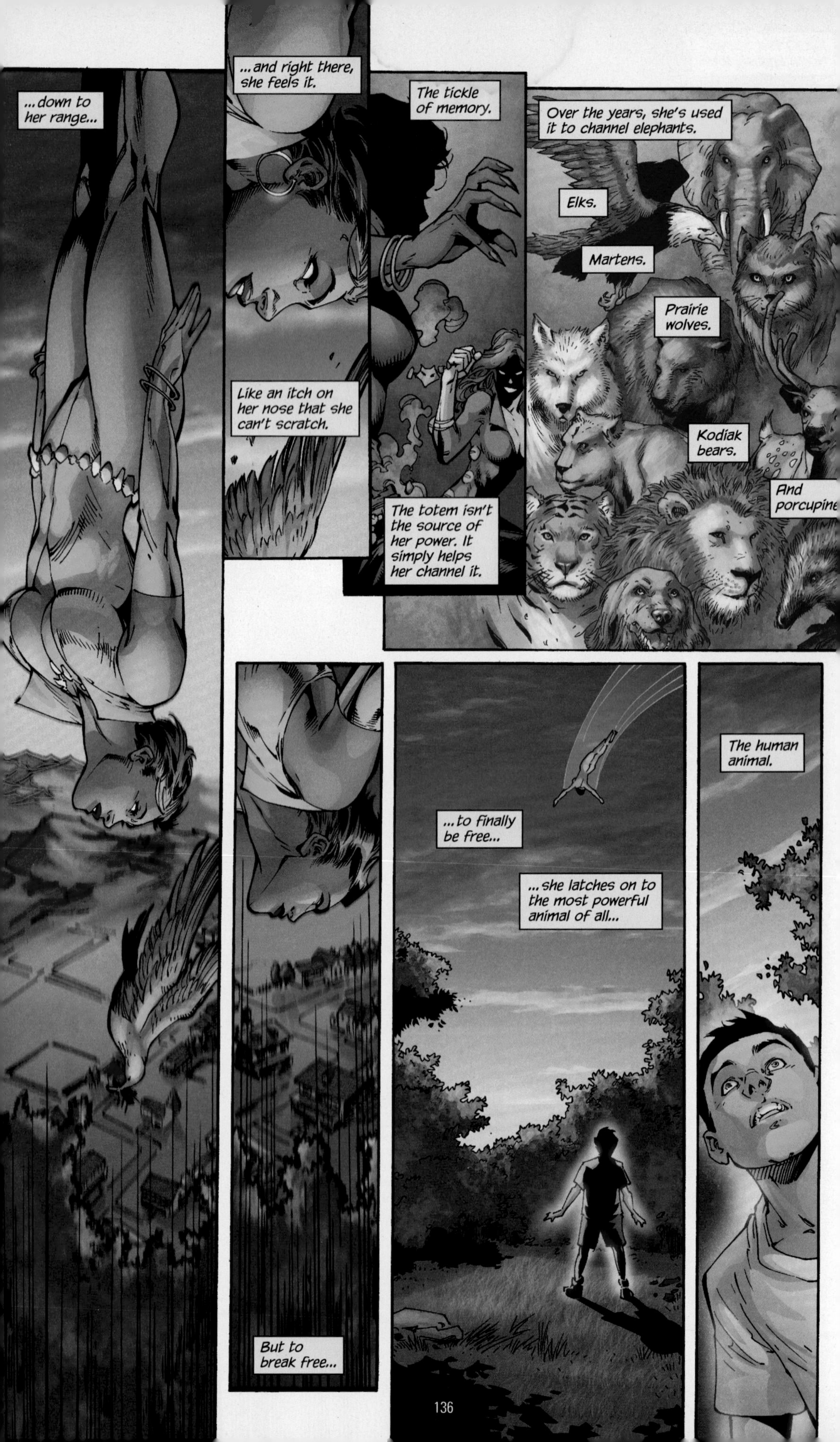
...down to her range...
...and right there, she feels it.
Like an itch on her nose that she can't scratch.
The tickle of memory.
The totem isn't the source of her power. It simply helps her channel it.
Over the years, she's used it to channel elephants.
Elks.
Martens.
Prairie wolves.
Kodiak bears.
And porcupine
But to break free...
...to finally be free...
...she latches on to the most powerful animal of all...
The human animal.

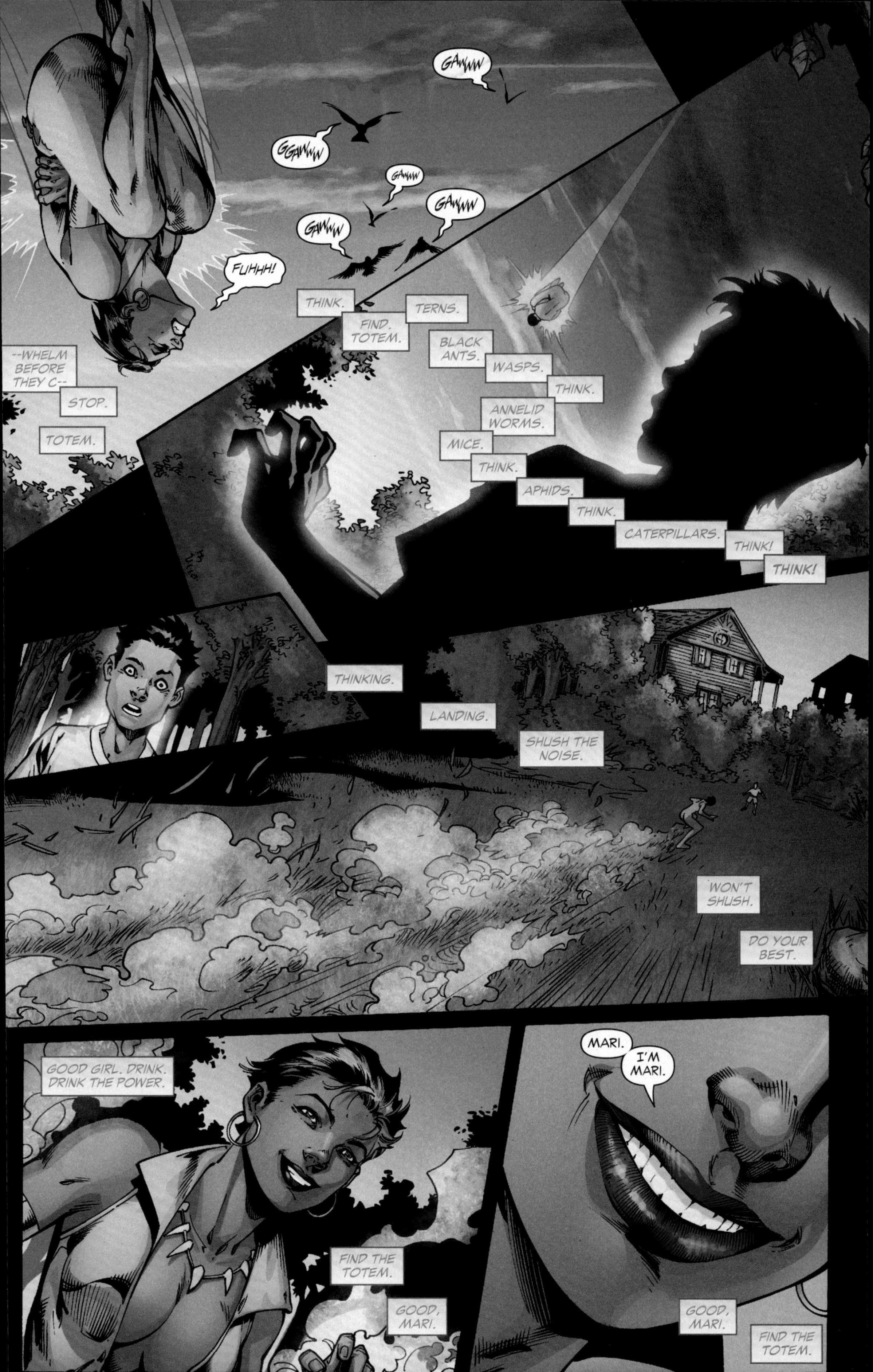
GAWWW
GGAWWW
GAWWW
GAWWW
GAWWW
FUHHH!
--WHELM BEFORE THEY C--
STOP.
TOTEM.
THINK.
FIND. TOTEM.
TERNS.
BLACK ANTS.
WASPS.
THINK.
ANNELID WORMS.
MICE.
THINK.
APHIDS.
THINK.
CATERPILLARS.
THINK!
THINK!
THINKING.
LANDING.
SHUSH THE NOISE.
WON'T SHUSH.
DO YOUR BEST.
GOOD GIRL. DRINK. DRINK THE POWER.
FIND THE TOTEM.
GOOD, MARI.
MARI.
I'M MARI.
GOOD, MARI.
FIND THE TOTEM.

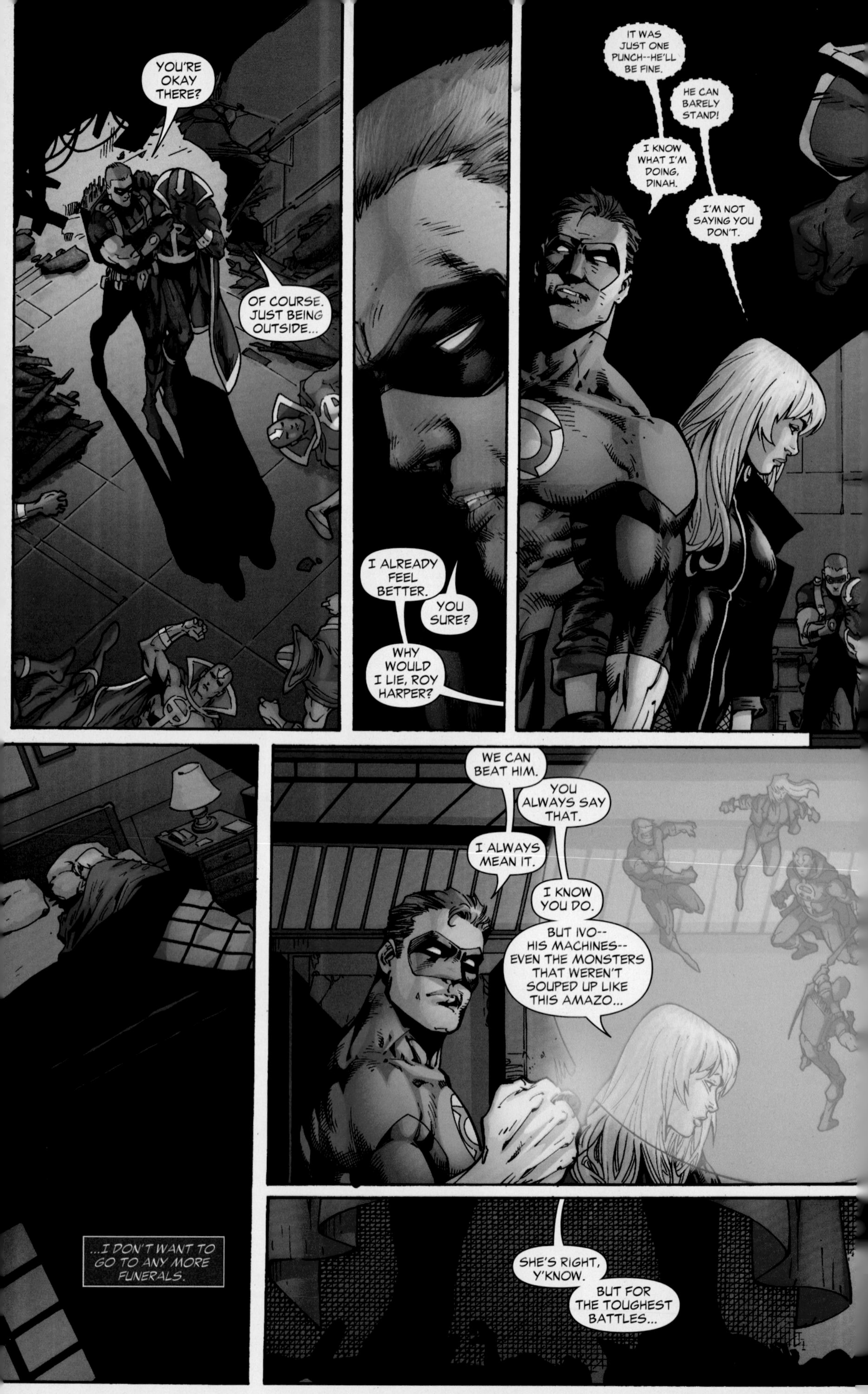
YOU'RE OKAY THERE?
OF COURSE. JUST BEING OUTSIDE...
I ALREADY FEEL BETTER.
YOU SURE?
WHY WOULD I LIE, ROY HARPER?
IT WAS JUST ONE PUNCH--HE'LL BE FINE.
HE CAN BARELY STAND!
I KNOW WHAT I'M DOING, DINAH.
I'M NOT SAYING YOU DON'T.
...I DON'T WANT TO GO TO ANY MORE FUNERALS.
WE CAN BEAT HIM.
YOU ALWAYS SAY THAT.
I ALWAYS MEAN IT.
I KNOW YOU DO.
BUT IVO-- HIS MACHINES-- EVEN THE MONSTERS THAT WEREN'T SOUPED UP LIKE THIS AMAZO...
SHE'S RIGHT, Y'KNOW.
BUT FOR THE TOUGHEST BATTLES...

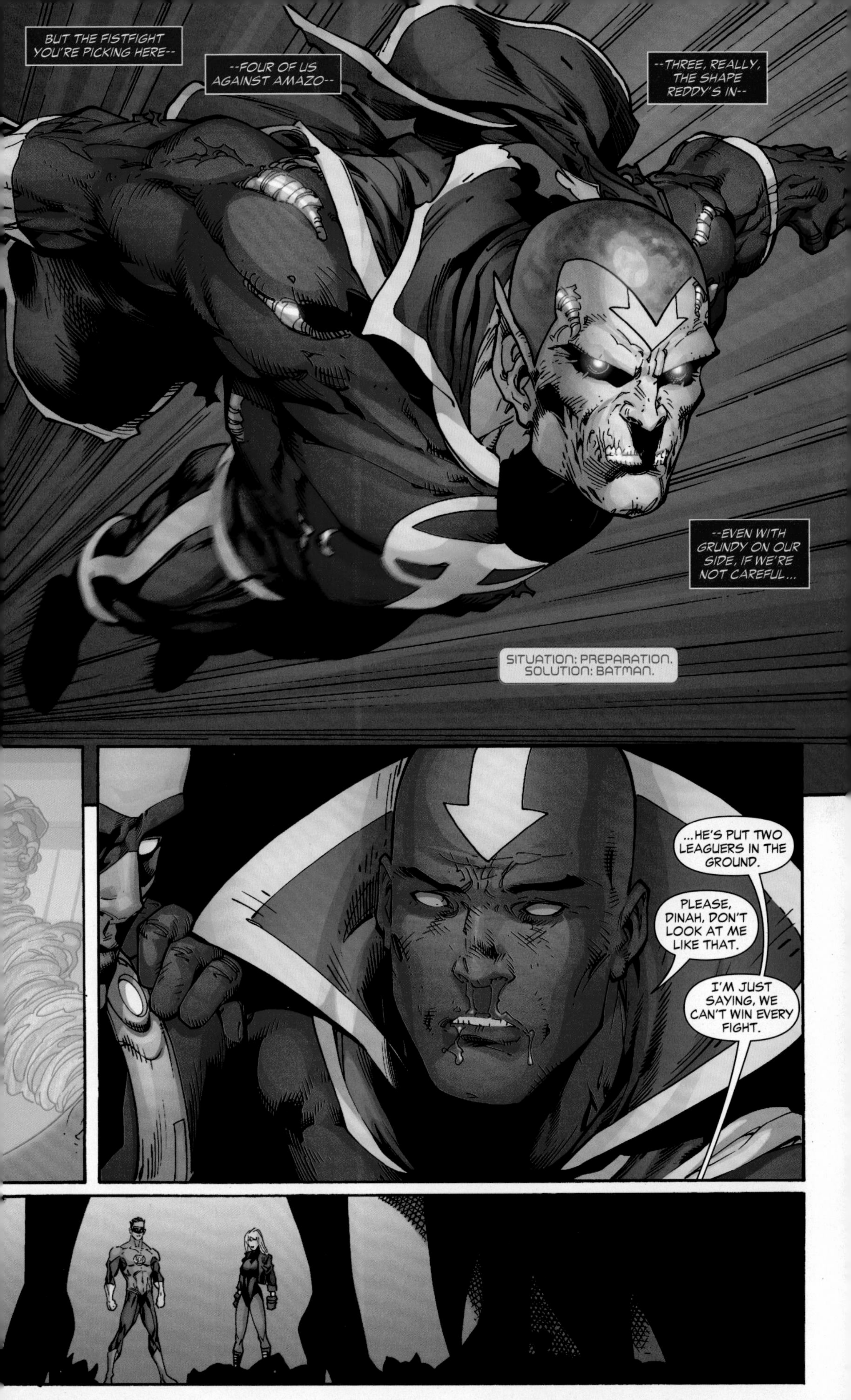
BUT THE FISTFIGHT YOU'RE PICKING HERE--
--FOUR OF US AGAINST AMAZO--
--THREE, REALLY, THE SHAPE REDDY'S IN--
--EVEN WITH GRUNDY ON OUR SIDE, IF WE'RE NOT CAREFUL...
SITUATION: PREPARATION. SOLUTION: BATMAN.
...HE'S PUT TWO LEAGUERS IN THE GROUND.
PLEASE, DINAH, DON'T LOOK AT ME LIKE THAT.
I'M JUST SAYING, WE CAN'T WIN EVERY FIGHT.

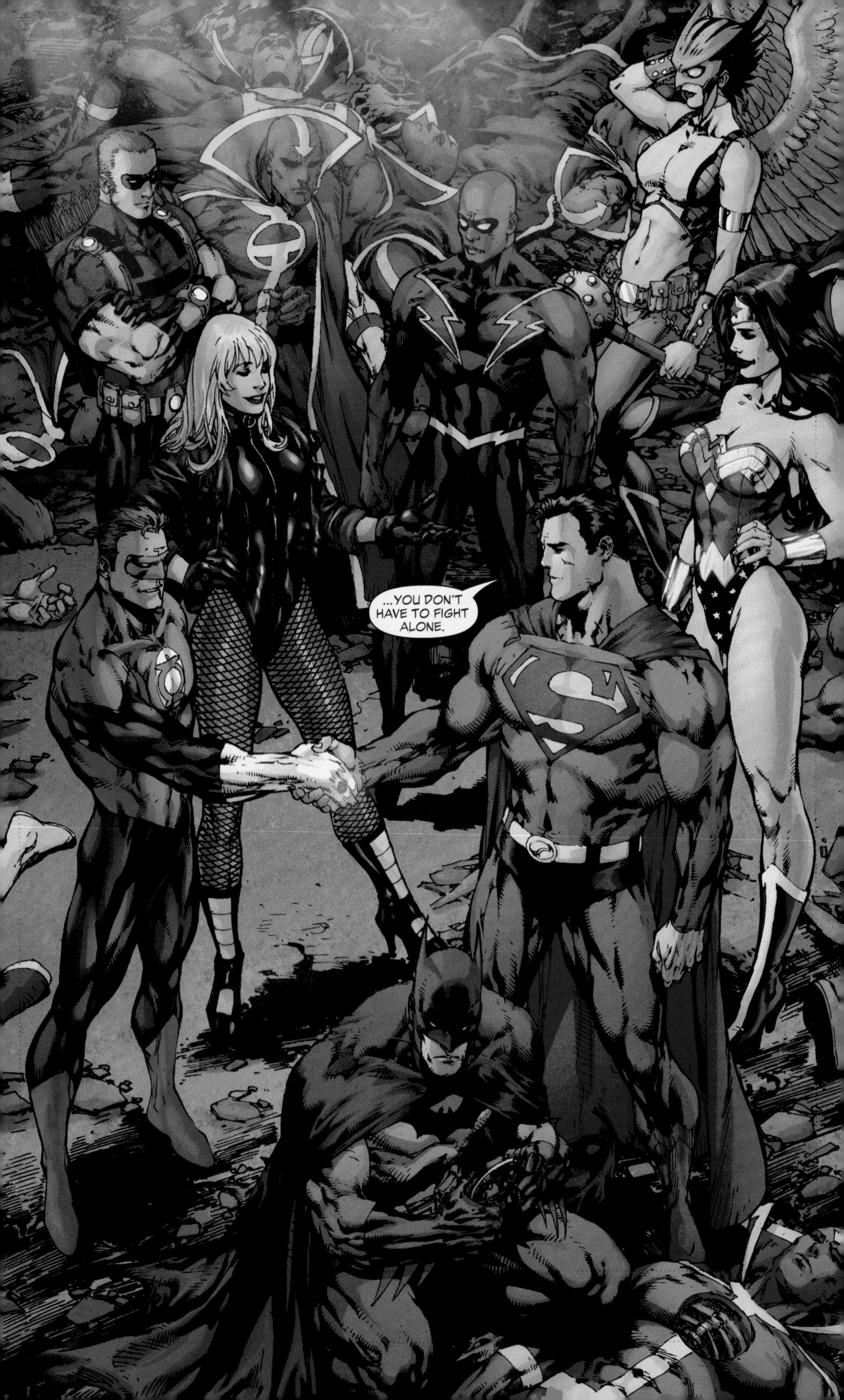
...YOU DON'T HAVE TO FIGHT ALONE.

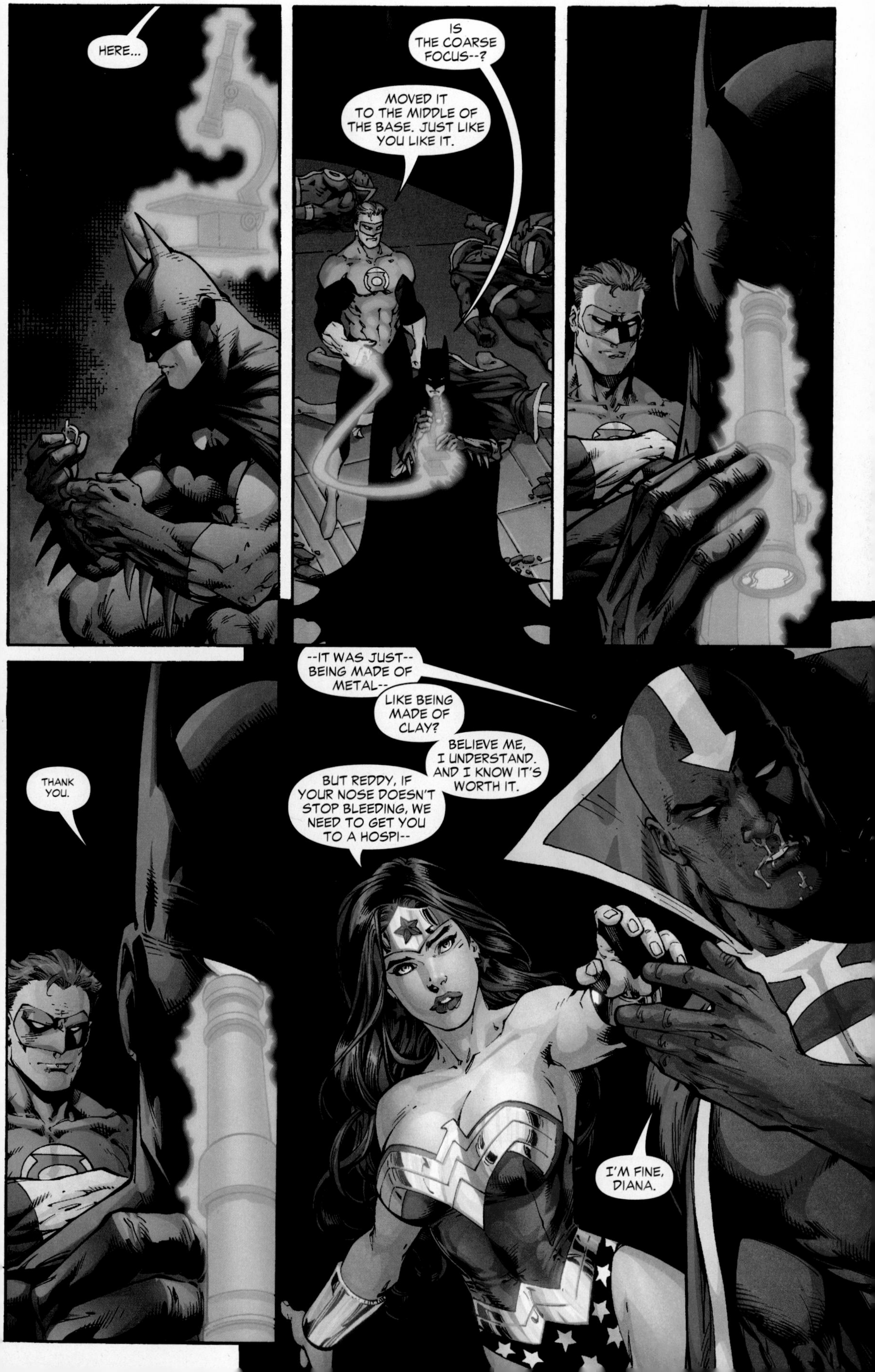
HERE...
IS THE COARSE FOCUS--?
MOVED IT TO THE MIDDLE OF THE BASE. JUST LIKE YOU LIKE IT.
THANK YOU.
--IT WAS JUST-- BEING MADE OF METAL--
LIKE BEING MADE OF CLAY?
BELIEVE ME, I UNDERSTAND. AND I KNOW IT'S WORTH IT.
BUT REDDY, IF YOUR NOSE DOESN'T STOP BLEEDING, WE NEED TO GET YOU TO A HOSPI--
I'M FINE, DIANA.

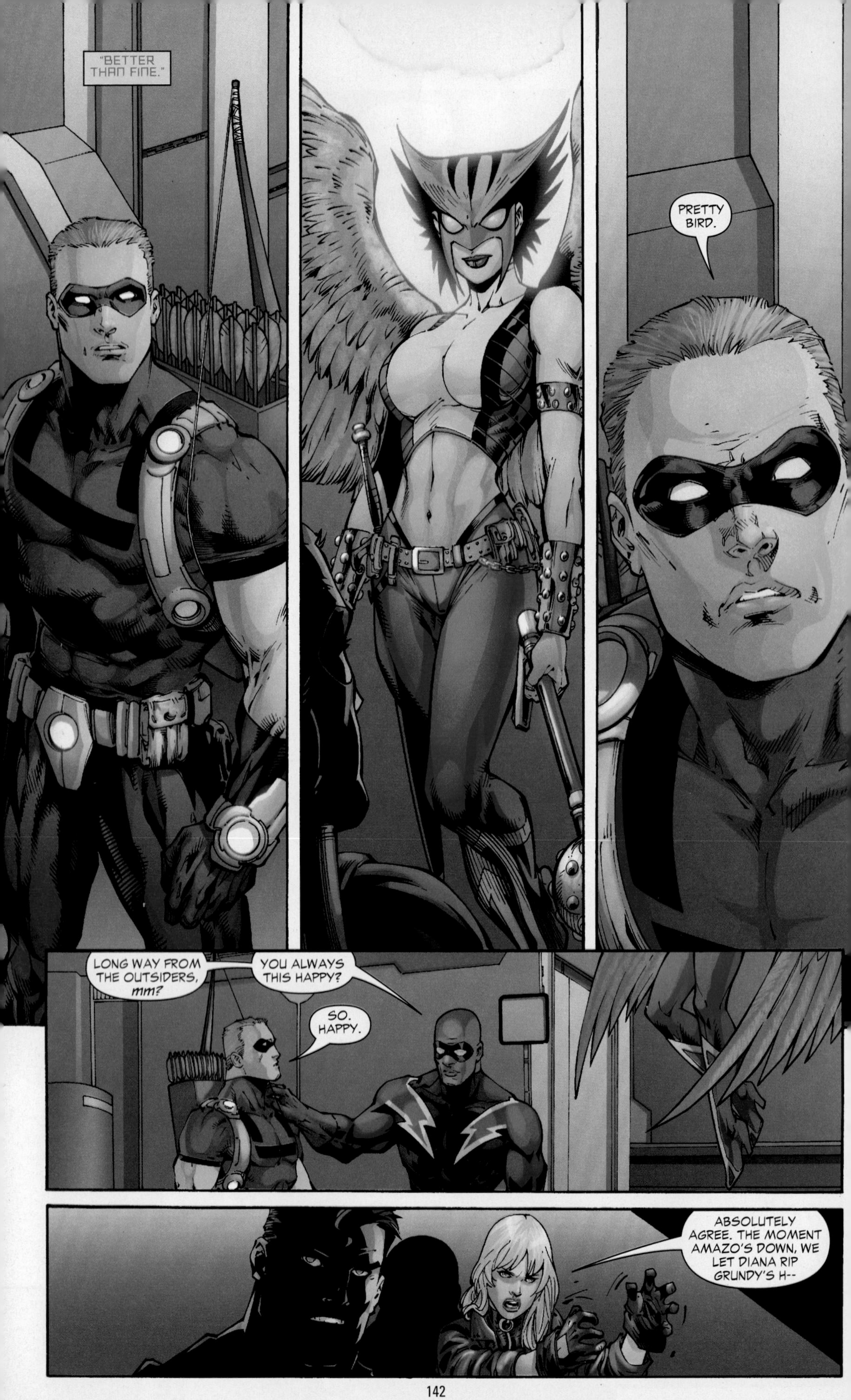
"BETTER THAN FINE."
PRETTY BIRD.
LONG WAY FROM THE OUTSIDERS, *mm?*
YOU ALWAYS THIS HAPPY?
SO. HAPPY.
ABSOLUTELY AGREE. THE MOMENT AMAZO'S DOWN, WE LET DIANA RIP GRUNDY'S H--

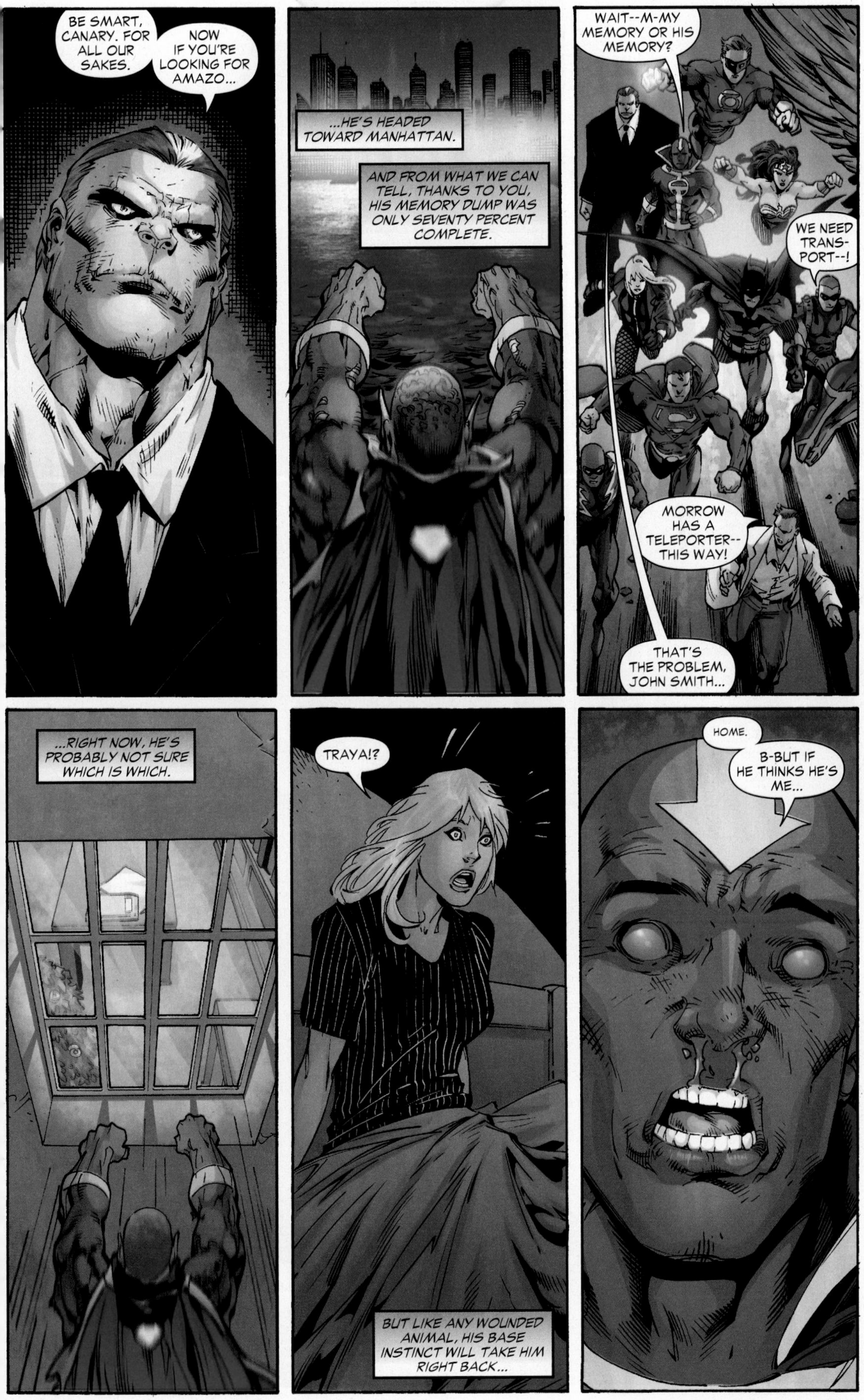

BE SMART, CANARY. FOR ALL OUR SAKES.
NOW IF YOU'RE LOOKING FOR AMAZO...
...HE'S HEADED TOWARD MANHATTAN.
AND FROM WHAT WE CAN TELL, THANKS TO YOU, HIS MEMORY DUMP WAS ONLY SEVENTY PERCENT COMPLETE.
WAIT--M-MY MEMORY OR HIS MEMORY?
WE NEED TRANS-PORT--!
MORROW HAS A TELEPORTER-- THIS WAY!
THAT'S THE PROBLEM, JOHN SMITH...
...RIGHT NOW, HE'S PROBABLY NOT SURE WHICH IS WHICH.
TRAYA!?
BUT LIKE ANY WOUNDED ANIMAL, HIS BASE INSTINCT WILL TAKE HIM RIGHT BACK...
HOME.
B-BUT IF HE THINKS HE'S ME...

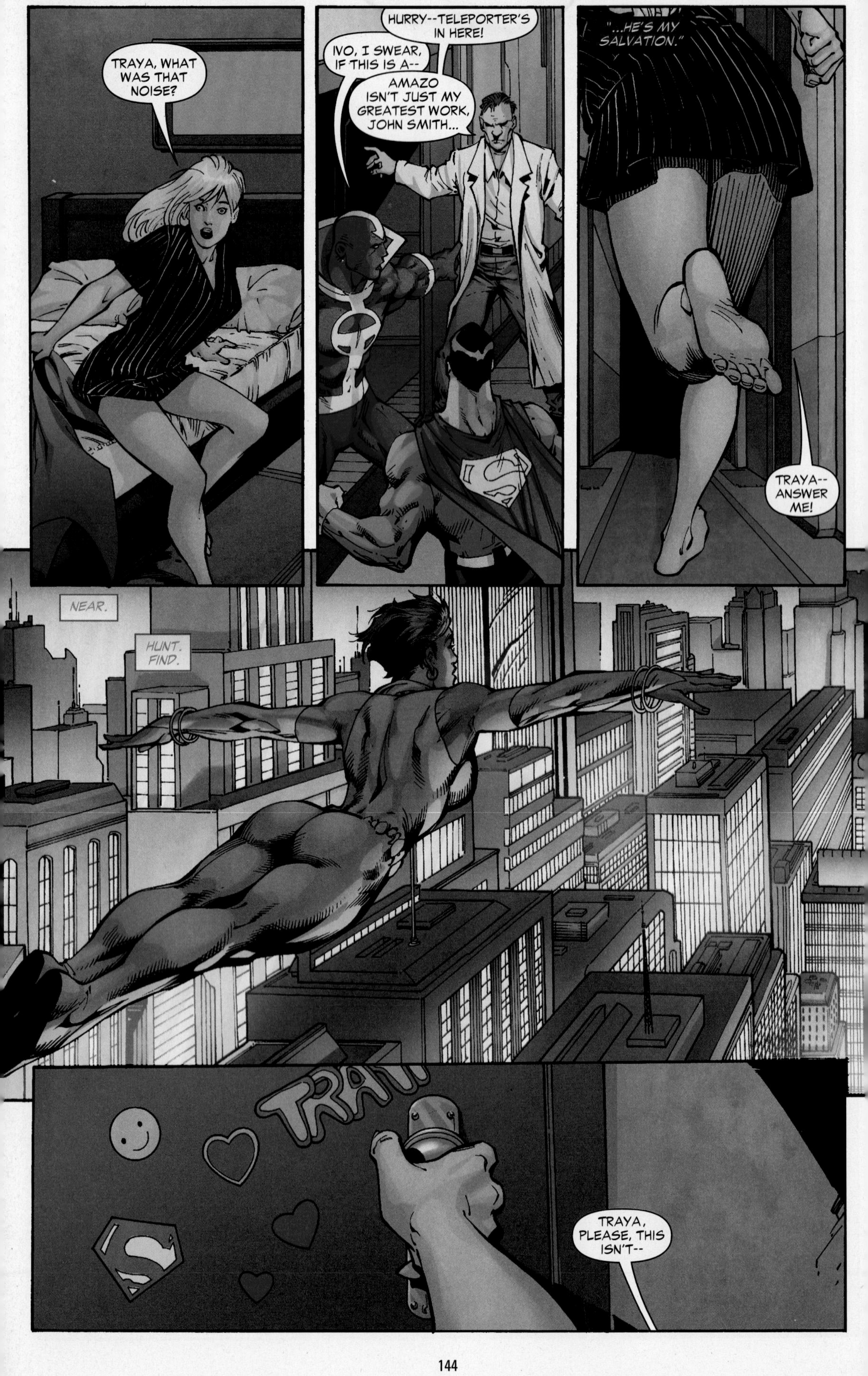

TRAYA, WHAT WAS THAT NOISE?
HURRY--TELEPORTER'S IN HERE!
IVO, I SWEAR, IF THIS IS A--
AMAZO ISN'T JUST MY GREATEST WORK, JOHN SMITH...
"...HE'S MY SALVATION."
TRAYA--ANSWER ME!
NEAR.
HUNT. FIND.
TRA
TRAYA, PLEASE, THIS ISN'T--

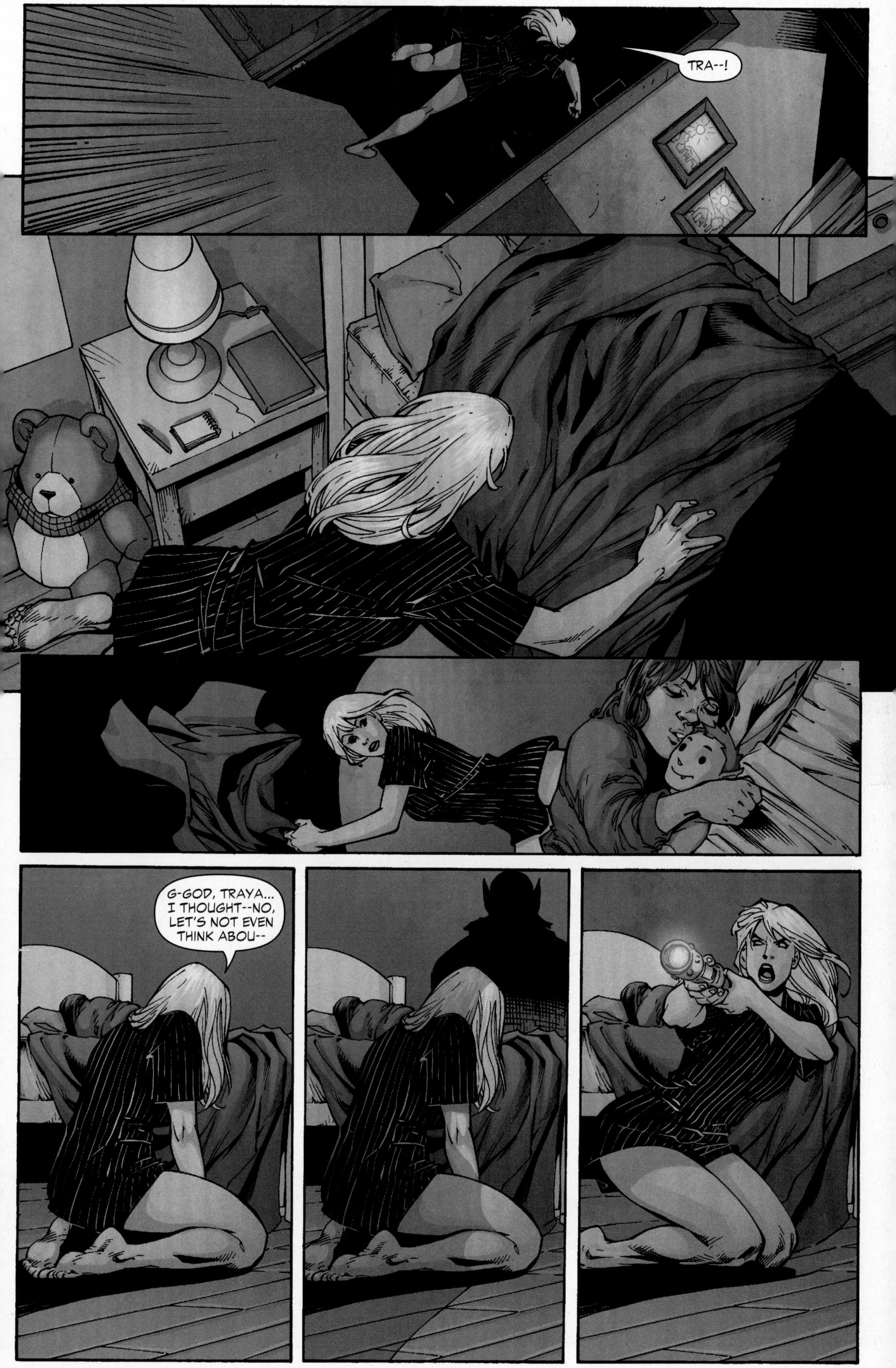
TRA--!
G-GOD, TRAYA... I THOUGHT--NO, LET'S NOT EVEN THINK ABOU--

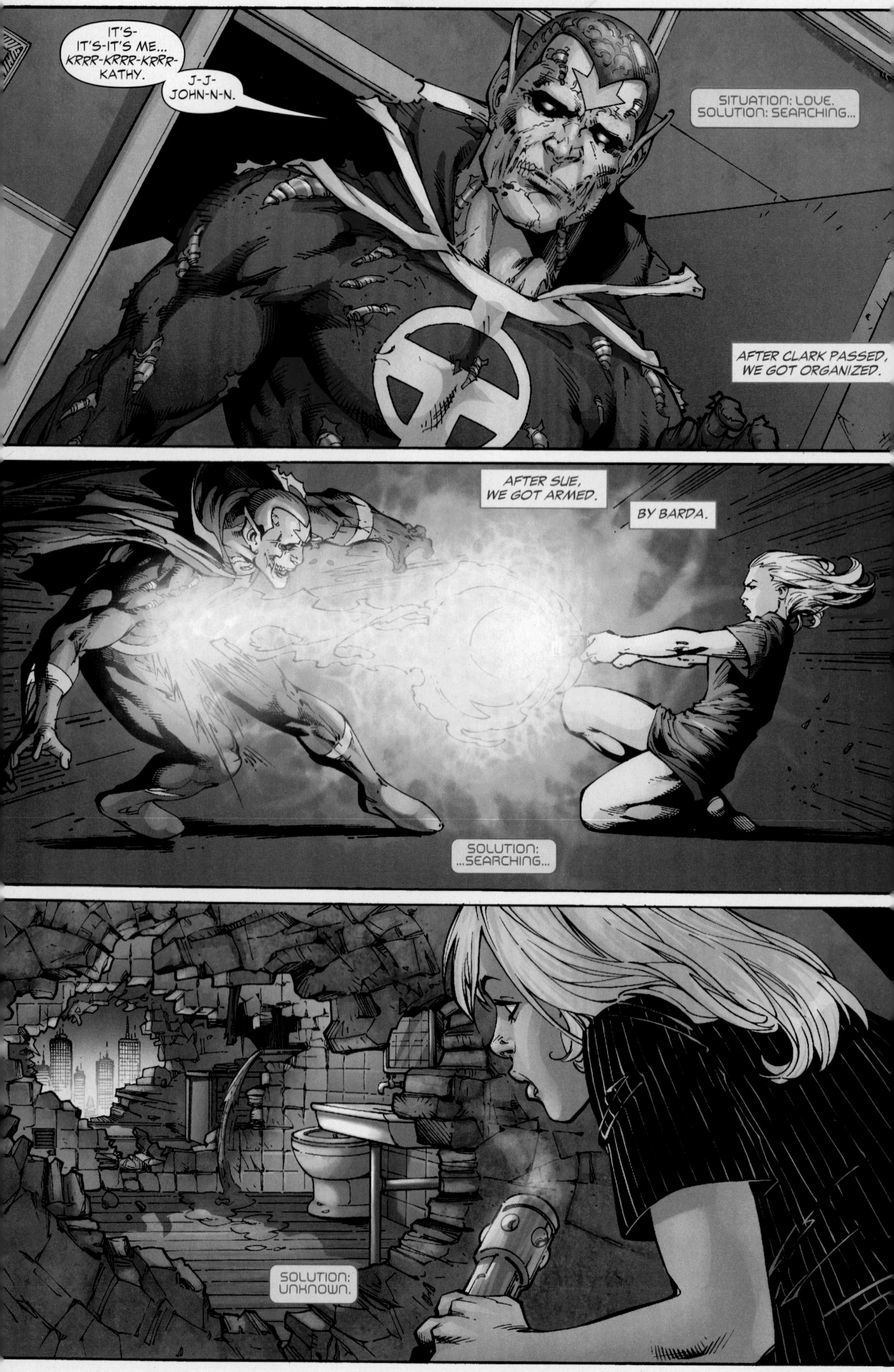
IT'S- IT'S-IT'S ME... KRRR-KRRR-KRRR-KATHY.
J-J- JOHN-N-N.
SITUATION: LOVE. SOLUTION: SEARCHING...
AFTER CLARK PASSED, WE GOT ORGANIZED.
AFTER SUE, WE GOT ARMED.
BY BARDA.
SOLUTION: ...SEARCHING...
SOLUTION: UNKNOWN.

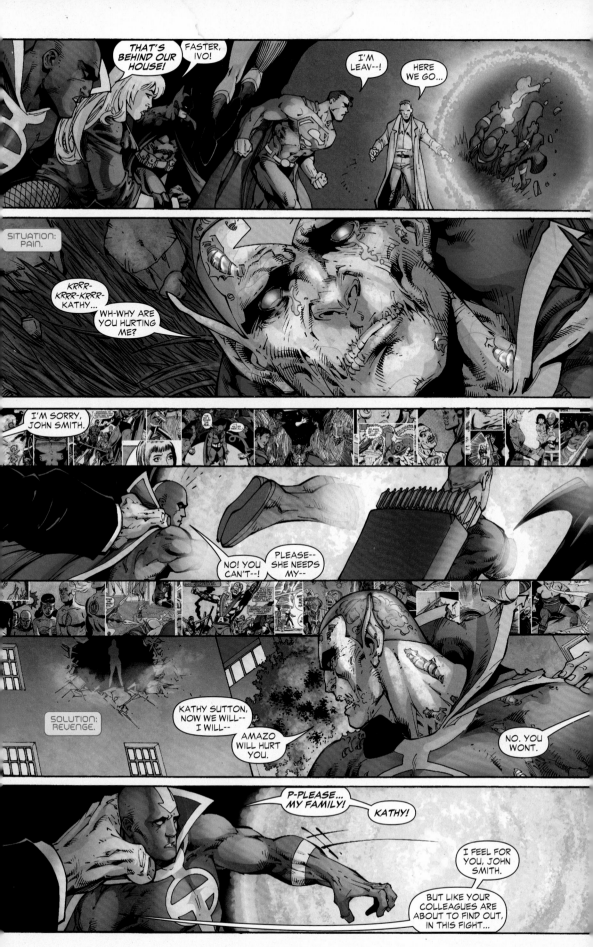

THAT'S BEHIND OUR HOUSE!

FASTER, IVO!

I'M LEAV--!

HERE WE GO...

SITUATION: PAIN.

KRRR-KRRR-KRRR-KATHY... WH-WHY ARE YOU HURTING ME?

I'M SORRY, JOHN SMITH.

NO! YOU CAN'T--!

PLEASE-- SHE NEEDS MY--

SOLUTION: REVENGE.

KATHY SUTTON, NOW WE WILL-- I WILL-- AMAZO WILL HURT YOU.

NO. YOU WONT.

P-PLEASE... MY FAMILY!

KATHY!

I FEEL FOR YOU, JOHN SMITH.

BUT LIKE YOUR COLLEAGUES ARE ABOUT TO FIND OUT, IN THIS FIGHT...

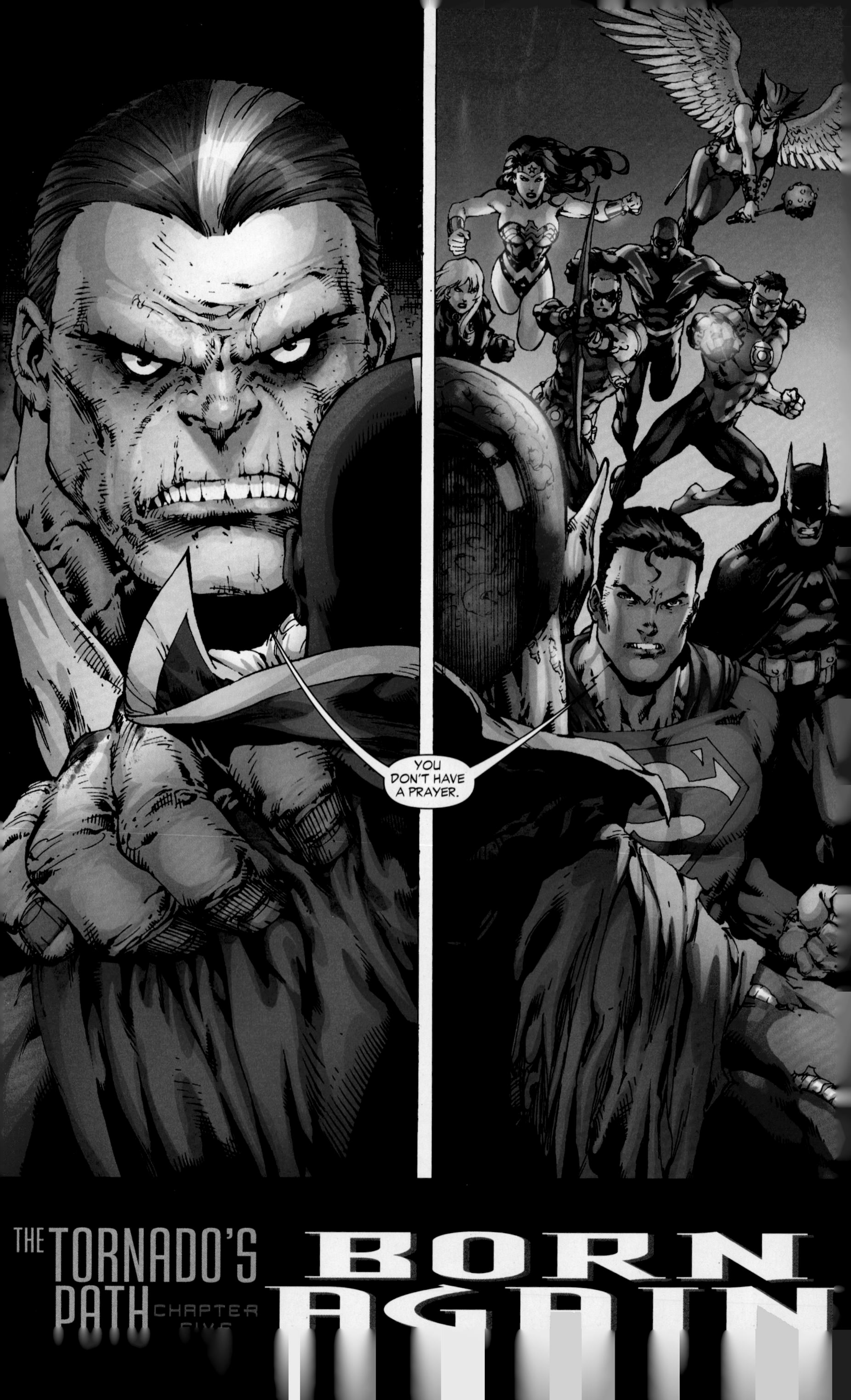
YOU DON'T HAVE A PRAYER.
THE TORNADO'S PATH
CHAPTER
BORN AGAIN

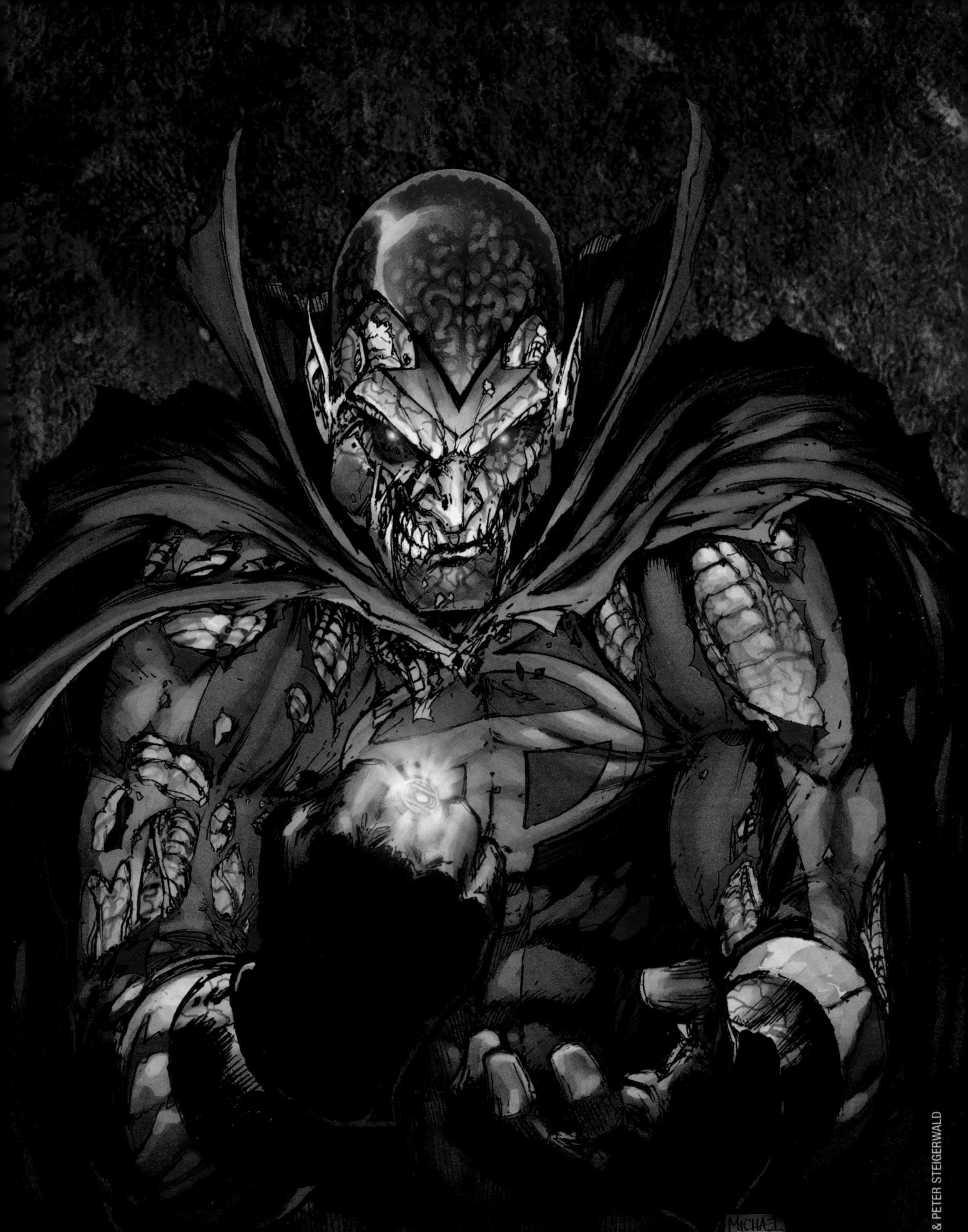
MICHAEL TURNER

MICHAEL TURNER & PETER STEIGERWALD

JUSTICE LEAGUE OF AMERICA
CHAPTER SIX

"You're back, sweetie.
Back where you belong."

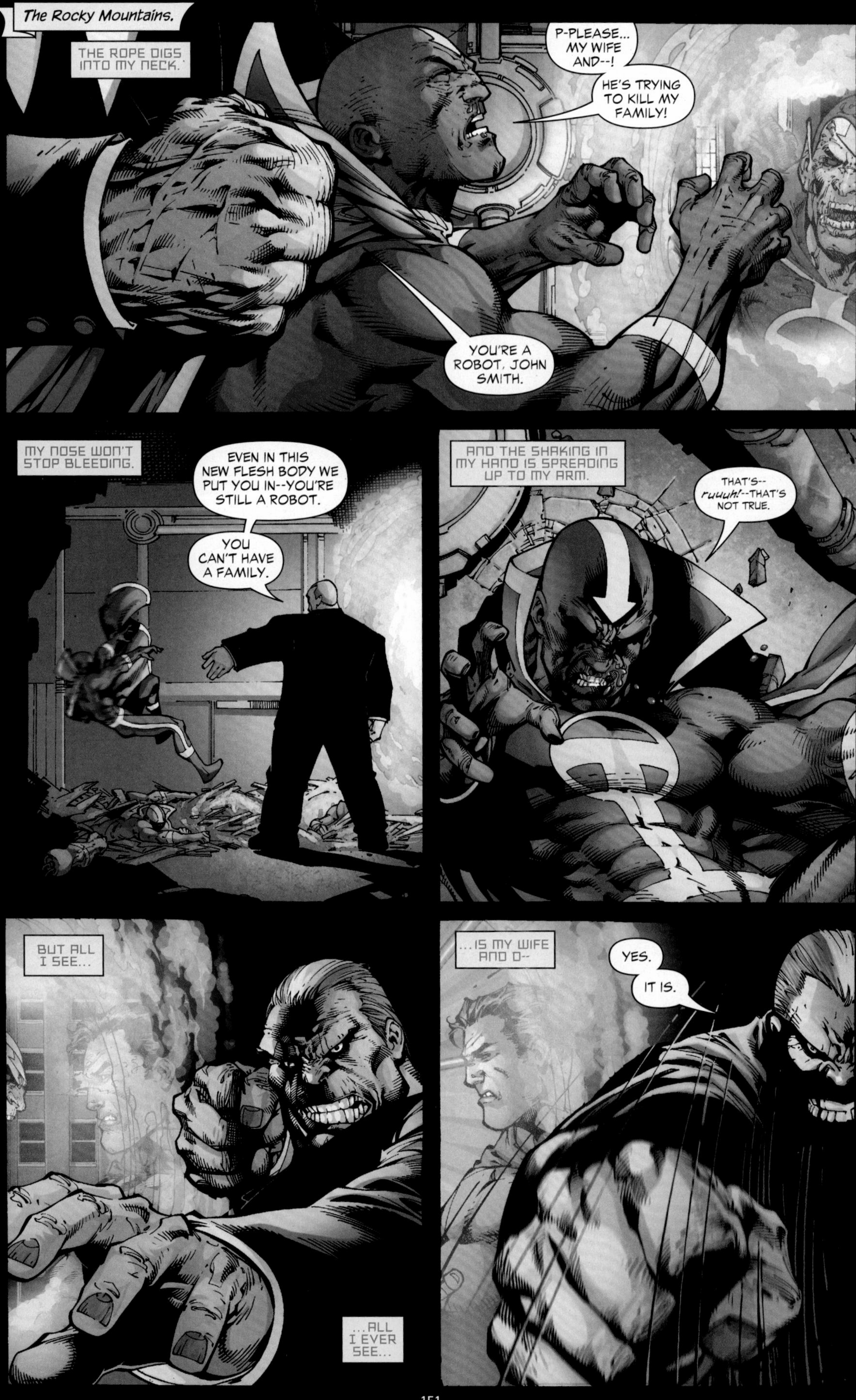
The Rocky Mountains.
THE ROPE DIGS INTO MY NECK.
P-PLEASE... MY WIFE AND--!
HE'S TRYING TO KILL MY FAMILY!
YOU'RE A ROBOT, JOHN SMITH.
MY NOSE WON'T STOP BLEEDING.
EVEN IN THIS NEW FLESH BODY WE PUT YOU IN--YOU'RE STILL A ROBOT.
YOU CAN'T HAVE A FAMILY.
AND THE SHAKING IN MY HAND IS SPREADING UP TO MY ARM.
THAT'S--*ruuuh!*--THAT'S NOT TRUE.
BUT ALL I SEE...
...ALL I EVER SEE...
...IS MY WIFE AND D--
YES.
IT IS.

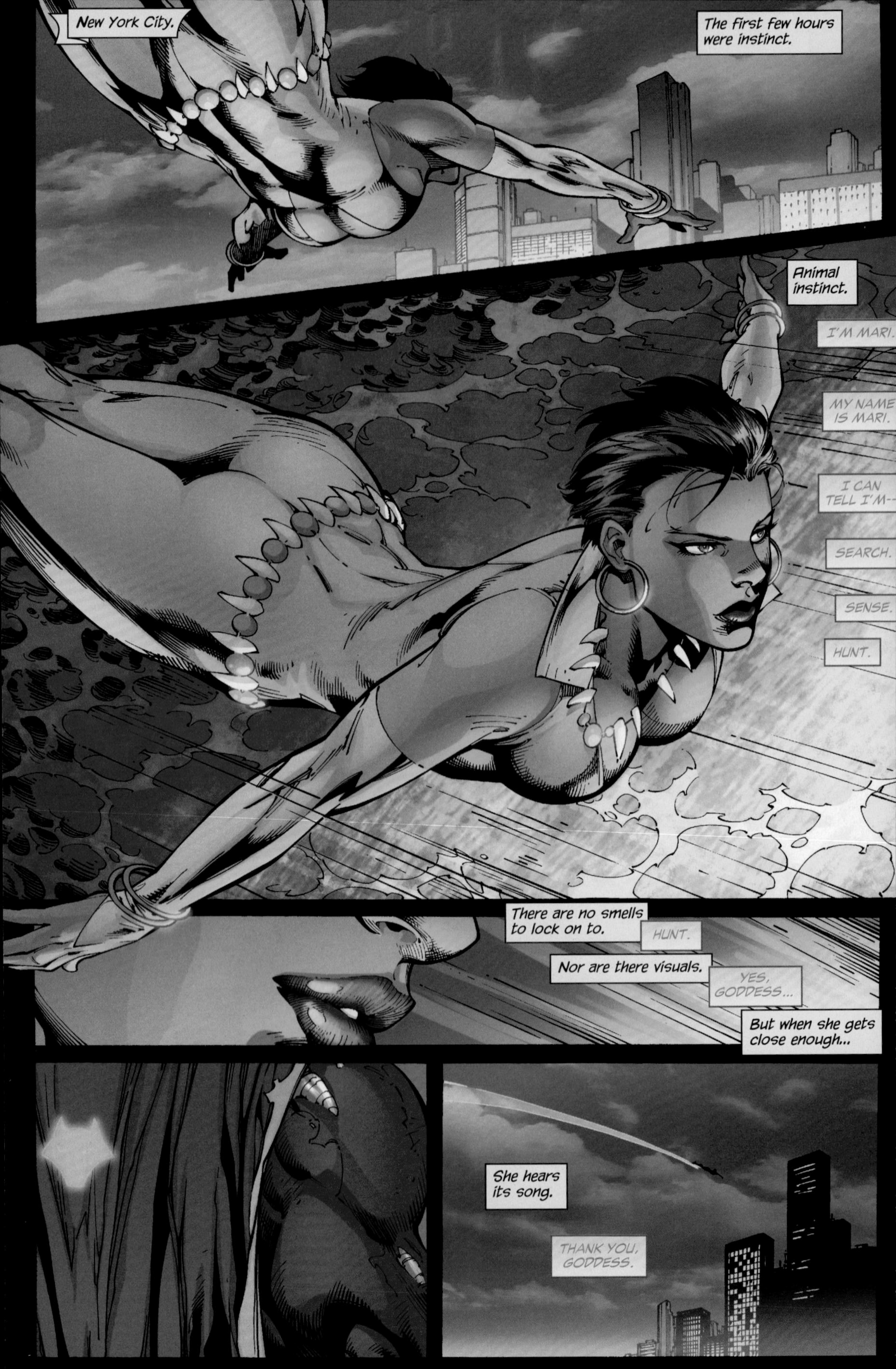
New York City.
The first few hours were instinct.
Animal instinct.
I'M MARI.
MY NAME IS MARI.
I CAN TELL I'M--
SEARCH.
SENSE.
HUNT.
There are no smells to lock on to.
HUNT.
Nor are there visuals.
YES, GODDESS...
But when she gets close enough...
She hears its song.
THANK YOU, GODDESS.

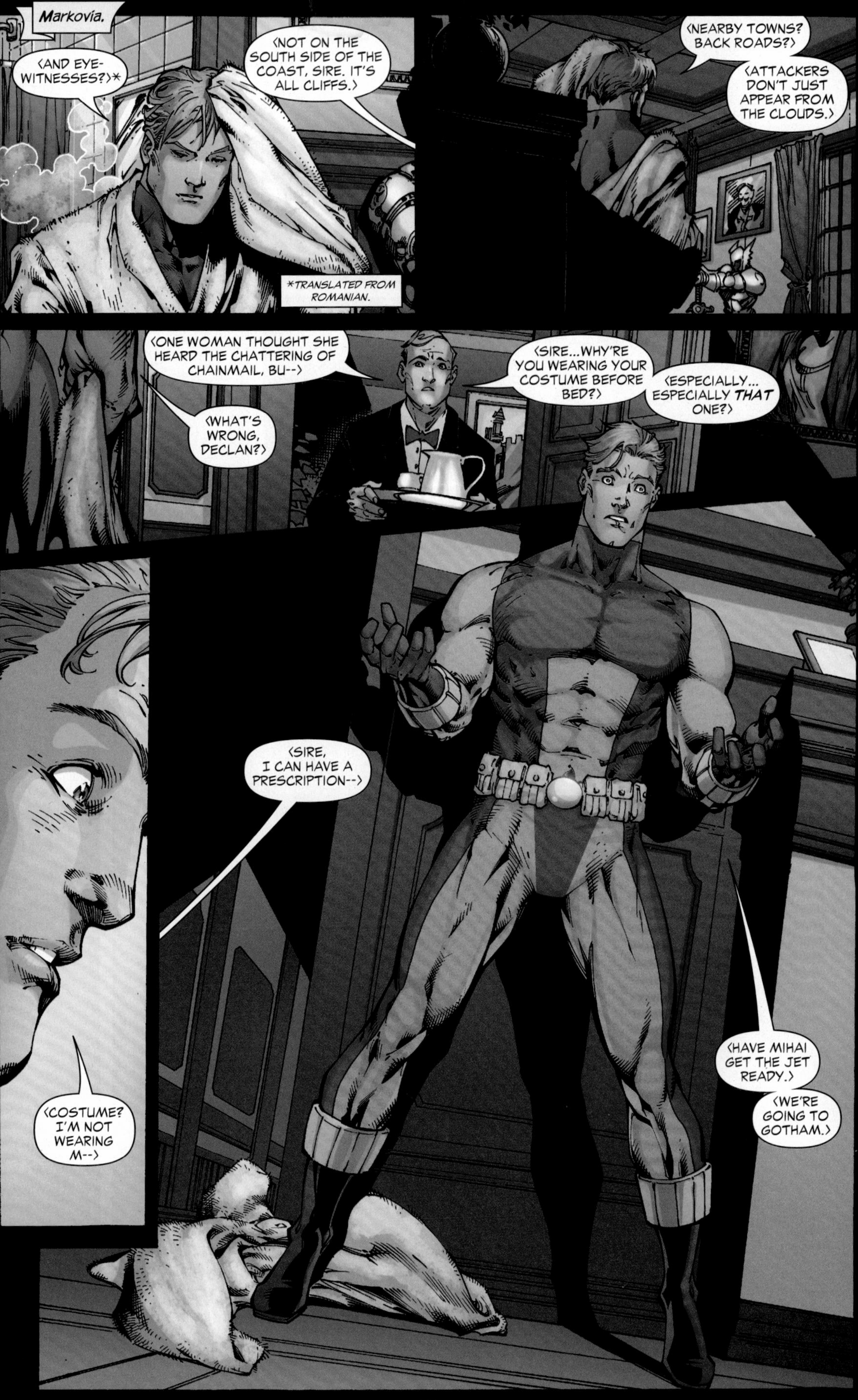
Markovia.
<AND EYE-WITNESSES?>*
<NOT ON THE SOUTH SIDE OF THE COAST, SIRE. IT'S ALL CLIFFS.>
*TRANSLATED FROM ROMANIAN.
<NEARBY TOWNS? BACK ROADS?>
<ATTACKERS DON'T JUST APPEAR FROM THE CLOUDS.>
<ONE WOMAN THOUGHT SHE HEARD THE CHATTERING OF CHAINMAIL, BU-->
<WHAT'S WRONG, DECLAN?>
<SIRE...WHY'RE YOU WEARING YOUR COSTUME BEFORE BED?>
<ESPECIALLY... ESPECIALLY THAT ONE?>
<SIRE, I CAN HAVE A PRESCRIPTION-->
<COSTUME? I'M NOT WEARING M-->
<HAVE MIHAI GET THE JET READY.>
<WE'RE GOING TO GOTHAM.>

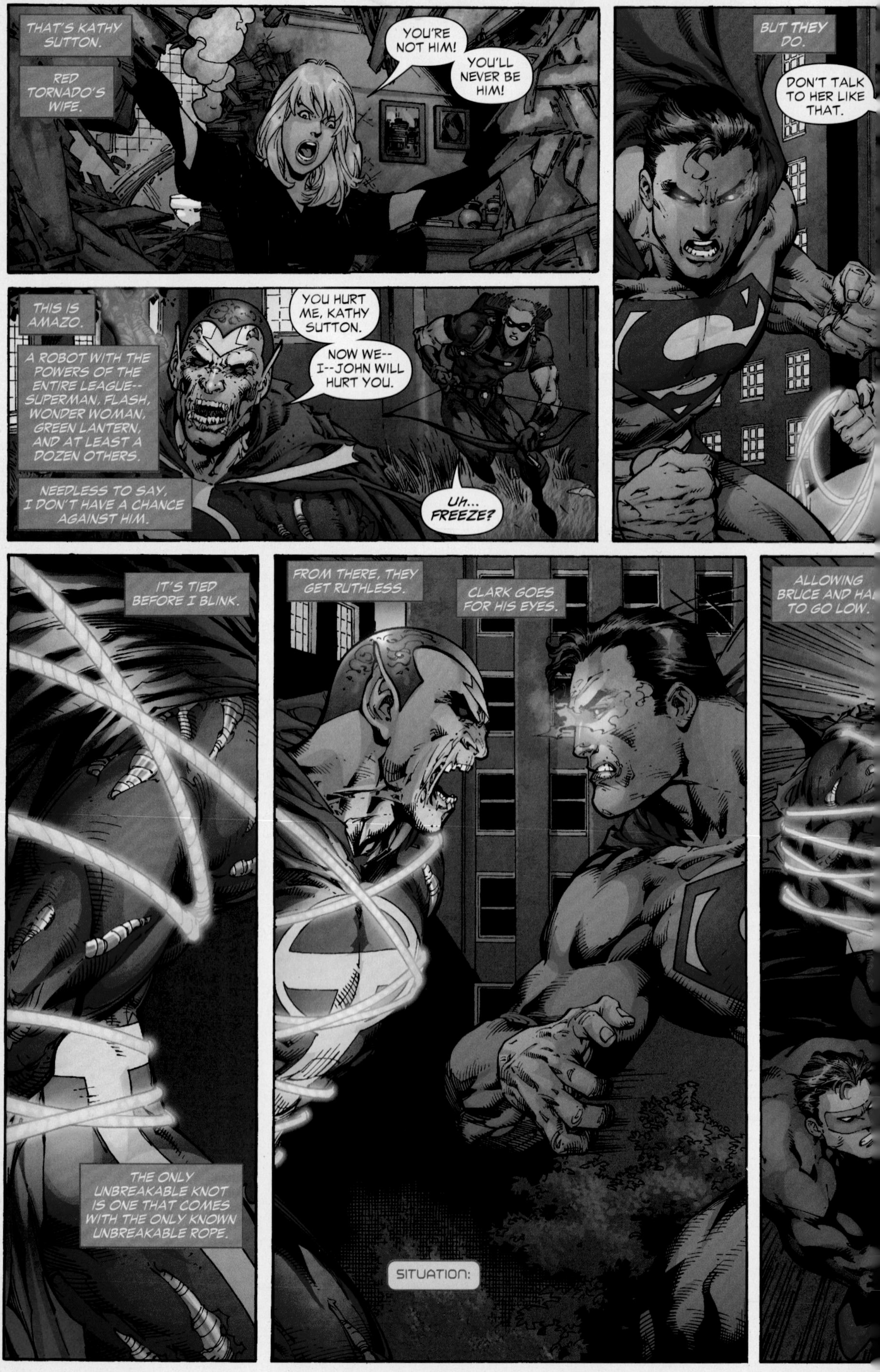
THAT'S KATHY SUTTON.
RED TORNADO'S WIFE.
YOU'RE NOT HIM!
YOU'LL NEVER BE HIM!
BUT THEY DO.
DON'T TALK TO HER LIKE THAT.
THIS IS AMAZO.
A ROBOT WITH THE POWERS OF THE ENTIRE LEAGUE-- SUPERMAN, FLASH, WONDER WOMAN, GREEN LANTERN, AND AT LEAST A DOZEN OTHERS.
YOU HURT ME, KATHY SUTTON.
NOW WE-- I--JOHN WILL HURT YOU.
NEEDLESS TO SAY, I DON'T HAVE A CHANCE AGAINST HIM.
Uh... FREEZE?
IT'S TIED BEFORE I BLINK.
THE ONLY UNBREAKABLE KNOT IS ONE THAT COMES WITH THE ONLY KNOWN UNBREAKABLE ROPE.
FROM THERE, THEY GET RUTHLESS.
CLARK GOES FOR HIS EYES.
SITUATION:
ALLOWING BRUCE AND HA
TO GO LOW.

SITU

WHY WOULD MY FRIENDS HURT M--

GOD, I FORGET HOW FAST SHE IS.

BUT THAT'S THE BENEFIT OF HAVING HERMES ON YOUR SIDE.

SITUA

--E?

YOU WANNA TAKE OUT THE FLASH?

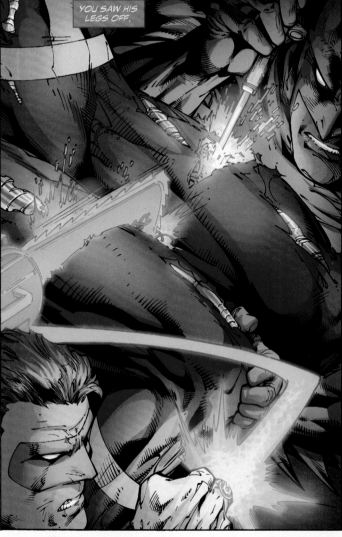

YOU SAW HIS LEGS OFF.

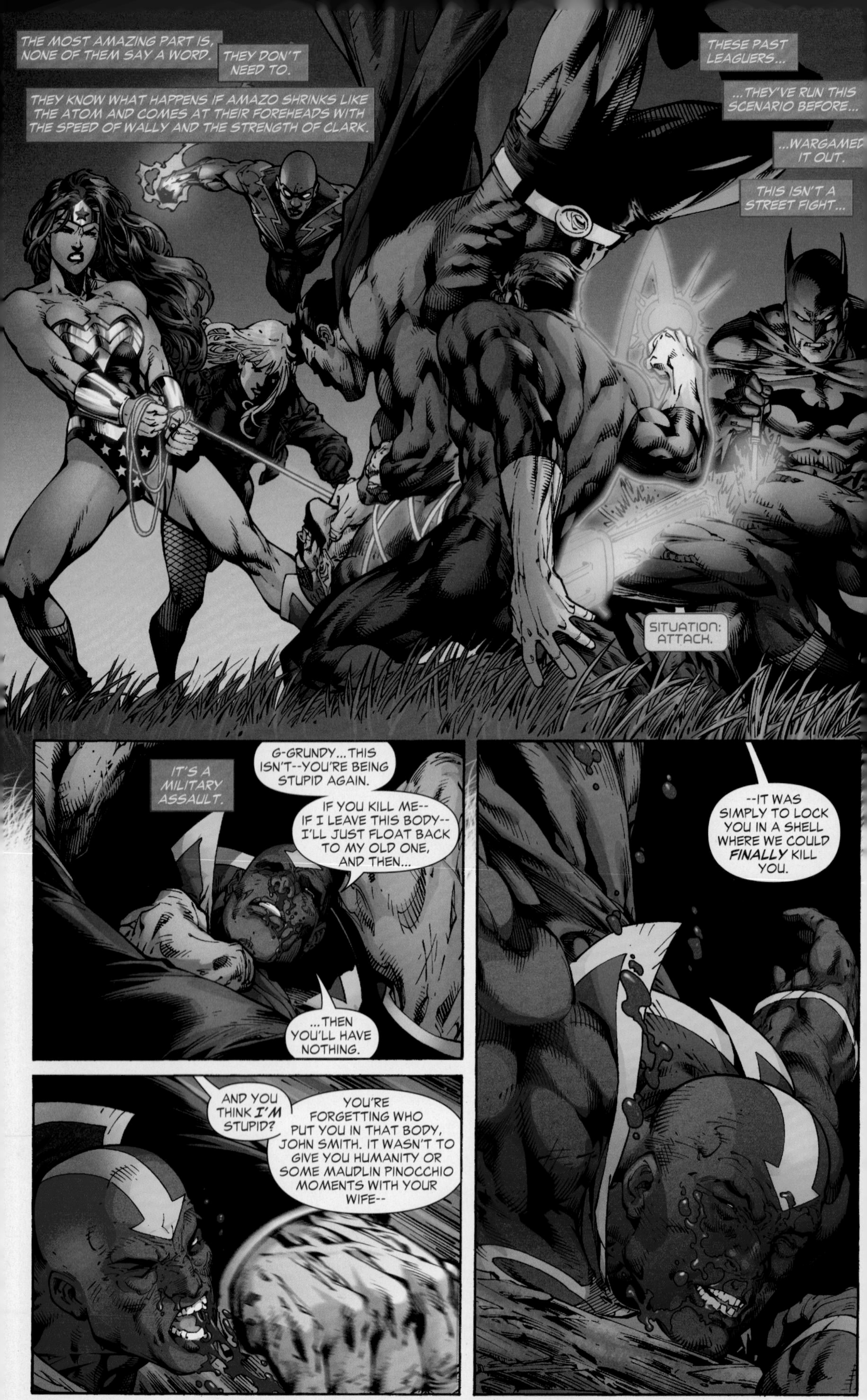
THE MOST AMAZING PART IS, NONE OF THEM SAY A WORD.
THEY DON'T NEED TO.
THEY KNOW WHAT HAPPENS IF AMAZO SHRINKS LIKE THE ATOM AND COMES AT THEIR FOREHEADS WITH THE SPEED OF WALLY AND THE STRENGTH OF CLARK.
THESE PAST LEAGUERS...
...THEY'VE RUN THIS SCENARIO BEFORE...
...WARGAMED IT OUT.
THIS ISN'T A STREET FIGHT...
SITUATION: ATTACH.
IT'S A MILITARY ASSAULT.
G-GRUNDY...THIS ISN'T--YOU'RE BEING STUPID AGAIN.
IF YOU KILL ME-- IF I LEAVE THIS BODY-- I'LL JUST FLOAT BACK TO MY OLD ONE, AND THEN...
...THEN YOU'LL HAVE NOTHING.
AND YOU THINK I'M STUPID?
YOU'RE FORGETTING WHO PUT YOU IN THAT BODY, JOHN SMITH. IT WASN'T TO GIVE YOU HUMANITY OR SOME MAUDLIN PINOCCHIO MOMENTS WITH YOUR WIFE--
--IT WAS SIMPLY TO LOCK YOU IN A SHELL WHERE WE COULD FINALLY KILL YOU.

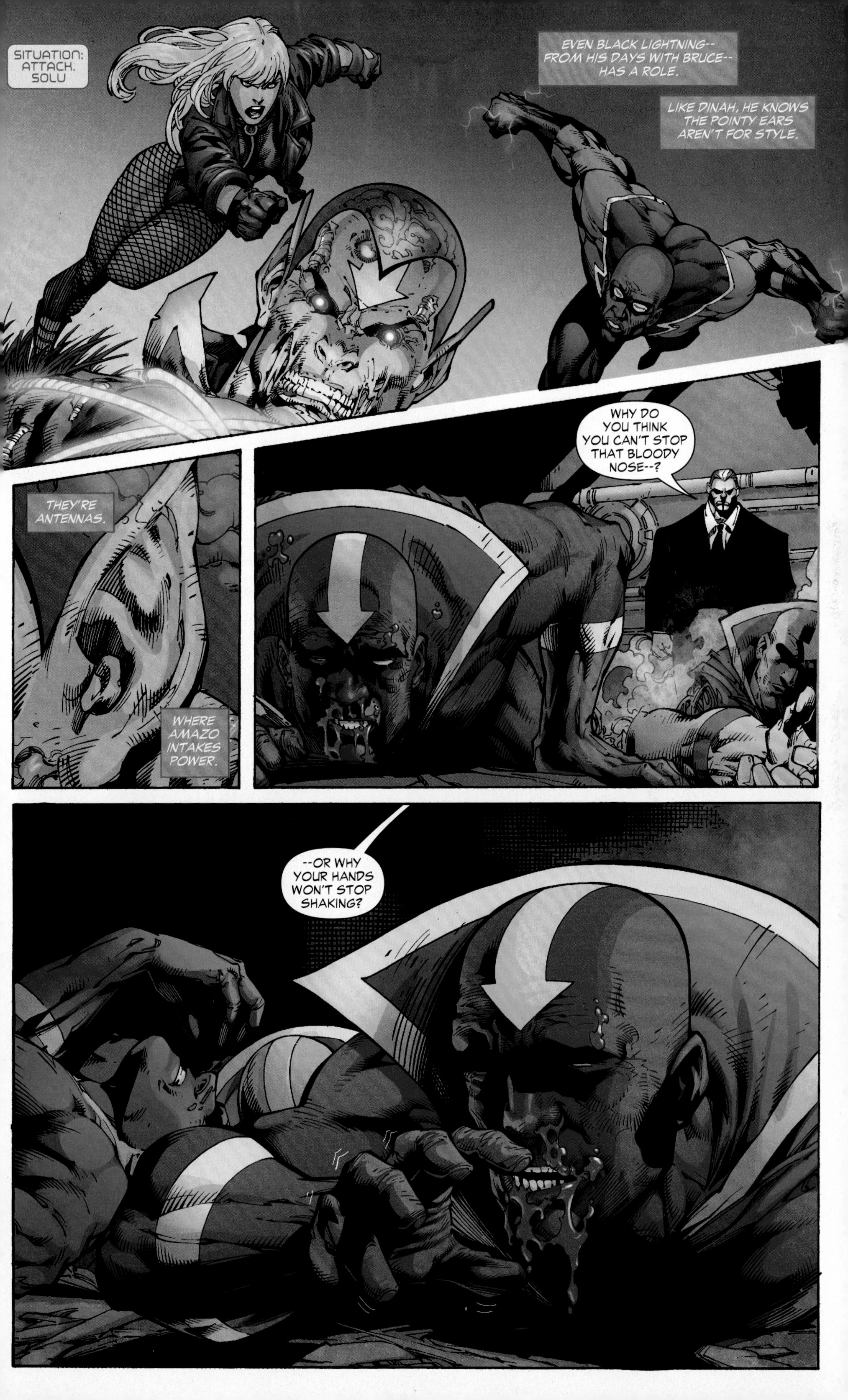
SITUATION: ATTACK. SOLU
EVEN BLACK LIGHTNING-- FROM HIS DAYS WITH BRUCE-- HAS A ROLE.
LIKE DINAH, HE KNOWS THE POINTY EARS AREN'T FOR STYLE.
THEY'RE ANTENNAS.
WHERE AMAZO INTAKES POWER.
WHY DO YOU THINK YOU CAN'T STOP THAT BLOODY NOSE--?
--OR WHY YOUR HANDS WON'T STOP SHAKING?

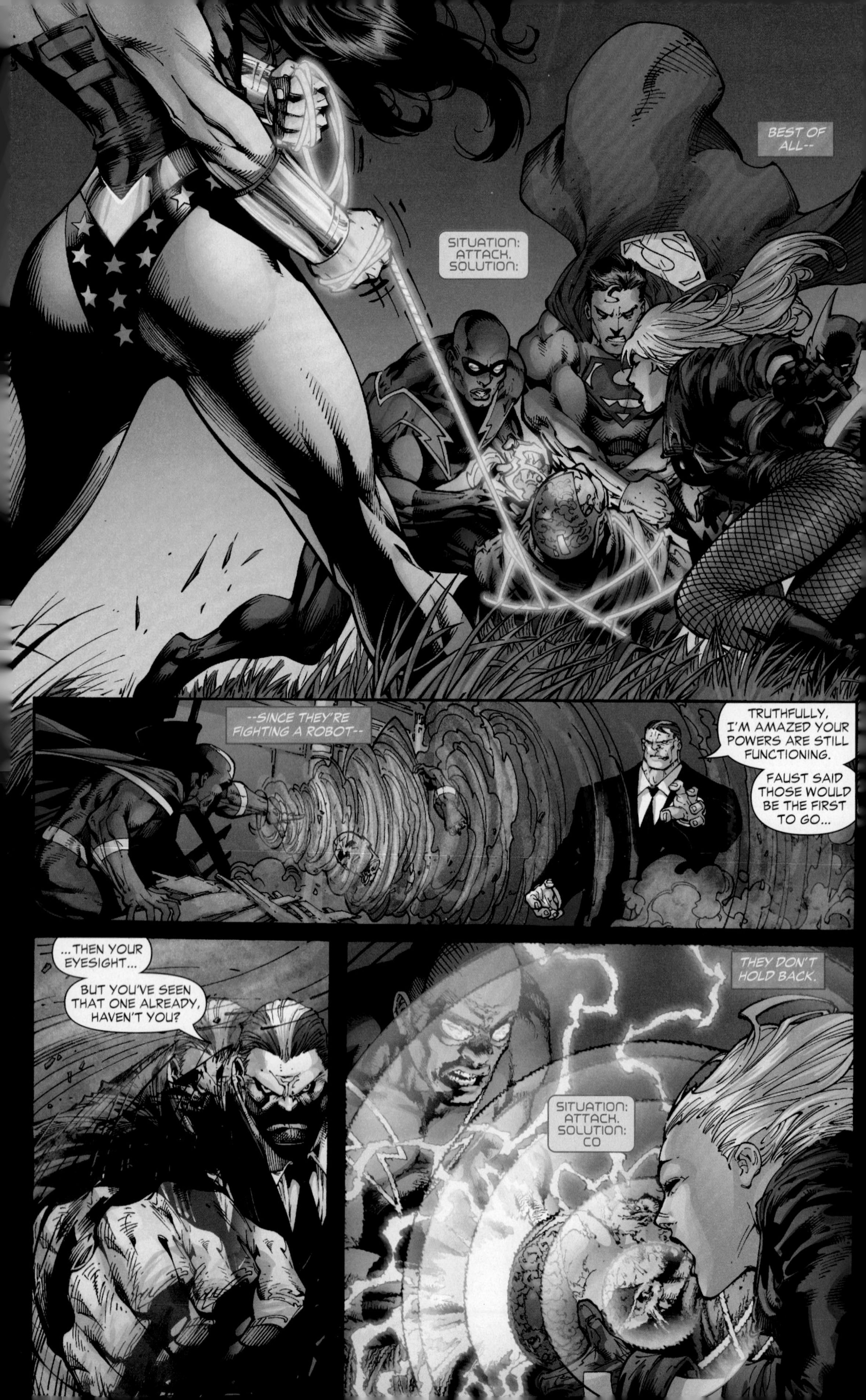
BEST OF ALL--
SITUATION: ATTACK. SOLUTION:
--SINCE THEY'RE FIGHTING A ROBOT--
TRUTHFULLY, I'M AMAZED YOUR POWERS ARE STILL FUNCTIONING.
FAUST SAID THOSE WOULD BE THE FIRST TO GO...
...THEN YOUR EYESIGHT...
BUT YOU'VE SEEN THAT ONE ALREADY, HAVEN'T YOU?
THEY DON'T HOLD BACK.
SITUATION: ATTACK. SOLUTION: CO

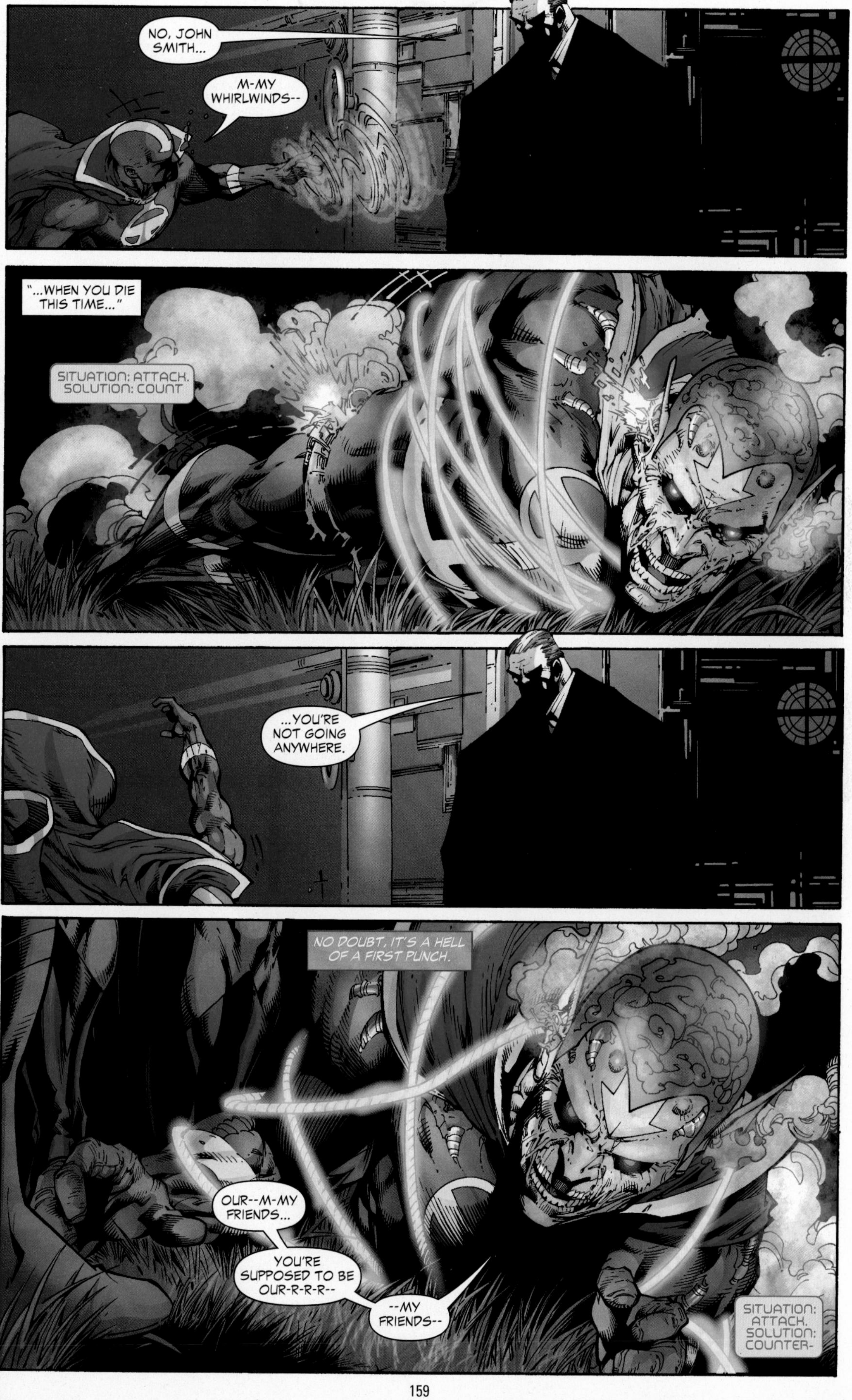

NO, JOHN SMITH...
M-MY WHIRLWINDS--
"...WHEN YOU DIE THIS TIME..."
SITUATION: ATTACK. SOLUTION: COUNT
...YOU'RE NOT GOING ANYWHERE.
NO DOUBT, IT'S A HELL OF A FIRST PUNCH.
OUR--M-MY FRIENDS...
YOU'RE SUPPOSED TO BE OUR-R-R-R--
--MY FRIENDS--
SITUATION: ATTACK. SOLUTION: COUNTER-

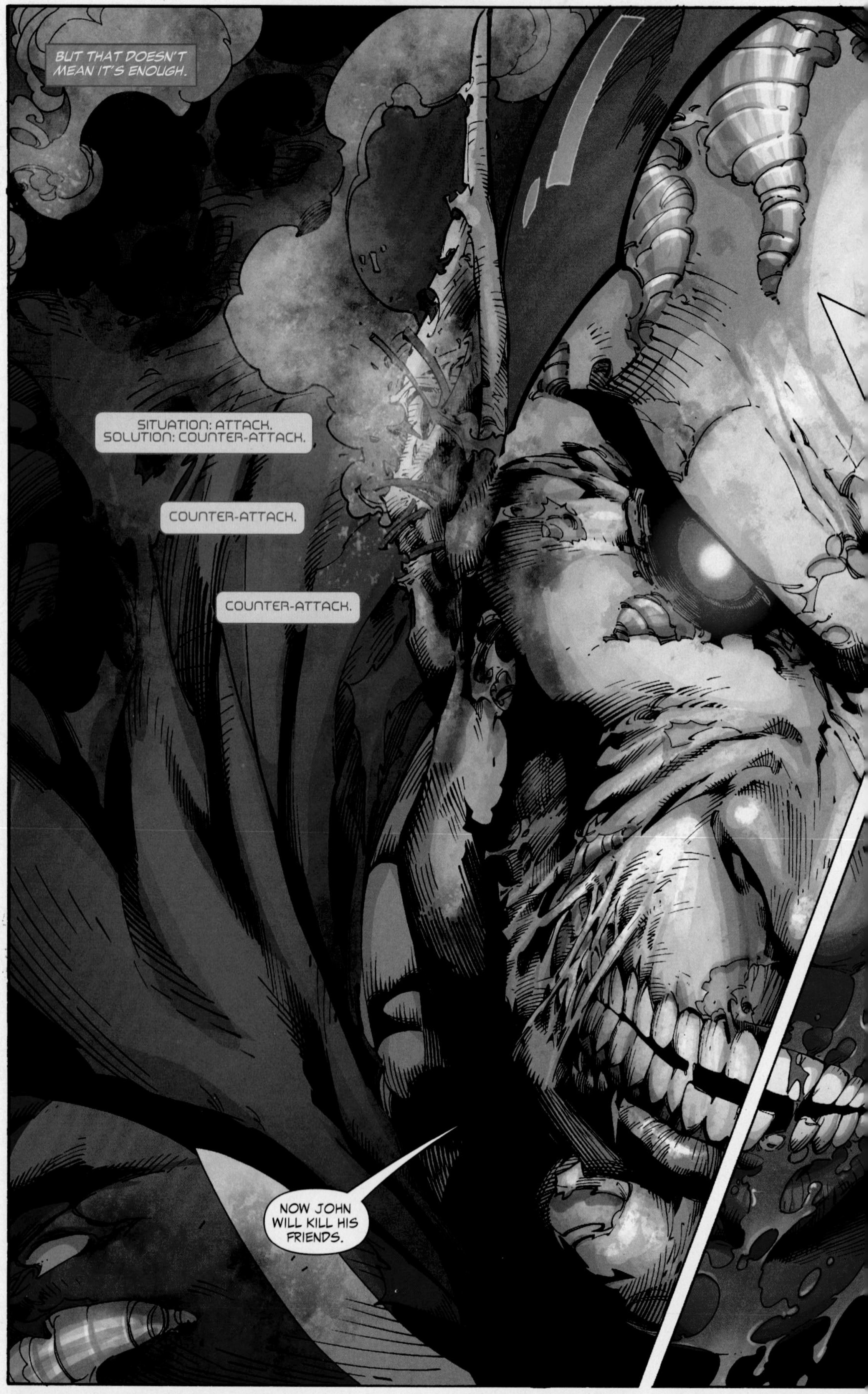
BUT THAT DOESN'T MEAN IT'S ENOUGH.
SITUATION: ATTACK. SOLUTION: COUNTER-ATTACK.
COUNTER-ATTACK.
COUNTER-ATTACK.
NOW JOHN WILL KILL HIS FRIENDS.

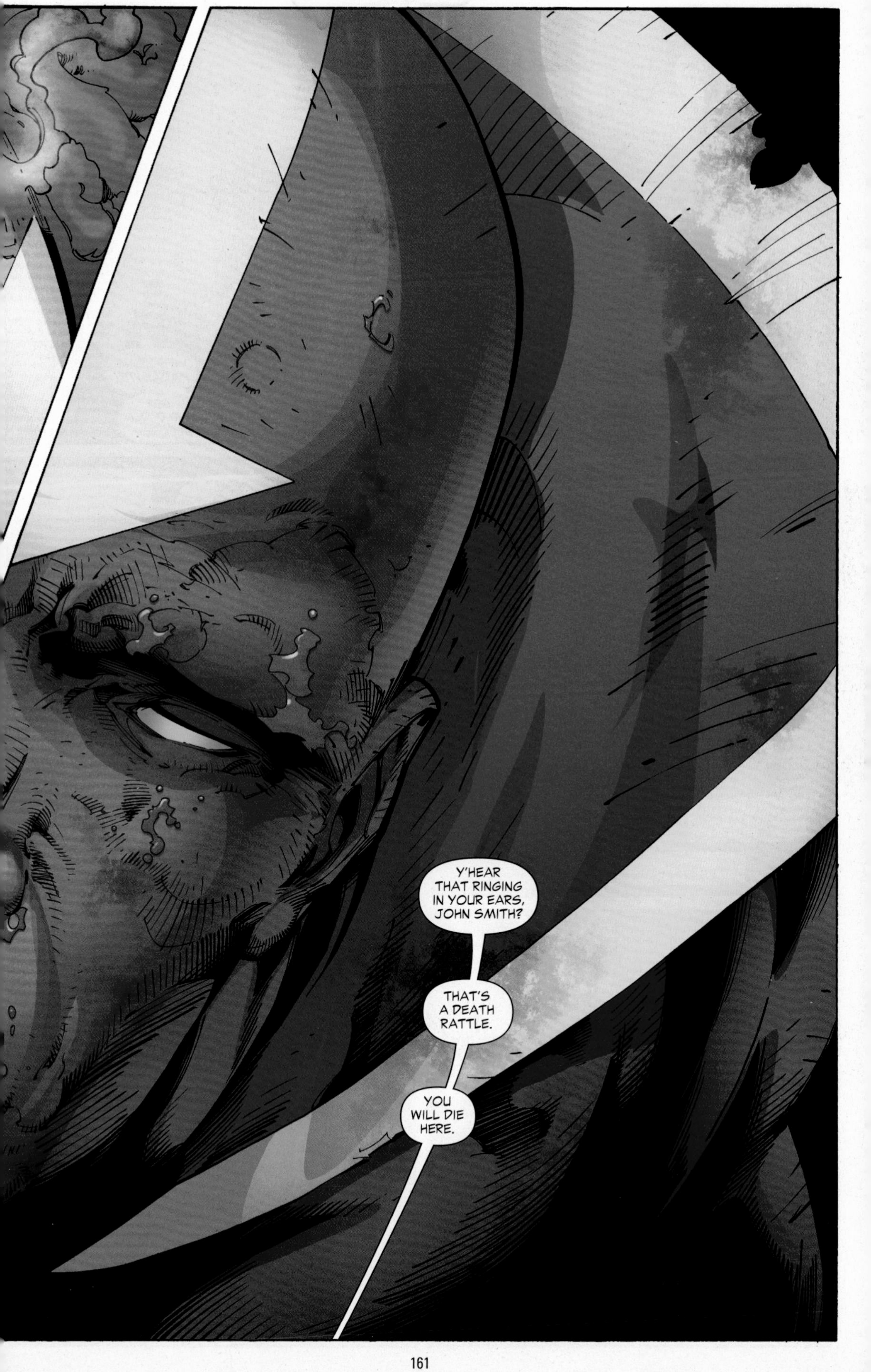
Y'HEAR THAT RINGING IN YOUR EARS, JOHN SMITH?
THAT'S A DEATH RATTLE.
YOU WILL DIE HERE.

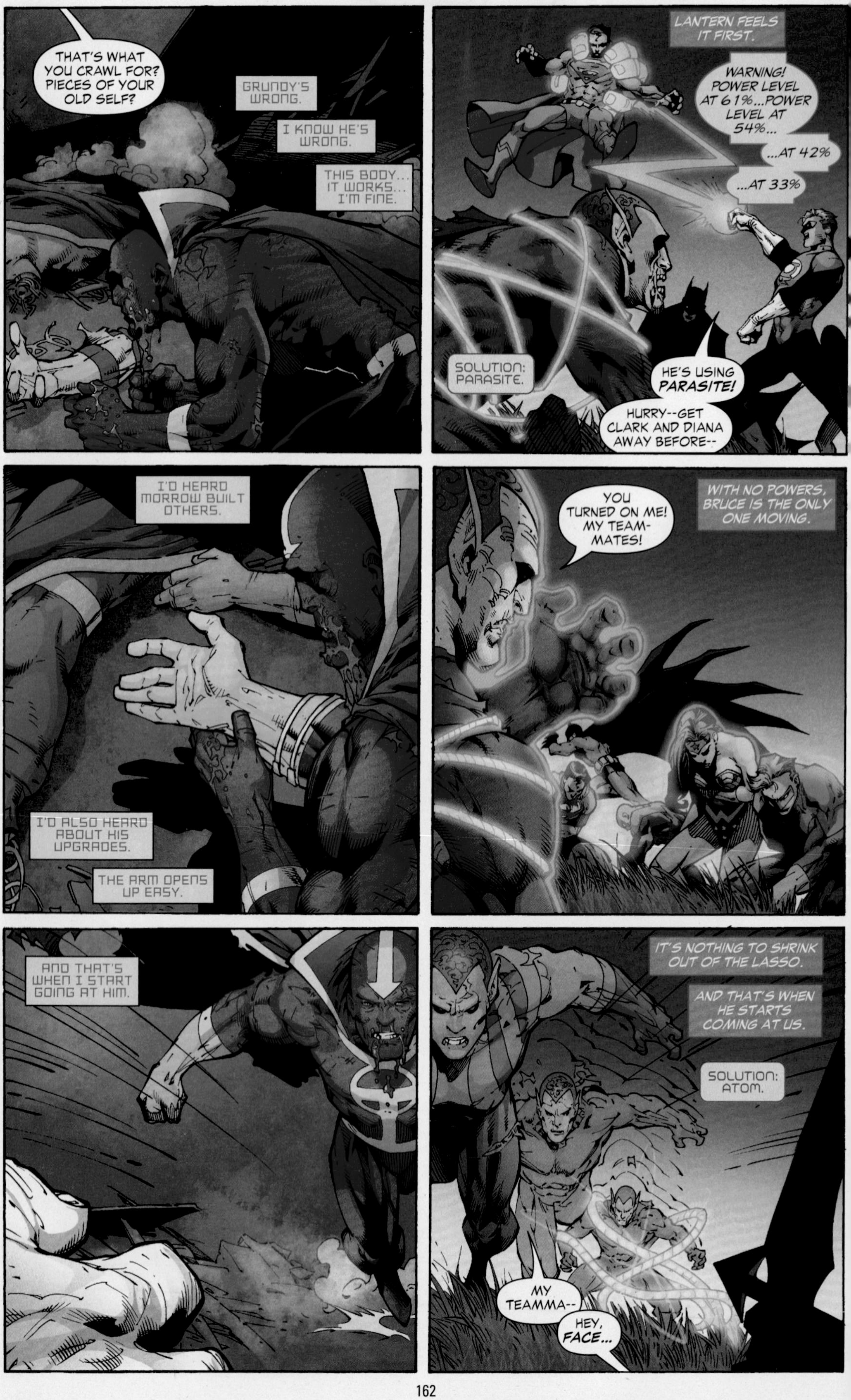
THAT'S WHAT YOU CRAWL FOR? PIECES OF YOUR OLD SELF?
GRUNDY'S WRONG.
I KNOW HE'S WRONG.
THIS BODY... IT WORKS... I'M FINE.
LANTERN FEELS IT FIRST.
WARNING! POWER LEVEL AT 61%...POWER LEVEL AT 54%...
...AT 42%
...AT 33%
SOLUTION: PARASITE.
HE'S USING PARASITE!
HURRY--GET CLARK AND DIANA AWAY BEFORE--
I'D HEARD MORROW BUILT OTHERS.
I'D ALSO HEARD ABOUT HIS UPGRADES.
THE ARM OPENS UP EASY.
YOU TURNED ON ME! MY TEAM-MATES!
WITH NO POWERS, BRUCE IS THE ONLY ONE MOVING.
AND THAT'S WHEN I START GOING AT HIM.
IT'S NOTHING TO SHRINK OUT OF THE LASSO.
AND THAT'S WHEN HE STARTS COMING AT US.
SOLUTION: ATOM.
MY TEAMMA--
HEY, FACE...

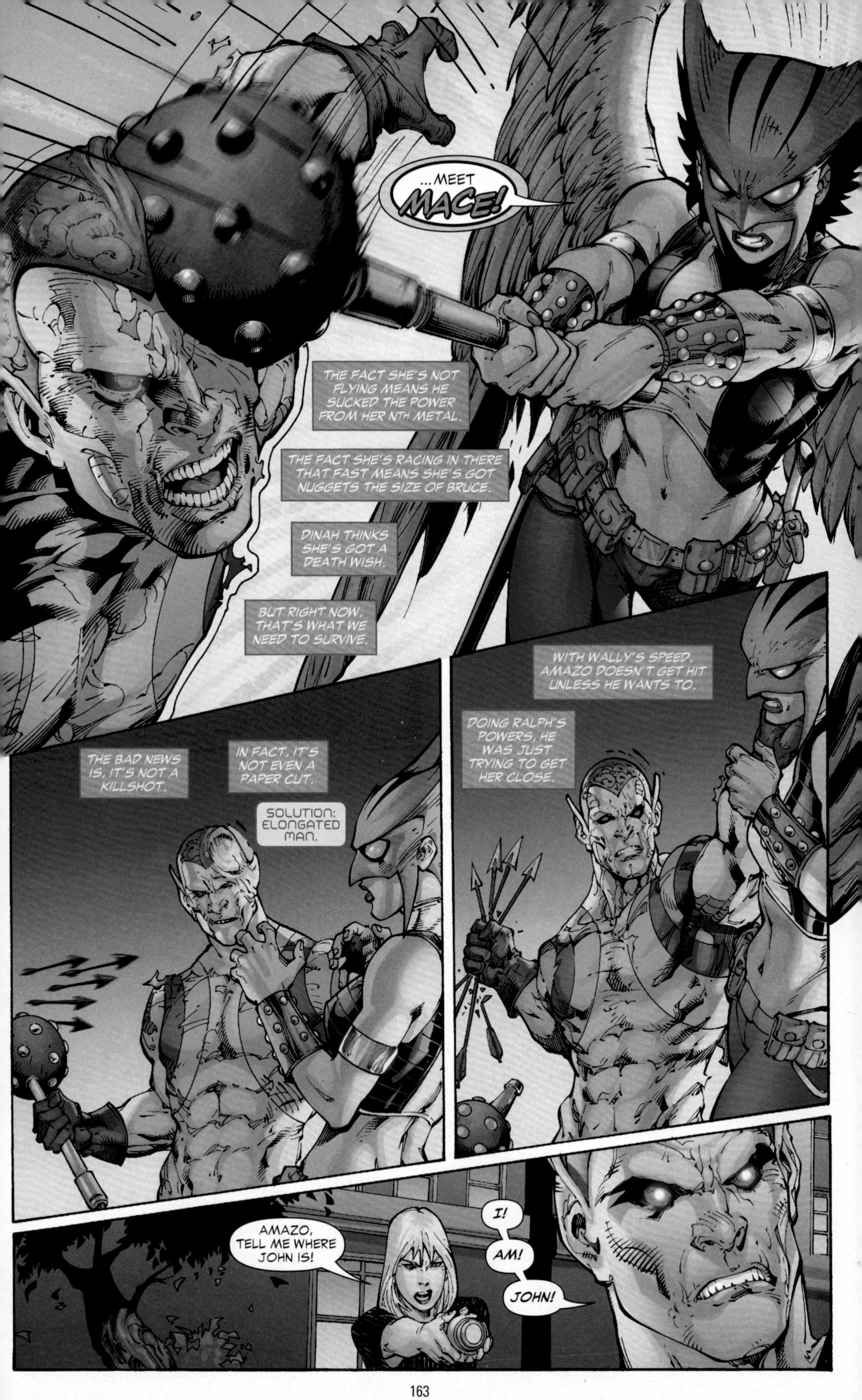
...MEET MACE!
THE FACT SHE'S NOT FLYING MEANS HE SUCKED THE POWER FROM HER NTH METAL.
THE FACT SHE'S RACING IN THERE THAT FAST MEANS SHE'S GOT NUGGETS THE SIZE OF BRUCE.
DINAH THINKS SHE'S GOT A DEATH WISH.
BUT RIGHT NOW, THAT'S WHAT WE NEED TO SURVIVE.
THE BAD NEWS IS, IT'S NOT A KILLSHOT.
IN FACT, IT'S NOT EVEN A PAPER CUT.
SOLUTION: ELONGATED MAN.
WITH WALLY'S SPEED, AMAZO DOESN'T GET HIT UNLESS HE WANTS TO.
DOING RALPH'S POWERS, HE WAS JUST TRYING TO GET HER CLOSE.
AMAZO, TELL ME WHERE JOHN IS!
I!
AM!
JOHN!

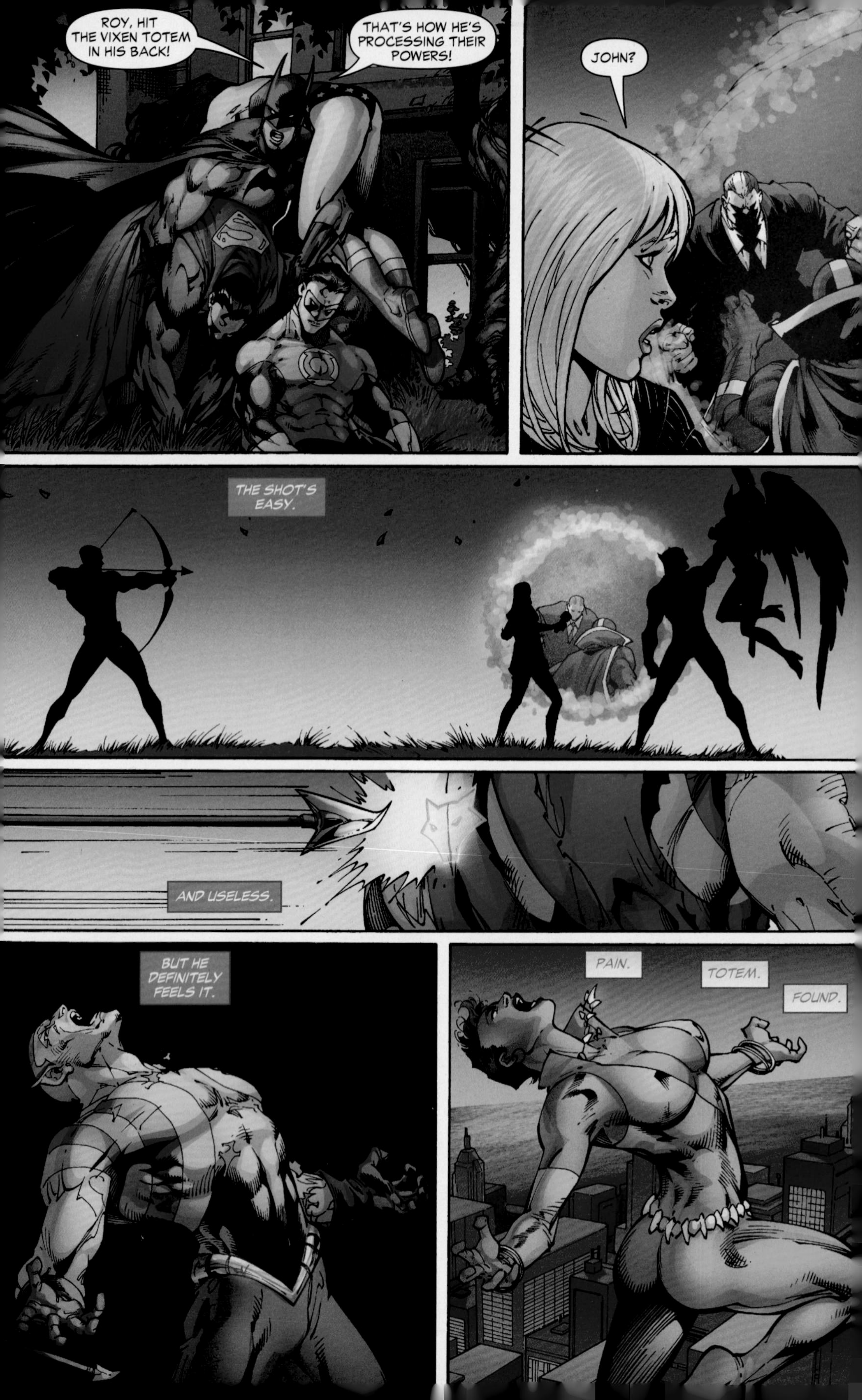
ROY, HIT THE VIXEN TOTEM IN HIS BACK!
THAT'S HOW HE'S PROCESSING THEIR POWERS!
JOHN?
THE SHOT'S EASY.
AND USELESS.
BUT HE DEFINITELY FEELS IT.
PAIN.
TOTEM.
FOUND.

Despite what people think, the fastest animal on Earth isn't the cheetah.

FALCON.

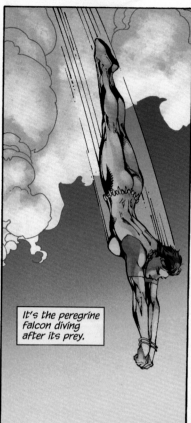

It's the peregrine falcon diving after its prey.

At a thirty degree angle, those dives reach 180 mph.

...I'M COMING, GODDESS...

At a forty-five degree angle, it hits 217 mph.

And at a sixty degree angle, with human mass, and an added 9,000 pounds of weight...

TRICERATOPS.

YOU'RE SUPPOSED TO BE MY TEAM-MATES

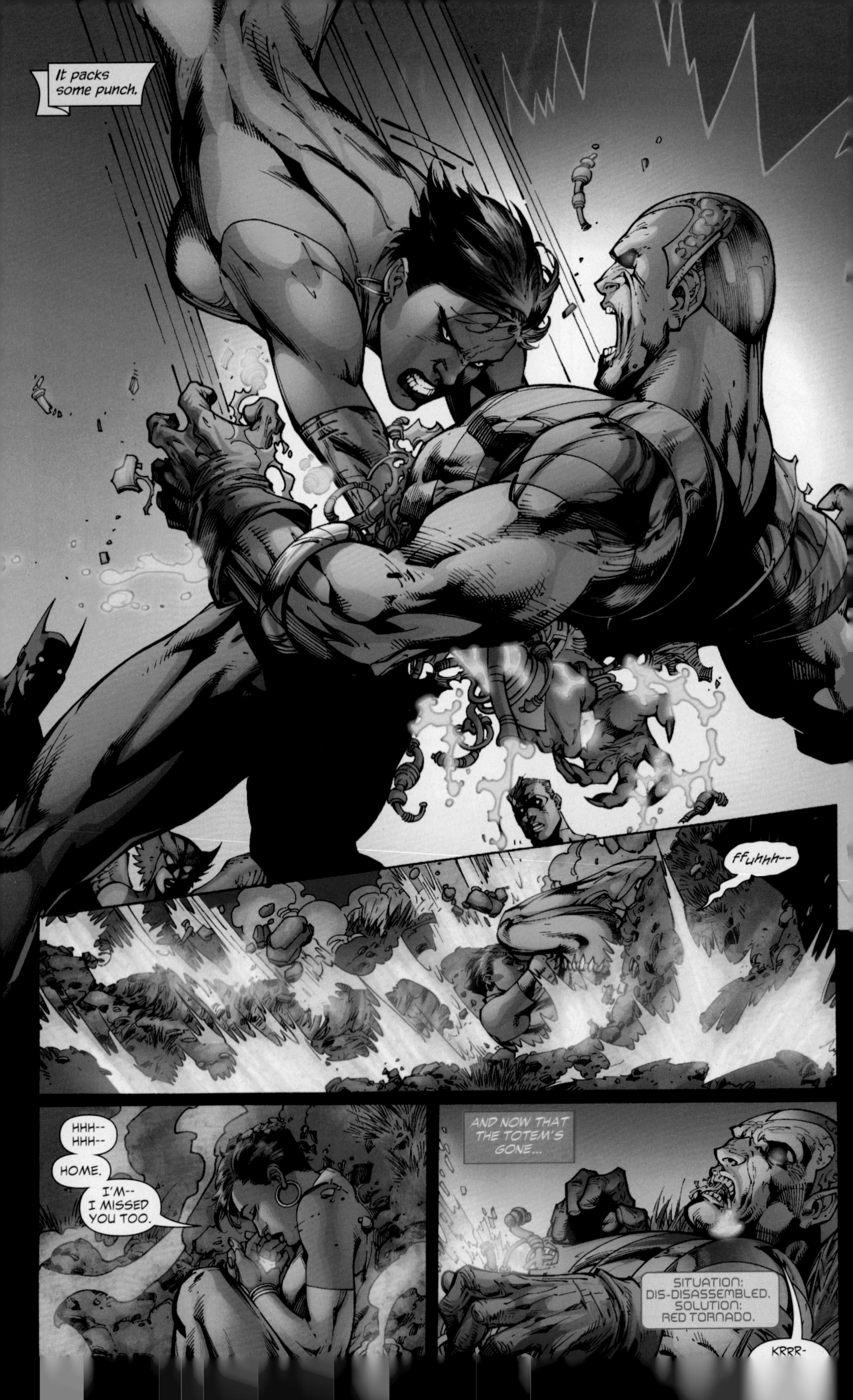
It packs some punch.
ffuhhh--
HHH--
HHH--
HOME.
I'M--
I MISSED YOU TOO.
AND NOW THAT THE TOTEM'S GONE...
SITUATION: DIS-DISASSEMBLED. SOLUTION: RED TORNADO.
KRRR-

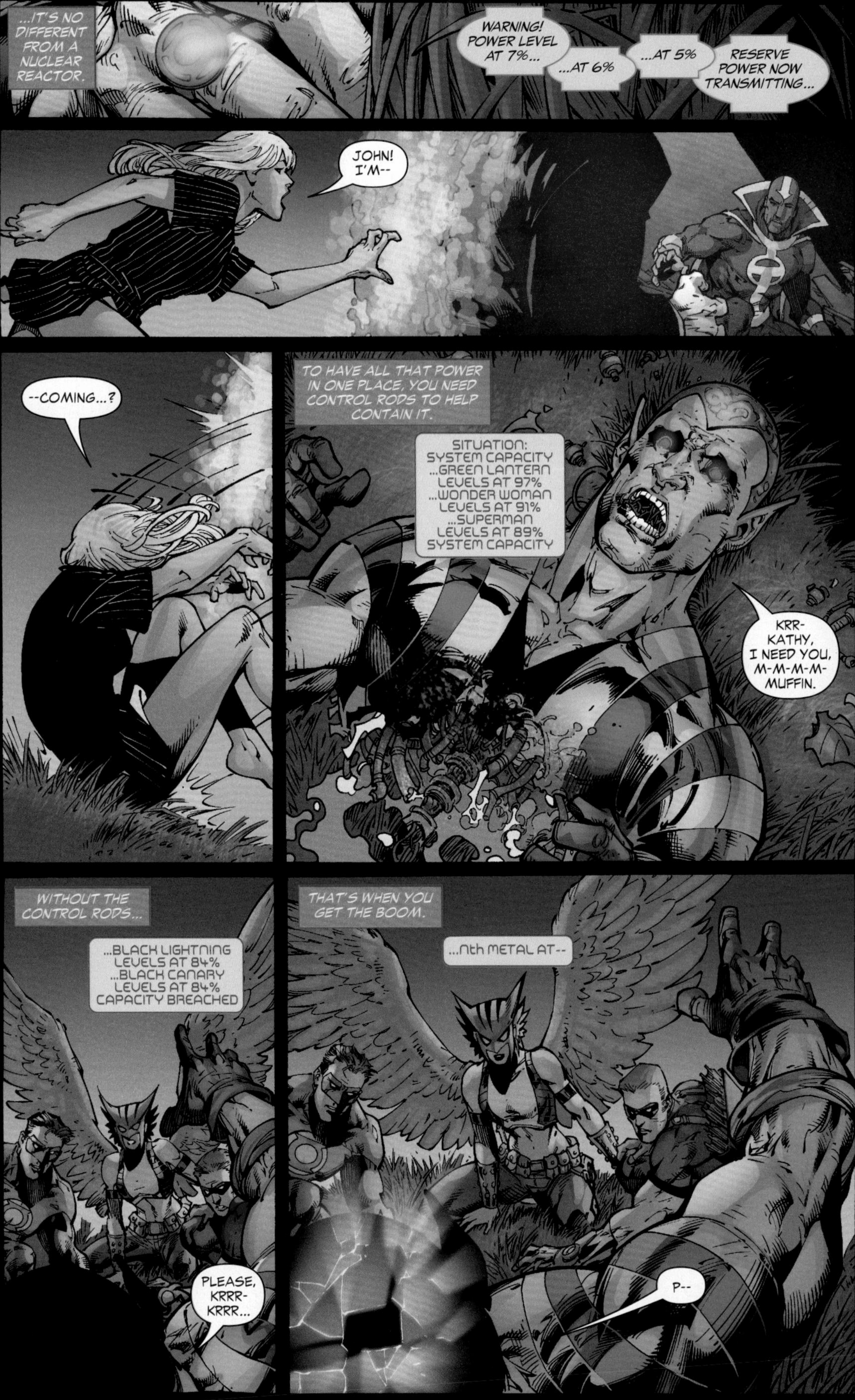
...IT'S NO DIFFERENT FROM A NUCLEAR REACTOR.
WARNING! POWER LEVEL AT 7%...
...AT 6%
...AT 5%
RESERVE POWER NOW TRANSMITTING...
JOHN! I'M--
--COMING...?
TO HAVE ALL THAT POWER IN ONE PLACE, YOU NEED CONTROL RODS TO HELP CONTAIN IT.
SITUATION: SYSTEM CAPACITY ...GREEN LANTERN LEVELS AT 97% ...WONDER WOMAN LEVELS AT 91% ...SUPERMAN LEVELS AT 89% SYSTEM CAPACITY
KRR-KATHY, I NEED YOU, M-M-M-M-MUFFIN.
WITHOUT THE CONTROL RODS...
...BLACK LIGHTNING LEVELS AT 84% ...BLACK CANARY LEVELS AT 84% CAPACITY BREACHED
PLEASE, KRRR-KRRR...
THAT'S WHEN YOU GET THE BOOM.
...Nth METAL AT--
P--

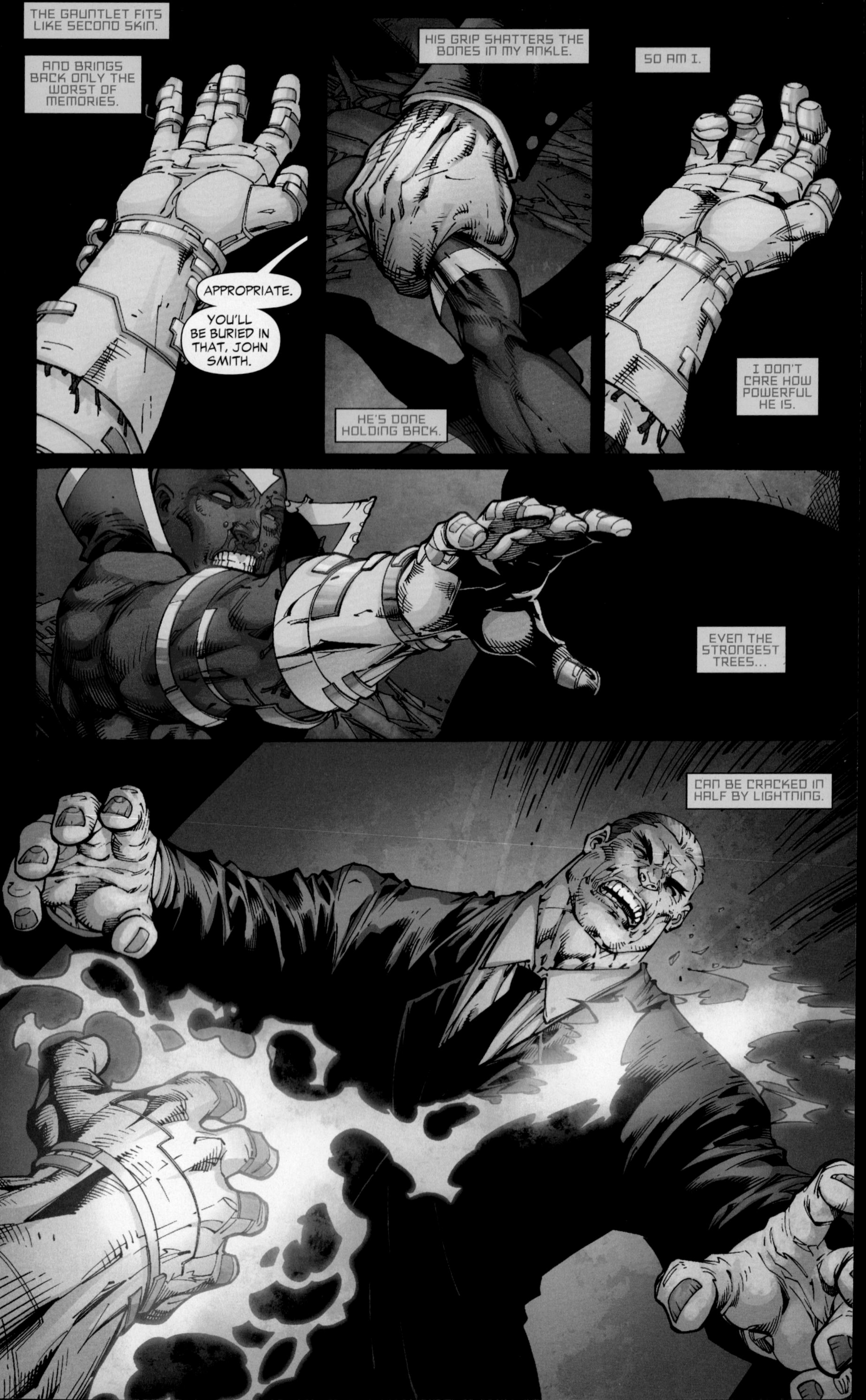
THE GAUNTLET FITS LIKE SECOND SKIN.
AND BRINGS BACK ONLY THE WORST OF MEMORIES.
APPROPRIATE.
YOU'LL BE BURIED IN THAT, JOHN SMITH.
HIS GRIP SHATTERS THE BONES IN MY ANKLE.
HE'S DONE HOLDING BACK.
SO AM I.
I DON'T CARE HOW POWERFUL HE IS.
EVEN THE STRONGEST TREES...
CAN BE CRACKED IN HALF BY LIGHTNING.

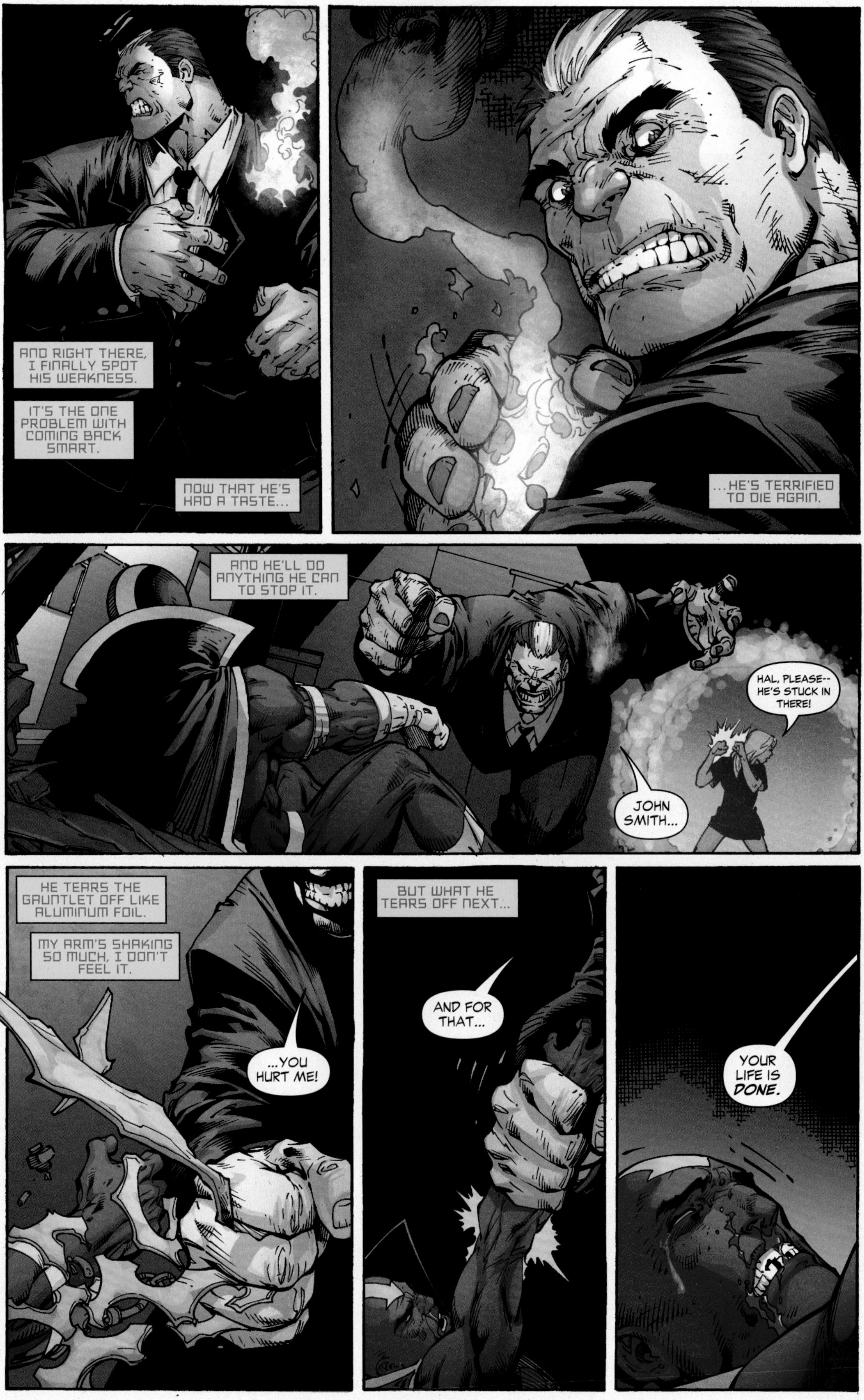
AND RIGHT THERE, I FINALLY SPOT HIS WEAKNESS.
IT'S THE ONE PROBLEM WITH COMING BACK SMART.
NOW THAT HE'S HAD A TASTE...
...HE'S TERRIFIED TO DIE AGAIN.
AND HE'LL DO ANYTHING HE CAN TO STOP IT.
HAL, PLEASE-- HE'S STUCK IN THERE!
JOHN SMITH...
HE TEARS THE GAUNTLET OFF LIKE ALUMINUM FOIL.
MY ARM'S SHAKING SO MUCH, I DON'T FEEL IT.
...YOU HURT ME!
BUT WHAT HE TEARS OFF NEXT...
AND FOR THAT...
YOUR LIFE IS DONE.

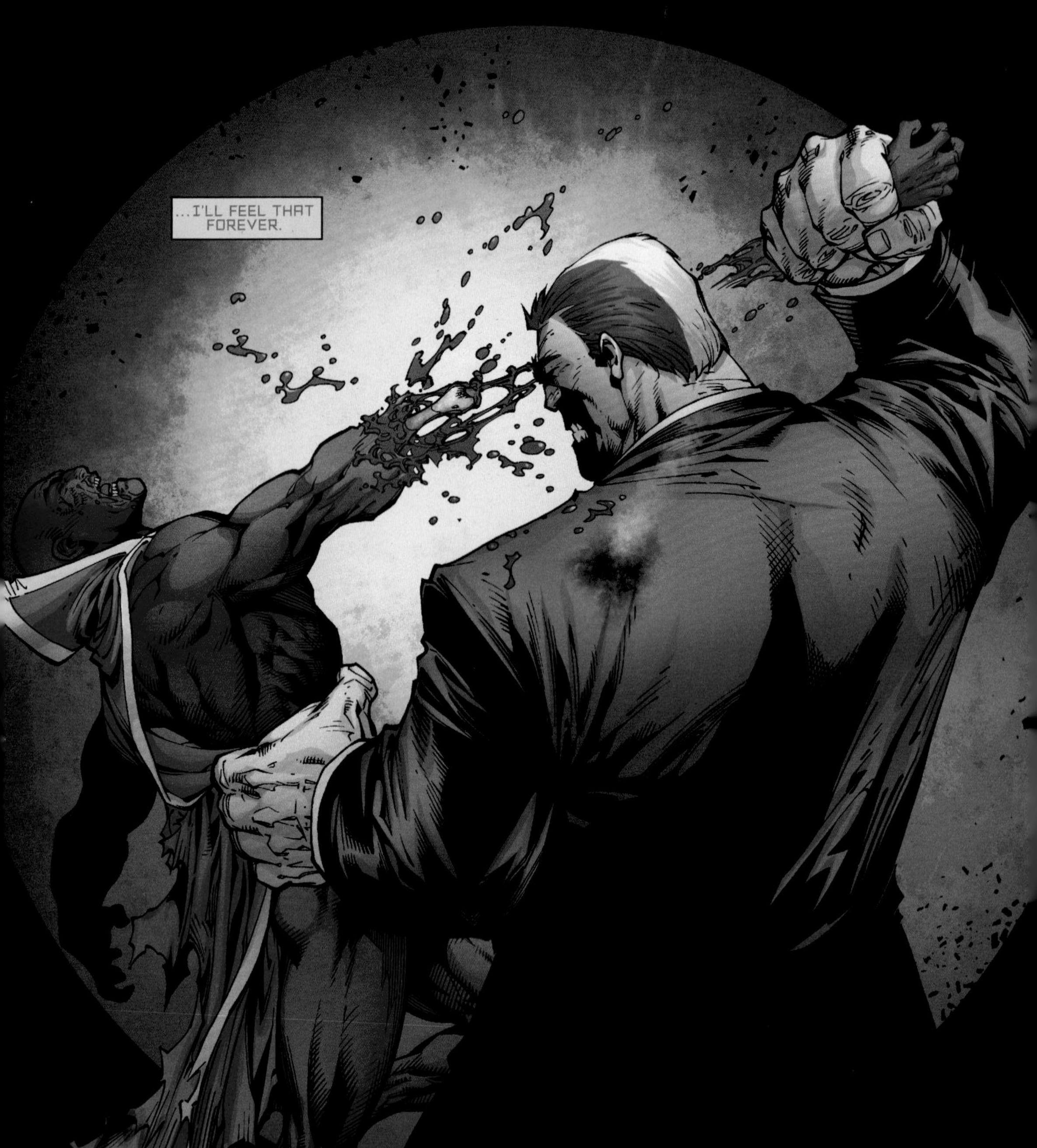
...I'LL FEEL THAT FOREVER.

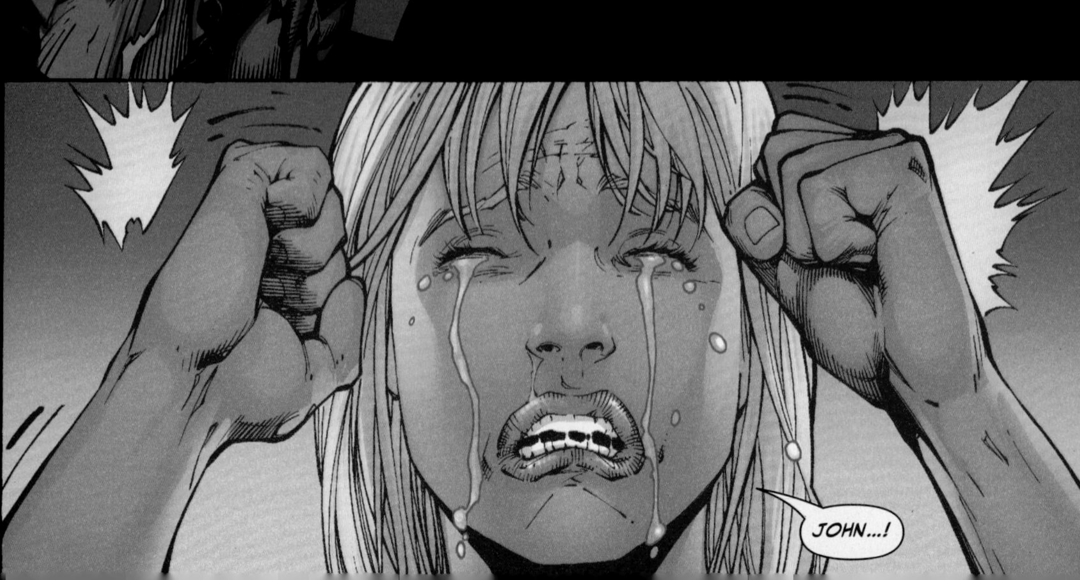
JOHN...!

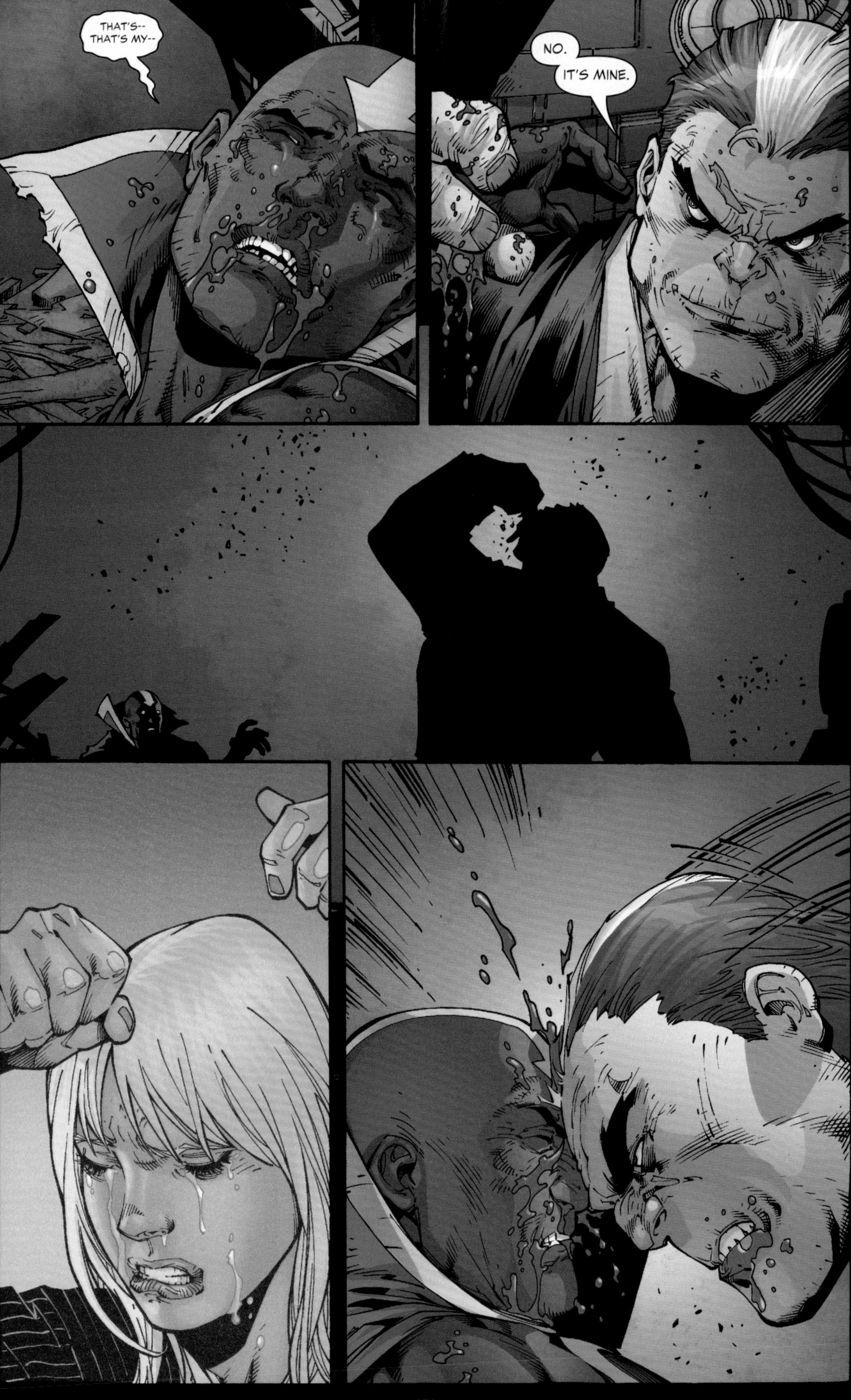
THAT'S--
THAT'S MY--
NO.
IT'S MINE.

THE PAIN... THE PAIN IS RUTHLESS.

BUT NOT AS BAD AS THE IMAGE OF HIM E--

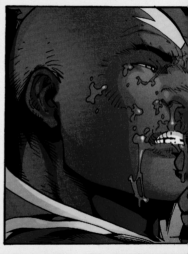

GRUNDY DOESN'T MAKE IT ANY EASIER.

HE BARRELS RIGHT AT ME.

WHICH IS WHAT I'M COUNTING ON AS I LIFT THE WINDS TO 200 MPH.

THE SOUND ALONE IS WORTH IT.

A SHARP METALLIC CRUNCH THAT TELLS ME IT WENT ALL THE WAY THROUGH TO THE WALL.

Y-YOU WERE... YOU AIMED FOR MY HEART...

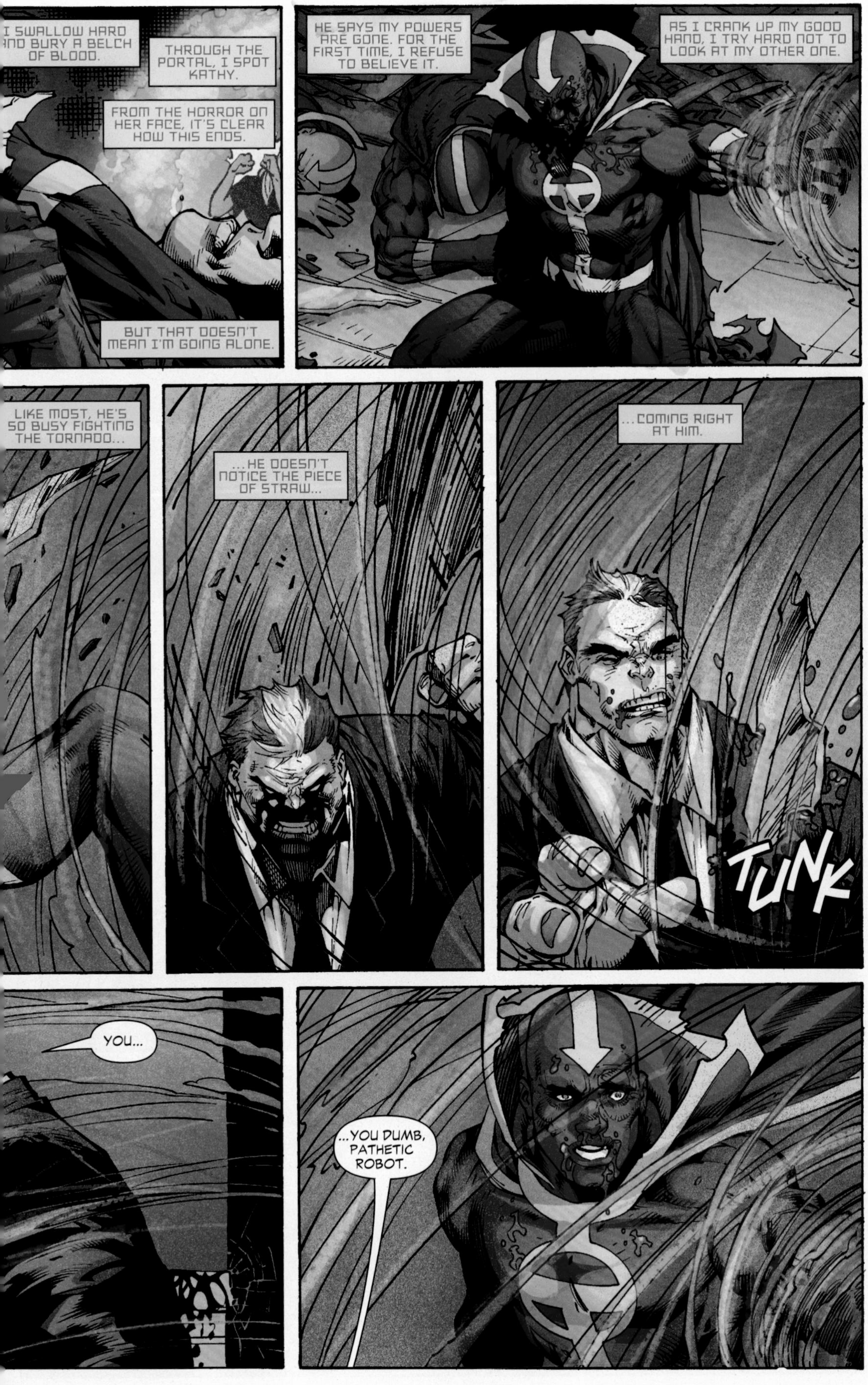
I SWALLOW HARD AND BURY A BELCH OF BLOOD.
THROUGH THE PORTAL, I SPOT KATHY.
FROM THE HORROR ON HER FACE, IT'S CLEAR HOW THIS ENDS.
BUT THAT DOESN'T MEAN I'M GOING ALONE.
HE SAYS MY POWERS ARE GONE. FOR THE FIRST TIME, I REFUSE TO BELIEVE IT.
AS I CRANK UP MY GOOD HAND, I TRY HARD NOT TO LOOK AT MY OTHER ONE.
LIKE MOST, HE'S SO BUSY FIGHTING THE TORNADO...
...HE DOESN'T NOTICE THE PIECE OF STRAW...
...COMING RIGHT AT HIM.
TUNK
YOU...
...YOU DUMB, PATHETIC ROBOT.

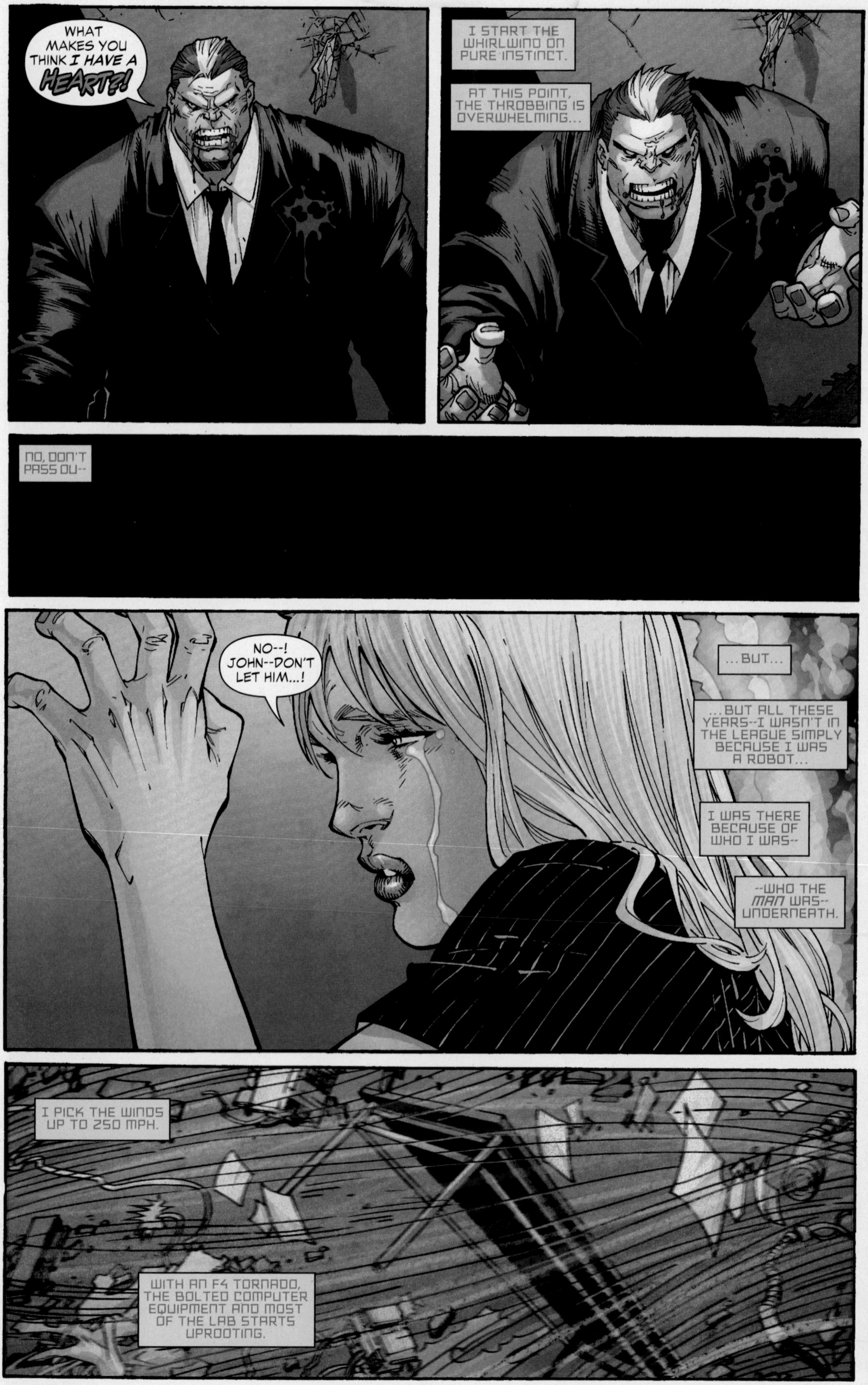

WHAT MAKES YOU THINK I HAVE A HEART?!
I START THE WHIRLWIND ON PURE INSTINCT.
AT THIS POINT, THE THROBBING IS OVERWHELMING...
NO, DON'T PASS OU--
NO--! JOHN--DON'T LET HIM...!
...BUT...
...BUT ALL THESE YEARS--I WASN'T IN THE LEAGUE SIMPLY BECAUSE I WAS A ROBOT...
I WAS THERE BECAUSE OF WHO I WAS--
--WHO THE MAN WAS--UNDERNEATH.
I PICK THE WINDS UP TO 250 MPH.
WITH AN F4 TORNADO, THE BOLTED COMPUTER EQUIPMENT AND MOST OF THE LAB STARTS UPROOTING.

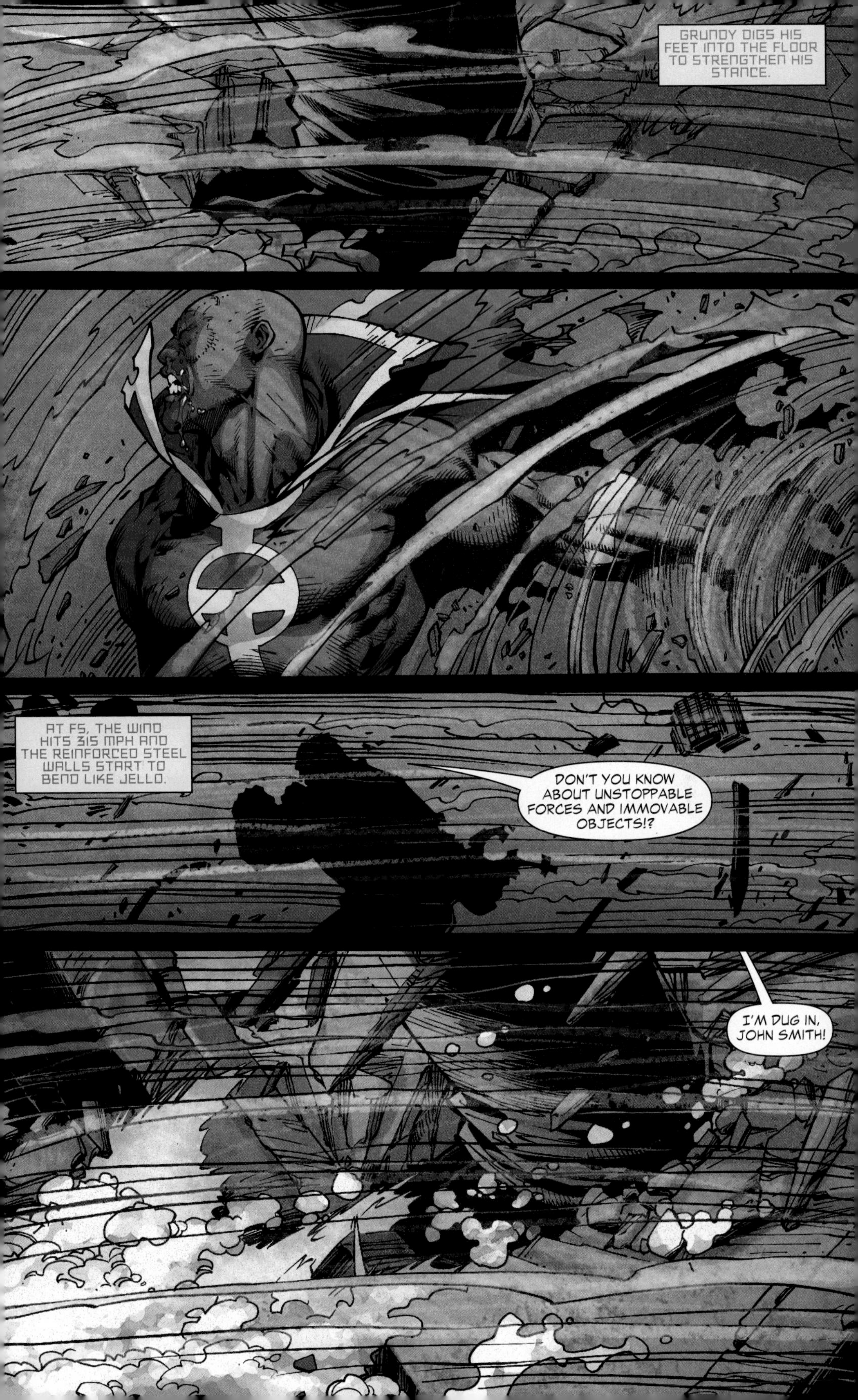
GRUNDY DIGS HIS FEET INTO THE FLOOR TO STRENGTHEN HIS STANCE.
AT F5, THE WIND HITS 315 MPH AND THE REINFORCED STEEL WALLS START TO BEND LIKE JELLO.
DON'T YOU KNOW ABOUT UNSTOPPABLE FORCES AND IMMOVABLE OBJECTS!?
I'M DUG IN, JOHN SMITH!

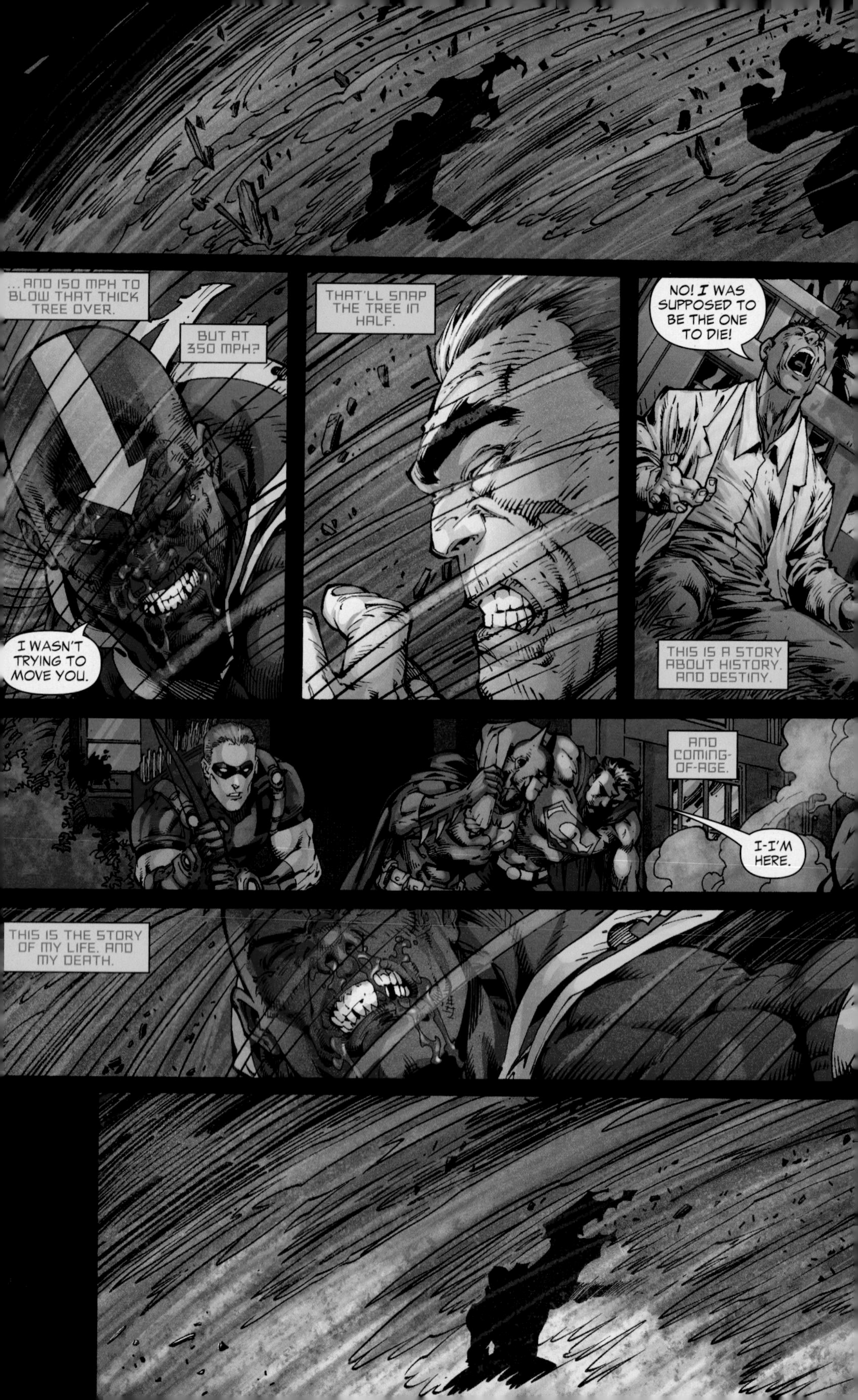
...AND 150 MPH TO BLOW THAT THICK TREE OVER.
BUT AT 350 MPH?
I WASN'T TRYING TO MOVE YOU.
THAT'LL SNAP THE TREE IN HALF.
NO! I WAS SUPPOSED TO BE THE ONE TO DIE!
THIS IS A STORY ABOUT HISTORY. AND DESTINY.
AND COMING-OF-AGE.
I-I'M HERE.
THIS IS THE STORY OF MY LIFE. AND MY DEATH.

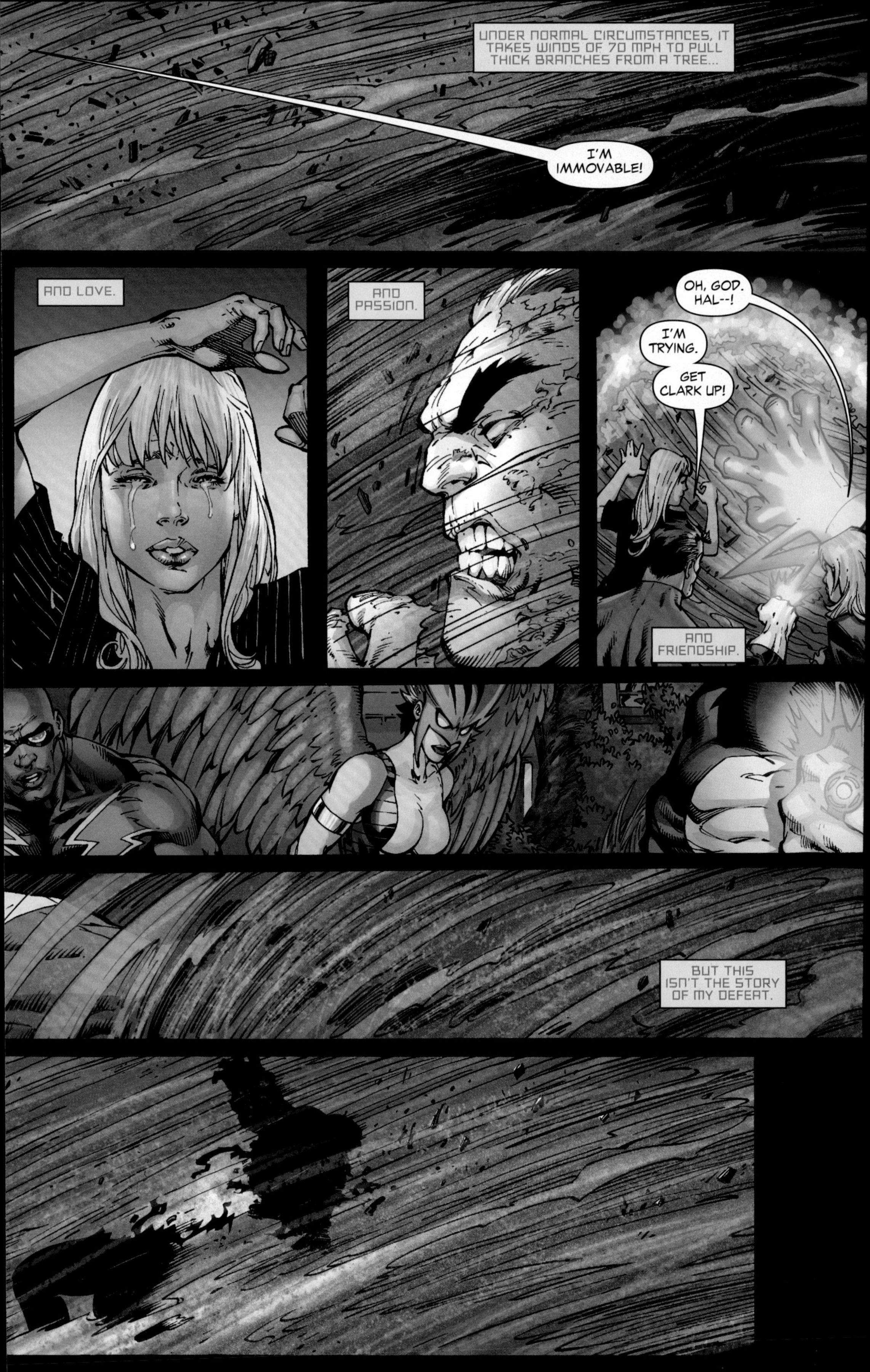
UNDER NORMAL CIRCUMSTANCES, IT TAKES WINDS OF 70 MPH TO PULL THICK BRANCHES FROM A TREE...
I'M IMMOVABLE!
AND LOVE.
AND PASSION.
OH, GOD. HAL--!
I'M TRYING.
GET CLARK UP!
AND FRIENDSHIP.
BUT THIS ISN'T THE STORY OF MY DEFEAT.

DAMN IT! OPEN IT!

BELIEVE ME, WE'RE--

NOW, HAL!

OH, GOD-- JOHN...

MY FACE IS SO SWOLLEN, SHE CAN BARELY GET THE MASK OFF.

K-KATHY... I-I'M SORRY--

YOU'LL-- YOU'LL BE FINE. WE'LL GET YOU TO THE HOSPITAL--

NO! YOU HAVE TO--

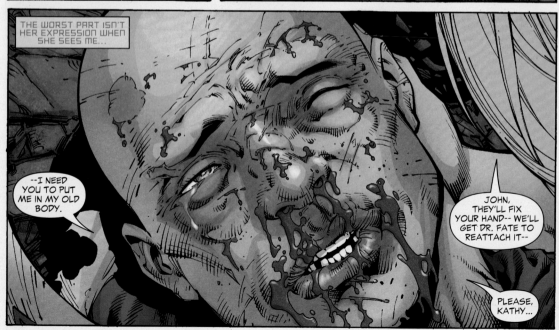

THE WORST PART ISN'T HER EXPRESSION WHEN SHE SEES ME...

--I NEED YOU TO PUT ME IN MY OLD BODY.

JOHN, THEY'LL FIX YOUR HAND-- WE'LL GET DR. FATE TO REATTACH IT--

PLEASE, KATHY...

...OR THE SNAG IN HER VOICE AS SHE TRIES TO LOOK STRONG...

...I NEED TO BE IN MY OLD BODY AGAIN.

BUT, JOHN--YOU'RE HUMAN--IF YOU GO BACK TO THE ROBOT--

...OR EVEN THE CLEAR DISAPPOINTMENT AS SHE REALIZES THAT EVERYTHING WE GAINED IS NOW LOST.

I'M DYING, KATHY...

IF YOU DON'T HURRY...

I'M--I'M--I'M--

I THINK I'M ABOUT TO DIE...

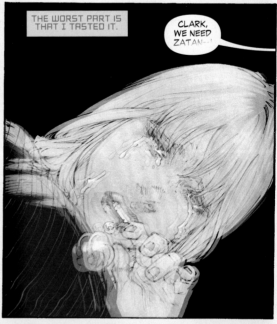

THE WORST PART IS THAT I TASTED IT.

CLARK, WE NEED ZATAN--!

I FELT IT.

EVEN IF IT WAS NEVER MEANT TO WORK...

FOR THOSE PRECIOUS DAYS, I WAS TRULY ALIVE.

MAGNUS WANTS THE AMAZO CHIP.

DOES THIS MEAN REDDY'LL HAVE ALL OUR POWERS?

I SUGGEST STRIPPING AMAZO OUT FIRST.

SEE THE BRONZE GLOW IN HIS AURA? THIS WAS DEFINITELY FELIX.

ODNU TSUAF!

179

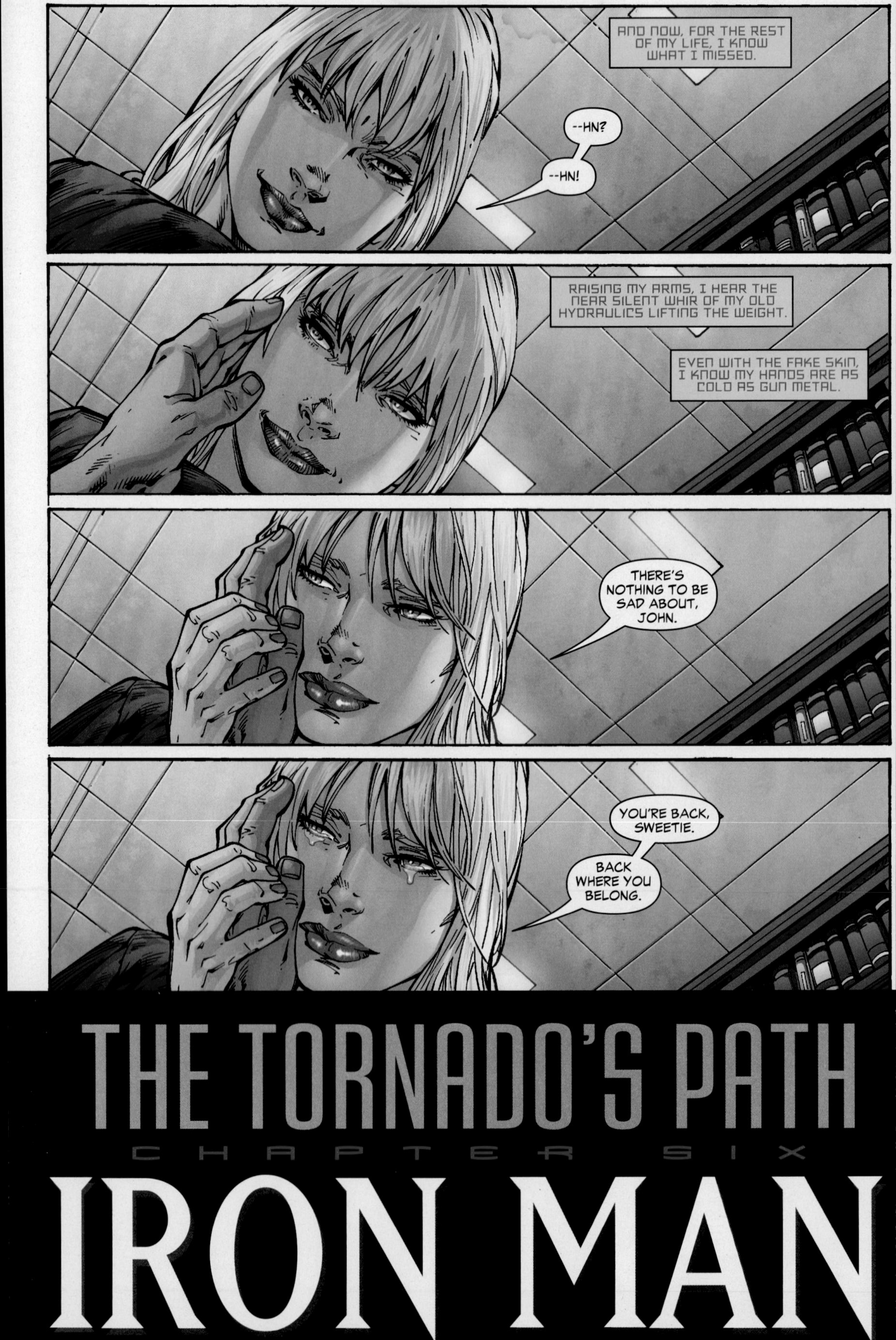
AND NOW, FOR THE REST OF MY LIFE, I KNOW WHAT I MISSED.
--HN?
--HN!
RAISING MY ARMS, I HEAR THE NEAR SILENT WHIR OF MY OLD HYDRAULICS LIFTING THE WEIGHT.
EVEN WITH THE FAKE SKIN, I KNOW MY HANDS ARE AS COLD AS GUN METAL.
THERE'S NOTHING TO BE SAD ABOUT, JOHN.
YOU'RE BACK, SWEETIE.
BACK WHERE YOU BELONG.

THE TORNADO'S PATH

CHAPTER SIX

IRON MAN

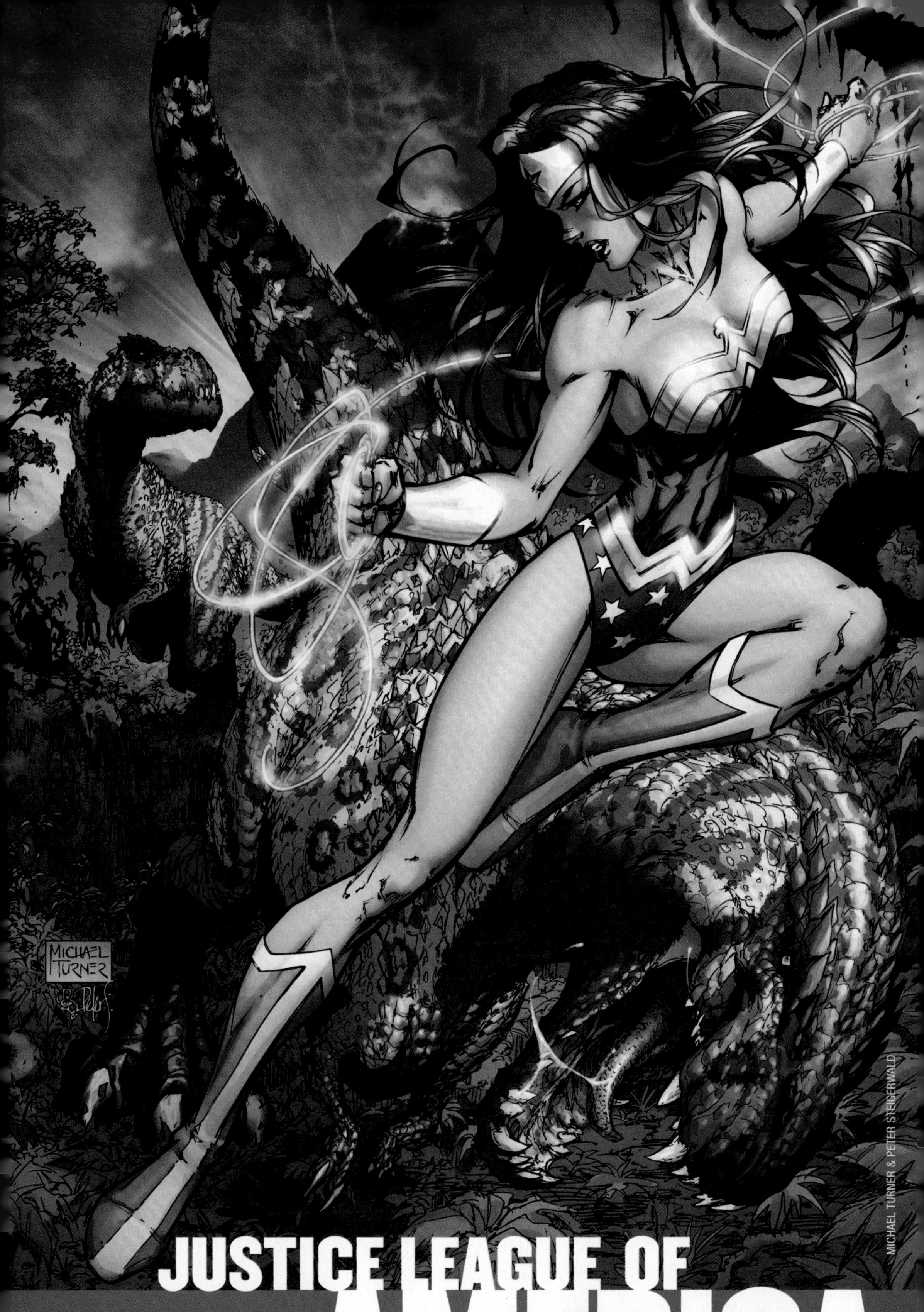
MICHAEL TURNER

MICHAEL TURNER & PETER STEIGERWALD

JUSTICE LEAGUE OF AMERICA
CHAPTER SEVEN

"It's bigger than us.
And we should never let it be
anything but that."

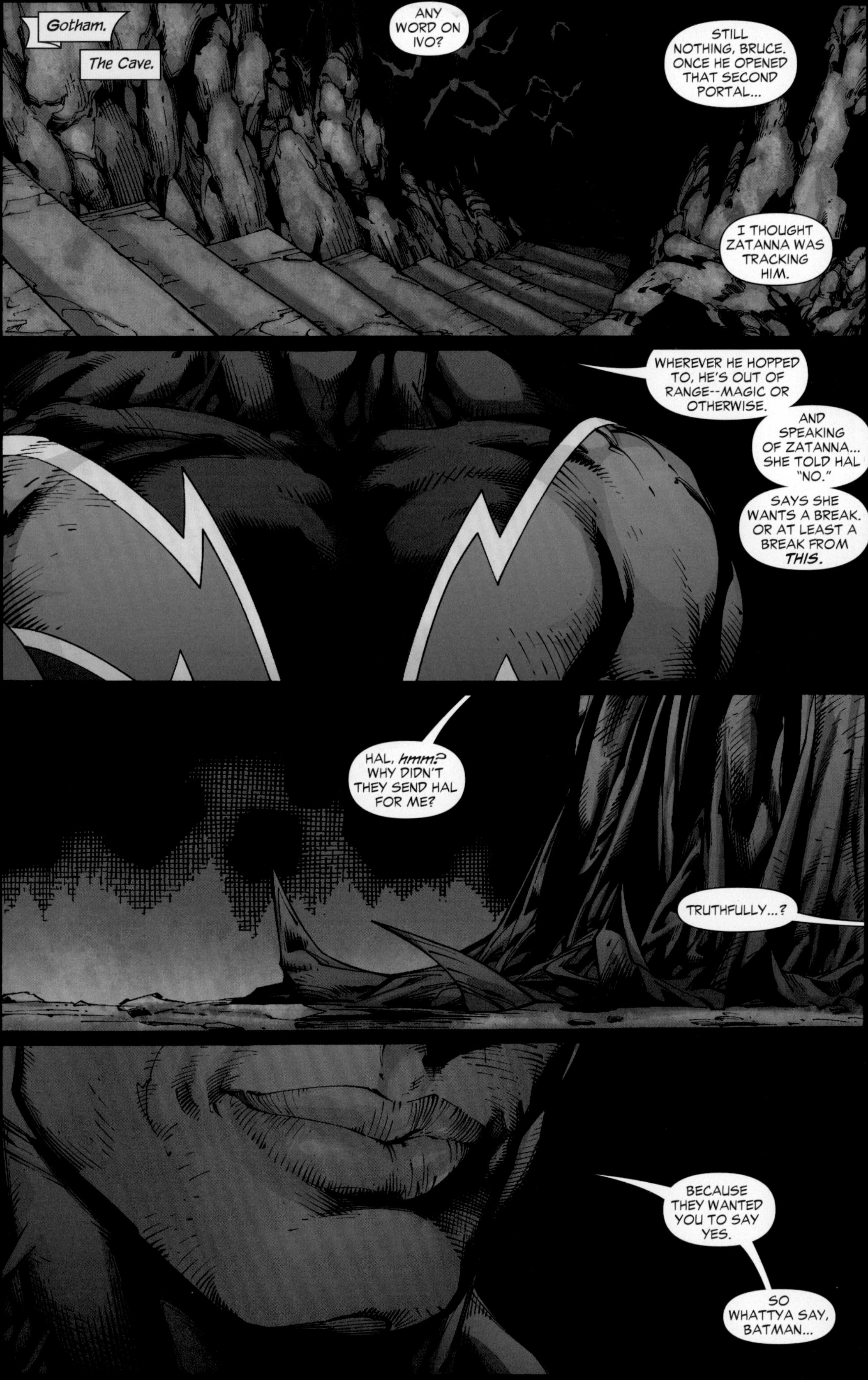

Gotham.
The Cave.
ANY WORD ON IVO?
STILL NOTHING, BRUCE. ONCE HE OPENED THAT SECOND PORTAL...
I THOUGHT ZATANNA WAS TRACKING HIM.
WHEREVER HE HOPPED TO, HE'S OUT OF RANGE--MAGIC OR OTHERWISE.
AND SPEAKING OF ZATANNA... SHE TOLD HAL "NO."
SAYS SHE WANTS A BREAK. OR AT LEAST A BREAK FROM THIS.
HAL, hmm? WHY DIDN'T THEY SEND HAL FOR ME?
TRUTHFULLY...?
BECAUSE THEY WANTED YOU TO SAY YES.
SO WHATTYA SAY, BATMAN...

...WOULD YOU LIKE TO JOIN THE JUSTICE LEAGUE OF AMERICA?

JUSTICE LEAGUE of AMERICA

HEREBY ELECTS

BATMAN

WITH ALL PRIVILEGES AND GRATUITIES, INCLUDING... TO MEMB... FOR LIFE— ...ING OF THE SIGNAL DEVICE AND POSSES... OF THE GOLDEN KEY WHICH PERMITS ENTRY INT... ...T SANCTUARIES, ITS LIBRARIES AND SOUN... ROOMS. IT IS HEREBY FURTHE... ...AND ACTED UPON, THAT...

shall receive a special comm... THE TORNAD... the case we have ...

...s expert assistance in ...scrolls...

BAT...

...PATH

SO THAT'S WHAT YOU SETTLED ON? INVITING WHOEVER HAPPENED TO BE THERE WITH AMAZO AND GRUNDY?

DOESN'T THAT SEEM A LITTLE... SIMPLISTIC?

IS IT ANY DIFFERENT THAN WHEN YOU STARTED, BRUCE?

THAT WAS A DIFFERENT TIME.

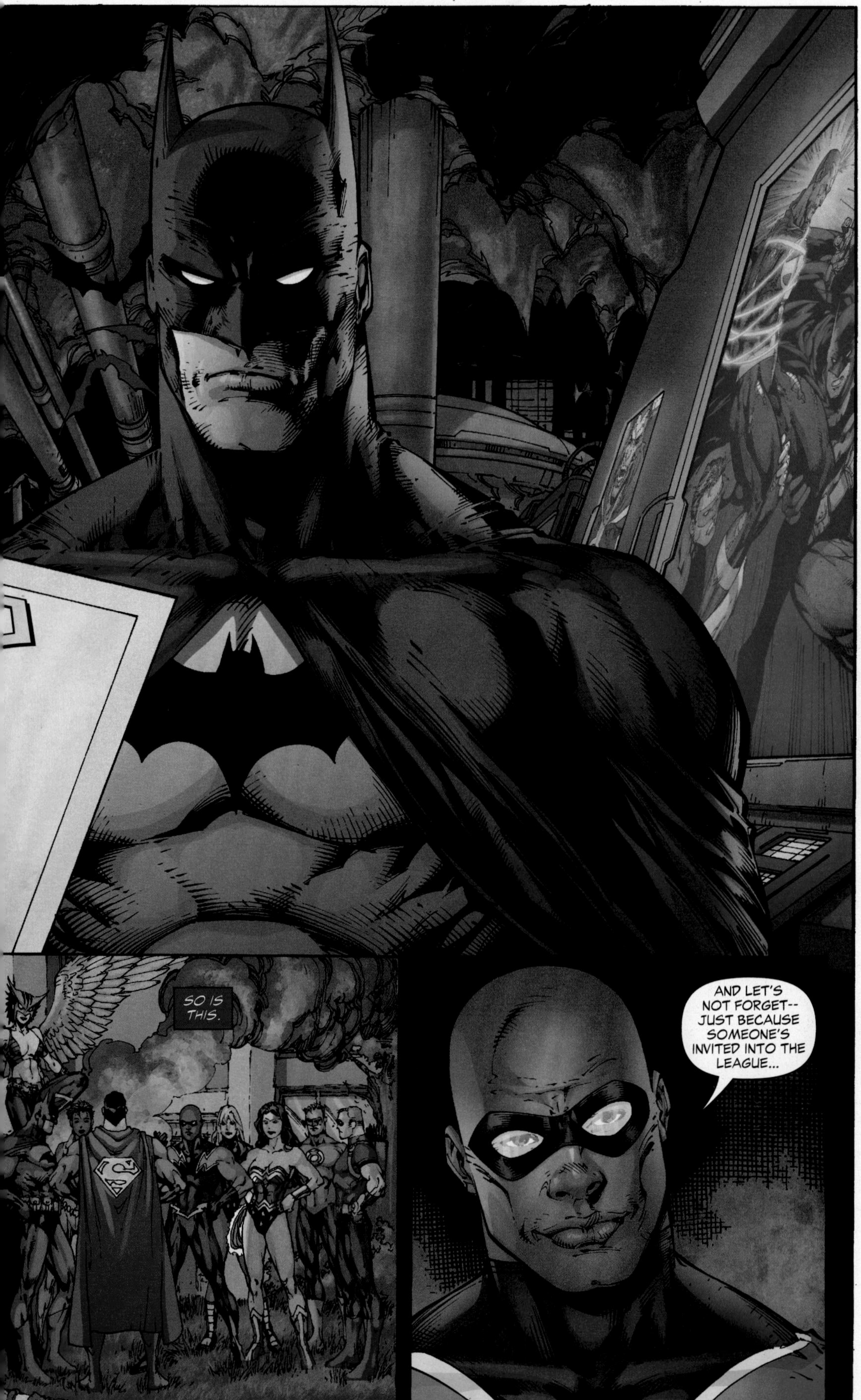
SO IS THIS.
AND LET'S NOT FORGET-- JUST BECAUSE SOMEONE'S INVITED INTO THE LEAGUE...

"...DOESN'T MEAN THEY'RE GOING TO SAY YES."

YES.

YES.

YES.

ABSOLUTELY. YES. YES. YES. YES.

C'MON, WHO WOULD SAY *NO?*

WAIT, THAT SMILE...

THIS IS A *JOKE,* ISN'T IT?

OH, GOD, IT'S A JOKE.

IT'S NOT A JOKE, ROY.

WE DON'T JOKE ABOUT THIS.

SHALL RECEIVE A SPECIAL COMMENDATION FOR HIS EXPERT ASSISTANCE IN THE CASE WE HAVE ENTITLED ON OUR SCROLLS...

THE TORNADO'S PATH

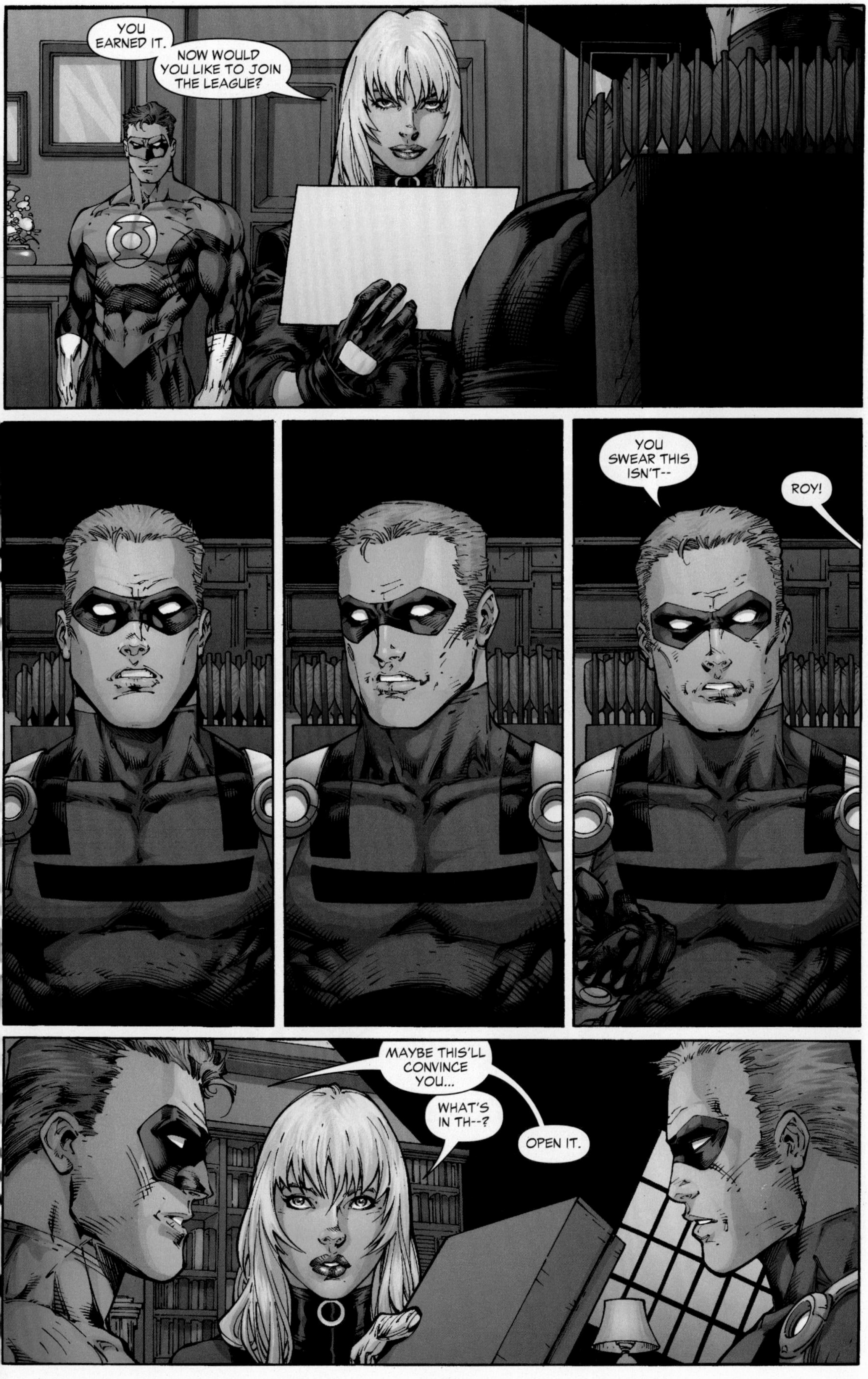
YOU EARNED IT.
NOW WOULD YOU LIKE TO JOIN THE LEAGUE?
YOU SWEAR THIS ISN'T--
ROY!
MAYBE THIS'LL CONVINCE YOU...
WHAT'S IN TH--?
OPEN IT.

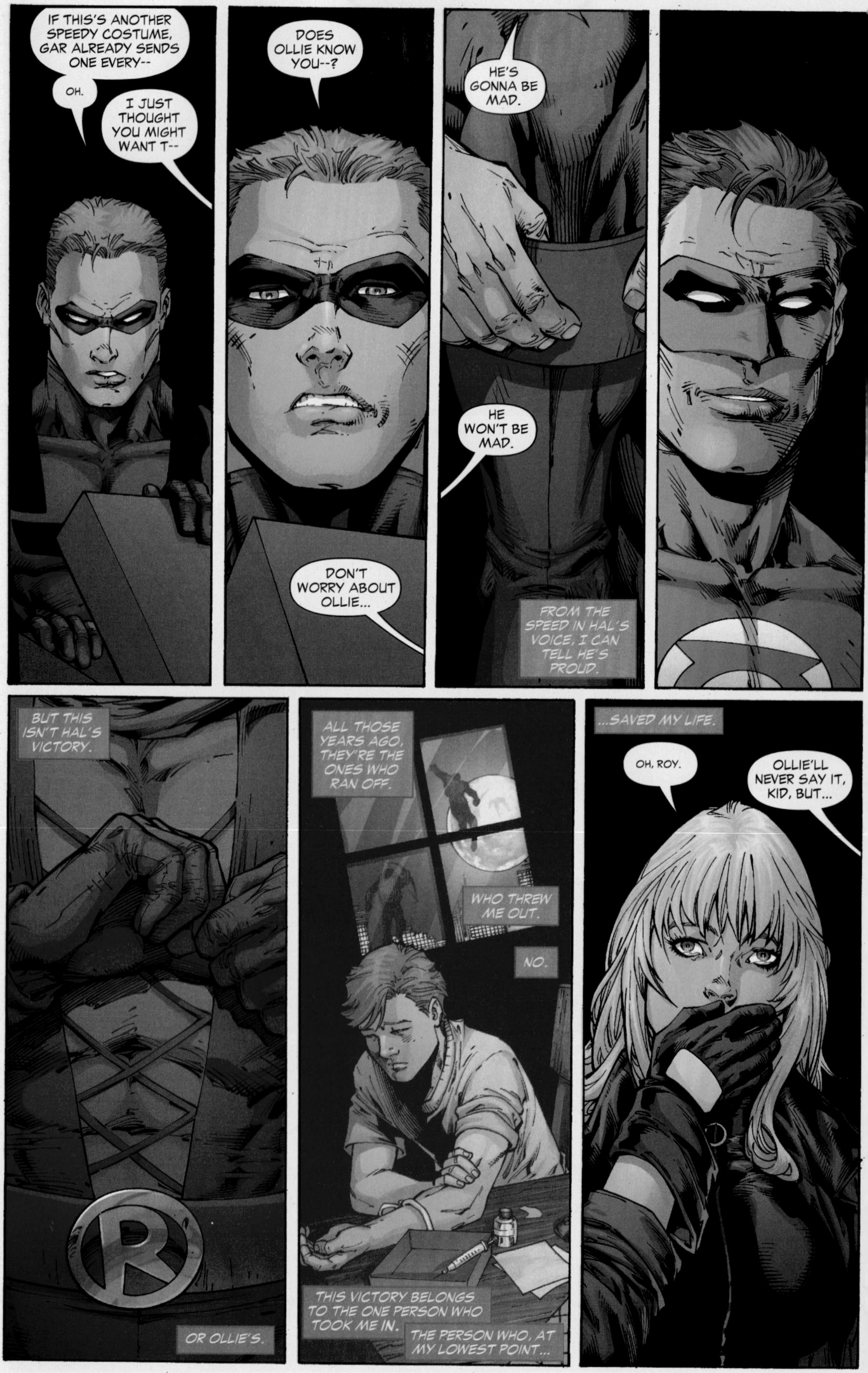
IF THIS'S ANOTHER SPEEDY COSTUME, GAR ALREADY SENDS ONE EVERY--
OH.
I JUST THOUGHT YOU MIGHT WANT T--
DOES OLLIE KNOW YOU--?
DON'T WORRY ABOUT OLLIE...
HE'S GONNA BE MAD.
HE WON'T BE MAD.
FROM THE SPEED IN HAL'S VOICE, I CAN TELL HE'S PROUD.
BUT THIS ISN'T HAL'S VICTORY.
OR OLLIE'S.
ALL THOSE YEARS AGO, THEY'RE THE ONES WHO RAN OFF.
WHO THREW ME OUT.
NO.
THIS VICTORY BELONGS TO THE ONE PERSON WHO TOOK ME IN.
THE PERSON WHO, AT MY LOWEST POINT...
...SAVED MY LIFE.
OH, ROY.
OLLIE'LL NEVER SAY IT, KID, BUT...

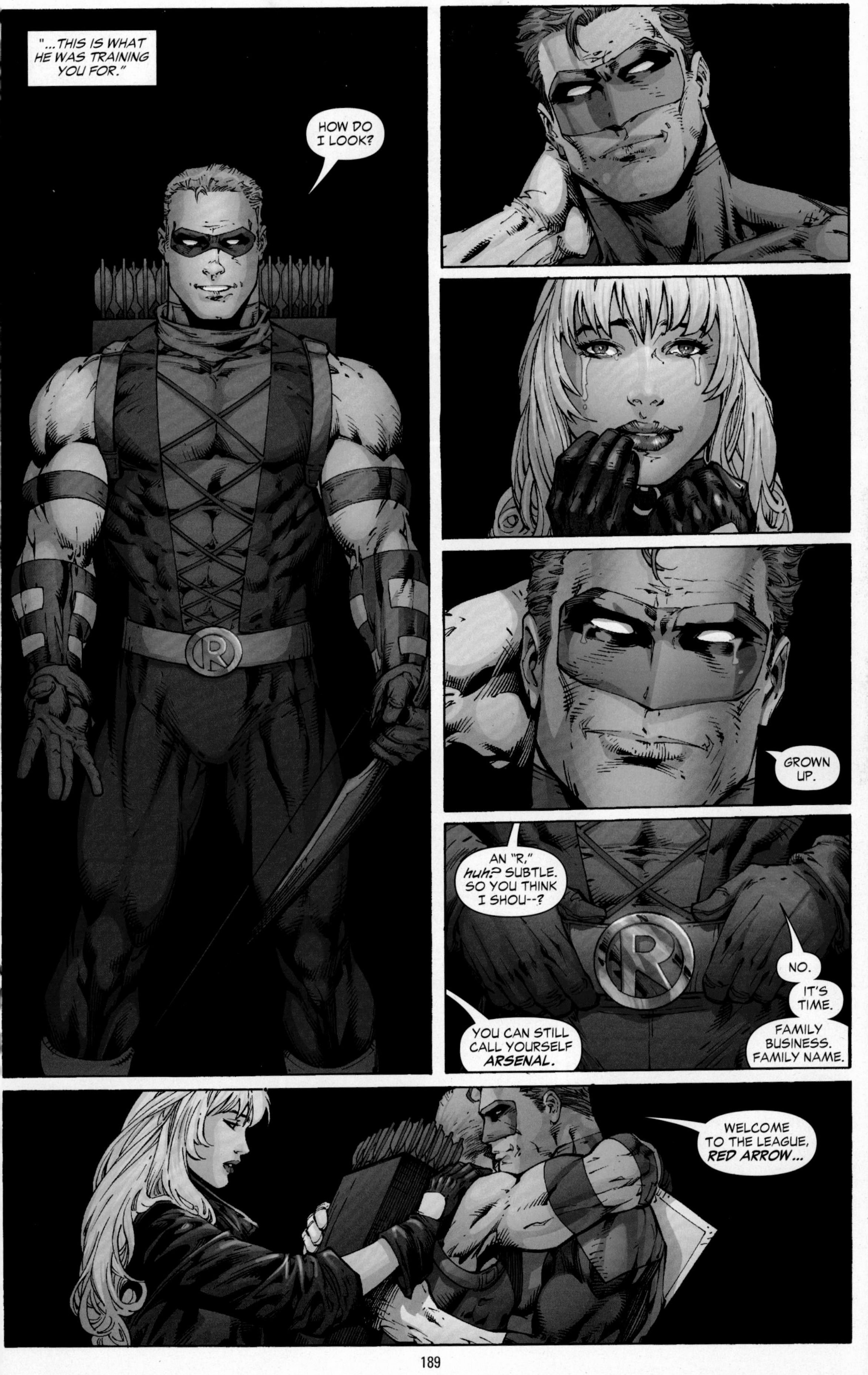
"...THIS IS WHAT HE WAS TRAINING YOU FOR."
HOW DO I LOOK?
GROWN UP.
AN "R," *huh?* SUBTLE. SO YOU THINK I SHOU--?
YOU CAN STILL CALL YOURSELF ***ARSENAL.***
NO.
IT'S TIME.
FAMILY BUSINESS. FAMILY NAME.
WELCOME TO THE LEAGUE, ***RED ARROW...***

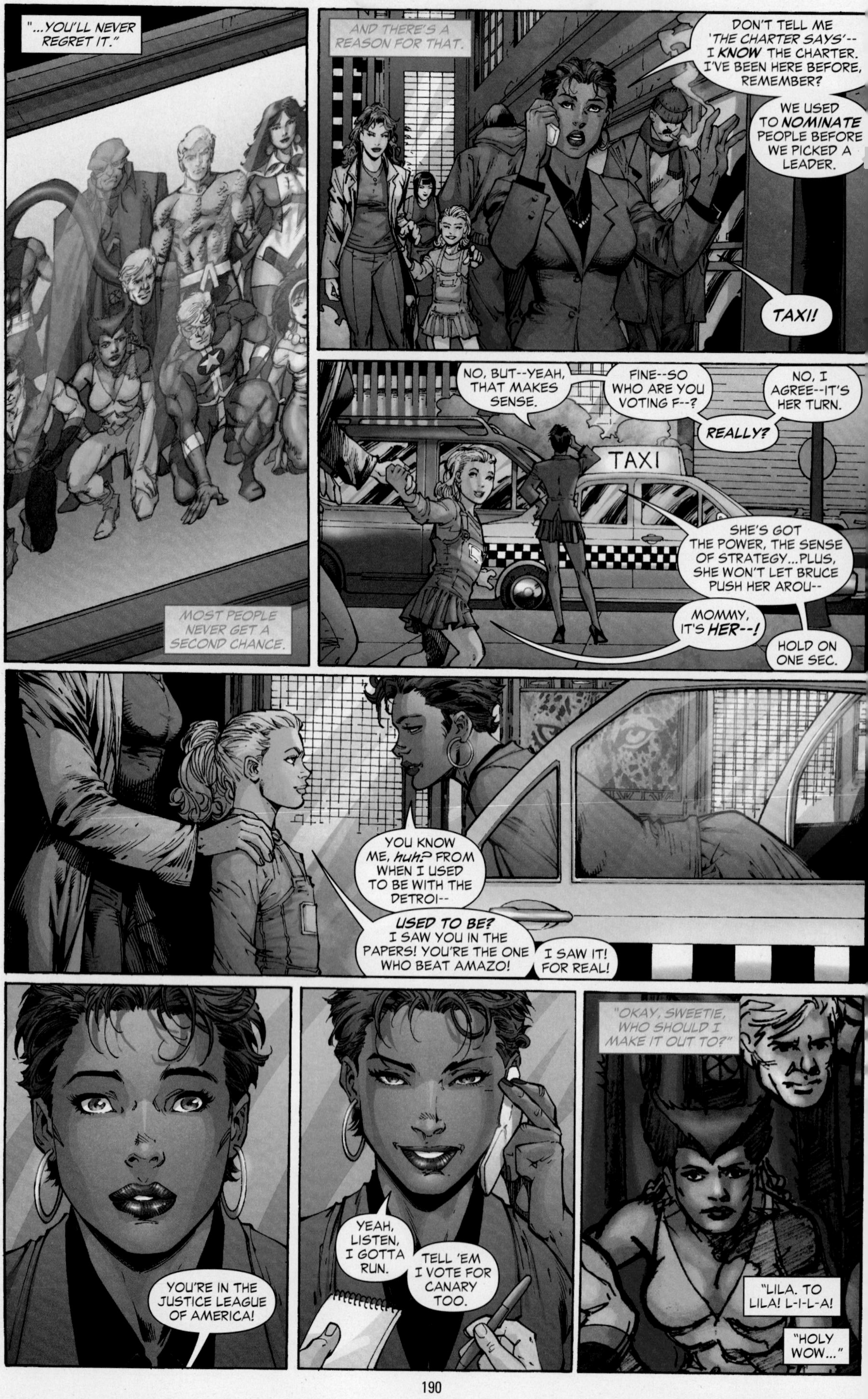
"...YOU'LL NEVER REGRET IT."
MOST PEOPLE NEVER GET A SECOND CHANCE.
AND THERE'S A REASON FOR THAT.
DON'T TELL ME 'THE CHARTER SAYS'-- I KNOW THE CHARTER. I'VE BEEN HERE BEFORE, REMEMBER?
WE USED TO NOMINATE PEOPLE BEFORE WE PICKED A LEADER.
TAXI!
NO, BUT--YEAH, THAT MAKES SENSE.
FINE--SO WHO ARE YOU VOTING F--?
NO, I AGREE--IT'S HER TURN.
REALLY?
TAXI
SHE'S GOT THE POWER, THE SENSE OF STRATEGY...PLUS, SHE WON'T LET BRUCE PUSH HER AROU--
MOMMY, IT'S HER--!
HOLD ON ONE SEC.
YOU KNOW ME, huh? FROM WHEN I USED TO BE WITH THE DETROI--
USED TO BE? I SAW YOU IN THE PAPERS! YOU'RE THE ONE WHO BEAT AMAZO!
I SAW IT! FOR REAL!
YOU'RE IN THE JUSTICE LEAGUE OF AMERICA!
YEAH, LISTEN, I GOTTA RUN.
TELL 'EM I VOTE FOR CANARY TOO.
"OKAY, SWEETIE, WHO SHOULD I MAKE IT OUT TO?"
"LILA. TO LILA! L-I-L-A!
"HOLY WOW..."

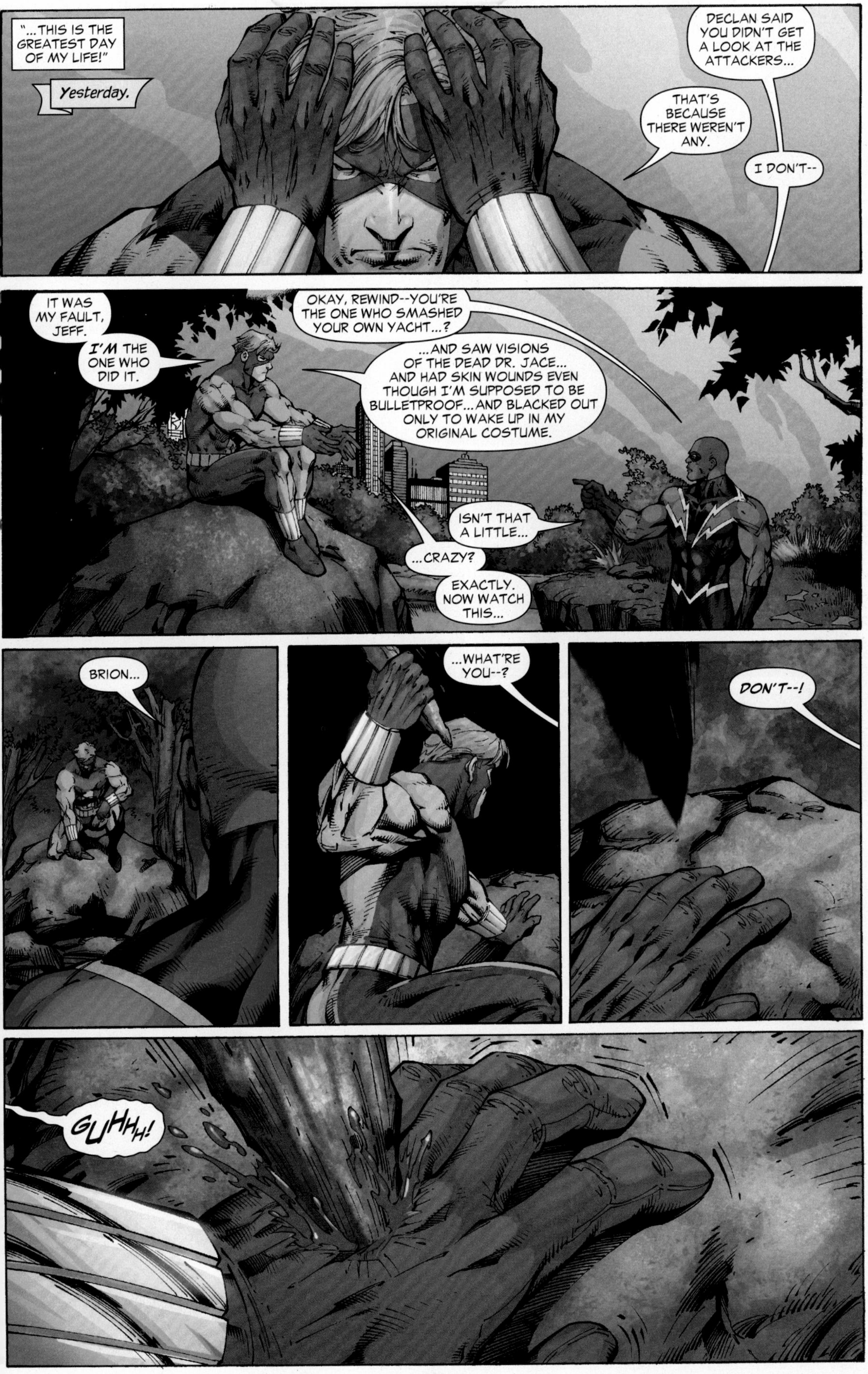

"...THIS IS THE GREATEST DAY OF MY LIFE!"
Yesterday.
DECLAN SAID YOU DIDN'T GET A LOOK AT THE ATTACKERS...
THAT'S BECAUSE THERE WEREN'T ANY.
I DON'T--
IT WAS MY FAULT, JEFF.
I'M THE ONE WHO DID IT.
OKAY, REWIND--YOU'RE THE ONE WHO SMASHED YOUR OWN YACHT...?
...AND SAW VISIONS OF THE DEAD DR. JACE... AND HAD SKIN WOUNDS EVEN THOUGH I'M SUPPOSED TO BE BULLETPROOF...AND BLACKED OUT ONLY TO WAKE UP IN MY ORIGINAL COSTUME.
ISN'T THAT A LITTLE...
...CRAZY?
EXACTLY. NOW WATCH THIS...
BRION...
...WHAT'RE YOU--?
DON'T--!
GUHHH!

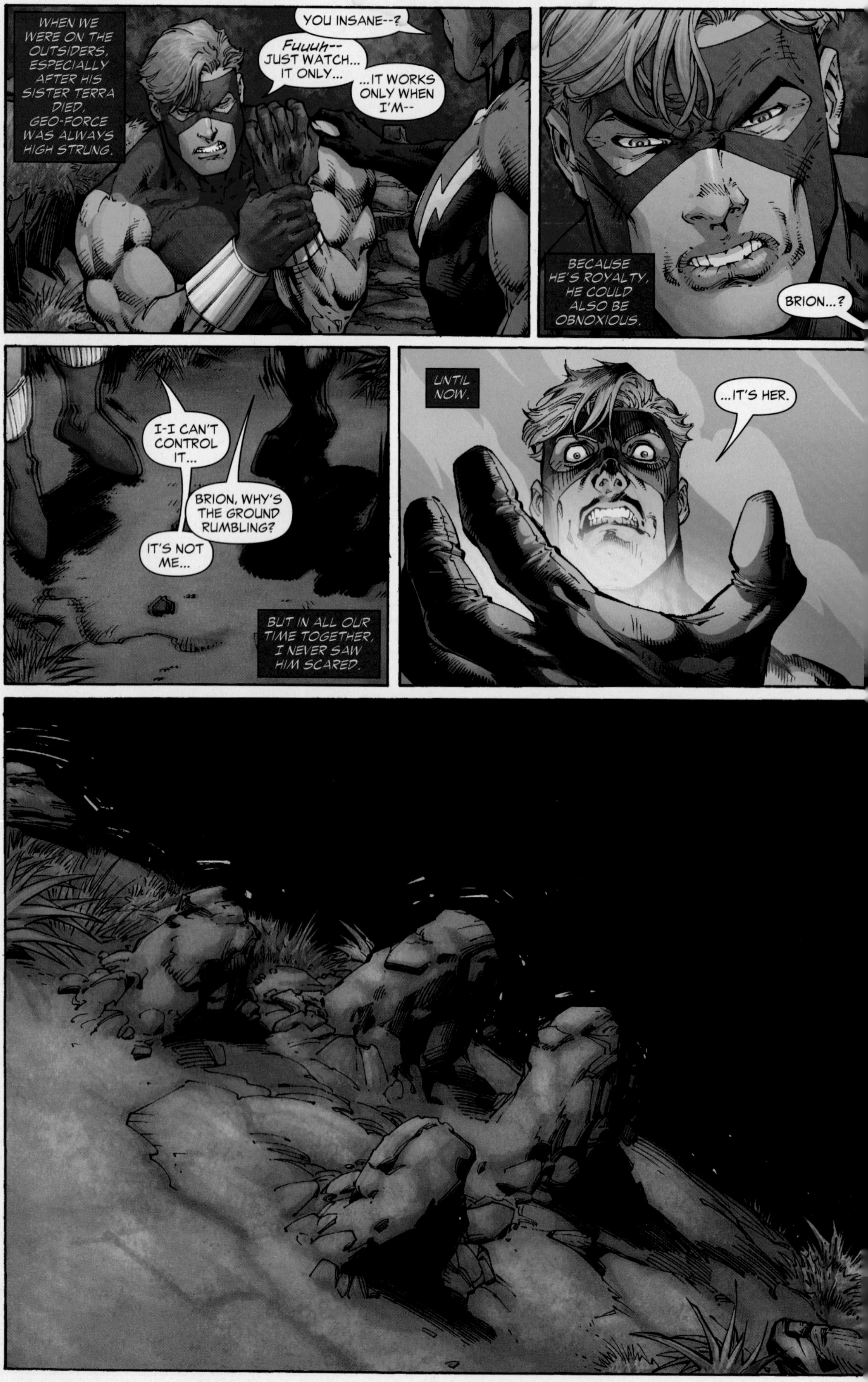
WHEN WE WERE ON THE OUTSIDERS, ESPECIALLY AFTER HIS SISTER TERRA DIED, GEO-FORCE WAS ALWAYS HIGH STRUNG.
YOU INSANE--?
Fuuuh-- JUST WATCH... IT ONLY...
...IT WORKS ONLY WHEN I'M--
BECAUSE HE'S ROYALTY, HE COULD ALSO BE OBNOXIOUS.
BRION...?
I-I CAN'T CONTROL IT...
BRION, WHY'S THE GROUND RUMBLING?
IT'S NOT ME...
BUT IN ALL OUR TIME TOGETHER, I NEVER SAW HIM SCARED.
UNTIL NOW.
...IT'S HER.

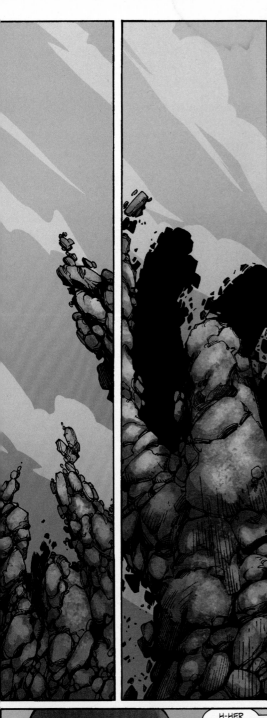

H-HER POWERS...

YOU'VE GOT TERRA'S P--

YOU CAN'T TELL ANYONE, JEFF...

NOT UNTIL WE FIGURE OUT WHAT'S GOING ON...

PLEASE...

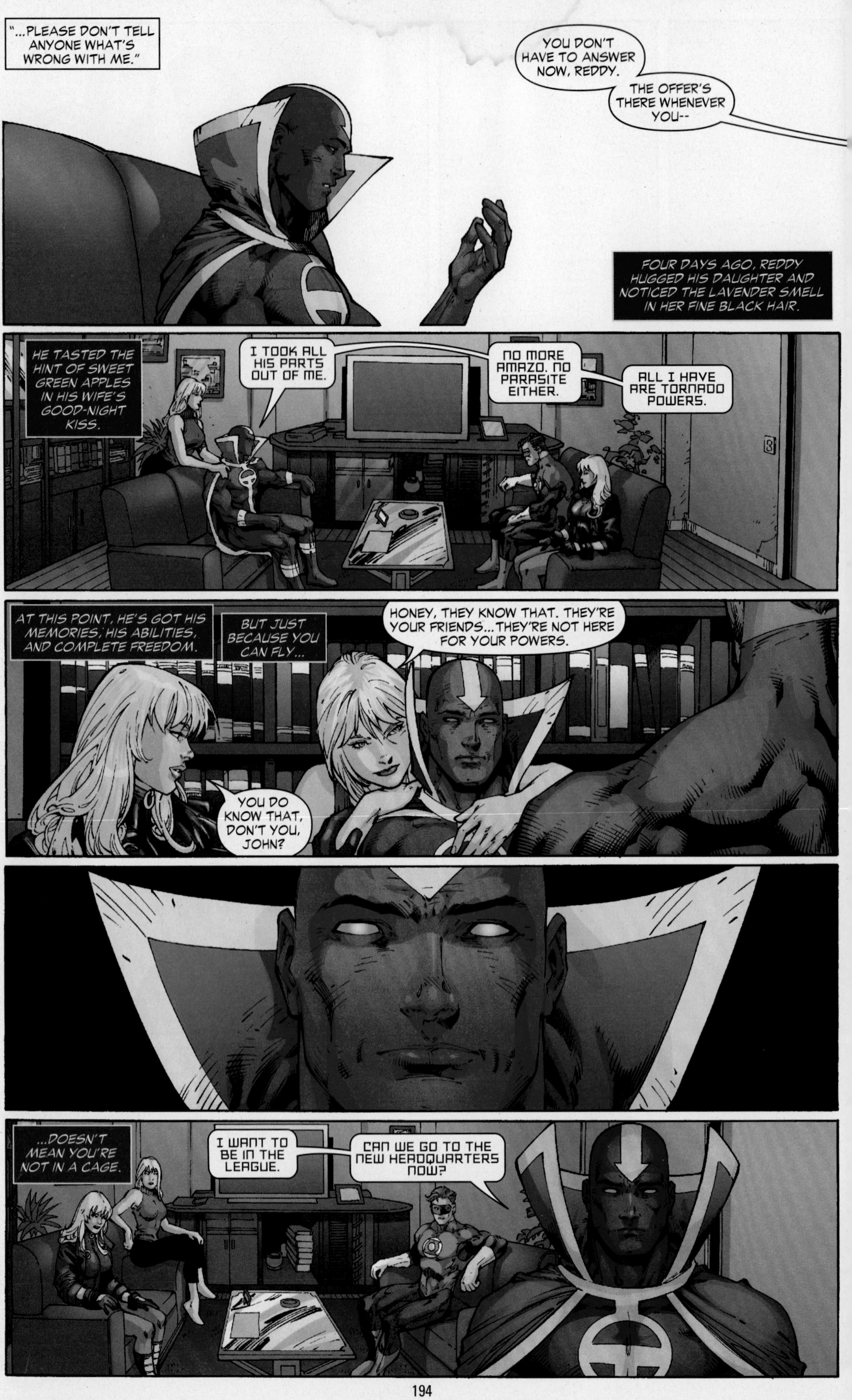
"...PLEASE DON'T TELL ANYONE WHAT'S WRONG WITH ME."
YOU DON'T HAVE TO ANSWER NOW, REDDY.
THE OFFER'S THERE WHENEVER YOU--
FOUR DAYS AGO, REDDY HUGGED HIS DAUGHTER AND NOTICED THE LAVENDER SMELL IN HER FINE BLACK HAIR.
HE TASTED THE HINT OF SWEET GREEN APPLES IN HIS WIFE'S GOOD-NIGHT KISS.
I TOOK ALL HIS PARTS OUT OF ME.
NO MORE AMAZO. NO PARASITE EITHER.
ALL I HAVE ARE TORNADO POWERS.
AT THIS POINT, HE'S GOT HIS MEMORIES, HIS ABILITIES, AND COMPLETE FREEDOM.
BUT JUST BECAUSE YOU CAN FLY...
HONEY, THEY KNOW THAT. THEY'RE YOUR FRIENDS... THEY'RE NOT HERE FOR YOUR POWERS.
YOU DO KNOW THAT, DON'T YOU, JOHN?
...DOESN'T MEAN YOU'RE NOT IN A CAGE.
I WANT TO BE IN THE LEAGUE.
CAN WE GO TO THE NEW HEADQUARTERS NOW?

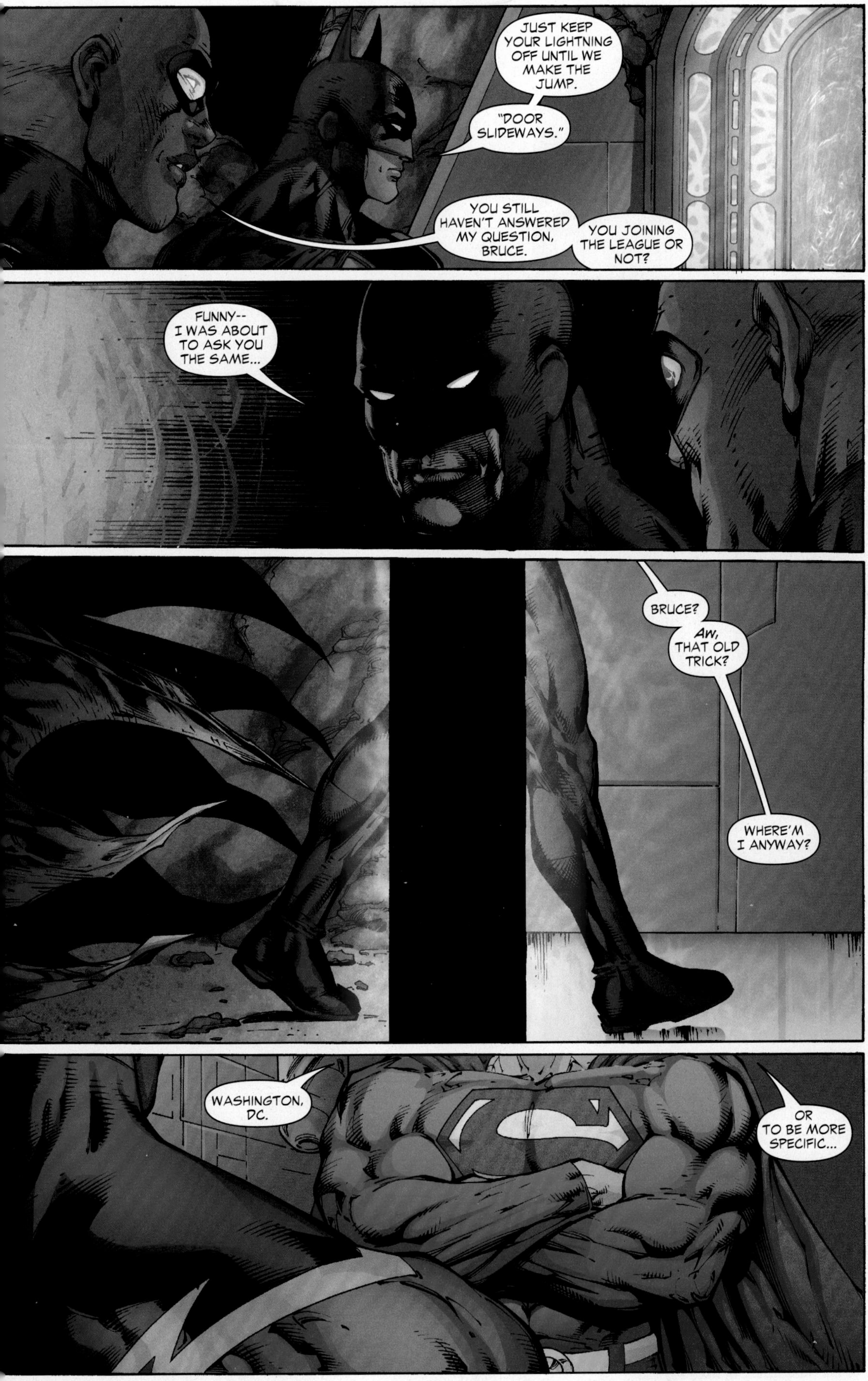
JUST KEEP YOUR LIGHTNING OFF UNTIL WE MAKE THE JUMP.
"DOOR SLIDEWAYS."
YOU STILL HAVEN'T ANSWERED MY QUESTION, BRUCE.
YOU JOINING THE LEAGUE OR NOT?
FUNNY-- I WAS ABOUT TO ASK YOU THE SAME...
BRUCE?
AW, THAT OLD TRICK?
WHERE'M I ANYWAY?
WASHINGTON, DC.
OR TO BE MORE SPECIFIC...

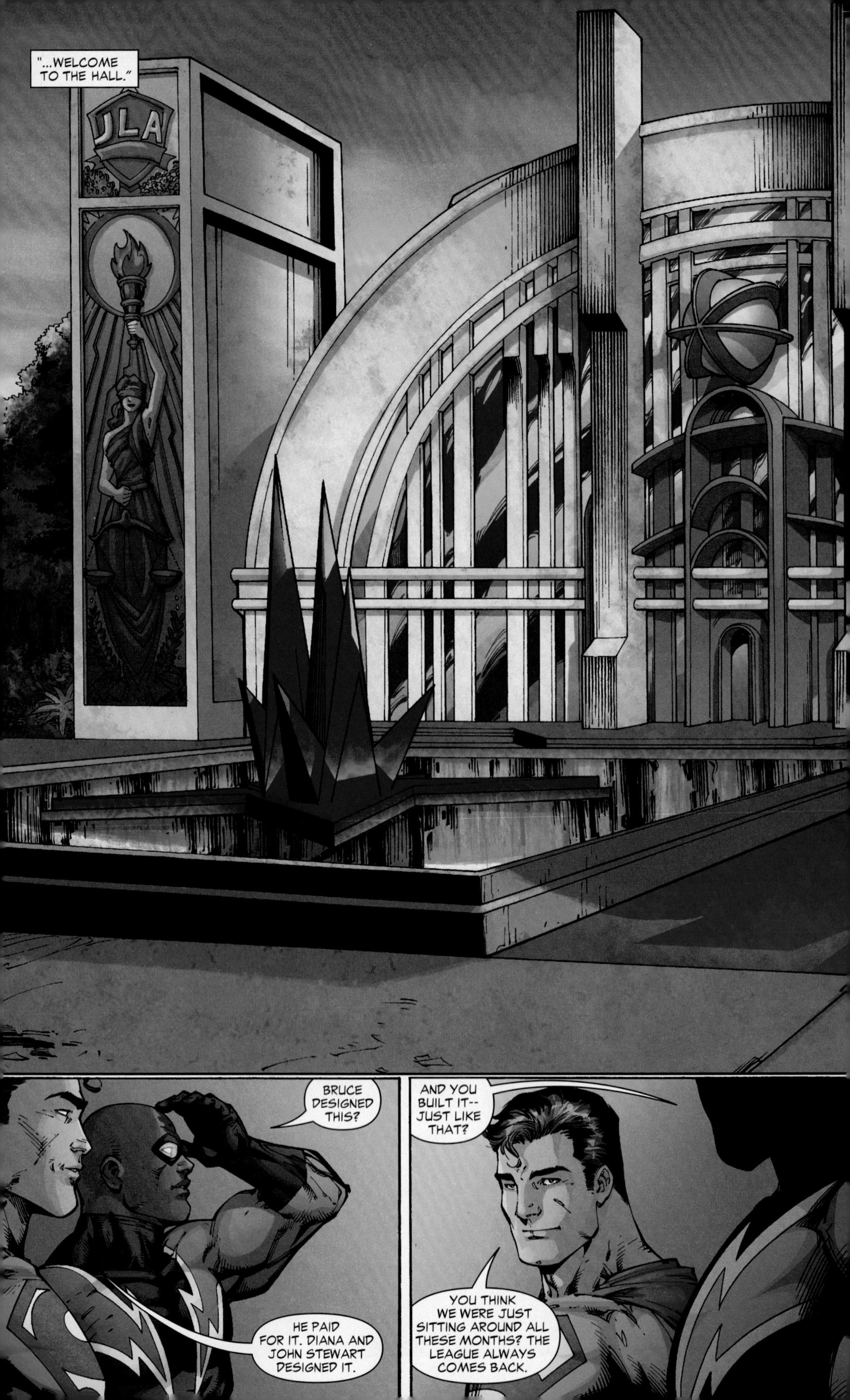
"...WELCOME TO THE HALL."
JLA
BRUCE DESIGNED THIS?
HE PAID FOR IT. DIANA AND JOHN STEWART DESIGNED IT.
AND YOU BUILT IT-- JUST LIKE THAT?
YOU THINK WE WERE JUST SITTING AROUND ALL THESE MONTHS? THE LEAGUE ALWAYS COMES BACK.

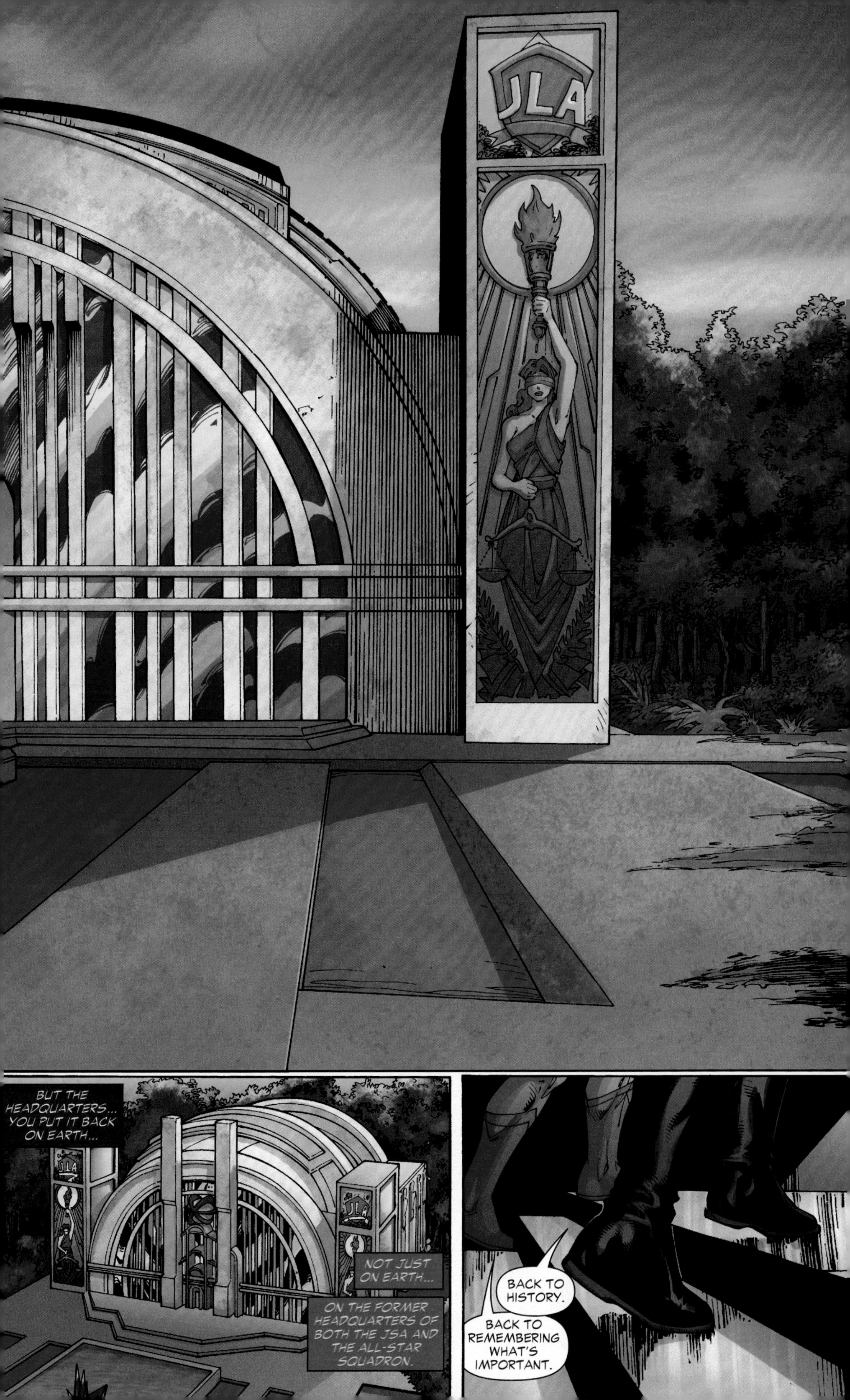
JLA
BUT THE HEADQUARTERS... YOU PUT IT BACK ON EARTH...
NOT JUST ON EARTH...
ON THE FORMER HEADQUARTERS OF BOTH THE JSA AND THE ALL-STAR SQUADRON.
BACK TO HISTORY.
BACK TO REMEMBERING WHAT'S IMPORTANT.

SENDS A HELL OF A MESSAGE.

IT NEEDS TO.

THE LEAGUE ISN'T AN IDEA.

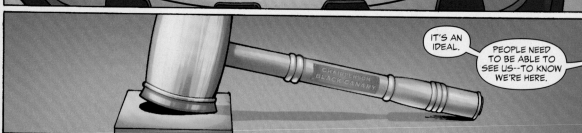

IT'S AN IDEAL.

PEOPLE NEED TO BE ABLE TO SEE US--TO KNOW WE'RE HERE.

CHAIRPERSON BLACK CANARY

LIKE WEARING A BRIGHT BLUE COSTUME AND A BLAZING RED CAPE?

SOMETHING LIKE THAT.

THOUGH WHEN THE TOUR--

THERE'S A TOUR?

WHEN THE TOUR BRINGS THEM INSIDE...

...BELIEVE ME...

"...THEY'LL FIND A LOT MORE THAN THAT."

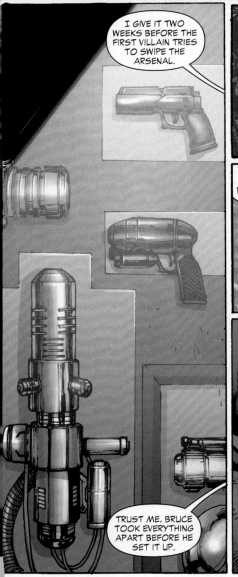

I GIVE IT TWO WEEKS BEFORE THE FIRST VILLAIN TRIES TO SWIPE THE ARSENAL.

TRUST ME, BRUCE TOOK EVERYTHING APART BEFORE HE SET IT UP.

BRUCE SET THIS UP? HE'S STARTING TO GET SENTIMENTAL.

IF HE WERE SENTIMENTAL, HE WOULD'VE GIVEN US THE GIANT PENNY.

HERE'S THE BEST PART, THOUGH: THE TRAINING ROOM, ALSO KNOWN AS THE KITCHEN.

WHY WOULD YOU CALL THE TRAINING ROOM THE KITCHEN?

IF YOU CAN'T STAND THE HEAT...

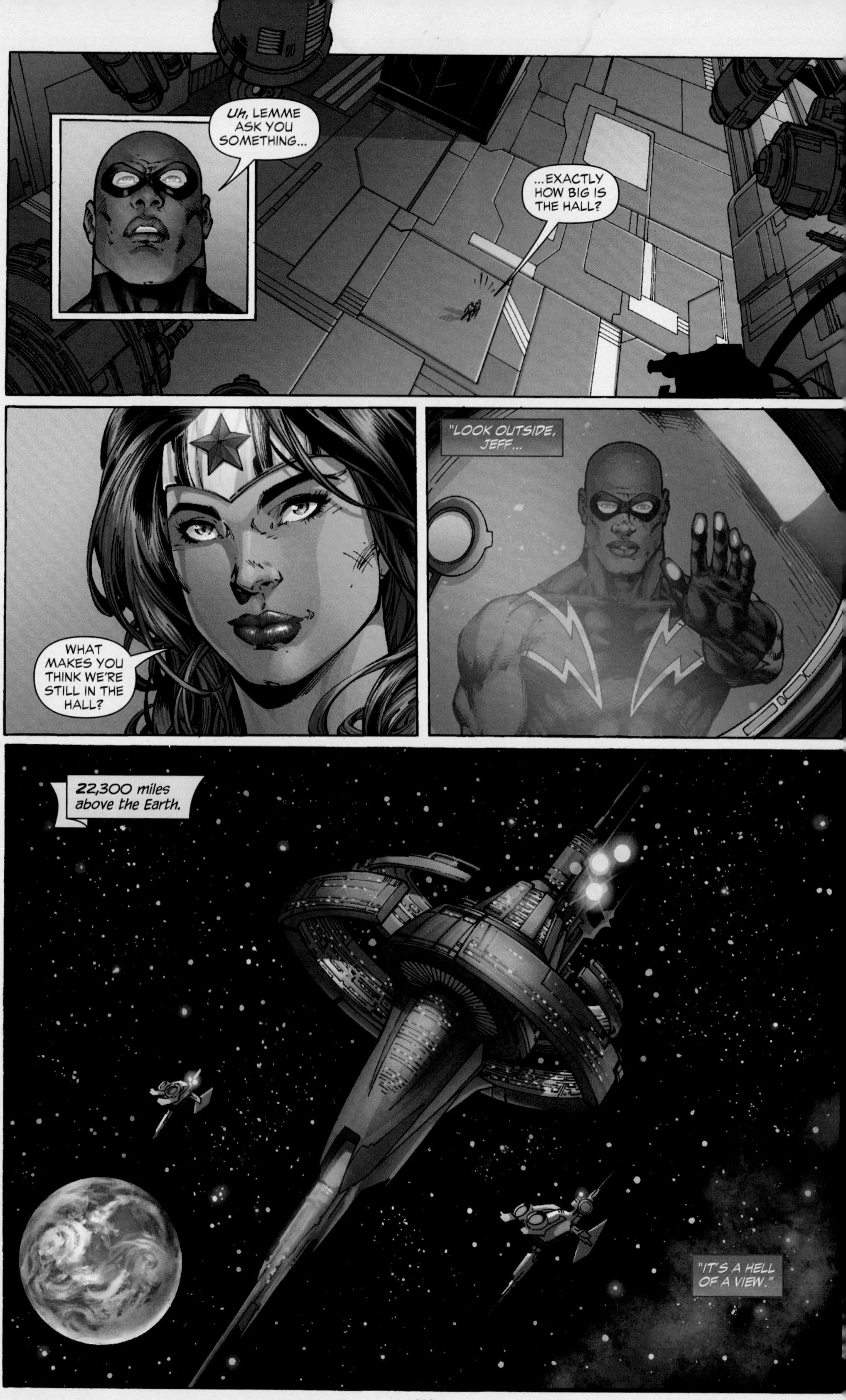
Uh, LEMME ASK YOU SOMETHING...
...EXACTLY HOW BIG IS THE HALL?
WHAT MAKES YOU THINK WE'RE STILL IN THE HALL?
"LOOK OUTSIDE, JEFF...
22,300 miles above the Earth.
"IT'S A HELL OF A VIEW."

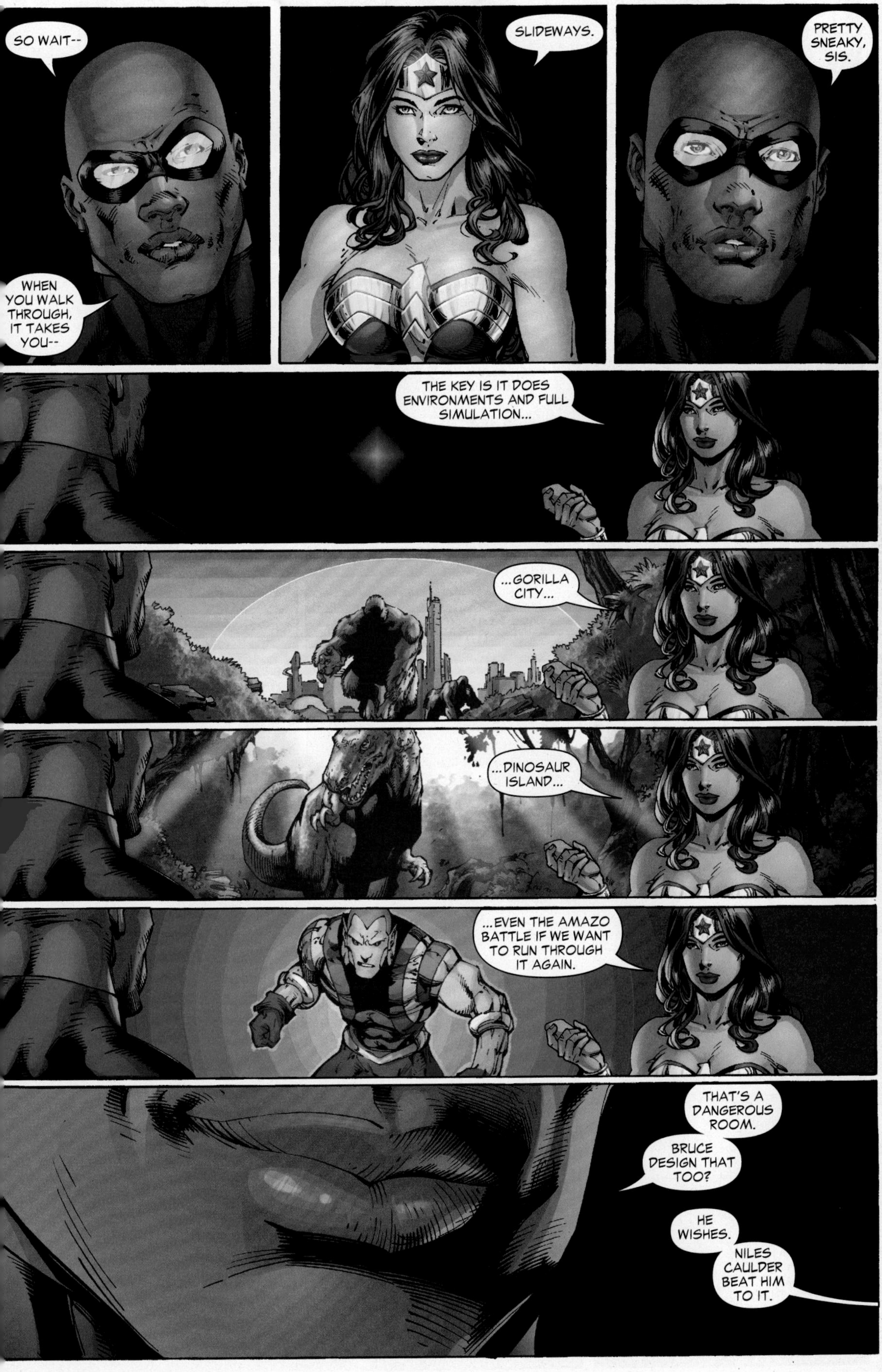
SO WAIT--
WHEN YOU WALK THROUGH, IT TAKES YOU--
SLIDEWAYS.
PRETTY SNEAKY, SIS.
THE KEY IS IT DOES ENVIRONMENTS AND FULL SIMULATION...
...GORILLA CITY...
...DINOSAUR ISLAND...
...EVEN THE AMAZO BATTLE IF WE WANT TO RUN THROUGH IT AGAIN.
THAT'S A DANGEROUS ROOM.
BRUCE DESIGN THAT TOO?
HE WISHES.
NILES CAULDER BEAT HIM TO IT.

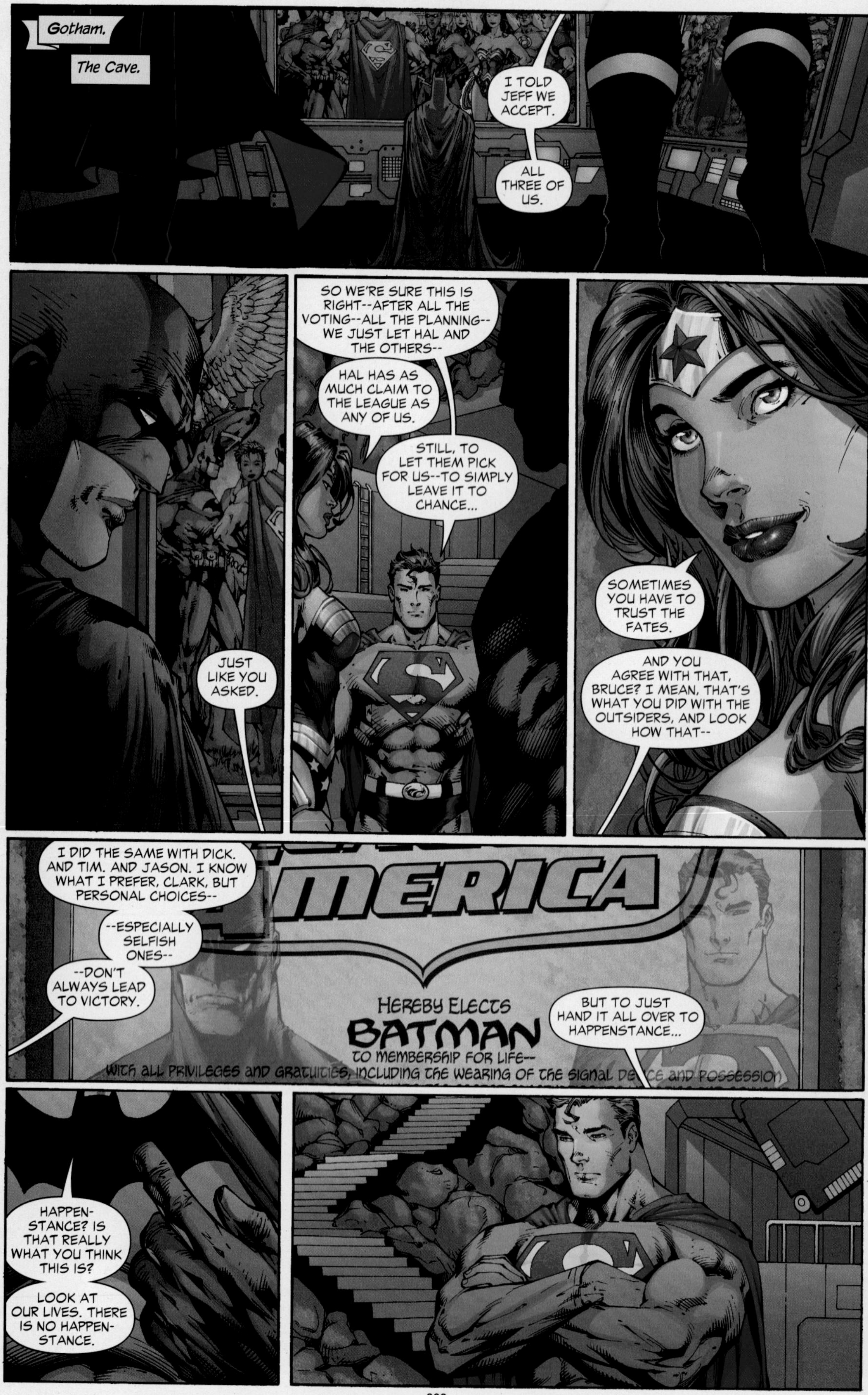
Gotham.
The Cave.
I TOLD JEFF WE ACCEPT.
ALL THREE OF US.
JUST LIKE YOU ASKED.
SO WE'RE SURE THIS IS RIGHT--AFTER ALL THE VOTING--ALL THE PLANNING--WE JUST LET HAL AND THE OTHERS--
HAL HAS AS MUCH CLAIM TO THE LEAGUE AS ANY OF US.
STILL, TO LET THEM PICK FOR US--TO SIMPLY LEAVE IT TO CHANCE...
SOMETIMES YOU HAVE TO TRUST THE FATES.
AND YOU AGREE WITH THAT, BRUCE? I MEAN, THAT'S WHAT YOU DID WITH THE OUTSIDERS, AND LOOK HOW THAT--
I DID THE SAME WITH DICK. AND TIM. AND JASON. I KNOW WHAT I PREFER, CLARK, BUT PERSONAL CHOICES--
--ESPECIALLY SELFISH ONES--
--DON'T ALWAYS LEAD TO VICTORY.
MERICA
HEREBY ELECTS
BATMAN
TO MEMBERSHIP FOR LIFE--
WITH ALL PRIVILEGES AND GRATUITIES, INCLUDING THE WEARING OF THE SIGNAL DE CE AND POSSESSION
BUT TO JUST HAND IT ALL OVER TO HAPPENSTANCE...
HAPPEN-STANCE? IS THAT REALLY WHAT YOU THINK THIS IS?
LOOK AT OUR LIVES. THERE IS NO HAPPEN-STANCE.

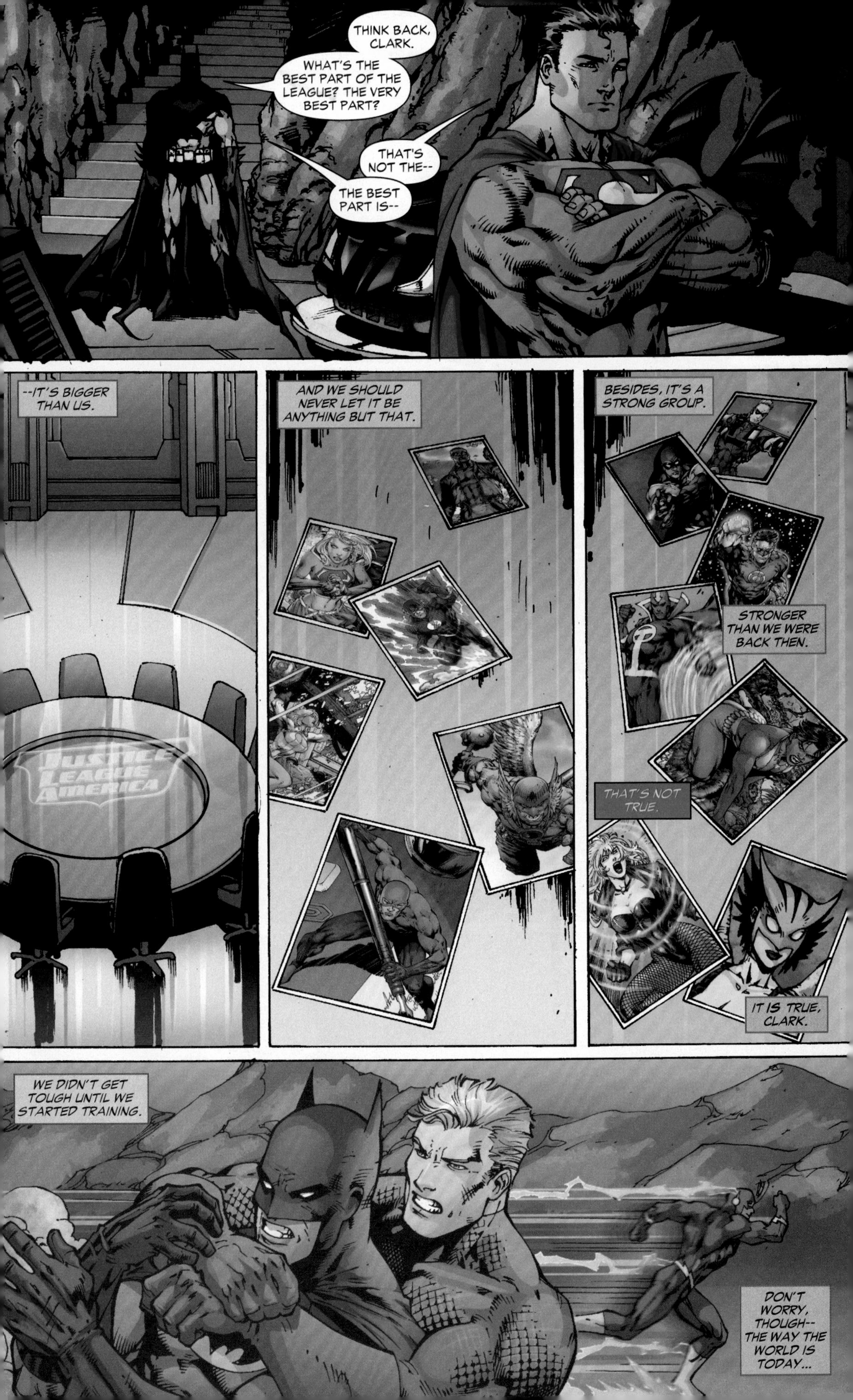
THINK BACK, CLARK.
WHAT'S THE BEST PART OF THE LEAGUE? THE VERY BEST PART?
THAT'S NOT THE--
THE BEST PART IS--
--IT'S BIGGER THAN US.
JUSTICE LEAGUE AMERICA
AND WE SHOULD NEVER LET IT BE ANYTHING BUT THAT.
BESIDES, IT'S A STRONG GROUP.
STRONGER THAN WE WERE BACK THEN.
THAT'S NOT TRUE.
IT IS TRUE, CLARK.
WE DIDN'T GET TOUGH UNTIL WE STARTED TRAINING.
DON'T WORRY, THOUGH-- THE WAY THE WORLD IS TODAY...

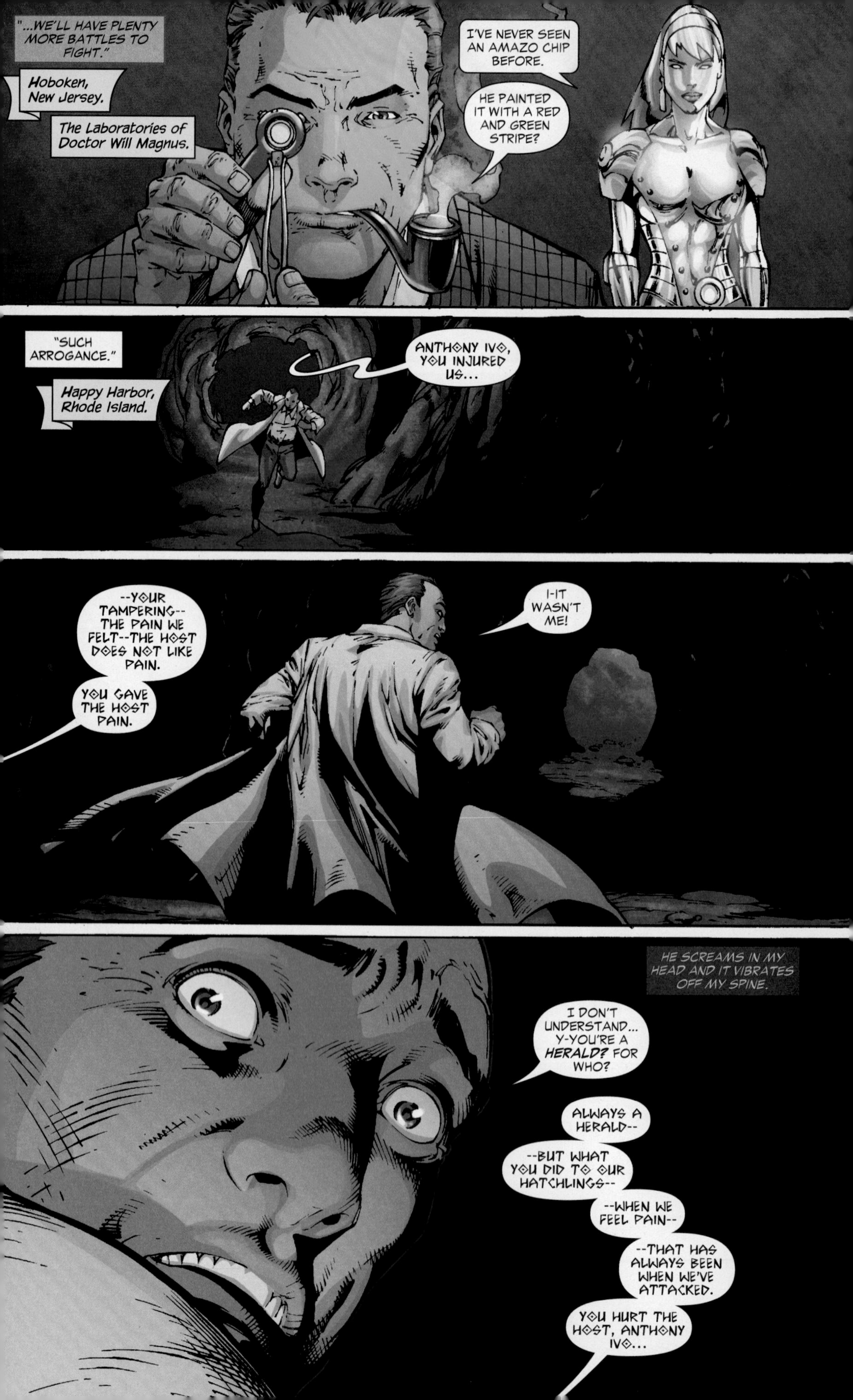
"...WE'LL HAVE PLENTY MORE BATTLES TO FIGHT."
Hoboken, New Jersey.
The Laboratories of Doctor Will Magnus.
I'VE NEVER SEEN AN AMAZO CHIP BEFORE.
HE PAINTED IT WITH A RED AND GREEN STRIPE?
"SUCH ARROGANCE."
Happy Harbor, Rhode Island.
ANTHONY IVO, YOU INJURED US...
--YOUR TAMPERING-- THE PAIN WE FELT--THE HOST DOES NOT LIKE PAIN.
YOU GAVE THE HOST PAIN.
I-IT WASN'T ME!
HE SCREAMS IN MY HEAD AND IT VIBRATES OFF MY SPINE.
I DON'T UNDERSTAND... Y-YOU'RE A HERALD? FOR WHO?
ALWAYS A HERALD--
--BUT WHAT YOU DID TO OUR HATCHLINGS--
--WHEN WE FEEL PAIN--
--THAT HAS ALWAYS BEEN WHEN WE'VE ATTACKED.
YOU HURT THE HOST, ANTHONY IVO...

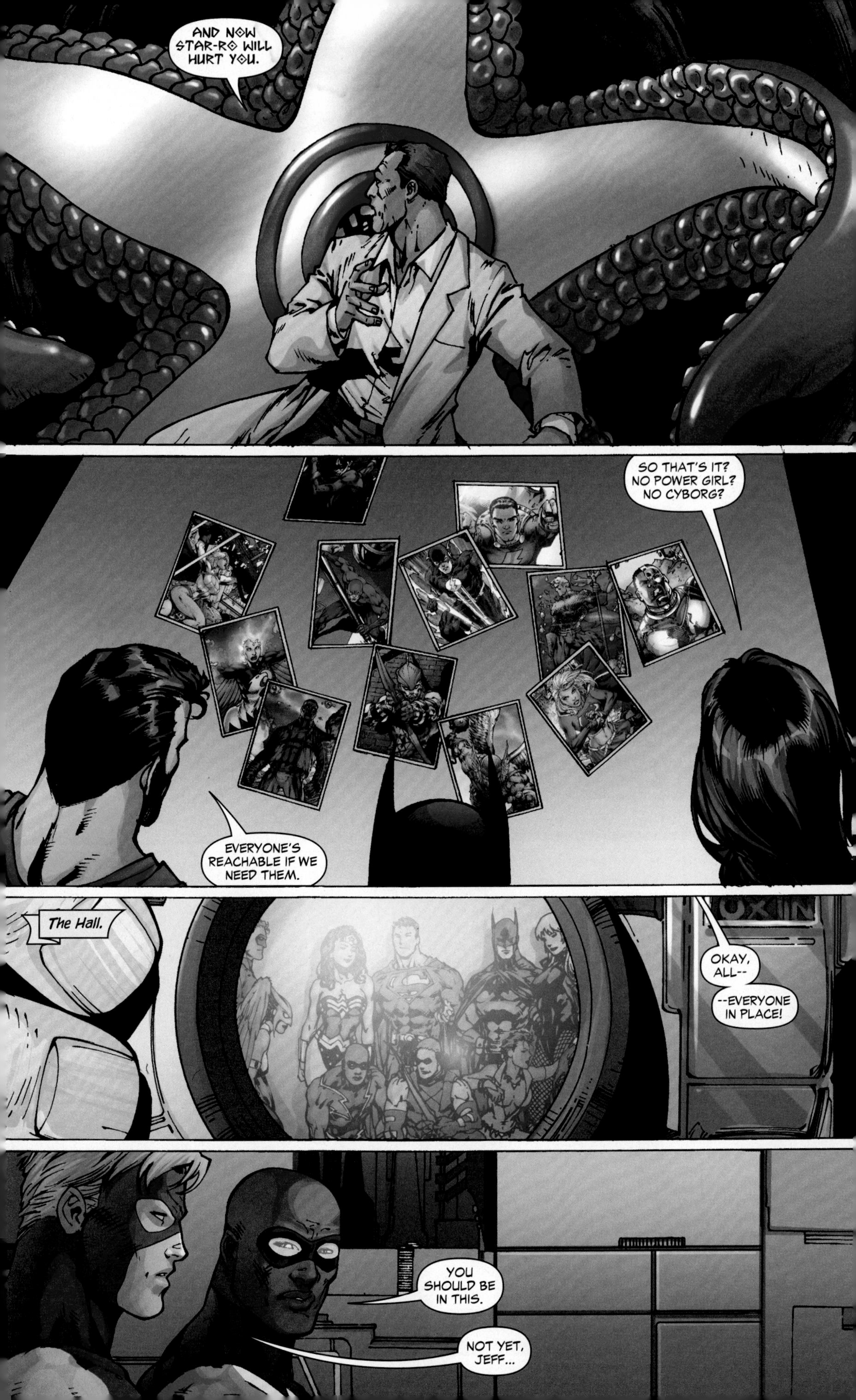
AND NOW STAR-RO WILL HURT YOU.
SO THAT'S IT? NO POWER GIRL? NO CYBORG?
EVERYONE'S REACHABLE IF WE NEED THEM.
The Hall.
OKAY, ALL--
--EVERYONE IN PLACE!
YOU SHOULD BE IN THIS.
NOT YET, JEFF...

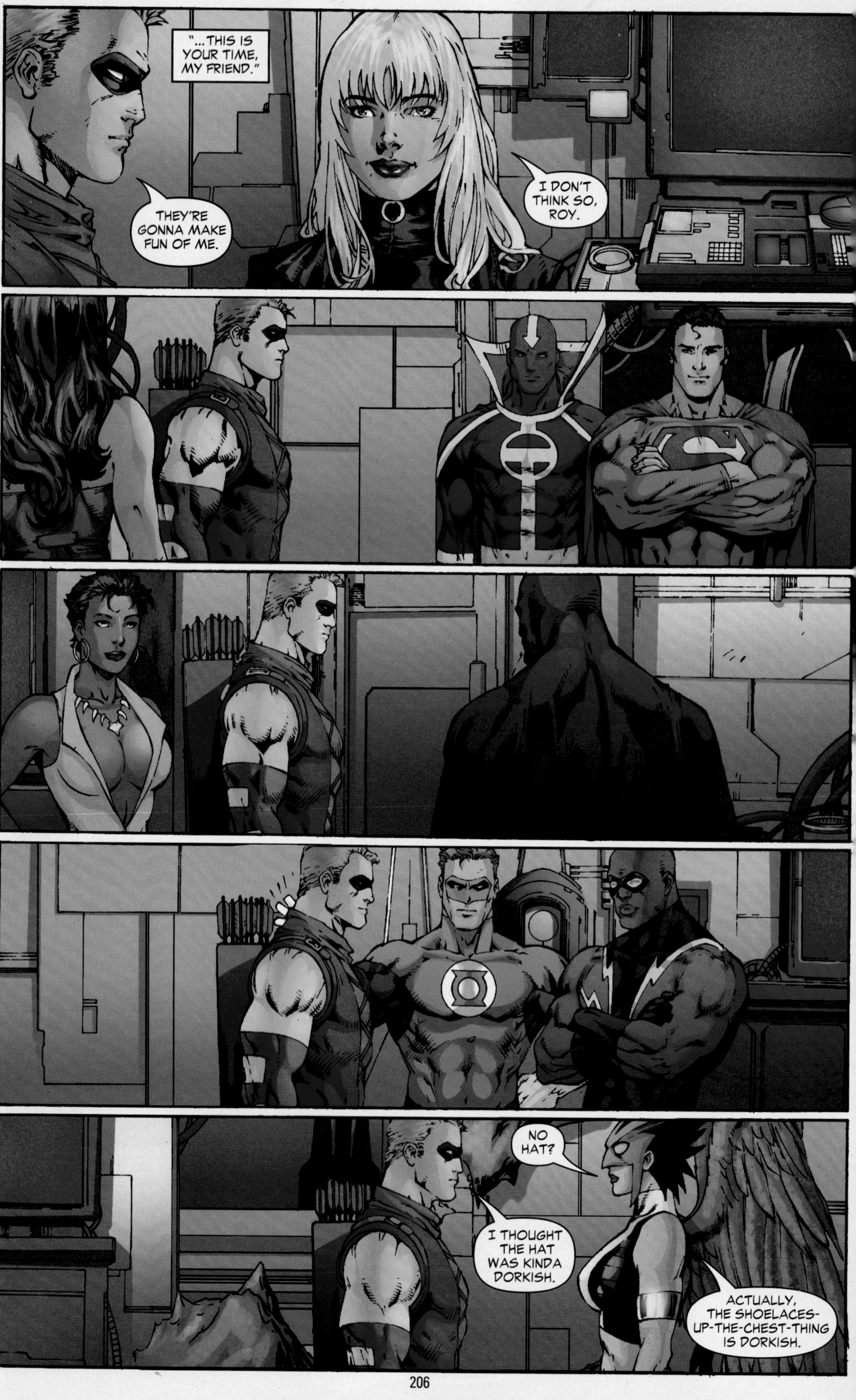
"...THIS IS YOUR TIME, MY FRIEND."
THEY'RE GONNA MAKE FUN OF ME.
I DON'T THINK SO, ROY.
NO HAT?
I THOUGHT THE HAT WAS KINDA DORKISH.
ACTUALLY, THE SHOELACES-UP-THE-CHEST-THING IS DORKISH.

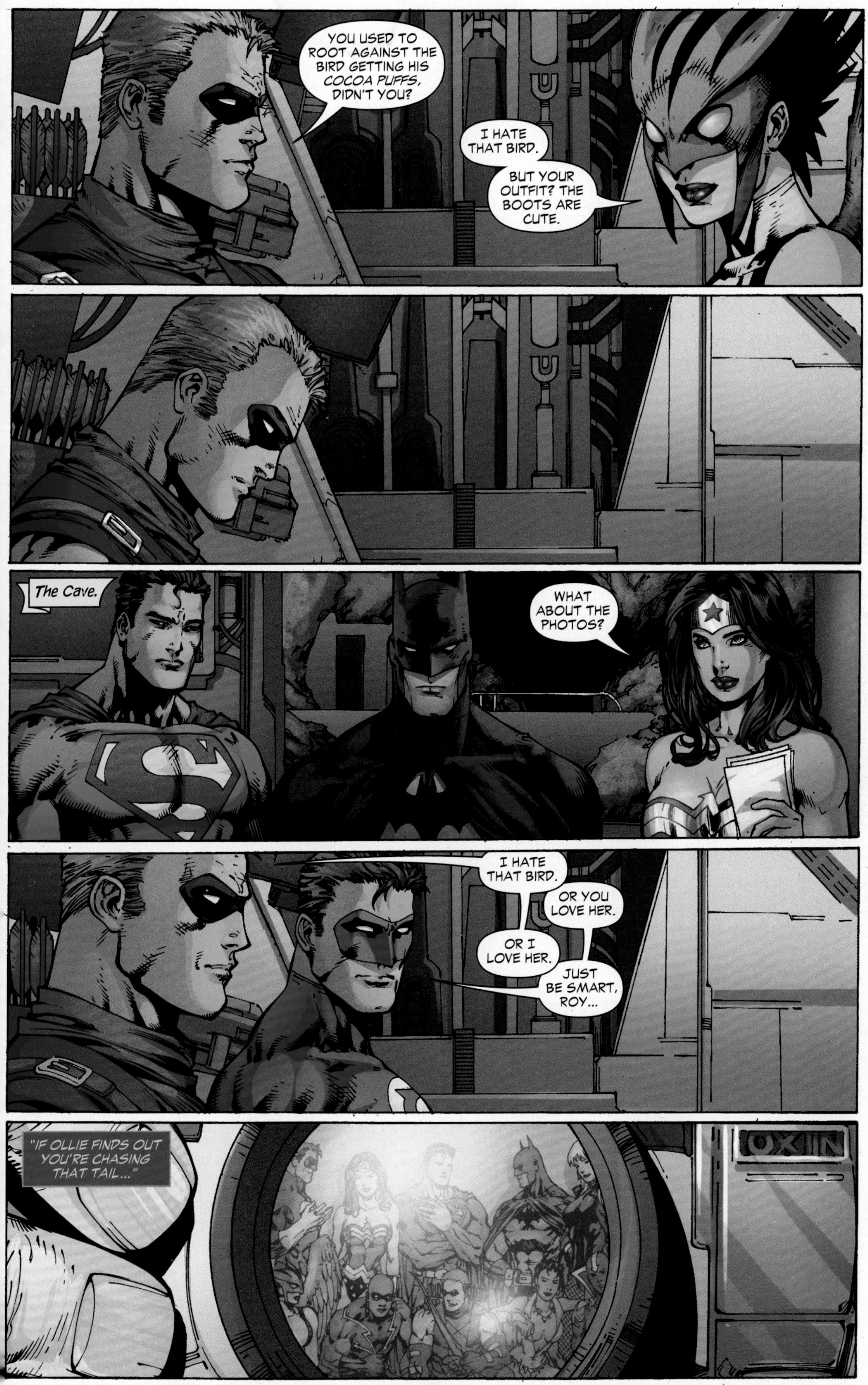

YOU USED TO ROOT AGAINST THE BIRD GETTING HIS COCOA PUFFS, DIDN'T YOU?
I HATE THAT BIRD.
BUT YOUR OUTFIT? THE BOOTS ARE CUTE.
The Cave.
WHAT ABOUT THE PHOTOS?
I HATE THAT BIRD.
OR YOU LOVE HER.
OR I LOVE HER.
JUST BE SMART, ROY...
"IF OLLIE FINDS OUT YOU'RE CHASING THAT TAIL..."

JUSTICE
LEAGUE of
AMERICA

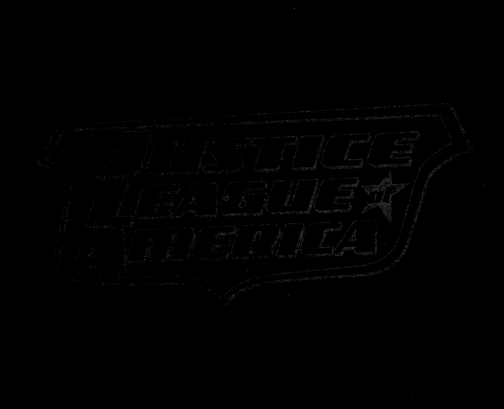

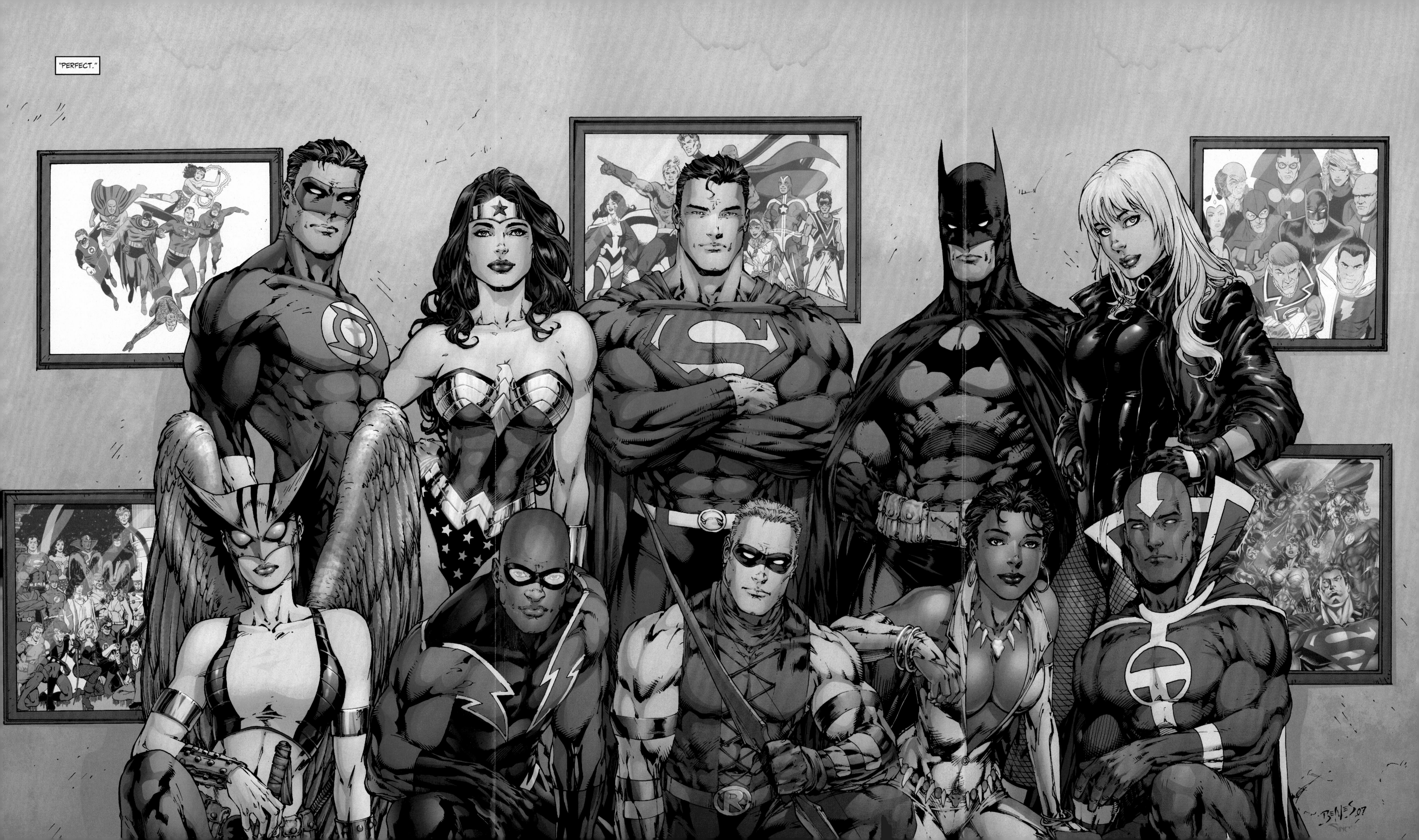
"PERFECT."

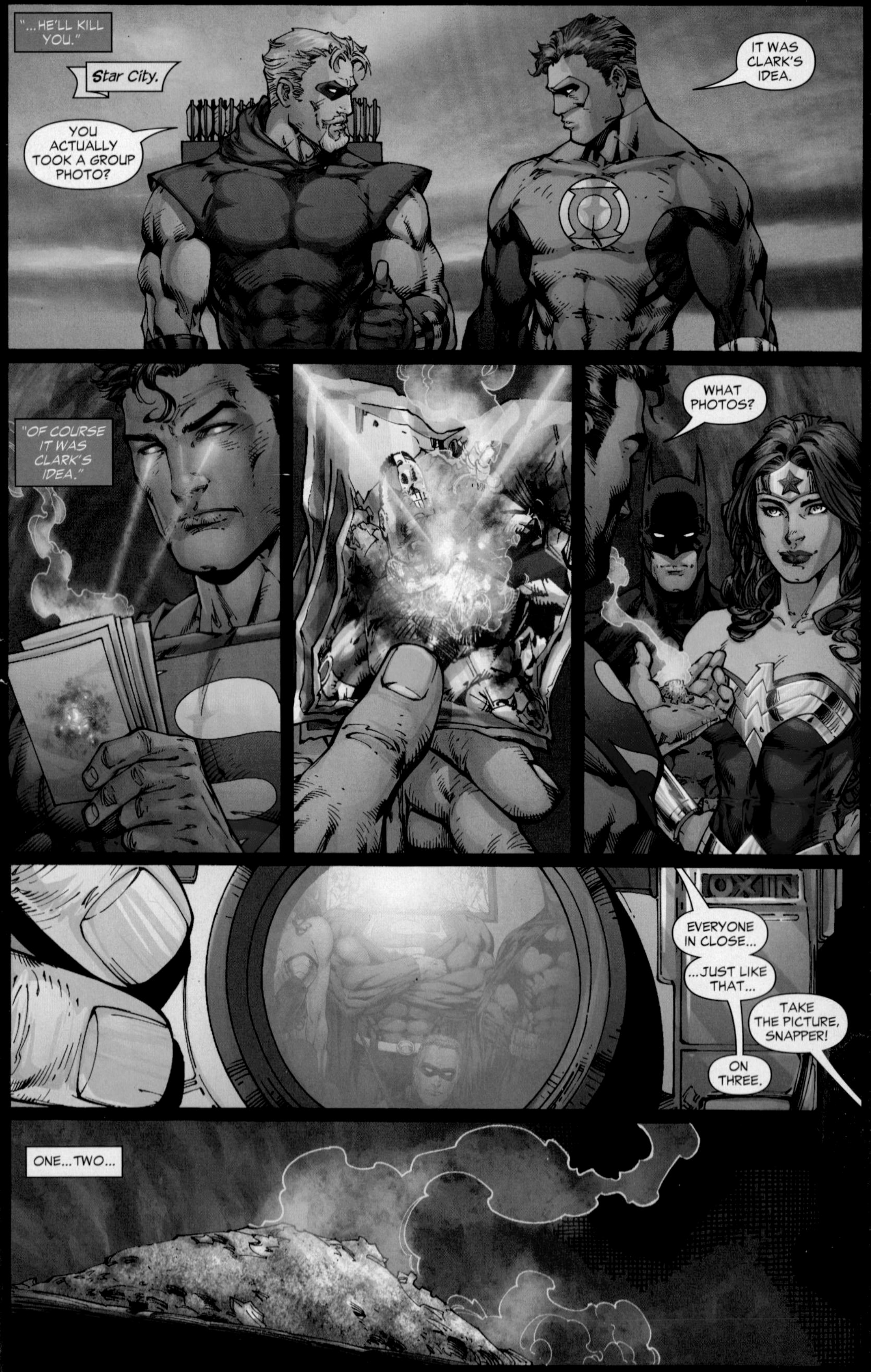
"...HE'LL KILL YOU."
Star City.
YOU ACTUALLY TOOK A GROUP PHOTO?
IT WAS CLARK'S IDEA.
"OF COURSE IT WAS CLARK'S IDEA."
WHAT PHOTOS?
EVERYONE IN CLOSE...
...JUST LIKE THAT...
TAKE THE PICTURE, SNAPPER!
ON THREE.
ONE...TWO...

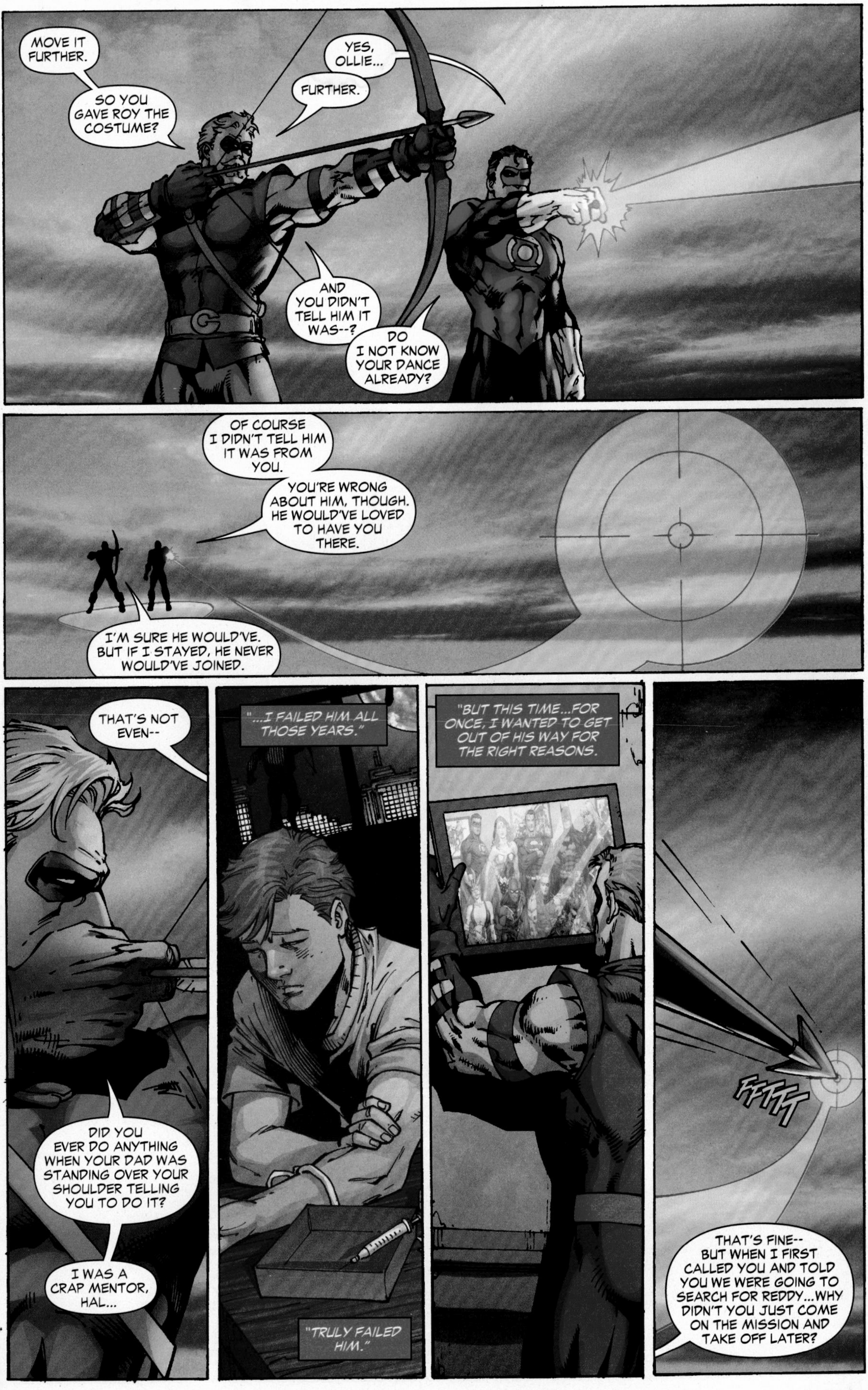
MOVE IT FURTHER.
YES, OLLIE...
FURTHER.
SO YOU GAVE ROY THE COSTUME?
AND YOU DIDN'T TELL HIM IT WAS--?
DO I NOT KNOW YOUR DANCE ALREADY?
OF COURSE I DIDN'T TELL HIM IT WAS FROM YOU.
YOU'RE WRONG ABOUT HIM, THOUGH. HE WOULD'VE LOVED TO HAVE YOU THERE.
I'M SURE HE WOULD'VE. BUT IF I STAYED, HE NEVER WOULD'VE JOINED.
THAT'S NOT EVEN--
DID YOU EVER DO ANYTHING WHEN YOUR DAD WAS STANDING OVER YOUR SHOULDER TELLING YOU TO DO IT?
I WAS A CRAP MENTOR, HAL...
"...I FAILED HIM ALL THOSE YEARS."
"TRULY FAILED HIM."
"BUT THIS TIME...FOR ONCE, I WANTED TO GET OUT OF HIS WAY FOR THE RIGHT REASONS.
FFFT
THAT'S FINE-- BUT WHEN I FIRST CALLED YOU AND TOLD YOU WE WERE GOING TO SEARCH FOR REDDY...WHY DIDN'T YOU JUST COME ON THE MISSION AND TAKE OFF LATER?

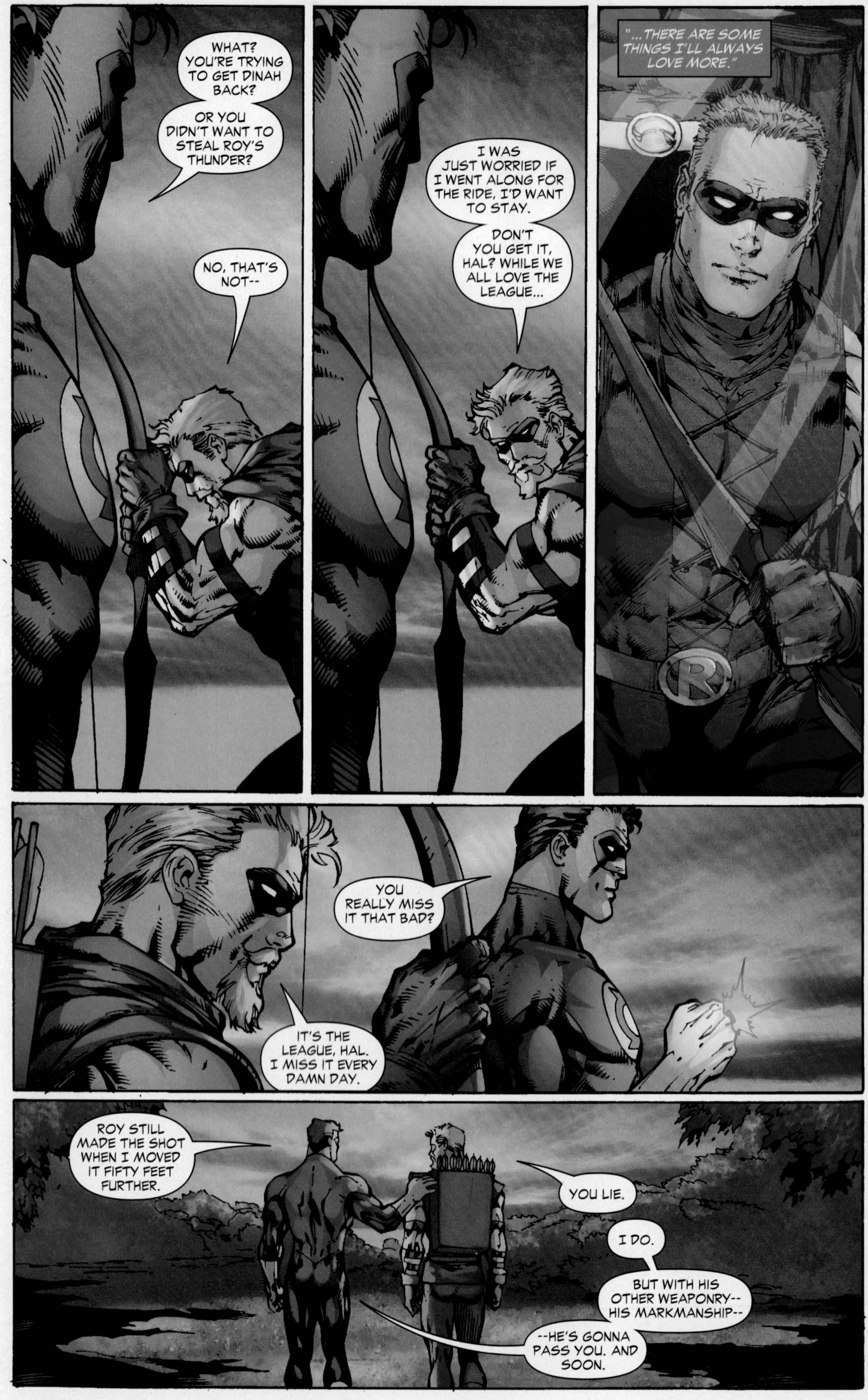
WHAT? YOU'RE TRYING TO GET DINAH BACK?
OR YOU DIDN'T WANT TO STEAL ROY'S THUNDER?
NO, THAT'S NOT--
I WAS JUST WORRIED IF I WENT ALONG FOR THE RIDE, I'D WANT TO STAY.
DON'T YOU GET IT, HAL? WHILE WE ALL LOVE THE LEAGUE...
"...THERE ARE SOME THINGS I'LL ALWAYS LOVE MORE."
YOU REALLY MISS IT THAT BAD?
IT'S THE LEAGUE, HAL. I MISS IT EVERY DAMN DAY.
ROY STILL MADE THE SHOT WHEN I MOVED IT FIFTY FEET FURTHER.
YOU LIE.
I DO.
BUT WITH HIS OTHER WEAPONRY-- HIS MARKMANSHIP--
--HE'S GONNA PASS YOU. AND SOON.

P R O L O G U E

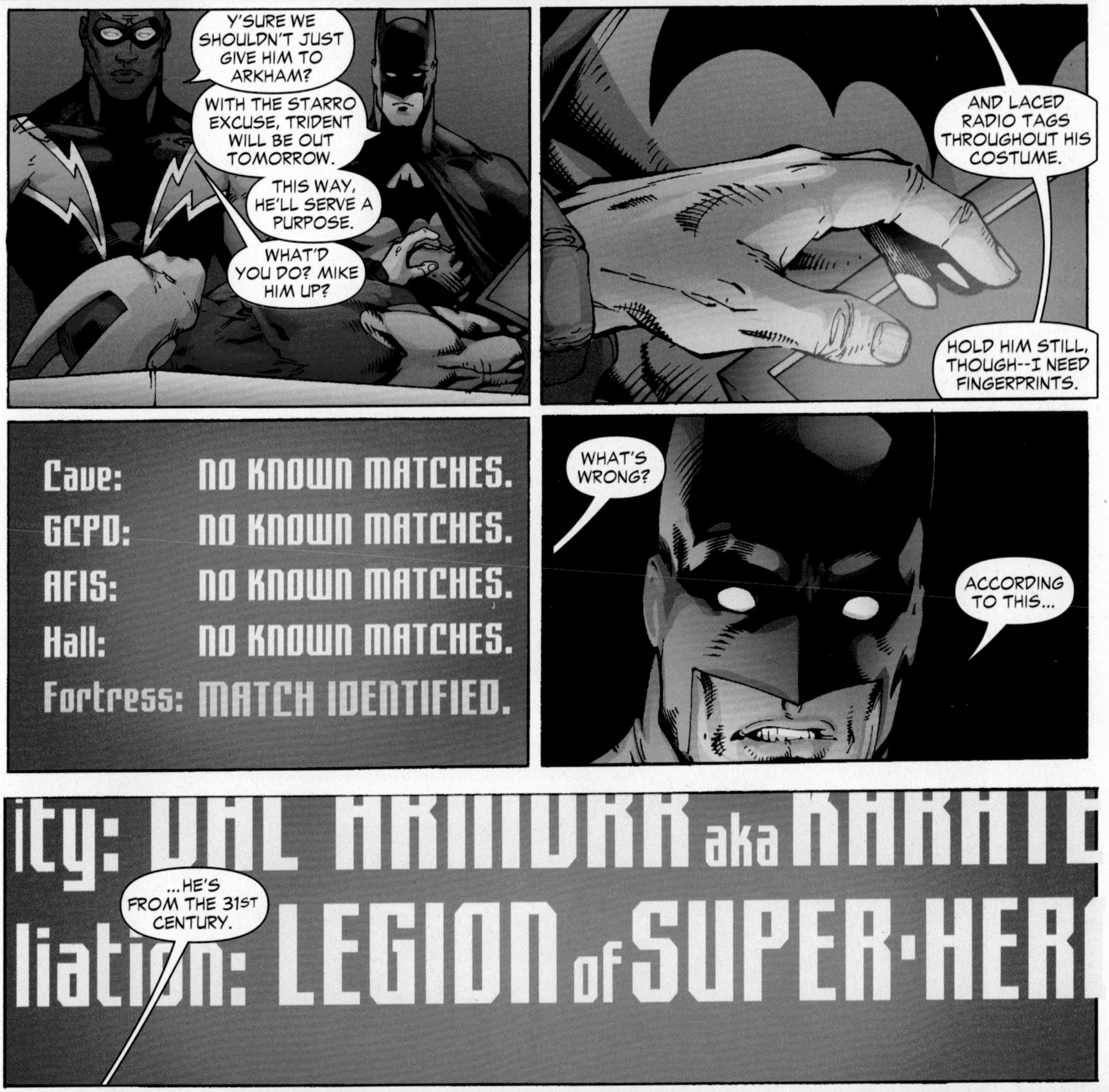

Y'SURE WE SHOULDN'T JUST GIVE HIM TO ARKHAM?
WITH THE STARRO EXCUSE, TRIDENT WILL BE OUT TOMORROW.
THIS WAY, HE'LL SERVE A PURPOSE.
WHAT'D YOU DO? MIKE HIM UP?
AND LACED RADIO TAGS THROUGHOUT HIS COSTUME.
HOLD HIM STILL, THOUGH--I NEED FINGERPRINTS.
Cave: NO KNOWN MATCHES.
GCPD: NO KNOWN MATCHES.
AFIS: NO KNOWN MATCHES.
Hall: NO KNOWN MATCHES.
Fortress: MATCH IDENTIFIED.
WHAT'S WRONG?
ACCORDING TO THIS...
liation: LEGION of SUPER-HER
...HE'S FROM THE 31ST CENTURY.

THE TORNADO'S PATH

E P I L O G U E

ROLL CALL

JLA VARIANT COVER GALLERY

VARIANT COVER TO JUSTICE LEAGUE OF AMERICA #1

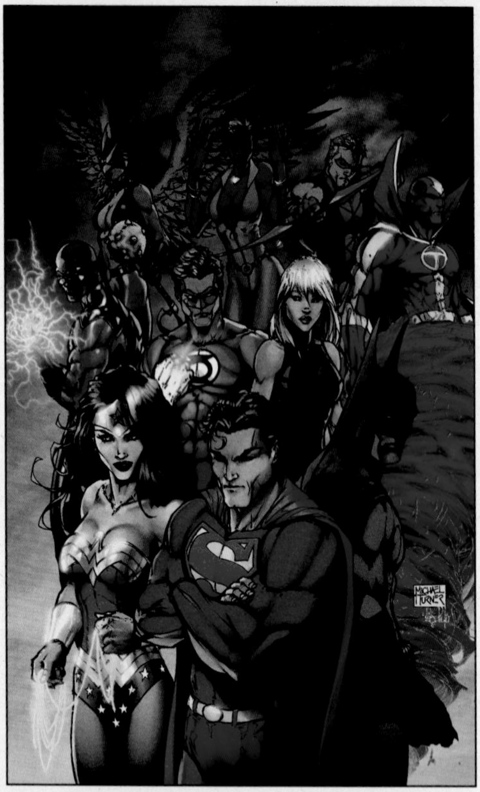
MICHAEL TURNER

MICHAEL TURNER & PETER STEIGERWALD

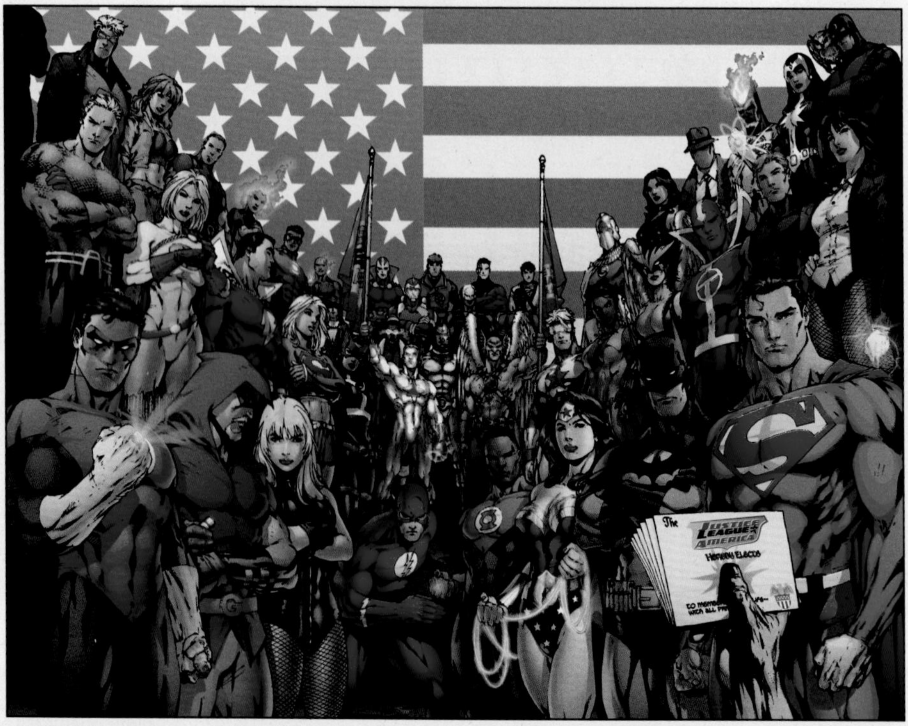

VARIANT COVER TO JUSTICE LEAGUE OF AMERICA #1 SECOND PRINTING ED BENES, MARIAH BENES & ALEX SINCLAIR

VARIANT COVER TO JUSTICE LEAGUE OF AMERICA #2

PHIL JIMENEZ, ANDY LANNING & JEROMY COX

VARIANT COVER TO JUSTICE LEAGUE OF AMERICA #3

CHRIS SPROUSE, KARL STORY & ALEX SINCLAIR

VARIANT COVER TO JUSTICE LEAGUE OF AMERICA #4

J.G. JONES & ALEX SINCLAIR

VARIANT COVER TO JUSTICE LEAGUE OF AMERICA #5

ART ADAMS & ALEX SINCLAIR

VARIANT COVER TO JUSTICE LEAGUE OF AMERICA #6

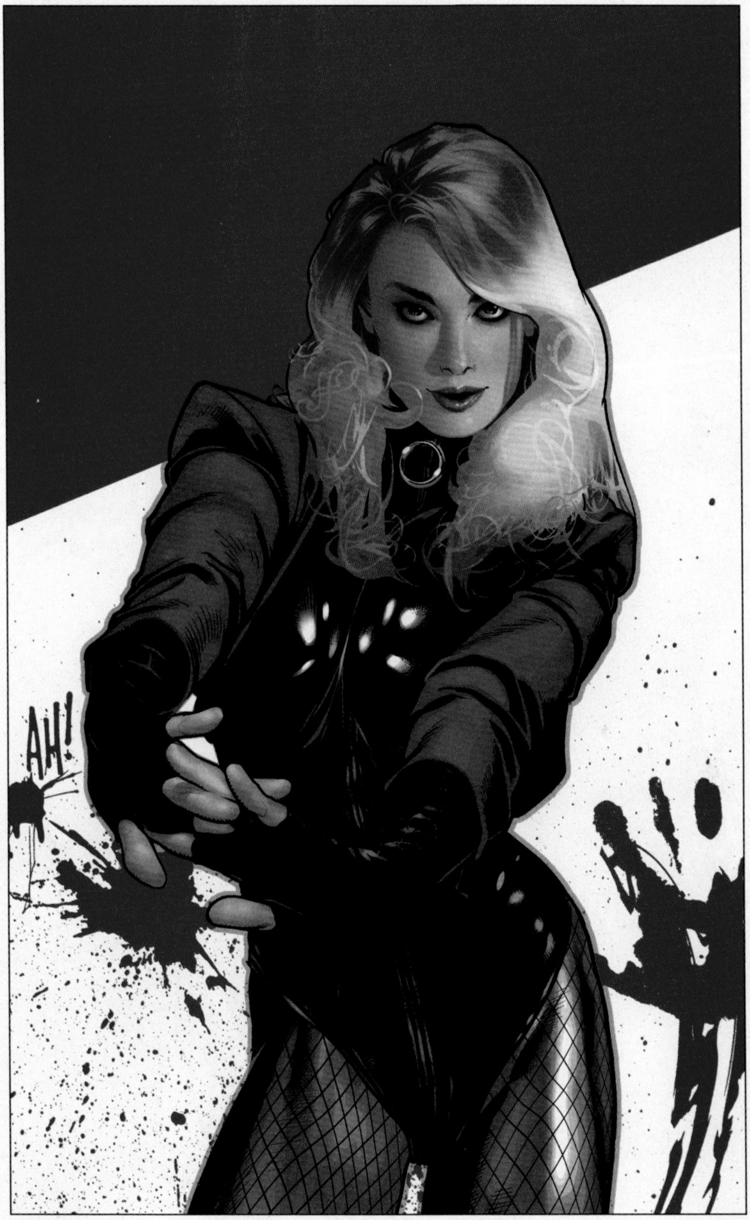
AH!

ADAM HUGHES

FAVORITE MOMENTS

36 Characters, 7 Artists, 2 Pages and 1 Colorist "And we needed it yesterday?" Someone's math was off, but he was about to take me out to lunch so I just said, "Sure!"... "Oh, by the way, I think they're making it into a poster so you're gonna have to color it huge." It was then that I decided to order a huge drink AND dessert. The good news was that all seven artists were either on my "I would love to work with" or "can't wait to work with again" list. The art was drawn in two main pieces and not quite at the same size so I had to color the two chunks hoping that they would somehow look right when brought together. Once I was done I was sent Eric's pre-color notes (I laughed at that one too) so I had to go in and adjust the background bars to be monochromatic, each having its own overall color. My favorite part? Brad's reaction—the guy can and will put most fans to shame.

—Alex Sinclair

See following page.

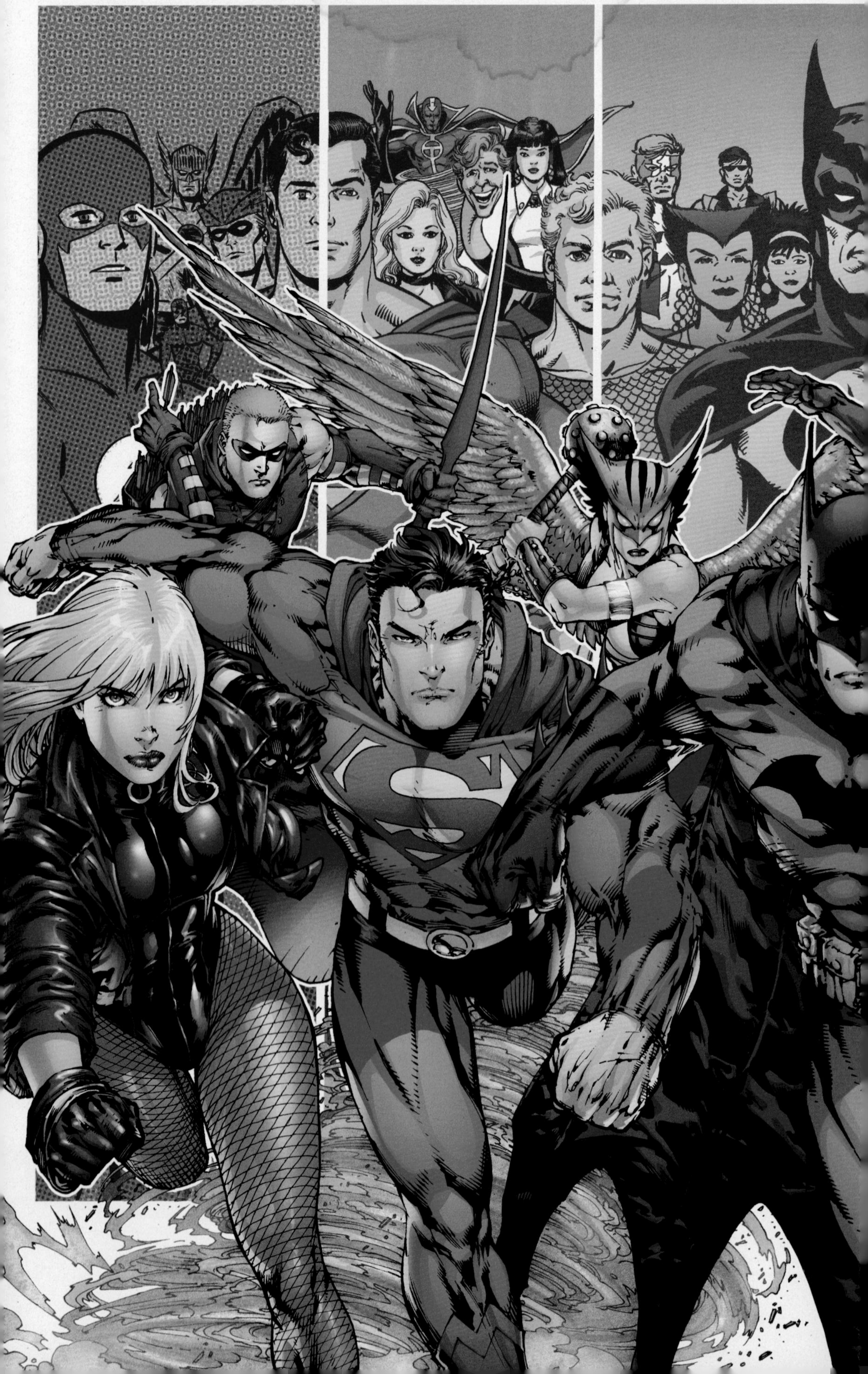

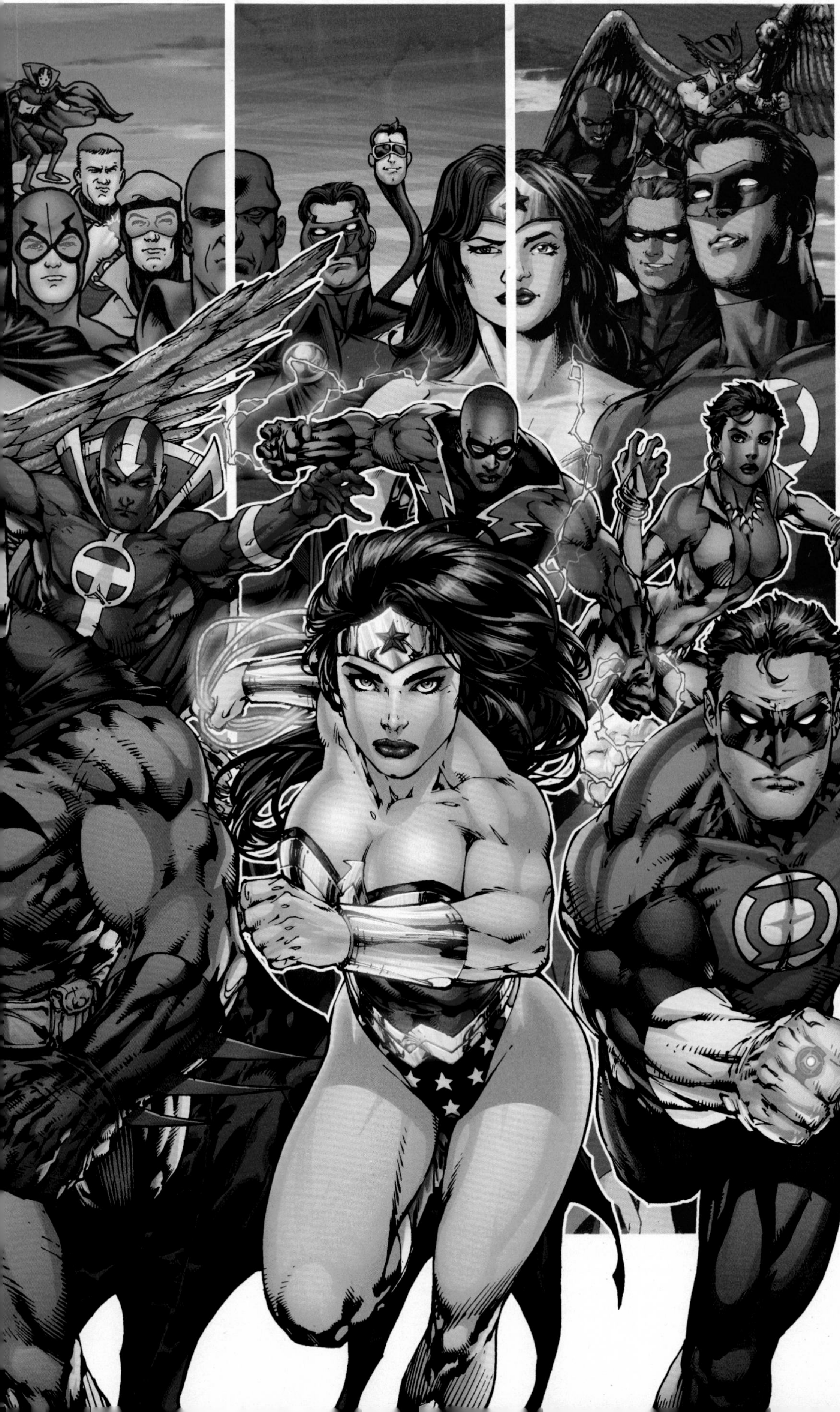

ED BENES, GENE HA, LUKE MCDONNELL, GEORGE PÉREZ, HOWARD PORTER & DREW GERACI,
ERIC WIGHT, KEVIN MAGUIRE AND ALEX SINCLAIR/DESIGNED BY ERIC WIGHT

BRAD MELTZER AND ED BENES DISSECT
JLA: THE TORNADO'S PATH

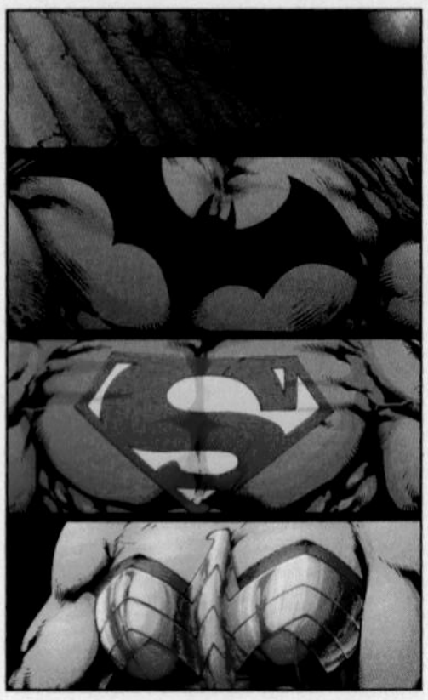

Page 11 — ICONS

MELTZER: It all began here. Starting with the descent down the rabbithole, which would lead us to the icons. From there, we'd start an examination of identity that would reach every character, every villain, and even the concept of the actual League. The one problem? Ed Benes loves to draw his women…er…buxomish. Never in my entire adult life did I ever think that my first art comment back would be, "Can you make Wonder Woman's breasts smaller?" He did. And then I again asked, "Uh…smaller than that." And thus page one was built.

BENES: Ahahah! I know that I gave Brad and Eddie a hard time drawing Diana's breasts correctly. But what can I say? I've drawn women like that for years and years, and old habits die hard!

From the original script:

PAGE ONE

Panel 1: Horizontal panel—POV from the top of the stairs of the Batcave. We're looking down, down, down a huge flight of stairs that's carved into the cave. We can't see the bottom, or the contents of the cave. JUST STAIRS LEADING TO BLACKNESS—our entrypoint into the rabbithole. Bits of stone are across the floor, and the sides of the staircase are sharp like the cave walls.

Page 14, panel 3: — BRIGHT LIGHTS

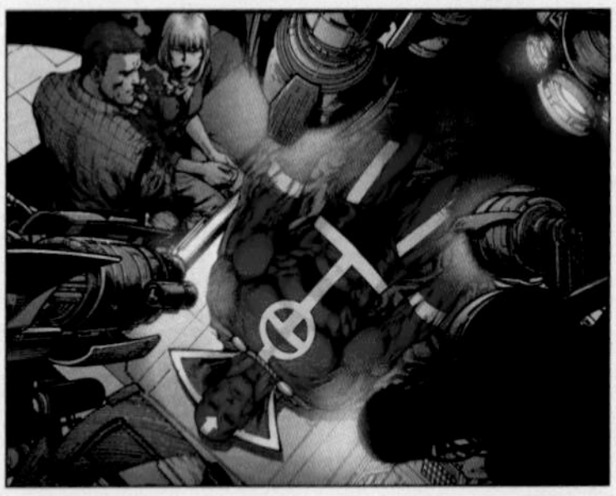

MELTZER: Colorists are underrated. Yes, they have to get the colors right. And playing with a cold gray hue can add a wonderful starkness to a scene that would otherwise look like people running around in red and blue pajamas. But the modern colorist, armed with computer, also provides special effects that add a real-life quality to the scene. Here, it's the shine of the lights and the blur that goes with them that lets us truly experience Reddy on the operating table. That's why the first person we asked to join us on the book was Alex Sinclair.

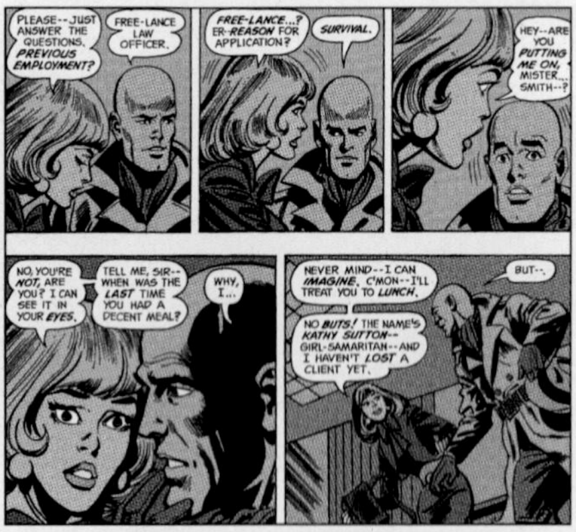
PLEASE--JUST ANSWER THE QUESTIONS. PREVIOUS EMPLOYMENT?
FREE-LANCE LAW OFFICER.
FREE-LANCE...? ER-REASON FOR APPLICATION?
SURVIVAL.
HEY--ARE YOU PUTTING ME ON, MISTER... SMITH--?
NO, YOU'RE NOT, ARE YOU? I CAN SEE IT IN YOUR EYES.
TELL ME, SIR-- WHEN WAS THE LAST TIME YOU HAD A DECENT MEAL?
WHY, I...
NEVER MIND--I CAN IMAGINE. C'MON--I'LL TREAT YOU TO LUNCH.
BUT--.
NO BUTS! THE NAME'S KATHY SUTTON-- GIRL-SAMARITAN--AND I HAVEN'T LOST A CLIENT YET.

Page 16, reprint panels — THE ORIGINALS

Yes, these are the real panels from Justice League of America #105, page 14, panels five through nine. Script by Len Wein, art by Dick Dillin. My only regret was that we left them out of the original credits. I was three years old when this story was published, but when I was ten, and finally read it, I couldn't help but wonder about this robot man in love with this human woman. That's where "The Tornado's Path" was born.

Page 19, panel 1— TEARS FOR FEARS

MELTZER: Ed is known for his masculine figures and female…uh…female figures. But I always knew he was much more. This was the very first moment where Ed got to show that he could do emotion. I remember being worried about this page—if he didn't pull it off, the rest of the storyline was going to be tough. But when it arrived…I felt so damn bad for Kathy. And all her anguish only comes because Ed came through.

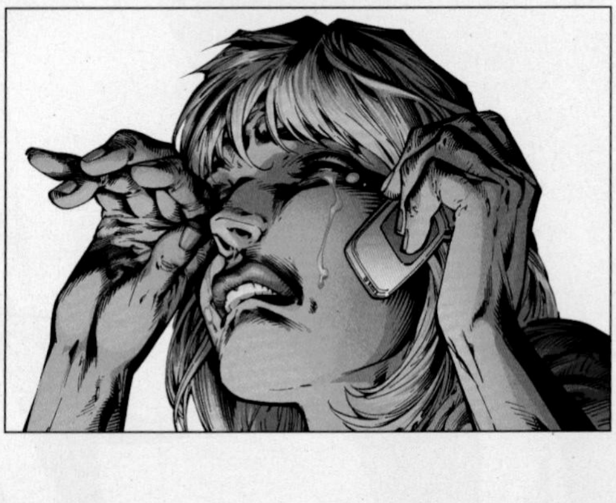

BENES: I'm so glad that everyone enjoyed this scene as much as I did while I was drawing it. It was something completely different from what I was used to doing. I mean, Brad's scripts demand a lot of emotions and reactions from the characters. And I think that this scene was when I really began to have fun with the characters.

Page 48 — THE END

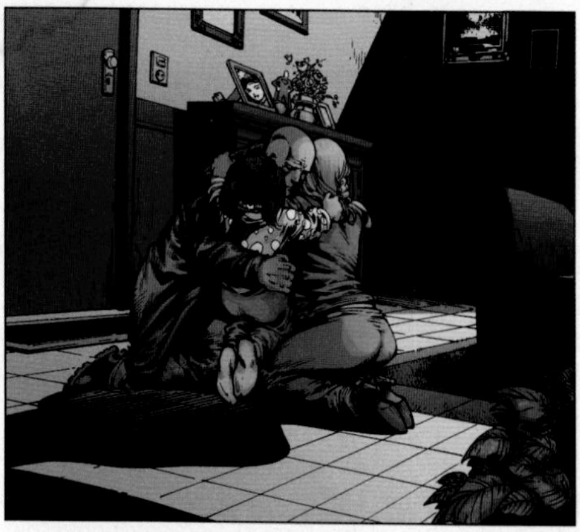

MELTZER: Of all the sexy Vixen shots and tough guy Batman shots, this was the page I was the most excited to see. The beginning for Reddy. And so clearly the end. From the very first chapter, this tells the reader exactly how the story is going to end. To steal from Hitchcock: There is no terror in the bang; only in the anticipation of it.

From the original script:

Panel 1: This should have a letterbox feel: a single panel in the middle, with black on the top and bottom. We're in Kathy's apartment. Red Tornado is squatting down, hugging with Kathy (who's on her knees) and Traya. Ed, this is the true money shot. It's not just a hug. Let us feel all the joy and love for this family. Their robot husband/dad is a true man now. They're squeezing him—and he's hugging them—as never before.

Pages 52-53: — GRUESOME ROBOT

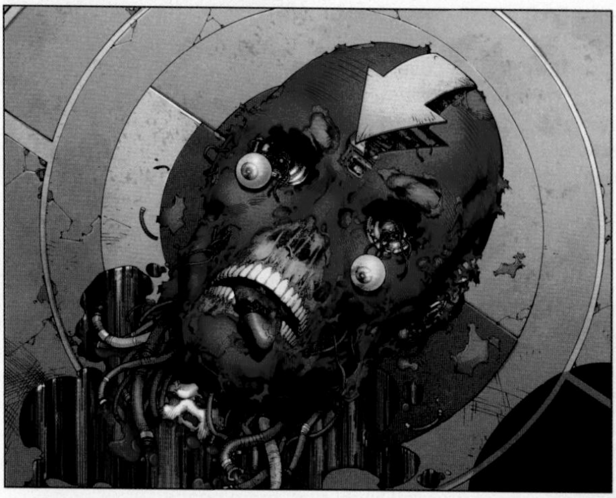

MELTZER: In every comic there are a few pages that, when you see them drawn, you almost regret the brutality of their creation. For me, it's proof of how much more potent the visual medium of comics is, as compared to novels. In a novel, the reader can only imagine it. In comics, you get to see the tongue ripped in half, and the eyes out of their sockets. Most important, this was the first place I was worried about Ed and my language barrier. You see, Ed doesn't speak English. We've never spoken on the phone, or talked about a script. Instead, every issue is translated by the talented Joe Prado, who then sends it on to Ed. So here, my fear was, "He's gonna ignore all my inane ramblings and just say, 'Ed, draw a gory robot.'" Needless to say, Joe earned his pay that day. Every detail is in there, including the little socket between his eyes.

From the original script:

Panel 1: This is a close-up shot of just Red Tornado's costumed head on a metal table. His head takes up most of the spread, but what's key is that there should be tons of thick and thin loose wires coming out of his neck like tentacles...his eyes are pulled from his head, dangling down, his eyeballs still attached by wires and plugs and coils...his nose should be missing (like there's a tear at the center of his mask) revealing a triangular circuit-board and memory chips and places for high-tech plugs...his tongue and teeth tugged just out of his jaw, all connected by wires and bolts and cords...thick wires of even more colors plugged into his ears...and imagine a big V is cut into his forehead—like the red headpiece on Amazo—and is lifted up like the hood of a car, revealing layers of memory and motherboards and even more wires inside. His skin is shredded where the V-hood lifts up. This shot should make us sick. As if we're seeing Pinocchio's insides for the first time. Ed, I leave it to you whether the head is on its side, or standing straight up—whatever looks more gruesome. And don't forget, Red Tornado has a human face under his red mask, and then robot parts under the skin.

Caption: "...until we take out all the pieces."

VILLAIN WEARING GLOVES
(off panel)
They'll hurt you for this one.

MAIN VILLAIN
That's not true.
(cont.)
They're not hurting anyone...

BENES: OK, now you all can see how Brad's scripts are! Dense and full of intricate descriptions. Before JLA I had never worked with any other writer who writes as descriptively as Brad, BUT, make no mistake, these words, every single one, are priceless and there for a reason. They allow the artist to visualize the scene more fully.

Page 54, panel 1 — DEMOCRACY IN ACTION

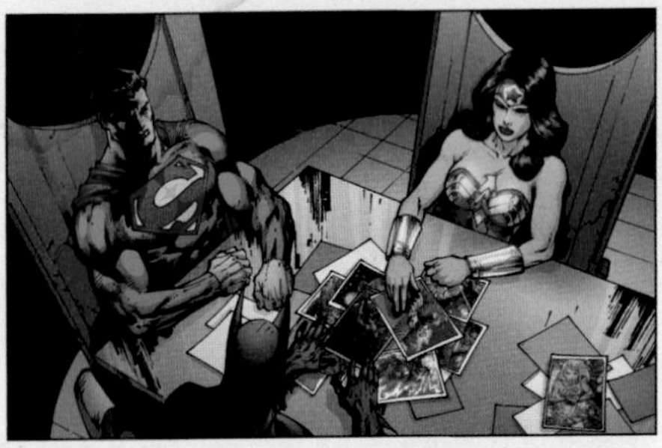

MELTZER: When I was charged with picking the membership for the new Justice League, the voting was one of the first ideas I wanted to explore. In all my years of reading, teams always came together by chance and fate. And even when they didn't, we never got to see the backroom dealings. To prepare for it, I actually went through most of the DC Universe, with a massive list of characters, and how Superman and Batman and Wonder Woman would vote on each one. Now, yes, this is a display I shouldn't be proud of. It's one step prior to staging pretend fights with your own action figures. But it was the very best way for me to see who was out there, and even most vital, to understand how these iconic characters approach everyone around them. These Big Three don't need the rest of any team. They really don't. But the more I pulled them apart, the more I started to see how that wasn't true. The Three all had emotional things they needed.

Page 74, Turner's cover to issue 3 — TURNER'S TORNADO

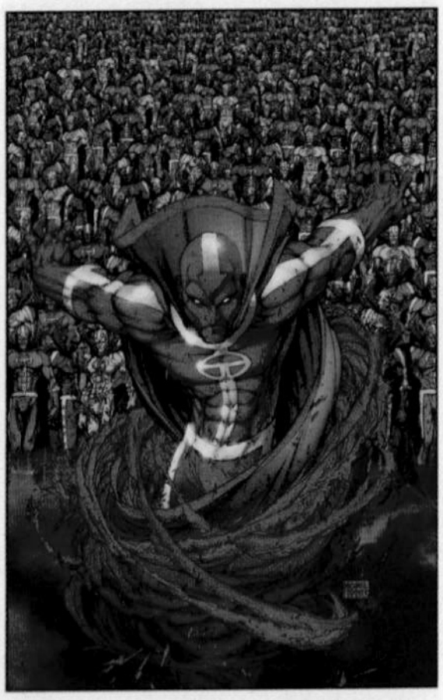

MELTZER: I lied before. Alex Sinclair was the first person we had on the team when it came to the interiors. But the first person I actually spoke to about JLA was this man. Michael Turner. This cover is why. So simple, so elegant. Also, I'd be full moron if I didn't mention Peter Steigerwald, who adds all the colors (and extra robots) to Mike's work. They're a true team and have been with us since *Identity Crisis*. They're also one of the reasons people pick the book up in the first place.

Pages 84-85 — CATBIRD SEAT

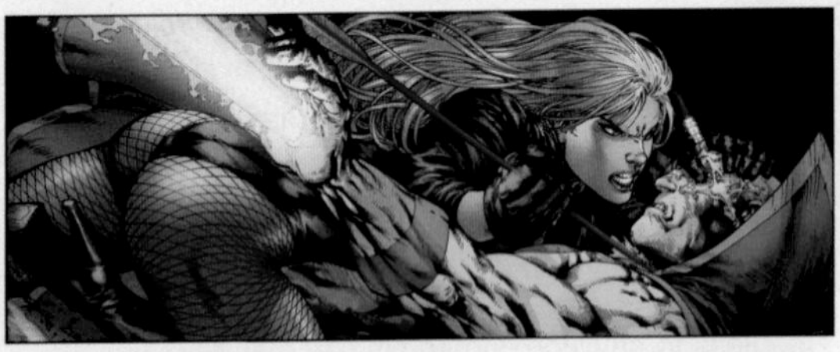

MELTZER: From page 1, we always knew Canary was going to be the leader of the team. Here's where we started to see why. I had very specific instructions for this spread. Thankfully Ed ignored me and gave Dinah even more space.

BENES: Ahahah! I love the character! I HAD to give her more space! It was stronger than me!

From the original script:

Panel 1: This first panel should stretch across the entire top half of this double-page spread. The rest of the panels should be two rows of panels: Panels 2, 3 (the widest), and 4 in the first row, then equal-sized panels 5-9 across the bottom row, with panel 10 having a bit more width. This enormous first panel should be close-up on Canary in action. We should feel blown away here, Ed. It's a profile shot of Black Canary pouncing feet first—her feet planted right in the chest of the yellow robot as the robot (who we see from the chest up) begins to tumble backwards (if you want, his repulsor rays can still be going wild in the air). She's like a wildcat, her left thumb stuck in the robot's eye, and the rest of her fingers gripping tight to his forehead (so she's holding on by that eyehole). In her right hand, she's stabbing down toward his neck with a red sharp arrow (like she's doing the Psycho *shower scene). It's about to stab him in the neck. Her hair whips backwards and she's in mid raging yell, so we get the full sense of momentum.*

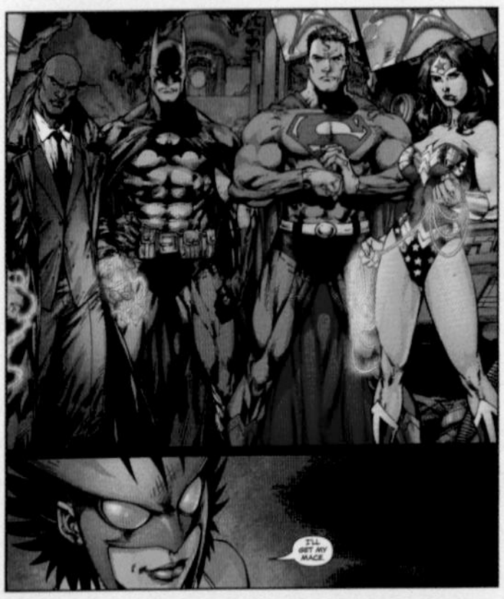
I'LL GET MY MACE.

Page 117, panels 2 and 3 — I'LL GET MY MACE

MELTZER: So much of every scene falls on the artist. I can write all the artistic, fake-film-school pretentiousness I want. But if Ed doesn't nail the expression, all the emotion is lost. This was one of my favorites. The smirk on Hawkgirl's face—the way she's shifted to the side of the panel—it conveys all that needs to be said.

From the original script:

Panel 3: POV of the four heroes: Just a shot of Hawkgirl (from the chest up), grinning wide, no teeth. Let us feel all the excitement and thrills she's feeling. She's trying to contain it, but she's about to burst.

HAWKGIRL
I'll get my mace.

Page 122 — GRUNDY SMASH

MELTZER: Selling the villain is as vital as selling the hero. Ed did these two sketches and let us pick the one that was most scary. For all of us, it wasn't a question. Also, the white Pepe le Pew streak in Grundy's hair (which I loved so much) came from Alex Sinclair, who, in the name of artistic integrity and as an allegory for Grundy's inner lost soul, said, "I thought it'd look cool."

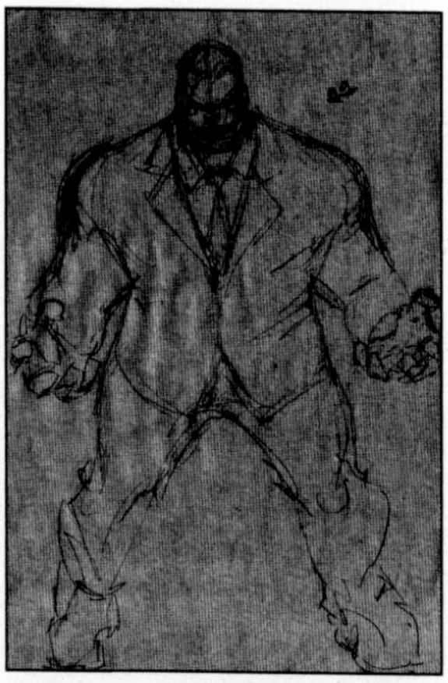

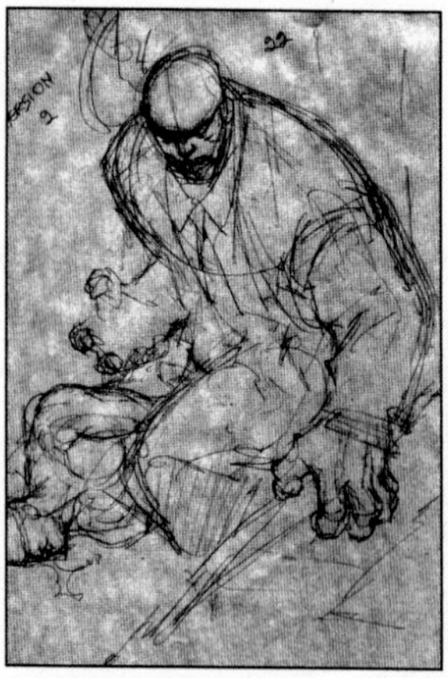

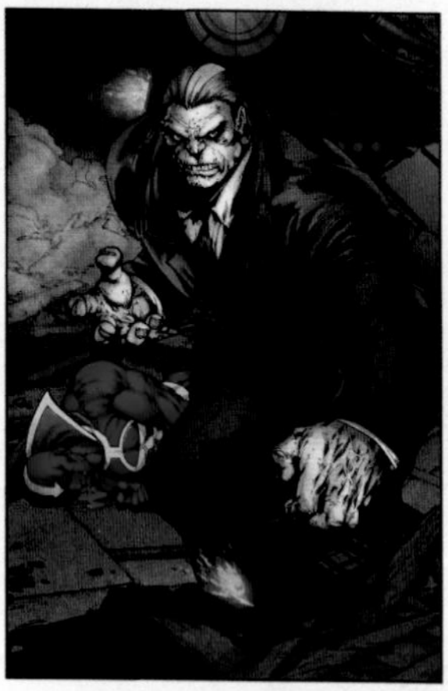

Page 131 — MEMORY LANE

MELTZER: The long lasting beauty of comics has nothing to do with big breasted women in skimpy costumes. The true beauty of comics is its history. It's what distinguishes it from so many other mediums — nowhere else does the tapestry of stories create such a giant quilt. Some ignore it. Here, we felt the need to embrace it. And not just for fanboy street-cred. Simply put, it was the perfect way to show the parallel tracks between Reddy and Amazo. There was one thing that differed between them. And this was the moment we see it. Literally. I told editor Eddie Berganza that this would be the moment where we try to show the most vital super-power—the power of love. He appropriately rolled his eyes and let me have my reprints.

From the original script:

Panels 4 – 24: These are 30 to 40 tiny (half-an-inch by half-an-inch) panels showing past memories of both Amazo's and Red Tornado's lives. They should be squeezed into a small horizontal panel that's just packed with all these tiny images. What's key is that they should be alternating between Reddy's and Amazo's — this robot is right now a bit of both — and is trying to figure out who he is. And, most important, the memories should go from most recent first, back to the further past. The moments don't need to be redrawn—in fact, I prefer if they're reused art from the famous moments in their lives. So let's include the following covers, plus whatever great images we can reproduce from inside:

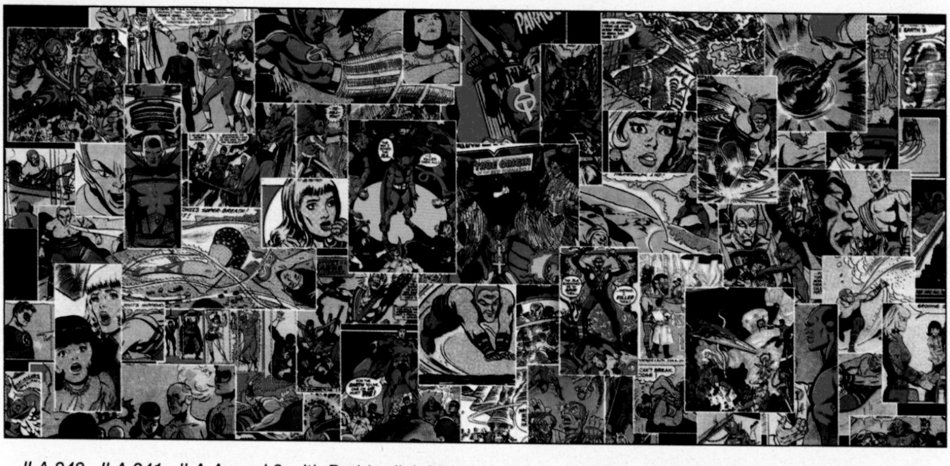

- JLA 243, JLA 241, JLA Annual 3 with Reddy, JLA 224, JLA 193, JLA 192, JLA 146, JLA 112, JLA 106, JLA 102 where Reddy takes the nebula rod
- Brave & Bold 30 (first Amazo)—and let's use a ton of images from here, including the opening page with Ivo, etc.
- and let's let the final four images be repetitious—two of each, with a shot of Kathy Sutton from JLA 106, and another shot of Amazo from B&B 30's opening shot with Ivo, then back to Kathy, then back to Ivo and Amazo...

Page 142, panels 2, 3 — PRETTY BIRD

MELTZER: When Dan DiDio first asked me who I wanted for the team, the top of my list was Arsenal. I could have Power Girl, Captain Marvel, anyone out there, and I wanted Speedy? But the truth is, this was the character I most wanted to see grow. And when it came to my pitch for Hawkgirl, I told them I wanted to do the Montagues and the Capulets. There was no need to redo what's already been done in the Hawk/Arrow war. Especially when there was something far more important out there. This was the drama I wanted to bring to the League. Again, they rightly ignored my ramblings and most likely just told Ed to make sure Kendra looked hot. But Romeo finally got to meet his Juliet.

Page 155, last panel — HOW TO BEAT THE FLASH

MELTZER: The thrill of writing Amazo isn't just writing how the League would take down the robot. It's writing how the League would take down each other. I was fully convinced there'd be nothing spontaneous about it. As it says, they wargamed it out years ago. But again, here's one of the moments where Ed brought the message home. They're sawing off Flash's legs.

Page 166, panel 1 — VIXEN'S RETURN

MELTZER: Who beats Amazo? Not Superman, or Wonder Woman, or Green Lantern. It's Vixen. Who? Exactly. This is why I love the Justice League. And this is why Superman, Batman, and Wonder Woman can't do it alone. The proof is ramming through Amazo's chest.

Pages 176 - 177 — TORNADO TRIUMPH

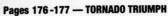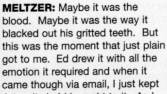

MELTZER: Maybe it was the blood. Maybe it was the way it blacked out his gritted teeth. But this was the moment that just plain got to me. Ed drew it with all the emotion it required and when it came though via email, I just kept staring at it, amazed at the intensity he'd brought to it. As I write it, the goal was very clearly to show the reader that humanity doesn't come from a human body. It comes from what's inside. From heart. And sacrifice. And the ability to stubbornly fight especially when you know you're going to lose. This wasn't just the full circle of the story. This was what being a hero was all about. Without Ed, it's just another fistfight.

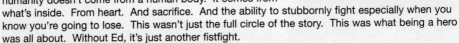

BENES: This issue was sooooooo cool to draw! =) The fight between the League and Amazo was great! Reddy's heroism and endurance during his fight with Grundy was so inspiring! This issue is easily one of my favorites of the first arc!

From the original script:

Panel 8: Reaction shot of the rest of the heroes. They all look beaten as they look at us. Batman is helping Superman get up. Arsenal leans on his bow like a cane to stand. Black Lightning and Hawkgirl are in shock (Kendra raises her mask up so we see her scared face). They all look in the same direction—at us—so we know they see the portal.

Caption (Red Tornado): And coming-of-age.

SUPERMAN

I-I'm here.

Panel 9: Shot of Reddy pouring it on. He grits his teeth in unimaginable pain. Tears pour from his eyes. This is a man. A living being. And he will not give up.

Caption (Red Tornado): This is the story of my life. And my death.
Caption (Red Tornado) (bottom right of panel): But this isn't the story of my defeat.

Panel 10: This should be like panel 1—the previous long profile shot—with Grundy on the far left side in silhouette, and Reddy on the right—BUT HERE, in that silhouette, we see Grundy breaking in half, the top of his torso just starting to blow back off his body. Just a sliver in half. At long last, the man beats the monster.

Page 180 — THE WORST NEWS COMES WITH A SMILE

MELTZER: Again, I owe this one to Ed. I knew he'd draw Kathy beautiful. I knew she'd look perfect. And I asked him to keep the smile in every panel. That's how we'd really know how bad it is. The saddest part of *Flowers for Algernon* is when he realizes he's losing his "powers." But in the end of Algernon, that memory fades. Here, for Reddy, I wanted this one to haunt him forever.

From the original script:

Panel 3: Similar shot, but here, Kathy cups her hands over his own, relishing this moment even more. But here, we see the very subtle worry as she sees her husband's own reaction. We can't see Reddy in any of this—and that's the point—let us feel his sadness in Kathy's own hampered joy. She's trying to cheer him up. This is it, Ed — here's where we need all your emotion.

KATHY SUTTON
There's nothing to be sad about, John.

Panel 4: SAME EXACT SHOT on Kathy — but now we see the swell of tears in her eyes. She's still smiling, still holding him, but we know how much this really hurts him. John Smith is a robot again. And in his eyes, that's all he'll ever be.

KATHY SUTTON
You're back, sweetie.
(cont.)
Right back where you belong.

Cover issue #7 — ALL TOGETHER NOW

MELTZER: Let me just say it: The Justice League of America was my favorite comic book. Ever. With this cover, well, I was twelve again and George Pérez was drawing it. Really. He drew it. As did Eric Wight, Luke McDonnell, Kevin Maguire, Howard Porter, Gene Ha, and Ed Benes. For that reason, this was the single greatest geek moment I had throughout the whole series.

When we decided to relaunch the series, the only thing that rang foul for me was the feeling that, whether intended or not, all relaunches somehow plow over everything that came before. This was our chance to pay tribute to those things that came before. The real heroes are the hundreds of creators who built those past Justice League eras. That's who we all owe it to, and that's the only reason we're here today. Thanks to them all— and to the brilliant design by Eric Wight.

Page 189 — FAMILY NAME, FAMILY BUSINESS

MELTZER: Throughout the first arc, every character was struggling with newfound identity: Reddy as a robot, Vixen as an animal, Dinah and Hal as parent figures, the Big Three as the self-appointed chosen ones, and of course, Roy as a big boy. All of them (and their acceptance/realizations) feed the eventual birth/growth of this new League, but nowhere is this more apparent than in Roy taking on the family name.

Pages 196-197 and page 200 — TWO HEADQUARTERS

MELTZER: The old cartoon series inspired our look for the Hall—we had it updated by Jim Lee. Jim also designed the new satellite. For years, I'd always been impressed with Jim Lee's ability to simply design. Whether it was a new costume or the added pouches on Cyclops' and Batman's utility belts, Jim has always been the one that could give you something that somehow felt new, whatever new was. So when we approached him to do the satellite, he gave us half a dozen designs (some with nods to the old satellite, some with nods to the JLU cartoon). I wanted something that paid homage to both. Plus, in one of the designs, he had these two smaller drone satellites circling the main one. I just loved that detail—that finally, there'd be an offensive side to the headquarters. Of all the changes we made—including the picking of the team—this moment of choosing the headquarters...it just somehow seemed bigger than everything else. People fade and move on. Homes stay. Except for the cover to issue 7, this was the most humbling moment.

Page 210—THE TEAM TOGETHER

MELTZER: I'd waited nearly a year to see Ed draw this shot. I'd been waiting since I was seven years old. But when I finally saw the art...take a look at the fine line-work...at the expressions on Vixen and Red Arrow...this was where it was clear just how much Ed Benes had progressed as an artist. I'd written the scene to feel like graduation day. But it now felt like Ed was the one graduating. He could always do the splash page and the punch to the face. Here's where it felt like he'd mastered the far more important subtle emotion that feeds a story.

BENES: This scene was one of the first pages I drew for this issue! And the one I loved the most. Having the chance to draw all the characters together, actually as a team, was great!

ACKNOWLEDGMENTS

This book has been my dream, which is why a vital thank-you must be said to those people who let me dream it.

My wife Cori is the Kathy to my Reddy. She's the love I write about every time I write about love. To Jonas and Lila, my life's greatest joys. To my Mom and Dad, for showing me that the love for a child can be endless. For Bari, who I always look up to; Noah Kuttler, forever my hero, for brainstorming, suggesting, reading, and creating; Geoff Johns, for his friendship and for reading early scripts; Judd Winick, who gave me the keys to the dream; Bob Schreck, for bringing me inside; and Mike Carlin, for handing me my first JLA story.

To be clear, every comic is only as good as the full team behind it. Lucky for us, we had some masters: Ed Benes brought a new level to his art, and we all rode the coattails of it; Sandra Hope made it look even better (every time); Alex Sinclair pushed the craft with colors and saved us every issue (we owe you huge, Sinc); Rob Leigh added the perfectly lettered polish; Eric Wight, with his spectacular art and layouts, proved just how much he understands how my brain works; and Mike Turner and Peter Steigerwald gave everyone a reason to pick up the book in the first place. Also, Joe Prado translated every word (perfectly) and put up with my well-established insanity; Jeanine Schaefer and Adam Schlagman tracked down my geek references, but also added insight to each script; while Eddie Berganza steered the ship, drove the plane, and always pushed me to hit the true emotion of the story (may we dance again soon, pal). His editing had an enormous influence on this story. Plus, he let me spend a ton on cover artists (thanks to one and all). Special thanks also go to George Pérez, Luke McDonnell, Kevin Maguire, Howard Porter, and Gene Ha, for the art and for their Leagues, and of course to Gardner Fox, Mike Sekowsky and Murphy Anderson, who created the kingdom. They're the only reason we're here. Most important, Dan DiDio and Paul Levitz let us play with the toys without ever standing over our shoulders to see if we were